DIALECTS AND AMERICAN ENGLISH

WALT WOLFRAM

Center for Applied Linguistics
University of the District of Columbia

A publication of **CAL** Center for Applied Linguistics

PRENTICE HALL REGENTS, Englewood Cliffs, New Jersey 07632

Library of Congress Cataloging-in-Publication Data
Wolfram, Walt,
    Dialects and American English/Walt Wolfram. p.
    cm.
    Includes bibliographical references and index.
    ISBN 0-13-210097-5:
    1. English language—Dialects—United States.   2. Americanisms.
I. Title.
PE2841.W64   1991   90-7391
427' .973—dc20   CIP

Editorial/production supervision and
    interior design: Margaret Lepera
Cover design: Ben Santora
Manufacturing buyer: Mary Ann Gloriande

©1991 by Prentice Hall Regents and Center for Applied Linguistics
Prentice-Hall, Inc.
A Paramount Communications Company
Englewood Cliffs, New Jersey 07632

Printed in the United States of America

10 9 8 7 6 5

ISBN   0-13-210097-5

Prentice-Hall International (UK) Limited, *London*
Prentice-Hall of Australia Pty. Limited, *Sydney*
Prentice-Hall Canada Inc., *Toronto*
Prentice-Hall Hispanoamericana, S.A., *Mexico*
Prentice-Hall of India Private Limited, *New Delhi*
Prentice-Hall of Japan, Inc., *Tokyo*
Simon & Schuster Asia Pte. Ltd., *Singapore*
Editora Prentice-Hall do Brasil, Ltda., *Rio de Janeiro*

CONTENTS

PREFACE

Students who have an interest in dialects often represent a wide range of backgrounds. Some are interested in the topic simply because it piques a natural curiosity about how different groups of people talk. Others feel that information about dialects may be relevant to an allied field of study, while still others are interested in dialect variation as a specialized concentration in linguistics or sociolinguistics. Given the diverse backgrounds and interests of students who end up in a course on dialects, the challenge is to fashion a curriculum of study that can meet the needs of this varied audience without compromising the inherent complexity of the subject matter. In my opinion, this course of study should combine an informed approach to the nature of dialect variation, descriptive detail about dialects, and a discussion of the application of dialect information to related fields. Two decades of wrestling with this challenge have led to the current version of "a textbook on dialects." This work has profited from other efforts to present information about dialects to students, including Wolfram and Fasold's *The Study of Social Dialects* (1974) and Wolfram and Christian's *Dialects and Education: Issues and Answers* (1989), but it offers an entirely fresh format. Furthermore, it should present a more balanced approach to the overall picture of dialect variation in American English than my earlier works on this topic.

Throughout the book, I have attempted to keep the diverse nature of the audience in mind, so that the text should be readable and relevant for students in English, education, speech and language pathology, anthropology, and various branches of linguistic studies. Lots of texts make this kind of broad-based claim in the preface; I hope that this will be one of those rare cases where the actual text matches the introductory boast. I have tried to keep technical linguistic terminology to a minimum, even with respect to phonetics. For convenience only, I have included a skeletal phonetics chart for readers; it should be used with the understanding that there is much phonetic detail eliminated. There are many aspects of vowels, in particular, that could have, and perhaps should have, been included, but I have worked under the assumption that the reader would not have an extensive background in phonetics. I can only apologize to those readers who find my phonetic discussions somewhat frustrating because they have a solid background in phonetics.

I have also tried to work to avoid linguistic formalism. To me, underlying principles of variation are much more significant than their formal representation. There are, however, times when technical terms are needed to convey essential constructs in the field. To help readers in this regard, a glossary of technical terms has been provided. Students also should be aided by exercises which are incorporated into the text at the point where they are relevant.

I have honestly attempted to write a text for all the students who enroll in my "course on dialects" rather than my professional colleagues who may wish to scrutinize my current state of sociolinguistic erudition. The text should be appropriate for both upper-level undergraduate and graduate students.

Conceptually, the text is divided into four major sections. The first section, consisting of the initial three chapters, is an introduction to the nature of dialects. The next section, Chapters 4 through 7, offers a descriptive account of some of the major factors accounting for variation in American English, including region, status, ethnicity, gender, and style. The third section, Chapters 8 and 9, presents the methodological and descriptive models underlying the study of dialects. I tried to balance the approach of traditional dialectology with the advances of variation studies without losing students in the technicalities of quantitative analysis. The final section, Chapters 10 through 12, discusses the applications of knowledge about dialects. The role of dialect in teaching Standard English, the impact of dialect on testing and other educational issues such as reading, writing, and language arts, are all considered in these final chapters. A summary appendix of diagnostic grammatical and phonological structures is included as a convenient reference for readers. The appendix shows an admitted bias in favor of socially significant structures over regionally significant ones, although some regional patterns are included.

The list of people to whom I am indebted starts with my first teacher in linguistics as an undergraduate student, Roger W. Shuy, and extends to my most recent class of students at the University of the District of Columbia. My students have patiently worked their way through some rough prose in manuscript form to try to figure out exactly what I meant. They have often helped me say it another way in order to save me from myself. On a weekly basis, students would bring in pages of helpful notes for me. My colleague, Donna Christian, meticulously worked through each chapter to exorcise the manuscript of its substantive and stylistic infelicities; she has been an invaluable collaborator on substantive and practical issues for many years now, and she has always been an available sounding board for ideas. Ron Butters field-tested the manuscript on students at Duke, as did Howard Mims at Cleveland State University and Donna Christian at Georgetown. These colleagues shared a draft of the developing manuscript with their students when it was a real pedagogical risk, but it provided critical feedback for my revisions. During these years of professional development I have been fortunate enough to associate with people who have taught me that professional colleagues can also be good friends: Guy Bailey, John Baugh, Elaine Bowman, Ron Butters, Donna Christian, Larry Davis, Ralph Fasold, Bob Johnson, Jane Koester, Howard Mims, Michael Montgomery, O. B. McCaleb, Joy Peyton, Dennis Preston, John Rickford, Roger Shuy, Nona Stokes, Dick Tucker, Wilhelmina Reverson, Fay Vaughn-Cooke, and Eugene Wiggins, among many others who should be named as well. Thanks for your support and friendship. This cast of characters has made academic inquiry much more fun than I ever thought it could be. If students reading this text can just catch a little bit of the excitement that academic inquiry in a real-world context can actually bring, I will be greatly satisfied. Thanks too, to the following reviewers of this text: Ronald R. Butters, John Fought, Mark Feinstein, Guy Bailey, and Howard A. Mims.

Special thanks go to my "ten-cow" wife, Marge, and our children, Tyler, Todd, Terry, and Tanya. Our "normal" teen-agers gave me invaluable access to a natural laboratory of adolescent peer cohorts over the last ten years by filling my workplace at home with a steady stream of friends who shared the computer, the refrigerator, the basketball court, the good and bad jokes, and everyday sociolinguistic dynamics. For keeping me in touch with another world out there, "Wanderin' Wally" would like to dedicate this effort to my family, as defined in the broadest sense of this term.

Walt Wolfram
University of the District of Columbia and
Center for Applied Linguistics

Phonetic Symbols
Consonants

Symbol	Key Words	Phonetic Description
[p]	pit, spit, tip	voiceless bilabial stop
[b]	bat, rabbit, rib	voiced bilabial stop
[t]	tip, stop, put	voiceless alveolar stop
[d]	doom, under, bud	voiced alveolar stop
[D]	butter, buddy	voiced alveolar flap
[k]	cap, skate, bake	voiceless velar stop
[g]	go, buggy, bag	voiced velar stop
[ˀ]	bottle, button (in some dialects)	voiceless glottal stop
[f]	fee, after, laugh	voiceless labiodental fricative
[v]	vote, over, love	voiced labiodental fricative
[θ]	thought, ether, both	voiceless interdental fricative
[ð]	the, mother, smooth	voiced interdental fricative

Symbol	Key Words	Phonetic Description
[s]	so, fasten, bus	voiceless alveolar sibilant
[z]	zoo, lazy, fuzz	voiced alveolar sibilant
[š]	shoe, nation, bush	voiceless palatal sibilant
[ž]	measure, closure	voiced palatal sibilant
[h]	hat, behind	voiceless glottal fricative
[č]	chew, pitcher, church	voiceless palatal affricate
[ǰ]	judge, ranger, dodge	voiced palatal affricate
[m]	my, mommy, bum	bilabial nasal
[n]	no, funny, run	alveolar nasal
[ŋ]	jungle, sing	velar nasal
[l]	look, bully, call	lateral
[r]	run, bury, car	retroflex
[w]	way, quack	labiovelar glide
[y]	yes, feud	palatal glide

Vowels

Symbol	Key Words	Phonetic Description
[i]	beet, leap	high front tense
[I]	bit, rip	high front lax
[e]	bait, egg	mid front tense
[ɛ]	bet, step	mid front lax
[æ]	cap, bat	low front tense
[ə]	about, afford	mid central tense
[ʌ]	shut, was	mid central lax
[a]	father, stop	low central
[u]	boot, through	high back tense
[U]	book, put	high back lax
[o]	no, toe	back mid tense
[ɔ]	oral, taught	back low tense
[aU]	crowd, bout	low central backing diphthong
[aI]	buy, lie	low central fronting diphthong
[oI]	boy, coin	low back fronting diphthong
[ɚ]	mother, bird	mid central retroflex

ILLUSTRATIONS

Figure 1–1.   A Continuum of Standardness.
Figure 1–2.   Progress of American Atlases (adapted from Wolfram 1981:42).
Figure 3–1.   A Typical Vowel Chart Indicating Different Tongue Positions.
Figure 3–2.   An Illustration of Chain Shifting in the Low Vowels of American English.
Figure 4–1.   Traditional Linguistic Atlas Map of *Pail* and *Bucket* in the Eastern United States (from Kurath 1949: Figure 66).

CHAPTER ONE

THE REALITY OF DIALECTS

Most of us have had the experience of sitting in a public place and eaves-dropping on conversations around us. As a matter of etiquette, we politely pretend to be preoccupied with the magazine or paper sitting on our laps, but we listen intently to people around us. And we form impressions of them, based not only on the topic of conversation, but on how they are discussing the topic. In fact, there's a good chance that the most critical part of our impression comes from *how* the people are talking rather than *what* they are discussing. We make judgments about social class, ethnicity, regional background, and a host of other social characteristics based simply on the kind of language the people are using. On those occasions when we get to check out our initial reactions, we are not surprised when many of our first impressions turn out to be relatively accurate.

Similar kinds of reactions are easy to document in telephone conver-sations, as we try to figure out who an unidentified caller might be and impute a set of characteristics that lead us to claim that "it sounds like a salesman of some type" or "it sounds like the auto mechanic." In fact, it is surprising how little conversation it takes to draw conclusions about a speak-er's "background"—a sentence, a phrase, or even a word is often adequate to trigger a regional, social, or ethnic classification.

Assessments of a complex set of social characteristics based on language differences are as inevitable as the kinds of judgments we make when we find out where people live, what their occupations are, where they went to school, and who their friends are. In fact, there are some who feel that language differences serve as the single most reliable indicator of social position in our society. When we live a certain way, we are expected to match that lifestyle with our talk. And when we don't match people's expectations of how we should talk, the apparent incongruity between words and behavior is itself a lively topic for conversation.

Language differences seem to be unavoidable in a society composed of a variety of social groups. In a broader context, of course, we must note that the inevitability of these differences is hardly peculiar to American society; any civilization with social and geographical dispersion can be expected to reveal language diversity, or "dialect differences." These differences are a fact of life. Like other "facts of life" passed on to us, these have sometimes come down to us with a peculiar mixture of fact and fantasy.

DEFINING DIALECT

Given the widespread awareness about language differences in our society, just about everyone has some notion of what the term *dialect* refers to. However, the technical use of the term in linguistics is different from its popular definition in some important, but sometimes subtle ways. Professional students of language typically use the term *dialect* as a neutral label to refer to any variety of a language which is shared by a group of speakers. Languages are invariably manifested through their dialects, and to speak a language is to speak some dialect of that language. In this technical usage, there are no particular social or attitudinal evaluations of the term (no "good" or "bad"); it is simply how we refer to any language variety that typifies a group of speakers within a language. The particular social factors which correlate with this diversity may range from geography to social class or age. Furthermore, it is important to understand that socially favored or "standard" varieties are every bit as much of a dialect as those varieties spoken by isolated, socially disfavored groups whose language differences are socially stigmatized. This technical definition is not rigorous, but it is a sufficient starting point in discussing language variation.

DIALECT: THE POPULAR VIEWPOINT

While linguists accept this technical definition of the term, happily arguing about what forms belong to a particular dialect or how two dialects differ, nonspecialists tend to use *dialect* in a somewhat different sense. At first glance, the differences between the popular and technical uses seem inconsequential, but closer inspection reveals that its popular uses carry connotations that give insight into how dialect differences are viewed in our society. Consider, for example, some commonly-held beliefs about dialects demonstrated by popular uses of this term:

1. "We went to the coast of Carolina for a vacation and the people there sure do speak a dialect."
2. "I know we speak a dialect in the mountains, but it's a very colorful way of speaking."
3. "The kids in that neighborhood don't really speak English; they speak a dialect."
4. "The kids in this school all seem to speak the dialect."

One popular use of the term *dialect* refers to those who simply speak differently from the local, native community of speakers (quote 1 in the preceding list). So, as a young native Philadelphian encountering speakers from other areas, I thought that these speakers spoke a dialect. I didn't speak a dialect; I spoke as a native Philadelphian should speak. Of course, I realized that this perception could be a two-way street when I attended college in the Midwest and was constantly chided by my new friends about speaking a dialect. Under close scrutiny, the perception that only other people speak dialects turns out to be a provincial and ethnocentric one, as one group's commonplace turns out to be another group's peculiarity.

Another common use of the term refers to those varieties of English whose features have, for one reason or another, become recognized throughout our society (quote 2). The society at large recognizes a "southern drawl" or a "Boston accent." In other words, if the variety contains features that are generally acknowledged and commented about by the society as a whole, then it may be recognized as a dialect even by the speakers themselves. If someone keeps telling you that you speak a dialect, after a while, you start to believe that you do. Thus, native New Yorkers often believe that they speak a dialect, because the dialect has become a topic of widespread public comment in American society. Similarly, speakers of an Appalachian dialect might recognize that they speak a dialect because of the caricatures and comments that so often appear in the media. On the other hand, the same perception does not hold true of the middle-class Midwesterners whose speech does not receive the same popular attention. This perception is, of course, simply an extension of the view that attaches the dialect label to some groups while excusing others from this designation. In the most extreme case (quote 3), dialect is used to refer to a kind of deficient or "broken" English. In this case, dialect is perceived as an imperfect attempt to speak "correct" or "proper" English. If, for example, members of a socially disfavored group produce a structure such as *three mile* instead of the Standard English structure *three miles* or *His ears be itching* instead of *His ears are itching*, it is assumed that they have attempted to produce the Standard English form but failed. The result is incorrectly perceived as a "deviant" or "deficient" form of English. Based on the careful examination of such forms, dialectologists take the position that dialects are *not* deviant forms of language, but simply different systems, with distinct subsets of language patterns.

During the late 1960s and 1970s, there were many heated debates in educational circles over the so-called "difference-deficit" controversy, with language scholars arguing passionately that dialect variation was simply a matter of *difference*, not *deficit*, and some educators arguing that this variation constituted a deficiency. The fires of this debate are still smoldering in some circles. This particular use of dialect has strong negative connotations, as many of the popular uses of dialect do. A clause such as "but the people use it in a colorful way" in quote 2 may offset this connotation, but it must be stated explicitly to counteract the more commonly-held belief that dialects aren't "as good as" another way of speaking. Without qualification, the popular use of the term *dialect* carries connotations ranging from mildly to strongly negative.

Finally, the term *dialect* often serves as an indirect label for a particular socially disfavored variety of English. A person speaking a recognized, socially stigmatized variety of English may be said to speak "the dialect" (quote 4). Such designations have, for example, been used to refer to the speech of low-income blacks, as a kind of euphemistic label for this variety. In this sense, with the definite article, *"the* dialect" behaves more like a proper noun. Notice that people would not refer to a socially acceptable variety as *the* dialect.

DIALECT MYTHS AND REALITY

What do these popular uses of the term *dialect* say about the general public's perception of dialect, as it varies from the neutral technical definition presented initially? As the preceding discussion points out, we have seen a popular mythology about dialect differences develop in our society which is at variance with the linguistic facts about dialects. Following are some of these myths, as they contrast with linguistic reality:

> MYTH: A dialect is something that *someone else* speaks.
> REALITY: Everyone who speaks a language speaks some dialect of the language; it is not possible to speak a language without speaking a dialect of the language.
> MYTH: Dialects always have highly noticeable features that set them apart.
> REALITY: Some dialects get much more attention than others; the status of speaking a dialect, however, is unrelated to public commentary about its special characteristics.

MYTH: Only varieties of a language spoken by socially disfavored groups are dialects.

REALITY: The notion of dialect exists apart from the social status of the language variety; there are socially favored as well as socially disfavored dialects.

MYTH: Dialects result from unsuccessful attempts to speak the "correct" form of a language.

REALITY: Dialect speakers learn their language by mimicking members of their speech community who speak the same variety, not by failing in their attempts to mimic speakers of the standard variety.

MYTH: Dialects inherently carry negative social connotations.

REALITY: Dialects are not necessarily positively or negatively valued; their social values are derived strictly from the social position of their community of speakers.

Exercise 1

Strike up a conversation about the term *dialect* with a group of friends unfamiliar with the technical definition presented in this chapter. Ask them who they think speaks a dialect by naming particular individuals (e.g., President of the United States, prominent political leaders from different regions, well-known newcasters, minority civic leaders, and so on). Also ask them if they think they speak a dialect. Finally, ask if different social and ethnic groups of people speak a dialect (e.g., native Californians, inner-city blacks, southern Appalachians). Do your observations about the way your friends use the term confirm the observations about its popular uses made in our discussion? Are there additional ways in which this term is used that are not mentioned in the presentation?

As we see, the popular uses of the term *dialect* strongly reflect the attitudes about dialect differences which have developed in the United States over the centuries. Whether or not we choose to use a currently neutral term as a euphemism for dialect, such as *language difference, language variety,* or *language variation,* we still have to confront the mismatch between the public perception of linguistic diversity and the linguistic reality. In fact, given the popular attitudes about dialect diversity, there is a good chance that whatever euphemism we use for the term *dialect* will eventually take on the kinds of connotations that dialect currently holds. I personally prefer to use the term *dialect* in its linguistically neutral sense, and to confront the issue of public education about language diversity as a separate matter. As we have seen, this matter constitutes an enormous challenge, one which we return to in our final chapters. For the time being, it is sufficient to set forth the technical and popular uses of this label and see how its popular uses have come to reflect predominant attitudes in American society.

STANDARDS AND VERNACULARS

In the preceding discussion, it was difficult to avoid reference to the dialect of English often referred to as *Standard English*. The notion of a so-called standard dialect is an important one, but one that is not always easy to define in a precise way for English. In some countries, such as France and Spain, language academies have been established and these institutions are responsible for determining what forms are considered acceptable for the normative "standard." They determine, for example, what new words are allowed to be included in official dictionaries and what grammatical forms and pronunciations are standard. However, in the United States we do not have such an institution, and the attempts that have been made to establish this type of agency have all failed (Heath 1976). Thus, labels such as *Standard English* and popular euphemisms such as "correct English" or "proper English" are commonly used but not without ambiguity. At best, we can discuss how this notion is used, and then offer a reasonable explanation as to how it seems to function in our society.

Exercise 2

Common popular labels for what we call Standard English here are "correct English," "proper English," and "good English." What do these labels tell us about the public perception of standard dialects in terms of the myths about dialects we discussed previously? What implications do these terms have for those dialects that are not considered "standard"?

Before we get too far into this discussion, we should note that whether or not there are specific institutions set up to guide the establishment of a standard variety, language standardization of some type seems inevitable. Ultimately, we can attribute this to underlying principles of human behavior in which certain ways of behaving (dressing, speaking, treating elders, and so forth) are established as normative for the society.

As a starting point, it is helpful to distinguish between the operation of standard English on a formal and informal level. In formal standardization, the norms are prescribed for language by recognized sources of authority, such as grammar and usage books, dictionaries, and institutions like the language academies. In the United States, we don't have a language academy, but we have many grammar and usage books that people turn to for the determination of standard forms. The key words in this definition are "prescribed" and "authority" so that the responsibility for the determination of standard forms rests largely outside the common users of the language. Whenever there is a question as to whether or not a form is considered Standard English, we can turn to authoritarian guides of usage. Thus, if we have a question as to where to use *will* or *shall*, we simply look it up in our usage guide which tells us that *shall* is used for first person future (*I/we shall*) and *will* for other persons. At that point, the issue of a particular usage is often considered settled.

Formal Standard English, or *Prescriptive Standard English,* tends to be based on the written language of established writers and is typically codified in English grammar texts. It is perpetuated to a large extent in formal institutions such as the schools, by those responsible for English language education. As a variety of English, it tends to be very conservative, so that it is the last language style to be reached by any changes going on in the language. For some of the forms, the usage will border on obsolescence. For example, the subjunctive use of *be* in sentences such as *If this be treason, I am a traitor* is a structure which is largely obsolete, yet may still be found in some prescriptive grammar books. Similarly, the maintenance of the singular form of *data* as *datum*, or even the *shall/will* distinction (e.g., *I shall read this chapter* versus *She will read this chapter*) has largely disappeared from spoken language, but is still prescribed in many usage guides and maintained in written language. Without an official agency responsible for the maintenance of a uniform Formal Standard English in the United States, there may be disagreement among prescriptive grammarians, but in most cases, there is fairly strong agreement among authorities. As set forth, Formal Standard English is most likely to be exemplified in formal kinds of written language and the most formal kinds of spoken language occasions, such as a speech that has been written first.

If we took a sample of everyday conversational style, we would find that there are virtually no speakers who consistently speak Formal Standard English as prescribed in the textbooks. In fact, it is not unusual to find the same person who prescribes a Formal Standard English form violating the norm. For example, one of the prescribed Formal Standard English rules prohibits the use of a pronoun following a subject noun, as in *My mother, she took me to the show,* and many teachers will correct children who use this form. Yet, we have documented these same teachers uttering a sentence such as *The students who returned late from recess yesterday and today, they will have to remain after school today* within a few minutes of correcting the child. The point of such illustrations is not to expose as hypocrites those who assume responsibility for perpetuating Standard English norms, but to show that the prescribed formal variety is, in reality, not maintained in natural spoken language. Does this mean that Standard English does not exist in our society, and that we should stop talking about this variety as if it were a real entity? On the contrary, we have evidence that people in our society do make judgments of standardness based on everyday, natural speech samples, but that it is apparently based on a more informal, nonprescriptive version of a standard variety used by real speakers.

Informal Standard English, without recourse to prescriptive authority, is much more difficult to define, and a realistic definition must take into account the actual kinds of assessments that the members of American society make as they judge other speakers' standardness. As a starting point, we must acknowledge that this notion exists on a continuum, with speakers ranging along the continuum between the standard and nonstandard poles (see Figure 1–1). For example, on such a continuum, speakers may be placed at the following points, with Speaker *A* using few, if any, nonstandard forms, and Speaker *E* using many.

Ratings of standardness not only exist on a continuum; they can be fairly subjective as well. Based on different sociopsychological experiences and dialect backgrounds in American society, one listener may rate a particular speaker as standard, while another listener rates the same speaker as nonstandard. This is particularly true when the regional and ethnic background of listeners are taken into account, so that a northern-born middle-class black might rate a southern white as nonstandard, while a native of the region might rate the same speaker as a standard speaker.

At the same time that we admit a subjective dimension to the notion of standardness, we find that there is a consensus in rating speakers at the more extreme ranges of the continuum. Thus, virtually all listeners will rate Speaker *A* in Figure 1–1 as a Standard English speaker and Speaker *E* as a nonstandard English speaker. On the other hand, there might be considerable difference in the rating of Speakers *B* and *C* in terms of a simple classification into standard or nonstandard categories. Furthermore, we have found that the classification of speakers at the extreme poles of the continuum (such as Speakers *A* and *E*) holds regardless of socioeconomic class background of the person making the judgment.

Classifications of standardness will also be somewhat flexible with respect to regional variation. Thus, both a distinct eastern New England or coastal southeastern pronunciation, without the pronunciation of the *r* in words like *car* and *bear,* may be judged as Standard English, as will some dialects that use *r* in these words. And people may be judged as Standard English speakers whether they *go to the beach, go to the shore,* or *go to the ocean* for a summer vacation. On this informal level, Standard English is a pluralistic notion, at least with respect to pronunciation and vocabulary differences. That is, there are regional standards which are recognized within the broad and informal notion of Standard American English. We have more to say about this in Chapter 12.

What is it about a speaker's dialect that is critical in determining whether

Speaker *A*   Speaker *B* Speaker *C* Speaker *D* Speaker *E*
 SE --|----------------|-----+-------------------|---------|-------------------------- NSE

FIGURE 1–1 A Continuum of Standardness

the speaker will be judged as a standard or nonstandard? There is no simple answer to this question, and the actual explanations that people give ("quality of voice," "correct grammar," "tone of expression") have to be viewed with considerable suspicion. However, there are aspects of the realistic operational definition which are noteworthy. One of these is the observation that Standard American English seems to be determined by what it is *not* more than by what it is. To a large extent, American English speech samples rated as Standard English by a cross section of listeners exhibit a range of regional variation in pronunciation and vocabulary items, but they do *not* contain grammatical structures that are socially stigmatized. If native speakers from Michigan, New England, and Arkansas avoid the use of socially stigmatized grammatical structures such as "double negatives" (e.g., *They didn't do nothing*), different verb agreement patterns (e.g., *They's okay*), and different irregular verb forms (e.g., *She done it*), there is a good chance they will be considered Standard English speakers even though they may have distinct regional pronunciations. In this way, Informal Standard English is defined negatively. If a person's speech is free of structures that can be identified as "nonstandard," then it is considered standard.

The definition of Informal Standard English tends to be supported by an additional observation about Americans' attitudes about dialects. For the most part, Americans do not assign strong positive, or prestige, value to any particular native American English dialect. The basic contrast exists between negatively valued dialects and those without negative value, not between those with prestige value and those without. (Interestingly, Americans do assign positive value to British dialects, which are not viable options for wide-scale use in the United States.) This observation is reinforced by the fact that Americans are much more likely to make comments about nonstandardness ("That person doesn't talk correct English") than they are to comment on standardness ("That person really speaks correct English"). We have seen that Informal Standard English is a real notion in American society, but it differs considerably from the Formal Standard English notion that is often taught as *the* standard. Our discussion throughout this book typically refers to this more informal definition of the standard language rather than the formal one, since it is the informal version that plays a predominant role in our everyday lives.

Exercise 3

We don't usually comment on Informal Standard English, but we may comment on a person's speech if it is either nonstandard or *too* standard, or "snooty." Forms which are too standard for everyday conversation are sometimes referred to as *Superstandard English*. Just as it is possible to call attention to speech because it contains nonstandard forms, it is possible to call attention to speech because it is too formal or "proper." In the following sets of sentences, identify the forms that are (1) Nonstandard English, (2) Informal Standard English, and (3) Superstandard English. What structures in the sentences are responsible for your assessment? Are there any sentences you're not sure about? Why?

1. a. He's not as smart as I.
    b. He's not so smart as I.
    c. He ain't as smart as me.
    d. He not as smart as me.
2. a. He's not to do that.
    b. He not supposed to do that.
    c. He don't supposed to do that.
    d. He's not supposed to do that.
3. a. I'm right, ain't I?
    b. I'm right, aren't I?
    c. I'm right, am I not?
    d. I'm right, isn't I?
4. a. If I was going to do that, I would start right now.
    b. If I were going to do that, I would start right now.
    c. Were I to do that, I would start right now.
    d. I would start right now, if I was going to that.
5. a. A person should not change his speech.
    b. One should not change one's speech.
    c. A person should not change their speech.
    d. A person should not change his or her speech.

Why do people sometimes comment about other people's speech because it sounds too proper? What does it say about its users?

VERNACULAR DIALECTS

At the other end of the continuum of standardness are the nonstandard English dialects, or, as I prefer to call them, *vernacular dialects.* The term *vernacular* is used here simply to refer to those varieties of the language which are outside the standard dialects, in this case, outside of Informal Standard English. The term is used in much the same way that the term *vernacular language* is used to refer to local or native languages of common communication which contrast with the official standard language of a multilingual country. Other students of English refer to these dialects as *nonstandard* or *nonmainstream dialects,* but the labels are not nearly so important as an understanding of the reference encompassed by these labels.

Exercise 4

Although the choice of a label for a vernacular dialect may not seem important on one level, it can become a very important consideration when the broader sociopolitical context of naming is taken into consideration. This is particularly true when we consider the emotive connotations of various labels. For example, in the past two decades, one vernacular dialect has endured the following labels, given here in approximate chronological sequence: *Negro Dialect, Substandard Negro English, Nonstandard Negro English, Black English, Afro-American English, Vernacular Black English, Black English Vernacular, Ebonics, African American English.* (Believe it or not, this is not the complete list!) Speculate about the factors that led to some of these labels and why so many changes have taken place in the short modern history of naming this vernacular cariety. Why is there continuing controversy over the labeling of this variety?

As with the standard dialects of English, there are a number of different social and regional factors that go into the making of a vernacular, and any attempt to define a vernacular dialect on a unidimensional basis is problematic. Invariably, it is a complex array of factors that ultimately accounts for the delimitation of the dialect, including dimensions of social class, region, ethnicity, situation, and so forth. Nonetheless, it is possible for both vernacular and nonvernacular speakers of English to identify paradigm speakers of the vernacular variety in a way that is analogous to the way that we can identify representatives of standard dialects. However, the continuum of standardness affects the classification of vernacular speakers, just as it affects standard speakers. Thus, Speaker *D* in Figure 1–1 may or may not be classified as a vernacular dialect speaker, but we can expect a consensus of people (from the same and different dialects) to recognize Speaker *E* as a representative of some vernacular variety.

Unlike standard dialects, which are largely defined by their *absence* of socially stigmatized structures of English, vernacular varieties seem to be characterized by the *presence* of socially obtrusive structures. In other words, vernacular varieties are the converse of standard dialects in that a set of nonstandard English structures mark them as being vernacular. These structures (such as multiple negation, verb agreement, and irregular verb forms we mentioned earlier) naturally coexist with other social factors such as region, age, style, and so forth. Although there seems to be a core of nonstandard structures, we have to be careful about saying that all speakers of a given vernacular variety exhibit this common set of structures. Not all speakers necessarily use the entire set of structures described for a given variety, and there may be differing patterns of usage among speakers of the variety. In fact, attempts to isolate *the* common core of structures for particular vernaculars often lead to heavily qualified, nonrigorous descriptions. This is typified by our attempt to delimit "Appalachian English."

> There may be some question as to whether it is justifiable to differentiate an entity such as AE [Appalachian English] from other (equally difficult to define precisely) varieties of American English, particularly some of those spoken in the South. Quite obviously, there are many features we have described which are not peculiar to speakers within the Appalachian range. On the other hand, there also appears to be a small set of features which may not be found in other areas. Even if this is not the case, we may justify our distinction of AE on the basis of the combination of features . . . Fully cognizant of the pitfalls found in any attempt to attach terminological labels to the varieties of English, we shall proceed to use the designation AE as a convenient, if loosely-defined notion. (Woolfram and Christian 1976:29–30)

Language scholars may sometimes have difficulty defining a set of features uniquely distinguishing a given vernacular variety, but it is easy to demonstrate that both professionals and nonprofessionals identify and classify quite accurately speakers representing the vernacular pole in the continuum of standardness. Vernacular dialects are very real and identifiable entities in American society, notwithstanding our inability to come up with a precise set of structures characterizing them. And this real-world recognition underlies the willingness of members of society to identify particular vernaculars even though linguists may encounter difficulty defining the dialect precisely. As we wind our way through the description of the dimensions of American English dialects, however, we will discuss a number of the specific factors that go into a definition of these dialects.

We can summarize the features that set apart standard dialects and vernacular dialects as follows:

> *Formal Standard:* applied primarily to written language and the most formal spoken language situations; objective standards prescribed by language "authorities"; standards codified in usage books, dictionaries, and other written texts; a single norm for acceptable usage, conservative outlook on language forms.
>
> *Informal Standard:* applied to spoken language; determined by actual usage patterns of speakers; listener judgment essential in determining socially acceptable norms; multiple norms of acceptability, incorporating regional and social considerations; defined negatively by the *avoidance* of socially stigmatized linguistic structures.
>
> *Vernacular:* applied to spoken language; determined by actual usage patterns of speakers; listener judgment essential in determining social *un*acceptability; stereotyping of speakers based upon linguistic forms; defined by the *presence* of socially stigmatized linguistic structures.

Since both formal and informal standard varieties are associated with middle-class, mainstream groups, they are socially respected, but since vernacular varieties are associated with the social underclass, they are not considered socially respectable. This association, of course, simply reflects underlying values about different social groups in our society and is hardly unique to language differences.

WHY STUDY DIALECTS?

There are a nuimber of reasons why the study of dialects is an attractive field of inquiry. First, there is a natural curiosity that stirs when we hear speakers of different dialects. If we are the least bit interested in different manifestations of human behavior, then we are likely to be intrigued by the artifacts of behavior revealed in language. On more than one occasion, the remark that I study dialects in a casual social gathering has been sufficient to elicit a steady stream of comments. They range from the challenge to identify where people come from originally (guaranteeing instant social notoriety) to the question of why particular groups of speakers talk as they do (usually a warning that you're about to be offered an uninformed opinion as to why). It is not uncommon to encounter individuals from varied walks of life who profess an interest in dialects as a "hobby," simply because they are so fascinating. The positive side to this curiosity is that the study of dialects can often sell itself; the negative side, as discussed earlier, is that the attendant set of attitudes and opinions about American dialects makes it difficult to deal with information about them in an objective way. In one form or another, most professional students of dialects have simply cultivated the natural interest that resides within us all. After decades of study, dialectologists still experience the same level of excitement at the discovery of another dialect feature as they did when they first set out to study the way people talk.

As a manifestation of human behavioral differences, dialects may be studied because they provide the opportunity to extend social science inquiry into language, a quite natural application for fields such as history, anthropology, sociology, psychology, and geography. Thus, as one of the most extensive series of studies ever conducted on the dialects of American English, the *Linguistic Atlas of the United States and Canada* carefully charted the geographical distribution of various forms of American English as a kind of linguistic geography. (In fact, it has become known by the label *linguistic geography*.) At the same time, these studies attempted to trace the settlement patterns of Americans through their language differences, as a kind of history. And these studies noted the distribution of forms in different social categories of speakers as a kind of sociology. It is easy to see how dialect differences can be seen as a natural extension of a number of different fields within the social sciences since these differences are so integrally related to all aspects of human behavior.

Other studies have shown how the cultural and historical heritage of particular cultural groups have been maintained through their dialects, such as the cultural isolation historically linked with regions such as Applachia and the island communities along the eastern seaboard of the United States (e.g., Tangier Island off the coast of Virginia or the Sea Islands along the South Carolina and Georgia coasts). From this perspective, interest in dialects may derive from a basic concern with the humanities found in fields such as folklore and literature. It is interesting to note that the U.S. government agency, The National Endowment for the Humanities, has been a primary source of financial support for traditional dialect surveys over the years.

The motivation for studying dialects may naturally go beyond the "objective" extensions of social science inquiry and the more "up close and personal" profiles of different social and ethnic heritages. In some cases, dialect differences may be studied as a kind of group or self-realization— a very subjective perspective related to the identity of the student. Thus, the members of a particular social group may seize upon language differences as part of "consciousness raising." It is no accident that the relationship of language and gender in English became a hot issue in the 1970s, as attention was drawn to the wide range of sex roles in our society. Similarly, the rise of interest in Black English coincided with the general development of black consciousness in other spheres of life in the late 1960s and early 1970s. This kind of focus on English dialect variation might strike majority, mainstream culture members as somewhat exaggerated, until we realize how central language is to the identification of self and group. Issues of nationalism and identity typically come to a head over language, as demonstrated by the attention paid to the French and English language issue in Canada. In a similar way, the status of the Dutch-based language, Afrikaans, in South Africa is hardly a simple language issue; it reflects deeper issues related to political and racial self-determination.

The historical consideration of the English language in the United States shows that the notion of American English was strongly vested in the nationalism of independence. Noah Webster, the father of generations of English dictionaries, in 1789, issued the declaration that "as an independent nation, our honor requires us to have a system of our own, in language as well as government," and that "a national language is a bond of national union" (Baugh 1957:426). In this context, studying American English as compared with British English might be motivated out of a feeling of patriotism and loyalty to the United States. It is easy to compile an impressive list of cases in which nationalism and group-consciousness movements were motivating factors for studying about languages and dialects.

At the other end of the spectrum, dialect differences might be justified on a theoretical basis—to examine language variation in an effort to understand the basic nature of language as a cognitive and human phenomenon. This theoretical concern may range from the investigation of how language changes over time and space to the representation of the cognitive capabilities of a speaker of a language. In this context, the examination of dialects may provide an essential and unique data base. William Labov, one of the pioneers in modern sociolinguistics, set forth this motivation in the published version of his doctoral dissertation (*The Social Stratification of English in New York City*) when he stated that "my own intention was to solve linguistic problems, bearing in mind that these are ultimately problems in the analysis of social behavior" (Labov 1966:v-vi). Empirical data from the study of dialects thus may contribute to central issues concerning the nature of language variation.

Finally, there is the applied motivation. Many students in education and allied health professions have become interested in dialects because of the "usefulness" of the information as it relates to another primary activity such as teaching or language assessment. Virtually all fields of education related to primary language activity (e.g., reading, composition, language arts) and language service professions such as speech and language pathology have recognized the need to understand both general principles and specific descriptive details about dialects. In fact, in one dramatic case of litigation which took place in 1979 in Ann Arbor, Michigan, the courts ordered teachers to attend workshops on dialects because of the potential impact of such information on the interpretation of reading behavior by vernacular dialect students. Application of such information may further be applied to the legal process itself. Knowledge of dialects has been relevant in cases ranging from language-based racial discrimination to the representation of verbatim testimony in transcripts of vernacular dialect speakers. The application of knowledge about dialects obviously has extensive and multifarious applications which have been considered by students of dialect differences, and we take up some of these in more detail later.

After reading the previous paragraphs, we might wonder if there is any justifiable reason for *not* studying dialects. The glib answer to this question is, "Probably not!" However, when we consider the full range of reasons for studying dialects, and the fact that there is a good historical tradition underlying each motivation, it is easy to see why there are scholars who feel that knowledge about dialects should be a central component of our educational process, as fundamental as many other "routine" topics covered in our education.

Exercise 5

On a personal level, consider which of the preceding motivations matches your interest most closely. Is there more than one reason that appeals to you? Rank in terms of priority the major reasons given earlier as they relate to your interest (basic curiosity, a kind of social science inquiry, a kind of humanities study, personal and group identity factors, an understanding of the nature of language, the application of knowledge about dialects to another primary field). Are there other reasons you can think of for studying dialects that have not been cited here (besides the fact that it may be a required course in the curriculum)? Has the need to study dialects been oversold? Why or why not?

A TRADITION OF STUDY

There is a longstanding tradition of collecting and studying data on variation in English, typically guided by the kinds of motivations cited previously. As we already mentioned, some of the earliest collections of American English were concerned with those aspects of American English which set it apart from British English, particularly with respect to vocabulary. Vocabulary is one of the most transparent ways for dialects to differ, and vocabulary collections are a common way in which dialect differences are profiled. Typical of these relatively early works was Pickering's 1812 work entitled *A Vocabulary, or Collection of Words and Phrases which have been Supposed to be Peculiar to the United States of America to which is Prefixed an Essay on the Present State of the English Language in the United States.* Some of the early collections of dialect structures of American English vis-à-vis British English were quite impressionistic, but others represented a fairly meticulous and exhaustive approach to the collection of dialect samples. It is also interesting to note that politicians and statesmen often became involved in language issues (for ex. mple, Benjamin Franklin suggested an early spelling reform and John Adams proposed an academy for establishing an American standard) as differences between British and American English began to emerge and the social and political implications of this divergence were considered.

As the United States became securely independent, the focus changed from the relationship between American and British English to the diversity within American English itself. Largely in connection with settlement patterns, data on geographical distribution came into prominence. Thus, the American Dialect Society was formed in 1889 for "the investigation of English dialects in America with regard to pronunciation, grammar, phraseology, and geographical distribution." Note that the concern with geographical distribution coincided with a period of fairly widespread migration and resettlement, and was motivated by a strong historical rationale. The initial hope of the American Dialect Society was to provide a body of data from which a dialect dictionary or series of linguistic maps might be derived. A considerable amount of data towards this end was published in the Society's original journal, *Dialect Notes*, but it was not until 1928 that a large-scale systematic study of dialect geography was undertaken, entitled the *Linguistic Atlas of the United States and Canada.* Along with the historical goals already mentioned, this survey aimed to correlate dialect differences with different social classifications, an incipient stage of social dialectology which would become developed much more extensively several decades later. A comprehensive set of *Linguistic Atlas* surveys for different areas of the United States and Canada was proposed and the initial survey of New England undertaken. New England was a logical starting place, given the project's focus on historical settlement patterns. Fieldworkers combed the region looking for older, lifetime residents from whom they might elicit particular items of pronunciation, grammar, and vocabulary. Quite typically, the fieldworkers ended up recording up to ten or twelve hours of elicited forms (of course, in the early stages these consisted of on-the-spot phonetic transcriptions without the aid of any mechanical recording equipment). Some of this work is still ongoing, despite severe criticisms about the techniques for gathering data and the approach to describing language variation that was the basis for these studies. The state of the various *Linguistic Atlas* projects is summarized in Figure 1–2, adapted from Wolfram (1981:42).

Almost a hundred years after the establishment of the American Dialect Society, one of its major goals is finally being realized, namely, the publication of the *Dictionary of American Regional English*. (The first volume, covering letters *A–C*, appeared in 1985; additional volumes are expected every few years.) The much-heralded, comprehensive work (over 1,000 pages in the first volume) dates its modern history to 1962, when Frederic Cassidy was appointed general editor. It taps a wealth of data sources, including its own extensive dialect survey of the United States, the various *Linguistic Atlas* projects, and the publications of the American Dialect Society, among others. The American Dialect Society remains a small but active organization. Its quarterly journal, *American Speech*, balances the traditional focus on regional variation with the more recent emphasis on social and ethnic variation in an attractive, readable format.

Beginning in the 1960s, research on dialects in the United States focused much more specifically on social and ethnic variation in American English than on regional variation. Part of this emphasis was fueled by the concern for language as a social problem, particularly as it related to educational issues of the American underclass. Many of the linguistic descriptions of vernacular dialects such as Vernacular Black English and Appalachian English became the basis for applied concerns in American education, and these remain a continuing issue up to the present. For some investigators, however, following the pioneering work of William Labov, the fundamental nature of linguistic variation as a theoretical issue in linguistics became a rationale for sociolinguistic inquiry. Although some current investigators motivate their dialect studies exclusively on a theoretical basis, the more typical rationale combines theoretical and applied or social perspectives. The last two decades have witnessed an unprecedented proliferation of studies of vernacular varieties of English of varying quality and

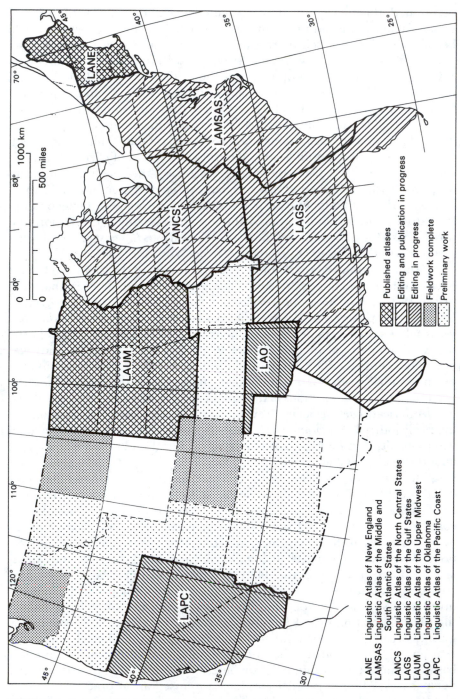

FIGURE 1–2 Progress of American Atlases (adapted from Wolfram 1981:42).

Legend (map):

- Published atlases
- Editing and publication in progress
- Editing in progress
- Fieldwork complete
- Preliminary work

LANE — Linguistic Atlas of New England
LAMSAS — Linguistic Atlas of the Middle and South Atlantic States
LANCS — Linguistic Atlas of the North Central States
LAGS — Linguistic Atlas of the Gulf States
LAUM — Linguistic Atlas of the Upper Midwest
LAO — Linguistic Atlas of Oklahoma
LAPC — Linguistic Atlas of the Pacific Coast

perspective. In fact, one comprehensive bibliography of black English (Brasch and Brasch 1974) listed over 2,400 entries related to black English alone; another annotated bibliography of southern American English (Mc-Millan and Montgomery 1989) listed over 3,800 references, the majority of which relate to the vernacular dialects of the South. The range of vernacular dialects considered over the past two decades has been extended to include Appalachian English, Ozark English, native American Indian English, Chicano English, Puerto Rican English, Italian English, Vietnamese English, and others. No vernacular dialect seems safe from descriptive scrutiny, and no social or ethnic group is assured of sociolinguistic anonymity.

Methods of data collection and the kind of data considered necessary for adequate analysis also shifted drastically during this period. Spontaneous, casual conversation became the favored kind of data for analysis, replacing the earlier emphasis on direct probes to elicit particular forms. Some fairly creative techniques were devised to enhance the possibility of recording good "naturalistic" data, aided by the advancing technology in audio and video recording equipment. In addition, more careful and systematic attention was paid to an array of social factors, ranging from the social relationships of speakers to the stylistic repertoire of the speaker. Such developments naturally were aided by perspectives from other fields in the social sciences such as psychology and sociology. In the analysis of data, advances incorporated more rigorous quantitative methods, including automatic data-processing programs for handling language variation. A traditional dialectologist, frozen in the time frame of the 1950s, would hardly recognize what takes place under the guise of dialect studies today. The different underlying motivations for studying dialects may be well established in historical precedents, but the specific development of the field has undergone some fairly profound changes in its focus and methods. There is also room for the entrepreneurial spirit now, as different specialists have carved out productive and useful niches for the application of information from the study of dialects, ranging from dialect training programs for actors adopting different regional and social roles to consultation services offering the analysis of language variation for legal deliberation of various types.

Further Reading

BAUGH, JOHN, "Language and Race: Some Implications for Linguistic Science," in *Linguistics: The Cambridge Survey IV, Language: The Socio-Cultural Context*, ed. Frederick J. Newmeyer. New York, NY: Cambridge University Press, 1988. Baugh considers the relationship between language and race from a linguistic perspective. A major portion of the discussion is a critical response to a 1983 paper by Thomas J. Farrell entitled "IQ and Standard English." The article demonstrates that the "difference-deficit" controversy is a persistent, current issue.

DANIELS, HARVEY, *Famous Last Words: The American Language Crisis Reconsidered*. Carbondale, IL: Southern Illinois University Press, 1983. This book is a response to those popular writers who decry the deterioration of the English language. It vividly illustrates the high level of emotion involved in the debate over language standards.

FINEGAN, EDWARD, *Attitudes Toward English Words: The History of a War of Words*. New York, NY: Teachers College Press, 1980. This work traces the concept of "good English" throughout the nation's history, showing how this notion has been used and abused.

LABOV, WILLIAM, "The Logic of Nonstandard English," Chapter 5 in *Language in the Inner City: Studies in the Black English Vernacular*. Philadelphia, PA: The University of Pennsylvania Press, 1972. This popular article, reprinted as a chapter in Labov's *Language in the Inner City*, deals with basic misconceptions about vernacular dialects. Historically, it constituted a critical argument for the linguistic and conceptual adequacy of vernacular dialects, and has been reprinted in numerous anthologies. A version was published in *Atlantic Monthly* (June 1972) under the title "Academic Ignorance and Black Intelligence."

MENCKEN, H. L., *The American Language: An Inquiry into the Development of English in the United States, Supplement I*. New York, NY: Alfred A. Knopf, 1962. The initial chapters of Mencken's classic work (Chapter 1 through 4, in particular) provide an intriguing account of the early developments of American English, with rich references to early commentary about this emerging variety by politicians and general observers of language.

CHAPTER TWO

WHY LANGUAGES HAVE DIALECTS

In one of Bill Cosby's classic routines, he asks the question, "Why is there air?" His answer: "to inflate footballs and basketballs!" When we wonder, "Why are there dialects?", a Cosby-like response could be, "to make conversations interesting!" Certainly, it would be dreadfully boring if we all spoke alike—as boring as if we all looked alike or acted alike. On a deeper level, the existence of dialects in a heterogeneous society is a natural manifestation of group differences. Dialects are as basic to social organization as the air we breathe is to the maintenance of our physical being. But what are the processes that make dialects so natural and inevitable? There are both social and linguistic factors to consider in answering this question. Socially, we look to some underlying principles that account for differences in other forms of social behavior (dress, social interaction, and so on), such as history, status, ethnicity, and so forth. Linguistically, we look to the way language systems are organized in the human mind and how we produce speech physically. Together, the linguistic and social factors conspire to work out the particular ways in which the dialects in society are ultimately manifested. In the following sections, we examine some social and linguistic considerations that help explain the natural development of dialect variation.

SOCIOHISTORICAL EXPLANATION

One side of the explanation for dialects is found in the social and historical conditions that surround language change. At the same time that language operates as a highly structured communicative code, it also functions as a kind of cultural behavior. It is only natural, then, that social differentiation of various types should go hand in hand with language differences. In the ideal situation for dialect development, both physical and social separation take place between groups of speakers. In the following sections, we discuss some of the primary factors that set the stage for dialect differentiation.

Settlement   One of the most obvious explanations for any dialect starts with the settlement pattern of the original groups of speakers. Thus, the history of American English does not begin with the initial landing of English speakers in the "New World." Instead, some of the dominant characteristics still found in varieties of American English can be traced to dialect differences that existed in the British Isles to begin with, to say nothing of the kind of English spoken in other English-speaking territories that contributed to the dialects of the Americas (for example, the kind of English spoken by West African and Caribbean blacks). The earliest Anglo settlers came from different parts of the British Isles, where dialects were already in place, and these groups tended to settle in different parts of America. Thus, many settlers from the eastern part of central and southern England settled in eastern New England and the Virginia Tidewater originally, settlers from the northern and western parts of England settled in the New Jersey and Delaware area, and the Scotch-Irish from Ulster settled in western New England, upper New York, and parts of Appalachia. From that point, the population fanned out in a way that is still represented in the dialect configuration of the United States today. The major dialects of American English to this day reflect the original sites of settlement, with cultural hearths such as Boston, Tidewater Virginia, and Charleston, South Carolina, still central foci in the delimitation of regional varieties of American English. Compare, for example, the configuration of the dialects of the eastern United States as given in Chapter 4 (Figure 4–4), which still reflects the distribution of early settlements.

Settlement patterns generally take place in several distinct phases. In the initial phase, a group of people moves to an area where there are attractive environmental qualities. The migrants bring with them the culture of their origin. In the next phase, the frontier of available land is occupied, and the identity of the new culture emerges, as a cohesive society develops in the region. In yet another phase, the population defines a role with respect to the more widespread systems of transportation and communication networks. A response to national commerce and culture becomes an important part of the definition of the population, as it maintains and adjusts aspects of its culture and dialect reflecting that culture.

The first settlers into a given region typically establish a cultural and linguistic area that persists in time, although the original features will change in a number of ways and other features may take their place. Much has changed in English over the centuries of its existence in America, but the initial settlement history is still reflected in prominent dialect features today.

Migration routes   Once settlement locations are established, dialect boundaries will often follow the major migratory routes from these initial points. Thus, the lines of demarcation in the classic delineation of American English dialects (see Figure 4–3) reflect both original settlement and migratory flow. It is no accident that many of the dialect boundaries show an east-west fanning pattern, since these were the major migratory routes taken from the earlier points of settlement along the east coast. For example, a major dialect boundary runs across the state of Pennsylvania, separating the so-called north from midland dialect. North of the line, speakers distinguished between the pronunciations of *horse* and *hoarse* and *which* and *witch;* south of the line, they did not. These pronunciation patterns went along with a number of traditional vocabulary differences such as the use of *pail* versus *bucket*, *teeter-totter* versus *seesaw*, and *stoop* versus *porch*. In the trough of the northern boundary through Pennsylvania and the southern boundary running through Delaware and Maryland a major early migration route existed. Actually, this high-density east-west flow is still reflected in major highway networks that run through the area. Major settlement areas such as Pittsburgh and Cincinnati carved out their own niche, but the reflection of early routes of movement in is still unmistakable in the present configuration of American English dialects.

The basic east-west migratory pattern reflects the movement of the Anglo population, but other groups show different patterns. The consideration of dialect areas for the black population shows a south-north route, emanating from different points in the South. There is a coastal route, in which black speakers from South Carolina and North Carolina migrated northward into Washington, DC, Philadelphia, and New York. The migratory route of inland blacks from the deep South, on the other hand, led into midwestern areas such as St. Louis, Chicago, and Detroit. The vernacular dialects of these areas still reflect differences attributable to these different migratory routes, cutting across the primary east-west route indicated for the Anglo population.

Physical factors   A number of physical factors may play a role in the development of dialects, not because of the topography per se, but because rivers, lakes, mountains, valleys, and other features of the terrain determine the routes that people take and where they settle. Important rivers such as the Ohio and Mississippi played an important part in the development of American English dialects, as pioneers established inland networks of commerce and communication. It is thus not surprising that a major dialect boundary runs in tandem with the course of the Ohio River. On the other hand, the Mississippi River, running a north-south route, deflected migration northward, creating a fault line both in settlement and dialect patterns.

Terrain which serves to isolate groups also can serve a critical role in defining dialects. Thus, Tangier Island and Smith Island, off the coast of Virginia and Maryland, have been the home of small fishing communities which historically were cut off from the mainland, as were the black inhabitants of the Sea Islands off the coast of South Carolina. In both of these cases, fairly distinctive localized English varieties were fostered, although the distinctive features in these two cases differed because of dialects of the settlers to begin with. On Tangier Island, distinctive vowel patterns have been maintained, along with older vocabulary items. On the Sea Islands, a historical creole language was perpetuated, which set off this variety from mainland black vernacular varieties as well as Anglo varieties. One of the most prominent vernacular dialects of English is found in the southern Appalachian mountain range, including West Virginia, western North Carolina and Virginia, eastern Tennessee and Kentucky, and, by migratory extension, northwest Arkansas and southern Missouri, where so-called Appalachian English can be found. Historically, settlers in these mountainous ranges were isolated and travel in and out of the area was relatively infrequent. The vestiges of this historical isolation, in tandem with other cultural and economic factors, are still very apparent in the maintenance of dialect differences.

When we cite the significance of physical boundaries, we are really talking about lines of communication, and the fact that discontinuities in communication have taken place between communities partly due to the physical conditions. The most effective kind of communication is face-to-face, and when a group of speakers does not interact with another, the likelihood of dialect divergence is heightened. Combined with other sociological conditions, natural boundaries of various types form a solid basis for different directions of dialect development.

Language contact   Along the paths of resettlement and migration, contact with other language groups often takes place. This contact can influence both general language and specific dialect formation as the languages borrow from each other. For example, in the seventeenth century, there was primary influence from American Indian groups, reflected in the general incorporation into English of words like *moccasin, raccoon,* and *chipmunk;* in the eighteenth century there was primary influence from French, giving English items like *bureau, depot,* and *prairie.* German gave English *delicatessen, kin-*

dergarten, and *hamburger,* while Spanish gave it *canyon, rodeo,* and *patio.* All of these items are now in widespread use across the varieties of American English so that they are no longer considered dialect-specific features.

In areas where contact with another language has been more intensive and localized, such as French in New Orleans, German in southern Pennsylvania, or Spanish in the Southwest, such borrowing may be more restricted to a given dialect, so that terms such as *lagniappe* (a small present) in New Orleans comes from the French influence, *stollen* (a kind of cake) in southeastern Pennsylvania comes from the German influence, and *arroyo* (a kind of gully) in the Southwest comes from Spanish. In many cases, words from other languages profile the influence of another group in terms of a particular cultural motif, such as the foods of New Orleans or the cowboys of the Southwest.

Exercise 1

Following are words borrowed from French, Spanish, and German. For the most part, these words are regionally restricted to areas where more extensive contact with native speakers of one of these languages took place. Identify the language that each of the words comes from, and where you would expect to find the item regionally.

> *coulee, aparajo grass, serape, foosnocks, cuartel, bayou, pumpernickel, zwiebach, levee, rathskeller, pirogue.*

Do you know the meanings of all of the preceding words? Which ones give you the most difficulty? Why?

Dialect influence from language contact is not limited to vocabulary items, although this is the most obvious type to the casual observer. Particular suffixes have been borrowed from other languages as well, such as German *-fest* in *songfest, slugfest,* and *gabfest* and the French suffix *-ee* (reinterpreted from its French feminine reference) in items like *draftee, enlistee,* and *trainee.* In southeastern Pennsylvania, with its heavy influx of German settlers, the use of the syntactic structure *Are you going with?* for *Are you going with us?* is most reasonably accounted for by tracing it to an analogous construction in German (*Gehst du mit?*). And in the South, the absence of *be* copula in forms such as *They in the house* or *We going to the store* among both blacks and whites can be attributed to the influence of language variety spoken by blacks originally. Forms taken from other language groups often blend into other features of dialect differentiation over time and thus become difficult to trace, but a careful examination of the history of English substantiates the importance other languages have had in molding both the common features of American English and its various dialects.

The historical facts of settlement, migration, and language contact constitute important bases for the development of dialects, but they are not the whole answer. For even if these factors were held constant, we would expect language differentiation. Large populations with similar settlement and migratory backgrounds still manage to establish dialects among different groups within the population. This is because there are sociological and psychological bases for talking differently that have to be recognized along with historical and physical factors.

Economic ecology   How people earn their living often goes hand in hand with how populations are distributed geographically and culturally. In the United States, there is a full complement of ecologically-based occupations, including fishing in coastal areas, coal mining in the mountains, and farming in the plains. Different economic bases not only bring about the development of specialized vocabulary items associated with different occupations; they also may affect the direction and rate of language change which molds dialects in grammar and pronunciation as well. The development of a rural, agriculturally-based lifestyle in some parts of the United States vis-à-vis the urban, industrialized focus of other areas is reflected in dialect differences on all levels of language organization.

In American society, metropolitan areas have become the locus of change, and rural areas have been slower to change. In this respect, language is just one of the areas in which this pattern of "cultural lag" is indicated. Thus, many of the retentions of older forms of English, such as the *a-* prefix in *He was a-hunting and a-fishing* or the [h] in *Hit's nice out today* are found currently only in rural areas. If dialectologists want to observe whether an older form of English is still in use in a particular area, they will typically seek out older, lifetime rural residents, and if they want to see if a recent language change has been adopted, they will seek out younger metropolitan-area speakers. Given the current demographics of many large metropolitan areas in the United States, this search for newer forms often focuses on suburbanites. Originally, the urban-rural distinction may have had a strong economic basis, but it has become much more than that in its linguistic reflection of regional and cultural differences.

Social stratification   Social stratification is a fact of life in American society. We may debate the number of distinct classes in the society and the precise basis for their delineation, but the reality of social status differences cuts across virtually all regional variation in English. The upper strata distinguish themselves from the lower strata in a whole range of social behaviors, including language, whether they reside in a southern community like Anniston, Alabama, or a large northern metropolitan one like New York City. The realization that a group from a different social stratum is getting "too close for comfort" may be sufficient reason to put distance between groups. One linguist went so far as to reduce the social basis for language change to a pattern indicating the "protracted pursuit of the elite by an envious mass, and consequent 'flight' of the elite" (Fisher 1958:2). It is not quite that simple, given the complex array of sociopsychological factors that can influence language change and the fact that both the upper and lower classes can initiate change, but the primacy of social strata as a basis for language differences is obvious.

It is difficult to talk about regional dialect differences in English without qualifying these in terms of social status considerations. When we talk about the *hit/it* or *a-hunting* found in Appalachia, as we did earlier, we need to qualify this observation in terms of different social groups of Appalachians. It is also important to note that there are a number of features of English language variation, such as double negation (e.g., *She ain't been nowhere/She hasn't been anywhere*), irregular verb forms (e.g., *She done it/She did it*), and comparative forms (e.g., *more bigger/bigger*), whose dialect distribution is best explained by starting with the consideration of social status differences. In these cases, social status is primary and other factors secondary in explaining the basis for the distribution of forms.

The one possible community exception to social stratification in American English is the small, homogeneous community isolated from the mainstream population, and we simply don't find very many communities like that. Maybe a couple of small isolated fishing communities found along the eastern seaboard qualify for this designation, but these certainly are the exception. The essential role of social status in defining the dialects of English is the rule in American society.

Communication networks   Who people talk to on a regular basis can sometimes be an important factor in the determination of dialect differences. The interactional patterns that typify people's conversational contact actually exist on a couple of levels. On one level, entire communities or regions may be affected by different patterns of intersectional transportational flow and population movement. As a general locale, areas like Washington, DC and Charleston, West Virginia, are very different in terms of population movement and, subsequently, "intersectional conversation." In fact, in Washington, DC, it is common to assume that "everybody's from someplace else," an assumption which clearly influences people's perceptions of those around them, as well as the definition of the dialect norm. People in the area are unsure of what a "native Washingtonian" is supposed to sound like, and the area has adopted a northern Standard English norm, even though the areas surrounding Washington, DC are southern. On the other hand, people in Charleston, West Virginia do not have difficulty distinguishing a native from a nonnative, and the standard norm is clearly a southern highland one. Certainly, the extent to which there is intersectional communication in the area, no doubt related to actual patterns of population transiency, has had a role in defining the present-day dialects of different regions.

On another level, the notion of communication network can be applied to the particular *social networks* which govern people's day-to-day conversation. On this level, we are concerned with the individual's pattern of social transactions within a community. Who are the kinds of people that a speaker interacts with on a regular basis? Is it family, neighborhood friends, friends of friends, or are there patterns of sustained contact with people outside the immediate community? There may be significant differences in the "density" of the various clusters of social networks, and these can have a direct relation to the dialect maintained by an individual speaker. For example, high-density networks, where speakers tend to interact with the same people in a number of different social transactions, correlate with the maintenance of vernacular forms.

Group reference   People want to be considered as a part of a particular social group as opposed to other groups, and part of this identity is symbolized by talking like other members of the group. The strength of this association may range from intense loyalty and pride to consigned membership in a cultural group without choice, and the levels of language involved may range from the relatively superficial adoption of certain vocabulary items to the maintenance of subtle pronunciation and grammatical patterns. For example, teen-agers may focus prominently on the so-called "slang" of age cohorts to distinguish themselves from older and younger groups, while an ethnic variety such as Vernacular Black English involves a complex array of grammatical, phonological, and lexical structures in its delimitation. In between, the native residents of Martha's Vineyard, an island off the coast of Massachusetts, rely on a restricted set of vowel distinctions to set apart the "locals" from tourists and other "outsiders." The level of language serving to represent the group, however, is not necessarily related to the depth of the symbolic significance. A teen-ager who does not adopt some of the terms of a peer group may be making a superficial language choice, but the choice may hold formidable consequences in terms of group acceptance.

In American English, the symbolic significance of an ethnic or regional variety may put a speaker in a bind between the primary social status associations of an external reference group and indigenous group identity. Thus, some features of Vernacular Black English may be associated with ethnic solidarity at the same time they are socially stigmatized by the mainstream culture; Appalachian English is associated with a rural, stigmatized vernacular at the same time it is associated with a person's native roots. Faced with the dilemma of choosing between group solidarity and external reference group status, it is not uncommon for speakers to attempt to balance their dialects carefully to live in two worlds. Native speakers of a vernacular dialect in eastern Tennessee who have moved away often feel constrained to shift to some degree back to the native dialect when visiting with family back home. Furthermore, the failure to make some linguistic accommodations may be interpreted as a kind of symbolic group rejection. An individual's dialectal range is often related to flexibility in terms of balancing status and solidarity constraints. Some speakers of American English dialects are amazingly adroit at balancing the dialects of English symbolically to live in different worlds—the world of meaningful group identity and the world of external and institutional mainstream status. Others are not as successful in balancing their dialects between competing marketplaces and pay the social consequences in terms of the vernacular group identity or the external reference group status.

The basis for group identity may be defined along a number of different social parameters, but the basic explanation for the language difference invariably reduces to the in-group and out-group. It may be teen-agers versus other age groups, ethnics versus others, or locals versus outsiders, but basically it is "us" and "them."

Character attributes   When a former president of the United States, Ronald Reagan, said in a nationally televised address that the United States "ain't gonna back down to nobody," he was not lapsing into a native dialect or solidifying his standing with a particular vernacular-speaking group. Instead, he seemed deliberately and consciously to choose a nonstandard form of English that has connotations of determination, toughness, and resolve. Particular dialects carry with them a set of connotations related to character attributes that may range from intellectual competence to moral resolution. These personality traits go along with the sociological and historical associations we have already discussed, such as social stratification and group identity. A vernacular dialect may thus be associated with the underclass at the same time as it carries connotations of strength and openness, whereas a standard variety may be socially prestigious at the same time as it carries connotations of duplicity and pretentiousness. In some cases, these character associations may outweigh sociological considerations as a motivation for dialect adoption. Thus, speakers may identify with or avoid particular dialects because of the set of character attributes associated with the forms rather than the group factors.

On several occasions in my academic experience, I have been surprised to hear native American academicians who sounded British, although they had never spent any significant time with British English speakers. My only explanation for the adoption of such forms is because of the positive associations that British English has with respect to erudition and academics in American society.

In the cases cited previously, the motivation for adopting a set of language forms seems to be more individual than group-based, but the force of character associations as a basis for molding groups of speakers cannot be discounted. New England schoolteachers in times past were known to drill students in a speech style which reflected directly the heritage of the British Isles, even though the forces of change in the area were making the dialect linguistically more distant from England. Some students of the history of American English cite this practice as a partial explanation for the Boston broad *a* pronunciation in *half* and *calf*, which is closer to the British production than most other American English varieties. And in Boston today, there remains a small subset of speakers who speak the so-called "Brahman dialect," a prestigious variety which has more resemblance to British English than other varieties of English.

It is important to understand that the motivation to learn Standard English may be based not on the desire to belong to the reference group of middle-class Standard English speakers, but because of an attendant set of attributes related to the association of competence, intelligence, and achievement that have grown around the Standard English mythology. In American society, it is possible to be dumb, but "talk smart," and conversely, to be smart but "talk dumb." Considerations of character associations may actually outweigh other factors in defining the linguistic presentation of self in the society. When I give a lecture using some nonstandard forms of English, I realize that some students will think I can't be very intelligent because of the character connotations that these forms carry. The associations between dialect and personal attributes can be very strong and difficult to overcome, and I have had students confide to me that it was initially very difficult for them to believe that I could be a competent teacher and still "talk like that."

Linguistic explanation   The other side of explaining dialects is rooted in the structure of language as opposed to the structure of society. It is sometimes assumed that the dialects of a language may differ in multifarious, random ways. This is not true! Instead, the evidence from actual dialect divergence suggests that there are higher-order principles of language structure that guide the ways in which the dialects of a language will differ from each other. Different kinds of social pressures may lead to the acceptance or rejection of potential changes leading to dialect divergence, but the differences themselves will be systematic and follow certain orderly principles of language development.

As a starting point, we need to understand that all languages are dynamic systems which are constantly in the process of changing. Certainly, the language Shakespeare used in his plays is different from today's English, as was the English of the Elizabethan period compared to a period several centuries earlier. The English language today is also undergoing change, and people several centuries from now will look back on the English of this period as "archaic," just as we look at the English of several centuries ago. In fact, the only language not undergoing change is a "dead language"— a language without speakers.

Under the constant pressure to change, some groups adopt a particular change and others do not. The end result of this selective adoption process results in a dialect difference if the adopted form stabilizes as a characteristic of some social group of speakers. The pressure for dialect variation may come from within the system itself, as the patterns within the language are adjusted and readjusted because of the way the system is organized. In other words, the patterns of the language itself direct change in certain ways. These kinds of developments are called *changes from within*, because they take place independent of outside language influences. Changes also may originate from contact with other language communities, as structures are *borrowed* or *transferred* from other languages or dialects. These are referred to as *changes from outside*. Although we distinguish the two sources of change, they often work hand in hand as the internal structure of the system may dictate what items from outside will be adopted and how.

Interestingly, some of the same principles of language organization that account for variation in the dialects of a language also account for the kinds of adaptation language undergoes in first- or second-language acquisition. In fact, one of the most frequently asked questions about the features of vernacular dialects is why some structures look so much like the kinds of modifications found in the developmental stages of language acquisition. In other words, we hear that certain endings are "dropped" in dialects or certain verb forms are changed and these same changes are found at various stages in the process of language acquisition. Unfortunately, this observation too often has led to the erroneous conclusion that vernacular dialects are nothing more than imperfectly learned versions of the standard variety. In reality, language learning and dialect variation are just two types of language situations that are subject to a set of underlying principles about how language is organized and how it changes.

We observe further that dialects without any apparent contact with each other often share certain features. For example, some patterns of subject-verb agreement such as *we was*, plural formation such as *oxes* and *deers*, and consonant combinations such as *tes'* for *test* are common to White Vernacular English spoken in Appalachia, native American Indian vernacular varieties spoken on reservations in the southwestern United States, and Vernacular Black English spoken in northern urban areas, despite the absence of significant contact between these groups. Why is it that these same structures are so far reaching in their adoption? As we said earlier, the answer lies in the way language structure is organized in our minds and the processes of physical production and perception. At this point, we consider some of the actual underlying principles that help us account for the systematic linguistic basis of dialect differentiation.

Generalization   Other things being equal (which, of course, they never are thanks to social pressures to accept and reject various natural developments), there is a tendency for language systems to become more general in the way their patterns operate. That is, a language pattern or rule may expand the linguistic context in which the pattern applies or may extend the class of items affected by the rule.

As an example, consider the current rule of negation in English in its more restricted (standard) and its more expanded, generalized (vernacular) versions. In Standard English, the negative is typically restricted to one element in the sentence, often within the verb phrase as in *The students were not reading the assignments*. This negative marking pattern is fairly straightforward, unless the sentence involves an indefinite word such as *anybody* or *any*. When these indefinite forms are involved in a sentence, an adjustment to the rule must be made. If the indefinite is placed before the verb, then the negative is marked on the indefinite, as in *Nobody was reading the assignments*. If, however, the indefinite comes after the verb, the negative may be placed in the verb phrase, as in *The students weren't reading anything*, with a stylistic option to mark only the following indefinite as in *The students were reading nothing*. A rule which allows the negative to appear on the indefinite *and* in the verb phrase, regardless of where the indefinite is placed, is a more general pattern than one which limits the negative to a single marking that must be adjusted when an indefinite occurs in the sentence. The following sentences in (2) are thus more general versions of the negation rule than those in (1).

1. a.   The dog *didn't* like anybody.
    b.   *Nobody* was there.
2. a.   The dog *didn't* like *nobody*.
    b.   *Nobody wasn't* there.

In the examples in (1), the negative is restricted to one element in the sentence as described previously, but in the examples in (2), the range of occurrences is expanded to include both the verb phrase and the indefinite, wherever it occurs. In other words, the rule that places the negative is applied without the restrictions of a single, selective negative marking, and is thus more general. This pattern, illustrated in (2), occurs in many vernacular varieties of English.

Exercise 2

So-called double negatives were quite common in earlier periods of the English language, as indicated in the following sentences from Early Modern English, the period that gave us Chaucer and Shakespeare, among others:

There was *no* man *nowhere* so vertuous.
He taketh *nothing* to hold of *no* man *ne* of *no* woman.

During this period, these double negatives were the only option available for forming particular negative sentences. Many other current languages also make exclusive use of multiple negative marking to form negative constructions, as in Spanish *"No* hizo *nada"* or French *"Il n'a rien* fait." Given the facts about the history of the English language and the formation of negation in other languages, how are we to react to the traditional, prescribed notion that the use of multiple negation is an illogical use of language? What are the consequences of such a position with respect to the status of earlier stages of English, and modern Spanish and French? Where do you think the prescriptive dictum that negatives in language cancel each other came from to begin with?

The more general version of the negative rule may also occur in the speech of first- and second-language learners of English, regardless of the kinds of contact these speakers have with other English dialects. It is amusing to hear concerned Standard English-speaking parents wonder where their children might have picked up double negatives when they have carefully limited the contact of these children to other middle-class children. The fact of the matter is that children don't need vernacular language models as a source for forms such as *She didn't do nothing.* All the child has to do is go through the normal language development process, and apply the underlying principles of language organization that guide all of us toward the generalization of patterns. That middle-class dialects have turned away from this more generalized version of the rule is a kind of linguistic accident that has somehow taken on social meaning.

Similar cases of rule generalization can be found in the pronunciation patterns of language as well, as rules found in a restricted linguistic context are expanded. For example, there is a rule in Standard English that operates to delete the unstressed, initial [w] in the modal *will* or *would,* giving us forms like *I'll go* for *I will go* or *I'd go* for *I would go.* This rule is quite restricted in its use; of all the words that begin with the sound [w], only those with *will* or *would* are eligible. A more general version of this pattern extends the deletion process to other classes of words beginning with [w], so that items such as *was* or *ones* (pronounced [wənz]) are produced without the [w] (e.g., *they's* for *they was* or *young 'uns* for *young ones*) in some American English varieties. The [w] that is lost is the same kind of phonetic segment as that found in *will* and *would,* but the linguistic class of items included in the pattern is broader.

We could cite many other examples of generalization accounting for variation in dialects, but the important point to understand is that all languages exert pressure to move towards more general versions of rules, and that this tendency is a major linguistic explanation for many kinds of language differences. For one reason or another, some of these generalizations are accepted by certain groups of speakers while rejected by others. Dialects will inevitably share many rules, with some of the differences simply related to more general and less general versions of a shared pattern. No inherent social value can be attached to how general or restricted a particular rule is, for a given dialect will contain both kinds of rules when compared with the other dialects of the language.

Analogy   The term *analogy* is typically used to refer to a similarity or likeness of things that are otherwise different. In the study of language, this notion is extended to refer to existing patterns of a language that are used as the basis for bringing other forms into conformity with these patterns. For example, most plurals in English are created by adding the suffix spelled -*s* or -*es*. (This is phonetically [s], as in *cats* [kæts], [z] as in *bags* [bægz], or [Iz] as in *dishes* [dIšIz].) Given this predominant pattern, we are not surprised to find forms such as *oxen* being changed to *oxes* in various language situations, including dialectal variation. Again, this is a natural process in terms of the organizational principles that characterize the human mind. In many cases, the prevalent pattern, also called "regular" forms, exerts pressure on patterns which apply only to a few items, or "irregular" forms. Shifts which eliminate exceptions, or irregular forms, are referred to as *regularization*.

Languages tolerate irregular patterns, but they don't really prefer them, so that there is a tendency to make the exceptions to dominant, productive patterns conform to the regular patterns. Present-day Standard English reveals that many of today's regular forms were yesterday's irregular forms, and it is only reasonable to expect the same process to continue working among the current dialects of English. For example, each of the sentences in (3) below illustrates a regularization of some type.

3.   a.   She *knowed* the woman.
      b.   The *oxes* pulled the cart.
      c.   *Mines* is here.
      d.   That is *badder* than this.

Example (3a) illustrates regularization of an irregular verb form, (3b) the regularization of an irregular plural, (3c) the regularization of the possessive suffix form (note the paradigm *yours, his/hers/its, ours, theirs*), and (3d) the regularization of the irregular comparative form. In each case, the prevalent pattern serves as the basis for the change of an exception. Again, we find that this kind of change is not unique to dialect variation, but is found in various language situations leading to language adaptation. It is a natural, expected, and predictable way in which language changes in a number of different situations.

Exercise 3

In present-day Standard English, person and number agreement between subject and verb have been greatly reduced from an earlier, more expansive system. For example, in Middle English, spoken from about 1300–1500, an -e suffix was used for first person (e.g., *I goe*), -*est* for second person (e.g., *thou goest*) and *eth* for third person singular (e.g., *he goeth*). The modern English system retains only an -*s* on third person singular forms, as in *She likes dialects.* Some vernacular dialects of English use a form without the -*s* as in *She like dialects.* Why might this be considered as a regularization of a prevalent pattern? Is it like the examples presented in the discussion? If not, how is it different?

Irregular patterns may also serve as the basis for analogic change, although these are not as common as regularization. In these cases, which we call *minority pattern analogy*, an irregular pattern is enhanced rather than the prevalent one. In present-day Standard English, the past and participle forms of *ring, rang,* and *rung* developed originally from a regular pattern by analogy with the minority pattern *sing, sang,* and *sung.* In an older form of English, *ring* was a regular verb form (e.g., *ring, ringed, ringed*), but over the years it was remodeled by analogy with the *sing/sang/sung* irregular pattern. In vernacular dialects of English, the forms *bring, brang,* and *brung* (e.g., *She brang them a present* or *She has brung them a present*) result from the process of one irregular pattern (*bring, brought, brought*) changing to conform to another.

We already pointed out that both analogical regularization and irregularization have left their mark on the development of English over time, thus maintaining a balance of regular and irregular forms in the language. The social judgments that rendered some changes by analogy socially acceptable, and thus standard, while others became socially stigmatized, and thus nonstandard, have nothing to do with the direction of language change itself, but only with the relative status of particular social groups in society who adopt and maintain particular linguistic changes. Thus, the standard variety has accepted *ring, rang, rung* while continuing to reject *bring, brang,* and *brung.* From the standpoint of strict linguistics, what forms become standard and what forms become nonstandard is purely accidental. From a sociological perspective, of course, it is no accident that the forms associated with socially favored groups become established as the standard and those associated with low-status groups remain the nonstandard.

Redundancy reduction   All languages contain considerable redundancy in their structure; that is, they mark at more than one point a particular grammatical function or form. Although languages are by no means organized for the most efficient transmission of information bits, there is pressure from within the system to eliminate some structural redundancy. A prime example of redundant marking in English is the agreement marker that is added to present tense verbs when they have a third person subject (e.g., *She likes the story*). Another redundant marker is the plural ending that is added to a noun even though a quantifier already indicates a plural (e.g., *many boys, four inches*). In fact, many of the inflectional suffixes of English are redundant in that they mark grammatical relationships that are indicated in other ways in the language as well. One of the focal points for variation in language is the set of redundant grammatical markings which may be omitted, resulting in differences in form but not necessarily any differences in meaning. For example, the sentences in (4) reflect the omission of such markers in English.

4. a. She like__ the class.
    b. The pole is four inch__ long.
    c. John__ hat is on the floor.
    d. The man __ ugly.

The first three examples (4a–c) illustrate the three structural functions of the English inflectional -*s* suffix: third person singular present tense (4a), the plural (4b), and the possessive (4c). All of these are, to a large extent, redundant in English since other factors in a sentence may signal the same structural information. In (4d), the present tense form of *be* is absent, since it redundantly marks the relationship between the noun *man* and adjective *ugly*, which already is shown by their positions in the sentence. It may be difficult for English speakers to think of the use of the linking verb, or copula *be* in this instance as "redundant," but there are many well-developed languages of the world where such a structure is, in fact, not used in this construction without any loss of meaning. Japanese and Russian are just two of the many languages of the world that are typified by the absence of the copula.

In English, many of the case forms of pronouns (e.g., subject forms such as *I, she* versus object forms such as *me, him*) have become redundant vestiges of a period in the development of the language when grammatical relationships were indicated by case endings rather than word order. As "fixed word order" (for example, the subject was consistently placed before the verb and the object after it) took over for "free word order" (where the positioning of subject in relation to the verb and object was more flexible), the case endings became redundant and thus vulnerable to change. This change is still ongoing in varying degrees in different dialects, ranging from the loss of objective forms on the relative pronoun in casual styles of Informal Standard English (e.g., *The man who I was talking about/The man whom I was talking about*) to the vernacular dialect extension of "objective" pronouns for coordinate subjects (e.g., *Him and me like football/He and I like football*), to the English-based creole languages which use virtually all case undifferentiated pronoun forms (e.g., *me like 'im/I like him*).

Redundancy reduction does not exist in isolation from other principles that govern change and variation, such as generalization and analogy, and there are lots of instances in which redundancy reduction may lose out to one of these other principles. For example, the vernacular dialect pattern of multiple negation as in *He didn't do nothing* involves generalization, but it also builds up redundancy by marking the negative at more than one point in the sentence. Furthermore, languages need a certain amount of redundancy to carry out efficient communication, since speakers and listeners do not attend to every "bit of information." The actual working out of the various principles involves a delicate balance of internal pressures which often complement but sometimes compete with one another.

Exercise 4

Consider the way in which some forms of the comparative and superlative in vernacular dialects of English increase rather than reduce redundancy, as in *more uglier* or *most beautifulest*. How might you explain these cases? How strong do you think the principle of redundancy is compared to the other principles just discussed? Are there any kinds of language situations in which redundancy reduction might become more prominent as a characteristic leading to language variation?

Naturalness   The principles introduced so far have been concerned with language change and variation that make the system "more sensible" from the perspective of how language is organized in the human mind. With respect to the pronunciation of a language, some segments or sequences of sounds appear to be more "natural" than others in terms of how they are produced or how they are heard rather than the organizational strategies of the human mind. The pressure to change toward physiologically more natural sounds or sequences of sounds may also guide the path of change leading to dialect differences.

In some cases, particular sounds may be physiologically more involved or complex than others, so that there is pressure to modify the sounds to more natural segments. For example, the *th* (phonetically [θ]) of *think*, *bath*, or *nothing* is more complex, and therefore not as common as sounds such as [t], [f], or even [s], in many phonetic contexts. As a result, speakers vary widely in their production of this sound, ranging from the accented production of *think* as *sink* or *tink* found among second-language learners of English to the native vernacular dialect production of *nothing* as *nuttin'* or *bath* as *baf*.

In other cases, the segments in a phonetic sequence may be changed so that they are more compatible with each other. The various combinations of consonants at the end of English words, as in items such as *test* [tɛst], *tests* [tɛsts], *tempt* [tɛmpt], *tempts* [tɛmpts] lead to some relatively complex and therefore "unnatural" sequences phonetically. There is thus a tendency to simplify some of these sequences by all speakers of English, which take slightly different roads among standard and vernacular dialects. Very few speakers of English, in informal style, will produce *tests* as [tɛsts] with all three consonants intact at the end of the word. Speakers of standard varieties may simplify the sequence by producing a lengthened [s:], such as [tɛs:] whereas vernacular speakers might produce it with two syllables, as in [tɛsɪz]. Similarly, Informal Standard English might reduce the cluster of [st] in *test* when the following word begins in a consonant (e.g., *test case* is produced as [tɛs kes]). Some vernacular dialects may extend this natural process to words beginning with a vowel, so that *test it* would become [tɛs ɪt].

Related to the tendency to make sequences of sounds more compatible with each other is the pressure to make the structure of syllables phonetically simpler. The universal and most natural syllable consists of a single consonant (C) and vowel (V), the CV sequence (as in *to* or *me*), and many variable features can be explained on this basis. In some cases, the pressure toward this "ideal" syllable may result in the insertion of a segment, as in the difference between *athletic* with and without the medial schwa [ə] (e.g., *ath*[ə]*letic* versus *athletic*) separating two consonants. In other cases it may result in a loss of a segment to form a CV sequence, as in the alternation between *p'ofessor* and *professor* where the CV variant at the beginning is simpler than the CCV.

Different pressures toward naturalness sometimes work at odds with each other, so that a natural change on one level may result in a less natural structure on another level. For example, many of the final consonant sequences, or clusters, of present-day English developed from the loss of a final vowel present at an earlier stage, so that the final consonant cluster of *soft* (from *sof-te*) or *kept* (from *kep-te*) resulted when the final vowel was lost in a natural process of "unstressed vowel reduction" (i.e., vowels that do not occur in a stressed syllable are modified or lost). The final consonant clusters are then subject to a natural tendency toward simplification into final single consonants, as in *soft* → *sof'* or *kept* → *kep'*. The persistent pressure toward naturalness thus subjects language to a continual process of adjustment and readjustment and accounts for the fact that the language change and variation do not simply take a unilateral course toward simplicity and naturalness.

Innovation   We have now considered explanations of linguistic diversity based on the internal organization of the cognitive system or physiology of speech production. But we must also understand that dialect diversity also comes from a linguistic response to physical and social conditions surrounding language and the need to label relevant categories of this environment. In its need to name new and different things, languages can be quite innovative, and this creative capacity to label objects and events is an important factor leading to dialect differences in the lexicon, or vocabulary, of the language. The adaptation of the English language to accommodate the space age or the computer generation is just another demonstration of this capacity, which ranges from the myriad of terms used for various agricultural designations in a rural setting to the jargon of urban athletics or the field of nuclear physics. A number of different processes within a language can be used to create new words, and words from other languages can be readily incorporated as well. Following is a list of some linguistic devices that can be used to create new labels, with examples. These words may be associated with social groups or regional groups of various types, including special interest groups. A new word typically starts out with a restricted range of usage, and if it persists only among a regional or social subset of speakers, it becomes established as a dialect form. If it spreads across a wide range of English dialects, then it emerges as a general characteristic of the English language. The examples in the following list illustrate both broad-based and dialectally restricted items as developed through the different processes available for new word creation.

Process	Definition	Examples
compounding	two or more existing words are combined to form a new word	*ingroup, honeysuckle, badmouth*
derivation	affixes are added to create new forms or change the part of speech	*forestry, badness, bewitched*
borrowing	words from other languages are incorporated into the language or dialect	*moccasin* (American Indian) *delicatessen* (German) *arroyo* (Spanish)
blending	parts of two words are combined to form a new word	*smog* (smoke/fog) *brunch* (breakfast/lunch) *sitcom* (situation/comedy)
acronyms	new words are formed by taking the initial sounds or letters from existing words	*radar* (radio detecting and range) *WASP* (white Anglo Saxon Protestant) *UN* (United Nations)
clipping	words are formed by shortening an existing word	*gas* (gasoline) *dorm* (dormitory) *perm* (permanent)
conversion	words are shifted from one part of speech to another without any change in their form	*run* (as a noun in "They scored a *run*.") *bottle* (as a verb in "She bottled the water.") *tree* (as a verb in "They treed a cat.")

Exercise 5

For each of the following English words, identify the process from the preceding list which accounts for its creation. Note that some of the items involve more than one process.

ingrown, prof, AIDS, selectric, avocado, motel, iguana, yuppyish, creampuff, phenom, picturesque, gym, NCAA, decaf, twirl, comeuppance, skyjacker, guestimating.

Do some of the sources of creation seem less apparent than others? If so, do you think it is related to the type of linguistic process involved or history (that is, how long the item has existed in its current form)?

Such innovative mechanisms represent only a partial list of the ways in which a language may be adapted to carry out communication needs under an ever-changing set of physical and social conditions. It is difficult to predict which creations will find widespread adoption and which will remain restricted to particular groups of speakers, but the continuous, active operation of the processes in dialect formation is undeniable. Many of the common English words of today started out as dialect-specific items, and then simply spread across dialects to the point where they have become identified as common items in English vocabulary. The next time you drive your car on the *interstate* to go to the *mall* to pick up *odds and ends,* you might think about all the common words of English that have entered or are entering the general lexicon of English through its dialectal roots.

By the same token, there are also present-day items which were once in widespread usage, but have since retracted to regional usage only. For example, the use of the *garrett* for *attic,* or *yonder* for *over there* in rural southern dialects are local retentions of older items which were once in much wider use in the English language. When a particular group of speakers does not participate in a change taking place elsewhere in the language, the result may lead to a retraction of a common language item to dialect-specific status.

THE FINAL PRODUCT

In the identification of important linguistic and sociohistorical factors accounting for dialects, we must consistently bear in mind that particular factors do not work in isolation. Basic linguistic and sociohistorical factors do not come in neat, self-contained packages in the real world. The exact weight of each linguistic and sociohistorical ingredient in the development of a dialect is difficult to specify with great precision. This does not, however, detract from the highly structured nature of the resultant variety and the different roles it fills in society.

Perhaps the work of a master chef is the best analogy we can draw to the interaction of the factors accounting for dialects. This chef identifies the basic ingredients in a dish and then describes its preparation by telling us to throw in a little handful of one ingredient, a big handful of another, and just a touch of still another while it is cooking. The resultant dish turns out to be a wonderfully tasteful concoction when prepared by the chef, but it is extremely difficult to replicate. Similar to the confections of high cuisine, dialects are formed by combining sociohistorical and linguistic factors in proportions that are sometimes difficult to measure precisely. The resultant language variety, however, turns out to be a uniquely molded dialect that is a matchless testimony to the dynamic nature of language as a sociolinguistic phenomenon.

Further Reading

KURATH, HANS, "The Origins of the Dialectal Differences in Spoken American English," in *A Various Language: Perspectives on American Dialects*, eds. Juanita V. Williamson and Virginia Burke. New York, NY: Holt, Rinehart and Winston, 1971. This reprint of an article originally published in 1928 offers a brief overview of the original British influences on American English and some of the migratory patterns that account for their geographical dispersion. As a summary of the state of dialect knowledge prior to the launching of the *Linguistic Atlas of the United States and Canada*, it is an important historical document.

LABOV, WILLIAM, *Sociolinguistic Patterns*. Philadelphia, PA: University of Pennsylvania Press, 1972. Several of the chapters in this collection, particularly Chapters 1, 4, 5, and 7, reveal how the processes of linguistic change interact with social forces to delimit the varieties of English.

PRESTON, DENNIS R., "Fifty Some-Odd Categories of Language Variation," *International Journal of the Sociology of Language* 57:9–48. (1986) This presentation provides a basic taxonomy of the types of social variables that may affect language variation, based on the sociolinguistic literature. It is a very helpful summary.

SHUY, ROGER W., "The Reasons for Dialects," Chapter 1 in *Discovering American Dialects*. Champaign, IL: National Council of Teachers of English, 1967. Shuy's chapter, which has been reprinted in several anthologies, summarizes the major historical reasons for dialect differentiation in a very readable presentation.

TRUDGILL, PETER, *On Dialects: Social and Geographical Perspectives*. New York, NY: New York University Press, 1983. This collection contains several chapters, in particular, Chapters 2 through 5, presenting the sociological and linguistic basis for dialect diversity. It presents linguistic and geographically-based models of explanation as an alternative to the traditional models which have an historical bias according to Trudgill. The examples are taken primarily from British rather than American English varieties, but most of the principles are broadly applicable.

CHAPTER THREE

LEVELS OF DIALECT

When we casually observe that a group of English speakers uses a different word for what we call a *submarine* sandwich, that some speakers pronounce the word *chocolate* differently from the way we do, or that speakers greet each other with *What's happenin'!* instead of *Hi!*, we are actually noting different forms of language variation. In one case, we notice a vocabulary difference, in another case a pronunciation difference, where speakers use the same word but produce it differently. Finally, "What's happenin' " and "Hi" represent different ways of accomplishing the function of greeting.

Languages are structured on several different levels and each of these can be subjected to dialectal variation. These levels include *phonology,* the sounds of language, *grammar,* the formation of words and combinations of words in sentences, *semantics,* the meaning of words, and *pragmatics,* the use of language forms to carry out particular communicative functions. We are not surprised to find dialect differences on all these levels; what is of greater interest is the specific ways in which these differences are worked out and the various social roles these differences are assigned in our society. In this chapter, we set forth these levels of dialect differences and how they function in the varieties of American English.

LEXICAL DIFFERENCES

One of the most transparent levels of dialect variation involves the vocabulary, or lexical stock of a language. Most of us can recount experiences in which our failure to identify the meaning of a term used by a regional or social group resulted in at least bemused confusion, if not communication breakdown. We may have been surprised when we traveled through the United States and ordered *sodas*, only to find that we received different drinks under this label in different regions, or surprised to discover that different people were referring to the same kind of animal when they talked about *mountain lions, cougars*, and sometimes even *panthers*. And many parents have shaken their heads in dismay when their teen-agers issued a compliment using the latest descriptive adjective such as *smooth, bad, fresh*, or *bumpin'*. Just about everyone has a collection of favorite anecdotes about lexical differences among the dialects of English, and these examples are a common topic for conversation.

There are a number of different ways in which lexical differences can manifest themselves. In one classic type, a different label is used for the same semantic referent; *skillet* and *frying pan* are simply different labels for the same kitchen utensil, and *quilt* and *comforter* refer to the same kind of bedding cover for some people. The source of the difference in labeling may take any of the innovative word formation routes discussed in Chapter 2. Thus, the piece of bedroom furniture variously labeled *dresser, chest of drawers*, and *bureau* reveals a derived form (*dresser*), a compound phrase (*chest of drawers*), and a borrowed item (*bureau*) among its dialect variants.

Another case of lexical differences involves shared words whose semantic reference has become more restricted or expanded for different groups of speakers. For example, *carry* and *take* are common English verbs, but in some southern areas, a person *carries* a date to the movies in the sense of escorting, whereas in the North, a person *takes* someone to the movies. Similarly, most American English speakers share the nouns *beach, shore*, and *ocean*, but along the New Jersey coast, a person takes a vacation (or *holiday*, if you will) at the *shore*, in Maryland and the Carolinas a person goes to the *beach*, and in still other regions a person may go to the *ocean*. In such cases, items share many semantic "senses" of a word, but one dialect expands or restricts the semantic reference.

At a given point in time, it may be difficult to trace the direction of semantic change, but a historical perspective on English word development can usually determine which of the current varieties have narrowed or broadened the semantic range of an item. The history of the English language tells us that *hound* was once used to refer to all dogs and that its use has narrowed historically in those dialects where it now refers to a particular type of dog (and for some dialects, the meanings may coexist, as speakers use *hound* informally to refer to any dog). By the same token, we know that *holiday* once referred only to religious "holy days" and that its use has since expanded to refer to any day of freedom from labor, and, in some cases, any vacation, as in *They are on holiday for a week*. Virtually all English words have narrowed or broadened their semantic range over time and this is an ongoing process. Some of these shifts, however, end up correlating with specific regional and/or social groups, and hence become dialect items. Others simply become part of the common stock of English words as their changing meanings spread among the dialects.

In another kind of semantic shift, a particular semantic feature of a lexical item is extrapolated and applied to a new class of items. This type of extension is more drastic in that it may involve the metaphorical transfer of a particular characteristic to a previously unrelated category. Thus, the term *submarine* for a particular type of sandwich may be related to the shape of the bread holding the sandwich contents as it compares with that of the submarine boat. Similarly, the term *plum* is applied to general color descriptions by extrapolating the characteristic color of the fruit. There are many instances of "new meanings for old words" across the dialects of English, although in many cases the original source of the semantic extrapolation may become quite obscure.

Exercise 1

Following are sets of lexical differences among the regional dialects of American English. For each of these sets, first attempt to determine whether the dialect difference is typified by a broadening or narrowing of a shared English word or an innovative labeling in different dialects. If the difference arose through innovative labeling, what basic processes discussed in Chapter 2 were used (e.g., derivation, borrowing, compounding, and so on)? Are there cases of labeling which look like they involved metaphorical extrapolation as discussed earlier?

1. *baby's breath/chalkweed/mist:* a type of plant, gypsophila
2. *pail/bucket:* a container holding water
3. *baby buggy/baby carriage/baby coach:* a vehicle for transporting a baby
4. *earthworm/angleworm/fishing worm/night crawler:* a type of worm used in fishing
5. *faucet/spigot/tap:* a device with a valve for regulating the flow of a liquid
6. *creep/crawl:* what babies do before walking
7. *kerosene/coal oil/lamp oil:* a petroleum derivative
8. *low lands/low ground/bottom land/savannah:* land that usually has standing water with trees or bushes growing on it
9. *armload/armful:* as much as can be carried with two hands together

10. *snap beans/string beans/green beans:* a type of vegetable with a stringy fiber on the pods

---

The inventory of lexical differences among the dialects of American English covers a wide domain of categories, and the number of dialectally sensitive words runs well into the thousands. In the questionnaire for eliciting items in the *Dictionary of American Regional English,* 41 different topical areas of lexical differences are delimited. Topography, food, furniture, animals, and equipment lead the list, but the range of possible differences is virtually unlimited and includes many descriptors of attitudinal and emotional states in addition to concrete items.

In the preceding discussion, we focused on lexical differences in so-called *content words*—words that carry primary semantic reference. There are also differences pertaining to *function words* such as prepositions (e.g., *in, on, under*) and articles (e.g., *the, a/an*), items more likely to indicate grammatical information than semantic content. In many cases, the differences in function words are confined to particular phrases, such as the differences in prepositions in *sick to/at/in/on my stomach, of/in the morning* to refer to the time of day, or the choice of articles in *have a/the toothache.* In other cases, the difference is between the use or nonuse of a function word in a particular phrase, as *live (at) Coal City* or *He was in (the) hospital.* Since content words in a language far outnumber the restricted set of function words in a language, dialect differences in the function words of English are not as common as those involving content words, but some of the function word differences can be quite diagnostic in setting apart varieties.

In most instances, the kinds of lexical differences we have discussed previously are considered to be regional curiosities of the American population, and little status significance is attached to them. There are associations related to other dimensions, such as rural-urban and cultural lifestyles considered to be "old-fashioned" or "modern," but people are not usually socially stigmatized purely on the basis of saying *soda* versus *pop* and *attic* versus *garret.* An exception to this observation are *taboo terms,* those "four-letter words" used to refer to bodily functions and various exclamations (e.g., *shit, fuck*). These items certainly stigmatize their users in particular social situations, but in American society, these items are viewed more in terms of socially appropriate behavior than social group differentiation. Speakers of any social class may be considered ill-mannered if they use these terms in inappropriate circumstances. In effect, all dialectal groups recognize taboo terms, although the conventions for usage may differ to some extent, and the identification of particular terms as taboo items may differ slightly from dialect to dialect. The use of *bloody* as an intensifier differs in its taboo status in American and British dialects (e.g., *Where is the bloody car?*) or *tits* to refer to female breasts differs in taboo status in some rural dialects as compared with nonrural dialects.

Some sets of vocabulary items characterize special interest groups rather than regional or sociocultural groups of speakers. These groups may range from technical fields such as computer technology and linguistics to recreational activities like baseball or football. Any novice computer *hacker* who has experienced *system crash* or looked for *user-friendly documentation* for a new *software* program is well aware of specialized vocabulary that has grown up around the personal computer technology. It is not unusual for a beginner to confront enough technical terms in a simple sentence so as to make it practically incomprehensible. By the same token, a casual observer of a Sunday afternoon football game may be told that "The Redskins' *nickel* defense *sacked* the Cowboys' quarterback in the *shotgun* formation with an all-out *blitz.*" Such cases of specialized terminology, or *jargon,* cut across many of the conventional social variables in society, including region, status, and ethnicity. Again, the mechanisms used for the development of these vocabularies follow the same principles of semantic change and innovative labeling that govern all other cases of lexical development in the language. In popular culture, the term *jargon* is sometimes used by confused or annoyed observers to refer to an unfamiliar vocabulary, and one person's technically precise terminology may be another person's jargon. From a more objective viewpoint, jargon simply refers to the specialized vocabulary characterizing a full array of special interest groups.

A more deliberately secretive jargon is referred to as an *argot,* such as a criminal argot. Some dialectologists and lexicologists have become outstanding specialists in the vocabulary of various special interest groups, although there are certainly special fieldwork problems associated with the investigation of "underworld" groups.

SLANG

Slang is one of those labels that gives dialectologists fits. In popular culture, the label is used freely to refer to everything from the general use of a vernacular dialect (e.g., "They don't speak Standard English, they speak slang") to specialized vocabulary words that are jargon (e.g., "Computer people use a lot of slang"), and words that are socially stigmatized (e.g., "*Ain't* is a slang word"). The rather loose, imprecise way it is often popularly used has caused many dialectologists to shy away from using this label at all. As one dialectologist put it, "Until slang can be objectively identified and segregated or until more precise subcategories replace the catchall label *slang,* little can be done to analyze this kind of lexis" (McMillan 1978:146). *The Dictionary of American Regional English* explicitly rejects the use of this label because it is "imprecise" and "too indefinite" (1985:xvii). At the same time, there are lexicologists who freely use this term to mark dictionary entries, with varying degrees of reliability among them, and there even exist special dictionaries devoted to slang, such as the *New Dictionary of American Slang* (Chapman 1986) and *College Slang 101* (Eble 1989).

From a strictly linguistic standpoint, words are words, and those that are labeled as slang are not unique in terms of the processes used to form them and the way their meanings come about. From the perspective of language as a kind of social behavior, however, there is a group of words labeled *slang* that have a special status in American culture, even though we can't come up with *the* definitive list or a single dimension for classifying these items. What distinguishes items classified as slang is their sociopsy-chological role rather than their linguistic composition. The notion of rel-egating some words to this special status has been around a long time (over 2,000 years according to some records). Sociolinguists and psycholinguists can hardly afford to continue dismissing this category of items on the basis of a lack of precision in its characterization. In recent years, several dialec-tologists have devoted themselves to the careful examination of this notion, and our discussion here follows closely the contributions of Dumas and Lighter (1976) and Eble (1983; 1984; 1985).

Part of the problem in defining slang comes from the fact that there appears to be a *set* of characteristics rather than a single attribute for clas-sifying slang. Furthermore, there seems to be a "slang scale," in which some items are more "slangy" than others. Just about everybody would agree that a term like *wus* for *fearful person* is a slang item and that *coward* is not, but a word like *chicken* seems to fall between the extremes. A realistic definition of this notion should take into account this continuous dimension, along with the understanding that some terms are categorically considered as slang or nonslang items.

One of the prerequisite features of slang items is their connotation of informality. Although formality and informality are not always easy to de-fine, there are certain social situations and status relationships between speakers that set the stage for formal and informal occasions. Slang items are always found at the informal end of the continuum. The reality of the formality dimension is illustrated by the fact that informal words in formal contexts are incongruous and vice versa. A cowardly person might be de-scribed variously as *pusillanimous, afraid, fearful, scared, chicken, spineless, gut-less, wimpy,* or *wussy,* but the conversational occasions considered appropriate for these different items differ drastically. Imagine the response of a football team if a coach called a player "pusillanimous," or even "fearful." These terms would be inappropriate because they are viewed as appropriate only for formal, serious occasions, not recreational or leisure activities. By the same token, it would be equally odd for a reporter questioning the President of the United States in a news conference to ask if he was a *chicken* or a *wus* about a particular political decision. Or imagine a minister opening a funeral service with a remark such as "Dearly beloved, we are gathered here to honor Mr. Jones, who has *kicked the bucket.*" To begin with, then, words classified as slang carry strong informal overtones. As Carl Sandburg put it, "Slang is language that rolls up its sleeves, spits on its hands, and gets down to business."

Another attribute of slang items is their potential for indicating a special familiarity with a group outside of the mainstream adult population. An item like *wus* is not only marked as informal, it is also associated with a relatively local and confined age group of speakers considered to be "less responsible" than the adult members of society—in this case, teen-agers and college students. Similarly, terms associated with vernacular groups might be labeled slang, such as the term *blood* as used by blacks (e.g., *He's a blood*) to refer to other blacks with a special in-group meaning. Interestingly, modern uses of the term *dude* to refer to a man or boy by nonmainstream groups of speakers (for example, blacks, teen-agers) apparently have transformed an older, nonslang use of this term (to refer to someone concerned with manners and appearance) into a slang item. Words associated with social groups outside of the mainstream have a high likelihood of being labeled slang, and items that are associated with local peer reference group identity are almost always considered slang. Slang items are often cultivated in peer group contexts, and the idea that the particular use of a term might be mysterious or secretive may make it even more appealing in its symbolic function. This is one reason why teen-agers and college students, with their emphasis on peer group relationships, are fertile grounds for the origin and cultivation of slang. That adults and people in other locales are totally unfamiliar with these terms is hardly a problem—in fact, a group of teen-agers may revel in the restricted sphere of usage of the terms. Not all items classified as slang have strong group identity associations, but many of the most extreme cases on the "slang continuum" do.

Another attribute of slang relates to its role as a special kind of synonym. Slang terms typically are associated with well-known, neutral, conventional synonyms. English speakers who use *kick the bucket* for *die*, *homeboy* for *special friend*, *wus* for *coward*, or *bumpin'* for *good* know that there is a ready alternate term but choose not to use it. Psychologically, or more properly, psycholinguistically, the slang term is thus viewed as an intentional replacement, or a "flouting" of the conventional, more neutral term, whether or not it is a conscious choice on the part of the speaker. Listeners would presume that a person who uses *wus* deliberately chooses not to use a neutral, conventional term such as *coward,* or that a speaker deliberately chooses to use *barf, puke, ralph, yak,* and so forth instead of *regurgitate, vomit,* or *throw up.* An association with synonymous items may not be a unique defining characteristic of slang, but most items carrying this label are considered deliberate replacements of a neutral, conventional term.

Finally, we should observe that slang items are often perceived as having a short life span. Certainly, some slang items have a short life span, particularly those associated with local peer groups. But many items have considerable staying power, so that *buck* for *dollar, beef* and *bitch* for *complain,* and *bull* for *insincere talk* have been around as long or longer than many other terms now incorporated as conventional words of English. Nonetheless, in popular culture, items considered slang are viewed as being ephemeral, and this perception (as opposed to reality) may contribute to the designation. Of course, many of yesterday's slang items were destined for obsolescence in the minds of the public, only to persist as more permanent fixtures in the language with all the privileges of the conventional lexical stock. It is difficult to determine which items will become part of the common lexical stock of English and which ones will die. Only time will tell if an item like *wus* catches on and is stabilized or whether it falls by the wayside of other short-lived slang items.

The discussion of slang may seem somewhat imprecise if we look for a categorical distinction between words that are slang and those that are not, but remember that slang tends to exist on a continuum, and that, to some extent, one person's slang may be another person's conventional lexicon. Some items, characterized by extremes in terms of the attributes mentioned earlier, are considered as slang by virtually all users of English, and others, sharing some but not all of the attributes, are more indeterminate in their status. This is, in fact, how the classification of slang seems to work out in American society. So far, I have yet to find a native speaker of American English who does not consider items like *wus* or *bumpin'* slang, but there is much more latitude in the classification of other items, such as *rip off* for *steal, sleazy* for *conniving,* or *buck* for *money.* The items *wus* and *bumpin'* are simply new labels for old notions that are associated with teenage peer usage in informal settings; no one expects them to be around very long. On the other hand, a term like *rip off* for *steal* is relatively informal, but not as informal as an item like *wus,* and it is now even found in more neutral contexts. Furthermore, any group identity it might have had is fast fading and it has now been around a while—at least compared with *wus.* We expect most people to consider *rip off* as slang but others may now consider it a conventional lexical item. In between slang and conventional lexical items on the continuum are items that are sometimes referred to as *colloquial.* These items share the attribute of informality with slang, but do not have as strong a connotation of group identity and flouted synonymy.

Exercise 2

Part one: Rate the following items in terms of how strongly you feel that each constitutes a slang item. Use a three-point scale, where *3* is the highest rating (you have a strong feeling that the item is slang) and *1* is the lowest rating (you don't believe that it is slang). For example, an item like *wus* might be given a rating of *3* and an item like *coward* a *1*.

1. *chicken* (afraid)
2. *zilch* (nothing)
3. *buck* (dollar)
4. *get it* (understand)
5. *frisk* (search)
6. *jerk* (undesirable person)
7. *awesome* (good)
8. *neat* (good)
9. *bumpin'* (good)
10. *cool* (good)

Part two: With your overall ratings of the above words in hand, now rate each item in terms of the four attributes given below. Rate items for each attribute, using a scale of *1* through 3; 1 represents the least and *3* the most extensive extreme of the attribute. For example, a rating of *1* for informality would indicate that an item is not informal (neutral or formal), a rating of *2* somewhat informal and a rating of *3* quite informal. In this rating scheme, *wus* would receive a *3* for informality, *2* or *3* for group identity, *3* for replacive word association, and *2* or *3* for its anticipated life span.

Attributes	Score		
Informality	1 (neutral)	2 (informal)	3 (very informal)
Group Identity	1 (none)	2 (limited)	3 (strong)
Replacive Word Association	1 (none)	2 (medium)	3 (strong)
Life Span	1 (long)	2 (medium)	3 (short)

Add the scores from the attribute scale for each item, so that all items have a cumulative rating between 4 and 12. At this point, you have two scores, one for the overall rating of each item and one for the cumulative attributes. Now compare the two scores with each other. Do you see a correlation with the ratings along these two dimensions? Do the words you rated *3* in the slang scale have strong values on all the attributes? If not, are there any attributes that seem to contribute less to the overall rating of a slang item than others? Which ones seem less critical in defining slang?

PHONOLOGICAL DIFFERENCES

Like lexical differences, phonological variation sometimes can be quite obtrusive among the dialects of American English. Many of the variations captured under the popular label *accent* focus on these characteristics, as listeners cue in on the vowels of "the southern drawl," the "broad *a*" and "dropped *r*" of Boston, or the "dropped *g*" of vernacular dialects. At the same time, some differences in phonology may be quite subtle, existing below the conscious level as they set apart various groups of speakers. Phonological patterns can be diagnostic of regional and social differences, and a person who has a good ear for dialects can often pinpoint a person's general regional and social affiliation with considerable accuracy based solely on phonology. Certainly, the use of a few critical pronunciation cues can narrow down a person's place of origin to at least general regions of the United States, if not to the precise county of origin.

There are several ways in which phonological differences may be manifested. One type involves the pronunciation of a shared, significant English sound unit, or *phoneme*. Although we don't want to engage in an extended discussion of phonological structure, it is important to recognize the phoneme as an essential construct in phonology, since it serves to contrast items. The basis for distinguishing between the words *bet* [bɛt] and *bat* [bæt] is found solely in the difference between the vowels /e/ and /æ/ since these words are identical in their other sounds. We thus say that these vowels have "phonemic status" in English and indicate this conventionally in linguistics by enclosing the sound in // brackets; these "phonemic brackets" are different from the "phonetic brackets," [], which conventionally are used to refer to the phonetic value of a sound apart from its phonemic status.

It is possible for different dialects to share a common phoneme, but to vary its phonetic production. For example, most varieties of English have a phoneme represented as the "open *o*" /ɔ/ of *bought, cough,* or *raw,* but the way this phoneme is produced phonetically varies widely from one dialect to another. In fact, the pronunciation ranges from a vowel as high as that found in words like *book* and *look* (phonetically [U]) to one as low as that found in *father* or *calm.* Similarly, the front vowel phoneme /æ/, found in words like *bat, bad,* and *man,* may range phonetically from a vowel close to the one found in *bit* or *rip* (phonetically [I]) to one close to that of *father.* Of the English vowels, the back /ɔ/ of *coffee* or *raw* and the front vowel /æ/ of *bad* and *ban* are probably the most dialectally sensitive vowels in the English language, although virtually all English vowels can be subjected to some degree of dialect variation.

Dialect differences in the phonetic quality of vowels typically affect a set of vowels rather than isolated vowels in the system. Phonetically, vowels represent points in a continuum of tongue height, fronting, and backing.

A typical charting of vowels sets forth these dimensions by the means of a vowel trapezoid such as the following, in which the dimensions represent a cross section of tongue height, lowering, and backing, as viewed from the side of the mouth. Major vowels of English are indicated in Figure 3–1, along with a "key" word in an idealized version of the standard variety, given here simply for the sake of convenience in terms of thinking about the different positions of the tongue in the production of vowels.

Given the nature of vowel production, it is convenient to view different vowels as occupying "phonetic spaces" in a continuum of vowel positions. The notion of phonetic space is important because the shift of one vowel in phonetic space often has an effect on adjacent vowels. As one vowel moves (e.g., becomes higher or more backed in its phonetic position) phonetically closer to or further away from an adjacent vowel, the next vowel may shift its phonetic value to maintain adequate phonetic distance in relation to the vowel that has moved initially. A whole sequence of vowel rotation may thus be set in motion. This overall shift in vowel systems may be illustrated by showing one dialectal pattern of adjustment in the vowels /ɔ/ (e.g., *bought*), /a/ (e.g., *pop*) and /æ/ (*bat*), where the phonetic lowering and fronting of the tongue height in [ɔ] works in tandem with the fronting of [a] and the raising of [æ], as illustrated in Figure 3–2.

The pattern of phonetic rotation in vowels, known as *chain shifting* or the *push-pull chain,* is actively involved in differentiating the current system of American English dialects. In other words, the lowering of a vowel like the [ɔ] of *bought* closer to that of the [a] of *father* may have the effect of moving the vowel of words like *pop* forward, closer to the [æ] of *bat*. This movement, in turn, may cause the vowel of *bat* to change its phonetic

FIGURE 3–1 A Typical Vowel Chart Indicating Different Tongue Positions

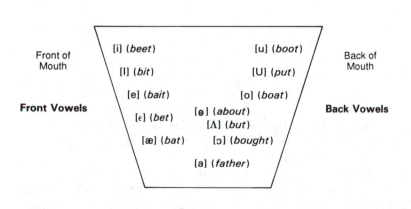

High Vowels

Front of Mouth

Front Vowels

[i] (*beet*)   [u] (*boot*)

[I] (*bit*)   [U] (*put*)

[e] (*bait*)   [o] (*boat*)

[ɛ] (*bet*)   [ə] (*about*)
          [ʌ] (*but*)

[æ] (*bat*)   [ɔ] (*bought*)

          [a] (*father*)

Back of Mouth

Back Vowels

Low Vowels

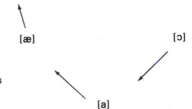

FIGURE 3–2   An Illustration of Chain Shifting in the Low Vowels of American English

position, moving closer to the [ɛ] of *bet*. The point here is that vowels are not functioning as independent units, but as a rotating system. There are actually a number of complex ramifications of such rotation for the developing system of English vowels, which we discuss more fully in Chapter 4. Chain shifting has also been quite active historically in the development of different stages of the English vowel system, as different varieties of English have systematically adjusted their vowels.

One of the well-known characteristics of English is its tendency to combine different vowels within a single vowel phoneme by gliding from one vowel into another. In these cases, there is a *nucleus*, or core vowel, and then a peripheral vowel, or *glide*. In a word like *time* or *buy*, the nucleus vowel may be like the [a] of *father* and the glide following that like the [I] of *bit*, so that *time* is pronounced [taIm]. These vowel combinations, or *diphthongs* are also quite susceptible to dialect differences. For example, the glide may be reduced or eliminated in some southern varieties (e.g., [tam] for *time*). The first part of the diphthong, or vowel nucleus, may also be quite sensitive to dialect differences, and the nucleus vowel of *boat* (phonetically a diphthong with an offglide of [U] as in [boUt] *boat*) phonetically can vary considerably in its production, from [o] to a vowel closer to the vowel of *but* [ʌ], or even the [ɛ] of *bet* in some varieties. The nucleus vowel of items like *out* (ranging from the [ɛ] of *bet* to the [æ] of *bat* and the [a] of *father*) may thus be dialectally quite diagnostic. Changes in the nucleus of the glide also may be subjected to principles of shifting as discussed previously. The change in the phonetic value of one nucleus in a diphthong (e.g., the first vowel in *house*, [aU]) may go hand in hand with other kinds of shifts, such as the shift in the nucleus vowel in *boy*, [oI]. The point here is not to elaborate all the principles of vowel rotation but to understand that dialectal differences in the phonetic value of the vowels are not typically isolated changes; rather, they involve shifts in subsystems of vowels. To a large extent, then, different dialects are distinguished on the basis of their participation in such shifts. For example, the Northern Cities Vowel Shift (an area extending from western New England through New York State, the northern tier in Pennsylvania, northern Ohio, Indiana, Illinois, Michigan and extending westward) is defined by a shift roughly approximated by that given in Figure 3–2, along with other subsystems of shifting phonetic value.

In some cases, contrasts between distinctive sound units, or phonemes, may be neutralized, or merged, in one dialect while maintained in another one. One of the well-known cases of merger in some dialects of American English involves the vowel of *caught* and *cot*. Do you hear a difference between those words when you say them? In some dialects, (e.g., an area centered around Boston, a region centered around Pittsburgh, and a vast area of the western United States), these items are pronounced with the same vowel, whereas in others, a distinction between the vowels in these items is maintained.

In many instances, a merger only takes place in restricted phonetic contexts. Sounds are highly sensitive to their surrounding phonetic context, such as the sounds they occur next to, the positions they occupy in words, and the stress patterns of syllables. It is quite common for a sound merger to take place in one phonetic context, but not in another. In one well-known case, the contrast between the vowels of *bit* [I] and *bet* [ɛ] is neutralized, but only when the following segment is a nasal sound such as [n]. Thus, in many southern dialects of English, there is no contrast between the items *pin* and *pen* (both usually pronounced as [pIn]), and *tinder* and *tender*. In these same dialects, the vowels of *pit* [pIt] and *pet* [pɛt] would remain distinct, illustrating how most cases of merger occur in some phonetic contexts (before [n] in this case) but not in others. Similarly, many northern dialects do not distinguish between *morning* and *mourning*, and others do not distinguish between *sure* and *shore*, but in these cases the critical phonetic environment for the neutralization is the following *r*. In American English, sounds that are followed by nasal sounds such as *m* and *n* and the *r* and *l* sounds are more likely to undergo changes than vowels in other phonetic environments.

Exercise 3

One of the interesting cases of vowel merger before *r* involves the vowels of the words *merry, Mary, marry,* and *Murray,* or *berry, beary* (acting like a *bear*), *Barry,* and *bury.* Ask several people who come from different regions of the country to pronounce these items and observe which items are pronounced the same and which are pronounced differently. What patterns of merger and distinction do you observe? What other sets of items fall into this general pattern? Can you identify any regional correlation among those you ask?

There are also cases in which differences between consonants may be neutralized. One classic case of neutralization is the so-called "*g* dropping." When the nasal segment represented phonetically as [ŋ] (often spelled *ng*) occurs at the end of a word in an unstressed syllable (as in *fighting*) it can be produced as the sound [n] (*fightin'*). This process makes the final nasal segment of *taken* [tekIn] and *takin'* [tekin] or *waken* [wekIn] and *wakin'* [wekIn] phonetically the same. Unfortunately, the popular term "*g* dropping" to describe this process is somewhat misleading, since the change of sound involves the substitution of one sound for another rather than the loss of a sound.

In many southern dialects, the voiced sounds [z] and [ð] of *wasn't* and *heathen* become *d* before a nasal, making them sound something like *wadn't*, and *headn*, respectively. Thus, the contrast between [z] or [ð] and [d] is neutralized before a nasal in these varieties. And, of course, there is the stereotypical *dese, dem,* and *dose* for *these, them,* and *those* and the vernacular neutralization between *f* and *th* (phonetically [θ]) so that *Ruth* and *roof* are both pronounced with a final [f]. While there are a number of cases of neutralization between segments across dialects, the phonetic contexts in which these processes occur are usually restricted.

The kinds of differences illustrated so far all concern instances in which a sound in one dialect *corresponds to* a different sound in another variety, or so-called *substitution processes*. There are also instances where basic segments are added or deleted in language variation, affecting the basic sequencing of sound segments. These are referred to as *phonotactic processes*. For example, there are cases of *l* and *r* absence in a number of dialects, such as the loss of [r] or [l] following a vowel, as in *ca'd* [kad] or *he'p* [hɛp] for *card* and *help*, respectively. As with substitution processes in phonology, such deletions are also highly sensitive to the surrounding phonetic context, so that the omission of *r* and *l* is restricted to instances in which the *r* or *l* follows a vowel. The complete absence of an [l] is confined to situations where it follows a vowel *and* precedes a labial sound such as [f] or [p], as in *woof* for *wolf* and *hep* for *help*. The case of initial [w] in unstressed syllables (e.g., *young 'uns* [yʌŋənz] for *young ones* [yʌŋ wənz] is another case of deletion but this pattern is sensitive to the position in the word and the lack of stress on the syllable.

Important phonological differences may also affect strings of consonants, or *consonant clusters*. One of the important dialect differences in English concerns the sequences of consonants at the end of words, where the cluster in items like *west* [st], *find* [nd], *act* [kt], or *cold* [ld] may be reduced to a single consonant, as in *wes'*[s], *fin'*[n], *ac'*[k], and *col'*[l], respectively. This kind of cluster reduction is found in the informal speaking styles of practically all speakers of English, but Standard English speakers tend to restrict this process to instances in which the word following the cluster begins with a consonant (e.g., *wes' point, col' cuts*). On the other hand, speakers of vernacular dialects may reduce the cluster regardless of the following segment (e.g., *wes' end, col' out*).

In another process relating to the sequencing of syllables, unstressed, syllables at the beginning of words may be deleted, resulting in *'lectricity* for *electricity* or *'member* for *remember*. There are also other cases in which the number of syllables in words differ across dialects because of reduction or insertion of vowels within the word. *Tire* and *fire* are two-syllable sequences in some dialects but single syllables in others. (They are produced something like *tar* and *far* in some Appalachian varieties.) An item like *baloney* consists of two syllables for some English speakers (*blo-ney*) but three syllables for others (*ba-lo-ney*).

As mentioned previously, one of the essential differences between some southern and northern vowel systems involves vowel glides. In some cases, these differences may lead to adjustments in the syllable sequences as well. In most northern varieties, words such as *bed* and *bill* are monosyllabic items and the vowels do not have an offglide, but in some southern varieties the vowel glides, even to the point of sounding more like a two-syllable sequence. For example, an item like *bed* (phonetically [bɛd]) in the North may be pronounced something like *beyud* [bIyəd] and *bill* (phonetically [bIl] in the North) something like *biyul* [biyUl]. This gliding, or vowel breaking, is actually becoming more distinct in southern varieties according to Feagin (1987), thus making these varieties more dissimilar from their northern counterparts.

Finally, we should mention the potential for melodic, or technically, *prosodic* differences in American English dialects. Differences in intonational contours of sentences, the timing of syllables, and stress patterns of words may certainly distinguish dialects, as well as the kinds of "segmental" differences set forth earlier, although they have generally been given less attention in dialect studies. Limited studies of intonational contours have, nonetheless, indicated some differences, so that Tarone (1973) concludes that the range of contours used by Vernacular Black English speakers is wider than those found in other American English dialects. It has also been noted that the relative intonational contours among women tend to exhibit a wider pitch range than those used by men, and that women have an extra-high pitch range not typically found among men (Brend 1975).

Variations exist in the stress patterns of words, mostly related to individual lexical items. For example, the differences in first- or second-syllable stress for items like *Júly/July*, *hótel/hotél*, and *théater/theáter* are dialectally diagnostic. Differences in the rhythm of syllables may also be involved in dialect distinctions. Thus, Spanish-influenced varieties of English often are characterized by what is referred to as syllable-timed rhythm, where each syllable in a sequence such as *in the garden* is given equal prominence. On the other hand, native English dialects tend to have phrase-timed rhythm, in which the stressed item in a phrase (in the example, the first syllable of *gárden*) is held longer than the other, less stressed syllables in the phrase.

The southern ungliding of diphthongs in items such as *time* and *ride*, along with the vowel breaking in *bed* and *bill*, have apparent consequences with respect to perceptions of the rate of speech production. The popular perception is that Southerners speak slower than Northerners. Given important qualifications (for example, the fact that it is a statistical pattern and may not hold for individual speakers), there do seem to be differences in speech rate that may correlate with the dialects of American English. Because speech rate features are sometimes exaggerated and stereotyped in popular perceptions, however, dialectologists tend to downplay such differences. The differences do not appear to be nearly as great as they are sometimes made out to be, but there may be some dialect variation related to speech rate and rhythm.

Phonological variation is usually considered interesting, but it is not always socially significant, particularly as it relates to vowel differences. Speakers may comment on the *o* of Wisconsin speakers or the broad *a* of Boston as regional peculiarities without attaching particular social stigma or prestige to them. Consonantal differences are more apt to be diagnostic socially, even to the point of stereotyping, as in the case of *dese, dem,* and *dose, baf* for *bath,* and *takin'* for *taking.* The symbolic choices of phonological patterns to indicate social differentiation among the varieties of English are difficult to explain from the standpoint of language organization, but once selected, the items may be perpetuated for generations as markers of social significance in American English.

GRAMMATICAL DIFFERENCES

Grammatical variation may be discussed in terms of two basic levels of organization. One level relates to the way in which words are formed from their meaningful parts, or *morphemes.* A word such as *girls* consists of two morphemes, the noun form *girl* and the plural suffix *-s;* a word such as *buyers* consists of three morphemes, the verb form *buy,* the agentive suffix *-er,* which changes the form from a verb to a noun, and the plural suffix *-s.* A suffix such as *-er* changes the grammatical word class from a verb to a noun, and is referred to as a *derivational suffix.* The plural *-s* does not alter the basic grammatical class and augments rather than changes meaning; it is referred to as an *inflectional suffix.* English has a relatively small set of inflectional suffixes that includes the plural *-s,* (e.g., *girls, houses*), possessive *-s* (e.g., *John's hat, girl's hat*), third person present tense *-s* (e.g., *She runs*), past tense *-ed* (e.g., *John guessed*), participle *-ed* (e.g., *have helped*), progressive *-ing* (e.g., *He is running*), and comparatives *-er* and *-est* (e.g., *smaller, smallest*).

Inflectional morphemes in English are susceptible to language variation in two ways, both of which make perfect sense in terms of the principles of language organization discussed in Chapter 2. In some cases, the inflectional morphemes found in one variety may be absent in another, whereas in other cases, the forms of inflectional morphemes differ. The third person -*s* suffix (*She run/She runs*), some plural forms (e.g., *four mile/ four miles*) and possessive -*s* (e.g., *John hat/John's*) may be absent in some vernacular dialects, illustrating the first type of dialect variation. This kind of difference is usually quite diagnostic in terms of the social differentiation of dialects. Less frequently, vernacular dialects may retain morphemes that are absent from other varieties, such as the *a-* prefix retained in some rural, particularly Appalachian, varieties (e.g., *He went a-hunting and a-fishing*). This prefix is now obsolete in most standard varieties. In another case, a suffix may be added as part of regularizing a paradigm, such as the possessive *mines* (by analogy with *his, hers, ours,* and so on) or the second person plural *youse* (by analogy with first and third person pronouns which distinguish singular from plural).

The regularization of irregular forms often illustrates the second type of inflectional variation. In this process, irregular plurals may be regularized (e.g., *oxes/oxen*) and irregular past tense forms may be regularized (e.g., *knowed/knew, throwed/threw*).

Morphological differences of the preceding types are among the most socially diagnostic structures in American English, and there is sharp differentiation of standard and vernacular speaking groups on the basis of these forms. In part, this may be attributed to the fact that the tendency toward regularization is such a strong organizing principle of language systems that many natural, predictable changes are resisted only by paying special attention to these irregular forms that must be learned by rote. This focused attention on learning these forms subsequently makes them sensitive to social marking. In effect, standard speakers pay special attention to the "unnatural" exceptions, and are rewarded socially for their efforts by their separation from their vernacular-speaking counterparts.

The other major level of grammatical organization, *syntax,* refers to the structuring of words into larger units such as phrases or sentences. Several different aspects of syntax may be involved in dialectal variation in English. First, there may be variation in how word classes such as verbs, verb auxiliaries, nouns, or articles are organized. In some cases, there may be different items included or absent within a basic word class. Verb auxiliaries are a major source of difference in the varieties of English, and some vernacular dialects contain forms not found in most standard varieties. These include the completive *done,* as in *He done forgot about the work,* habitual *be,* as in *Sometimes my ears be itching,* and counterfactual *liketa* as in *I liketa died, when I found out it was you.* Auxiliaries may also be clustered in different ways, such as the "double modals" found in some southern varieties, as in *She might could finish the project* or the *useta didn't* of other vernacular varieties in sentences like *We useta didn't do that a lot.*

The way in which word classes may combine with other structures in a sentence can also be sensitive to dialect differences. For example, the kinds of complements that occur with different verb types may differ from dialect to dialect. Some verbs take a particular kind of object in one dialect and a different kind of object, or no object at all, in another dialect. Thus, some vernacular dialects of English use the verb *beat* without an object (e.g., *The Cowboys beat*), whereas other varieties only use it with a direct object, as a transitive verb (e.g., *The Cowboys beat the Redskins*). In a similar vein, the verb *learn* may be used with a personal object in some dialects, as in *The teacher learned the students how to do the project*, whereas in other dialects it can only be used with inanimate objects, as in *The students learned the material*. In still another case, which is regionally rather than socially differentiated, the participle complements of verbs differ, so that one dialect uses an *-ing* form with the verb *need*, as in *The house needs painting*, while another dialect uses an *-ed* form, as in *The house needs painted*.

Another type of syntactic variation involves co-occurring relations between forms, where the use of one form is governed by the use of another form. Such relationships are typically referred to as *agreement* or *concord* patterns. For example, agreement patterns between subjects and verbs in modern English have changed substantially from earlier periods in the language, and there is continued movement in reducing, or "leveling," the extent of agreement in some vernacular dialects. Thus, many vernacular dialects level the agreement pattern in one way or another, ranging from the highly frequent use of *don't* with third person singular subjects (e.g., *She don't like it here/She doesn't like it here*) to the regularization of the conjugated forms of *be* (e.g., *We was here/We were here*) and the absence of the third person present tense *-s* form (e.g., *She go to work*). Many of the strongest social markers of vernacular dialects in American English relate to these *morphosyntactic forms,* in which the occurrence of a particular suffix is governed by the syntactic relationship between structures in a sentence such as a subject and verb.

The stereotyped double negative form of *She didn't have no money to do nothing* actually involves a relationship of syntactic agreement, in which the occurrence of a negative in a sentence governs the use of particular indefinite forms. In standard dialects, *any* is used with the postverbal indefinite (that is, the form comes *after* the verb in the sentence, such as *He didn't have any money*) whereas *no* may be used in most vernacular dialects (e.g., *He didn't have no money*). Many of the distinctive dialect differences of syntax involve agreement patterns between words or morphemes, and they are among the most prominent social markers within American English.

Finally, syntactic differences may involve the basic linear arrangement of words in phrases or sentences. Although languages may vary considerably in their sequencing of different syntactic categories, and this factor can have a substantial influence on second-language learners, this is a relatively minor area of difference in the dialects of English. Nonetheless, there are occasions where the ordering differs across regional or social varieties. The simple inverted or uninverted order of questions may vary, as in *What that was?/*

What was that? or the placement of adverbs may differ slightly in different dialects, as in *We'd all the time get into trouble/We'd get into trouble all the time.* Given the possibilities for sequencing differences in the basic units of the sentence, however, this kind of variation is relatively unexploited by American English dialects.

Exercise 4

The following sentence pairs represent different kinds of syntactic variation as discussed earlier. These types include the following: (1) the organization of grammatical categories (e.g., how the verb phrase is organized), including the addition or deletion of items in the pattern, (2) co-occurring privileges of structures (e.g., whether a verb needs an object), (3) agreement patterns (e.g., agreement between subjects and verbs), and (4) variation in the linear order of structures. Identify the type of syntactic variation indicated by the following sentence pairs according to the categories set forth. For example, a sentence pair such as *The Redskins beat/The Redskins beat the Cowboys* would be classified as *Type 2* in this classification, as the pattern relates to whether or not the verb *beat* takes an object. In your description of the difference, be as specific as possible about the pattern.

1. *Did ever a stray animal come to your house/ Did a stray animal ever come to your house?*
2. *Some people makes soap from pig fat/ Some people make soap from pig fat.*
3. *They started to running/ They started a-running/ They started running.*
4. *There's six people in our family/ There're six people in our family.*
5. *They made him out the liar/ They made him out to be a liar.*
6. *We once in a while will have a party/ We will have a party once in a while/ Once in a while we will have a party.*
7. *The dog ugly/ The dog's ugly.*
8. *The man been met him/ The man met him a long time ago.*

LANGUAGE USE AND PRAGMATICS

Knowing a language involves considerably more than knowing the meanings of the words and the phonological and grammatical structures of the language. In every language and dialect, there are various ways available to convey the same information, and the choice of *how* to say something may depend on *who* is talking to *whom* under *what* social circumstances. For example, a person might use any of the following ways to direct another person to do a particular exercise.

Do this exercise!
Can you do this exercise?
I would like for you to do this exercise.
You need to do this exercise.
Would you mind doing this exercise?
Let's try this exercise.
Doing this exercise will help.

Each of these sentences may be used to accomplish the same action in directing the person to do the exercise, but in varying degrees of directness. They also differ in terms of relative politeness and situational appropriateness. Thus, a person in a superior-status relationship (e.g., teacher, parent) could use the most direct form, the imperative *Do this exercise!*, whereas a person of subordinate status might not have the same option. Knowledge as to when and how to use certain forms is just as important to communication as the knowledge of particular forms, and the failure to abide by the conventions for language use can have important implications for how people are perceived within and across social groups.

In some cases, differences may exist in the use of so-called speech acts. In its technical sense, a *speech act* refers to the social action accomplished through the use of language, such as directing a person to carry out an activity, making a promise to someone, or apologizing for a behavior. In some case, the directness of a speech act may correlate with regional and social designations. For example, Heath (1983) showed that adults in rural working-class communities in the Piedmont region of the Carolinas used more direct commands with their children than their middle-class counterparts. Thus, one community of parents would be apt to state a command by using a direct imperative such as "Bring me the broom!" whereas another community would phrase the same order through a question such as "Would you like to bring the broom to me?" In both cases, the underlying function was an order for the child to perform an action, but the directness of the command differed. Similarly, one study (Goodwin 1980) showed that boys use more direct commands (e.g., *Give me the toy!*) than girls in play groups. Girls were more apt to use less direct forms such as *why don't* and *let's* (e.g., *Why don't you give me back the toy now?* or *Let's see the toy now*).

Conventions for the literal and nonliteral use of language may also differ across dialects. A statement such as *What are you doing?* may have both a literal and nonliteral interpretation depending on the context. It may be interpreted literally as a request for explanation, such as in a classroom when a student asks this question of a teacher conducting an experiment. However, if a teacher utters this sentence upon entering a classroom of rowdy children, it is not intended as a literal request for an explanation. Instead, it is an indirect way of telling the students to stop what they have been doing. In fact, in this context, its interpretation as a literal request on the part of the children (e.g., "We're throwing chalk at each other") would only aggravate the situation and would probably just evoke a further, more direct reprimand (e.g., "Don't act smart!").

The failure to distinguish between literal and nonliteral intention in communication is particularly subject to misinterpretation and, in some cases, cross-cultural conflict. For example, the kind of exaggerated boasting that was associated with the language style of the boxer Muhammad Ali was not to be taken literally, but simply as a kind of humorous inventiveness in language style. The problem was that some people, particularly those in mainstream Anglo culture, found this boasting offensive, since it did not match their literal demands for deeds to match words when talking about physical prowess. In fact, from this vantage point, any mismatch between word and deed is expected to be understated rather than overstated, in accordance with a cultural value placed upon the projection of personal humility about physical capabilities. Obviously, underlying cultural values enter into the determination of situational appropriateness, reinforcing the notion that knowledge about a dialect also involves knowledge about a people. Distinctions between directness and indirectness and literalness and nonliteralness are important dimensions of language use that have to be considered across varieties of English.

Although there is a full range of language use differences that goes along with other levels of dialect differences, a couple of areas are particularly sensitive to variation. One involves address forms, where the determination of appropriate titles for people is prescribed along different regional and social groups. In the South, a wide range of adults are addressed with the respect labels *Sir* and *Ma'am*, including parents, whereas in the North only a few adults with special status would ever be addressed by these forms. Although the different usage patterns simply constitute a kind of language use difference, they are quick to evoke evaluative judgments, as Southerners view Northerners as "rude" and Northerners view Southerners as insincerely deferential in their address forms. In reality, of course, it simply represents a language use difference in assigning respect titles. Similarly, the use of a first name in address is subject to considerations of status, personal familiarity, and age, but the relative weighting of these factors may differ from community to community. In some groups, age is a more significant variable than status, so that older people would be addressed as *Mr./Mrs.* regardless of their relative status; in other groups, status is more important than age, allowing low-status individuals to be addressed on a first-name basis regardless of age.

Related to address forms are the conventions for greeting and leave-taking, which involve ritualized forms that are not to be interpreted literally. In most cases, the greeting routines simply involve rote memorization of a limited set of formulaic exchanges, and understanding the appropriate circumstances for their use. Thus, an appropriate response to "What's happening?" as a greeting is simply learned (e.g., "Nothing to me") for a black speaker, just as "Not much" is learned as the response to "What's up?", or "Fine" is learned as the response to "How you doing?" Of course, there are different routines for different settings, so that telephone greetings are different from face-to-face encounters, and service exchanges in restaurants or shops are different from peer group encounters. What is important to recognize, however, is that there are a number of routines which may be distinguished on the basis of region, ethnicity, and class differences in American society. As such, they are simply another kind of language variation in the dialects of English.

Topics of conversation also may differ according to the social or regional group. The delimitation of "safe" topics of discussion may vary according to situational context and social relationships. A middle-class Anglo might consider a question like "What do you do for a living?" as an appropriate information question to initiate a conversation at a casual social gathering, but the same question might be considered inappropriate by some minority groups in the same situation. Direct questions about income and cost (e.g., house, car, and so on) may also vary from group to group. The determination of what topics can be talked about in what situations is learned like any other aspect of the socialization process, but it cannot be assumed that the determination of appropriate and inappropriate topics for conversation is shared among groups. While these differences are ultimately tied in with underlying cultural values and beliefs, many of them follow distributional lines that follow the same kind of social, ethnic, and regional differences that correlate with differences in linguistic form, and thus should be treated legitimately as a dimension of dialect variation.

Once a topic is chosen and a conversation initiated, keeping the exchange going may involve certain kinds of behaviors on the part of the participants. Some of the signals are nonverbal (e.g., physical distance, gestures, facial expressions), but there are also spoken signals and conventions dictated by different dialect communities. In mainstream varieties of English, forms like *Mmms* and *Uh-huhs* serve this function, as do words like *Yeah, Right,* and so forth. Different groups naturally vary in terms of the kinds of reinforcement offered to speakers by their listeners and signals used to "take a turn" in a conversation. In some American Indian groups and some Asian American groups, there may be less verbal reinforcement, or *backchanneling* by listeners in a conversation than is found in mainstream speaking groups, and there are fewer "interruptions" in the conversation. Furthermore, there is a greater tolerance for silence in the pauses between the turns of a conversation—silences that Anglos often rush into and fill. On the other hand, backchanneling in some black groups may occur more frequently and verbally at different points than found in other groups. Anglo mainstream speakers, accustomed to their learned style of backchanneling, may find both kinds of differences discomforting. In the former case, they may feel that participants are not following the conversation, whereas in the other case they may not feel in control of the conversation. Such an effect may be created simply on the basis of different verbal interactional styles and, in themselves, have very little to do with basic interest or concern. In American society, these kinds of differences often trigger strong evaluative reactions which can be quite negative and intolerant, since they are measured against what is assumed to be a single scale of propriety. In many cases, however, these differences are simply a type of dialect difference with respect to language use conventions.

Exercise 5

Think of social behaviors of another American social group that you have traditionally thought of as offensive from the standpoint of your native group. Classic cases might involve talking to the opposite sex, service encounters at stores, cross-ethnic encounters, and so forth. What kinds of language use tend to go along with this behavior? In what ways might the language use conventions contribute to your impression? What is different about the conventions of your cultural/dialectal group compared to this group? Are there aspects of your perception that, upon further reflection, might simply be related to how you interpret the language routines rather than the intentions of the speakers?

As we have seen, there are a number of different rules or conventions that govern our conversational format and interactional style. Furthermore, there are a variety of factors that have to be considered, ranging from broadbased cultural values about who can talk to whom about what to intricate details concerning how certain behavioral intentions must be expressed in a given community. Given the number and significance of the factors that enter into the selection of a strategy for carrying out conversation, the likelihood of misinterpretation is almost staggering. Certainly, there are many shared areas of American English with respect to language use, but there are also some subtle but important differences between groups that can lead to a significant misunderstanding across dialects, whether they be regionally or socially based.

The acknowledgment of language use differences as a legitimate domain of dialect studies is relatively recent compared to the traditional focus of dialect studies on language form, but its social significance cannot be understated. In fact, some of the major areas of social dissonance and conflict between social and ethnic groups in American society are reflected acutely in the failure to understand how language is being used in different situations and the intentions that underlie particular language uses.

Further Reading

American Speech, A Publication of the American Dialect Society. University, AL: The University of Alabama Press. This quarterly journal contains articles on all levels of dialect differences in American English dialects, balancing more technical treatments of dialect forms with shorter, nontechnical observations. A regular section entitled "Among the New Words" contains lists of items related to word innovation patterns.

CASSIDY, FREDERIC G., ed., *Dictionary of American Regional English, Volume 1: Introduction and A–C.* Cambridge, MA: The Belknap Press of Harvard University Press, 1985. The introductory articles by Cassidy and James Hartman set forth some of the major phonological and grammatical processes involved in differentiating American English dialects, whereas the dictionary listing of dialect items from *A* through *C* provides more than an adequate sampling of lexical differences.

DUMAS, BETHANY AND JONATHAN LIGHTER, "Is Slang a Word for Linguists?" *American Speech,* 51:5–17 (1976). Dumas and Lighter isolate some of the major attributes of slang, concluding that it is a valud sociolinguistic construct. This is an important conclusion, since most dialectologists prefer to dismiss the term because of the loose, imprecise way in which it is used in popular culture.

EBLE, CONNIE C., *College Slang 101.* Georgetown, CT: Spectacle Lane Press, 1989. Eble's collection of slang combines linguistic insight with an expansive inventory of examples from her studies of slang use by college students. It is a readable, entertaining treatment.

LABOV, WILLIAM, "The Three Dialects of English," in *Quantitative Analysis of Sound Change in Progress,* ed. Penelope Eckert. New York, NY: Academic Press, forthcoming. Labov views differences from the perspective of the overall vowel system as opposed to the traditional viewpoint in which each vowel is considered as a separate entity. It is a critical article which forces a reconsideration of the basis for delimiting dialects.

WILLIAMS, JOSEPH M., *The Origins of the English Language: A Social and Linguistic History.* New York, NY: The Free Press, 1975. The middle chapters of this book, Chapters 5 through 8, summarize the underlying principles of word formation and semantic development which lead to lexical differences in language. Although the focus of the text is not on dialects per se, the discussion is applicable to the study of dialects.

CHAPTER FOUR

REGIONAL DIALECTS

In describing distinct regions of the United States, it is common for Americans to mention dialect differences. In some cases, where the regional variety is fairly marked, this may be one of the first characteristics noted. It is not uncommon for people to open a conversation about Boston, New York City, or Atlanta with a comment about the dialect of the area. Regional variation is one of the most transparent factors associated with dialects, and there is a well-established tradition for studying regional varieties of English. For over a half century now, regional surveys of the *Linguistic Atlas of the United States and Canada* have been underway. While the traditional focus on regional variation took a back seat to other concerns for a number of years, there has been a resurgent interest in the regional dimension of American dialects. This revitalization was buoyed by the publication of *DARE* (*Dictionary of American Regional English*) and the centennial celebration of the American Dialect Society in 1989, the organization most prominently associated with the focus on regional dialects.

Linguists have long debated the precise place of regional dialect studies in the overall investigation of language variation, given the traditional concentration on geographical patterning. The focus on cartographic plotting in such studies has led some to the conclusion that regional dialect study is really a branch of geography rather than a kind of linguistic study. Certainly, studies of regional variation may be informed by models from the fields of cultural and historical geography, but there is no inherent reason why the study of regional variation cannot mesh models from geography with the rigorous study of linguistic variation proper. In fact, recent studies of language variation have integrated models from these distinct vantage points in insightful and informative ways.

One of the initial questions asked about the regional dialects of American English is "How many dialects are there?" The answer to this question seems as if it should be simple to the casual inquirer, but an honest response turns out to be full of qualifications. Discrete boundaries between dialects are often difficult to determine and the types of differences that uniquely set apart regional varieties are not always easy to establish. As a result, the answer really depends on how thinly a dialectologist chooses to slice the pieces of dialect from the language pie. A realistic answer may range from two to two hundred, depending on the criteria used to delimit a regional dialect.

One basis for this complexity stems from the fact that there are many variants on different levels of language organization that are regionally distributed. But what is the relative contribution of these differences in setting apart distinct regional varieties? An eastern New Englander might show characteristic phonological traits such as *r*-lessness as in the stereo-typical *pa'k the ca'*, the merger of vowels in *cot* and *caught*, and lexical features like *panfried potatoes* (*homefried potatoes*) or *dropped egg* (*poached egg*), but do all these variants contribute equally to the identification of a Bostonian? It seems that both the quantity and the quality of the differences have to be considered in distinguishing regional varieties. Furthermore, items may show varying regional lines of demarcation, and even the "classic" dialect items mentioned earlier do not show identical regional distribution.

An appeal to dialect speakers' subjective classifications does not help us out much in enumerating the dialects of American English. Studies of "perceptual dialectology," that is, how speakers themselves view dialect boundaries, may show considerable variation from area to area (Preston 1986), and even from speaker to speaker. For example, I have heard classifications of Appalachian dialects that range from "everybody in Appalachia talks the same way" to "every hollow has its own dialect"—and these assessments were given by speakers in the same community. So we have to conclude that the issue of determining clear-cut regional dialects is considerably more complex than it appears at first glance, and this is why most dialectologists hesitate to answer the question of how many regional dialects there are. Notwithstanding these qualifications, there is actually considerable agreement among dialectologists about some of the major regional varieties of English. This consensus is particularly remarkable, given the fact that quite different models for describing language variation have been used and different aspects of language organization have been focused on in analyses.

Exercise 1

Think about your own perceptions of regional dialects of American English. What major regional dialects come immediately to mind? How about the dialect(s) where you live? Are there major and minor regional dialects where you live? What kind of features do you associate with such differences? Ask several other people about their perceptions of the area, including both natives and nonnatives of the area. Ask them what characteristics they associate with the speech of the area and how it is distinguished from other areas.

MAPPING REGIONAL DIALECTS

We can anticipate our discussion of gathering dialect data in Chapter 8 by noting that the traditional approach to charting regional dialect patterns starts with the elicitation of diagnostic dialect forms from speakers representing local communities within a broader geographical area. In most major projects conducted under the aegis of the *Linguistic Atlas of the United States and Canada*, the targeted area constituted a major region of the United States, such as New England, the Upper Midwest, the Gulf States, and so forth, but studies run the full gamut of regional size.

Once the data have been collected from community representatives, the variants are plotted on a map in some fashion. In the typical plotting, distinct symbols are used to indicate different variants of the diagnostic item given by subjects. In a classic example of this cartographic method as shown in Figure 4–1, the distribution of *pail* and *bucket* is charted for subjects interviewed in the 1930s and 1940s (as part of one of the initial phases of the *Linguistic Atlas* project). In this map, the larger symbols represent four or more communities in the area that used the variant in question.

The work involved in superimposing the variants for each item and community on a map can be quite time consuming, and it involves careful attention to cartographic detail. In more recent years, this process has been aided through the use of computer-generated cartographic plotting. One of the noteworthy accomplishments of *DARE* was its utilization of computerized cartographic methods, particularly impressive given the fact that this project was initiated in the early 1960s. Illustrated in Figure 4–2 is a comparison of a conventional, hand-drawn map and a computer-generated one from *DARE*. An extra demographic wrinkle in the *DARE* map is its proportional representation of states on the basis of population density, rather than geographical area. Accordingly, a state such as Texas is not nearly as large as New York, even though it is much more expansive geo-

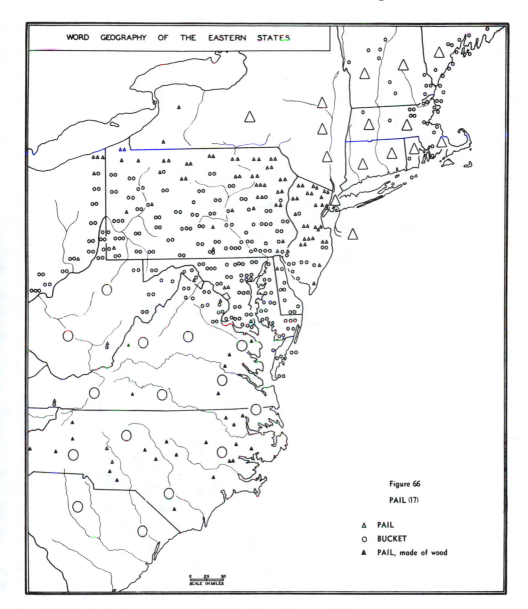

Figure 66

PAIL (17)

△ PAIL
○ BUCKET
▲ PAIL, made of wood

SCALE IN MILES

FIGURE 4–1 Traditional Linguistic Atlas Map of *Pail* and *Bucket* in the Eastern United States (from Kurath 1949: Figure 66)

graphically, since New York represents a higher proportion of the population of the United States than Texas. The proportional map seems distorted compared to the traditional map based solely on physical size, but it adds the important dimension of population distribution to the consideration of regional variation.

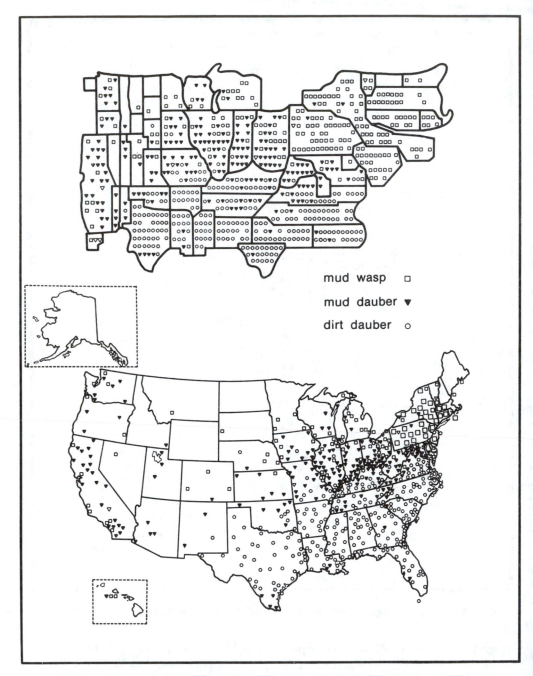

mud wasp □

mud dauber ▼

dirt dauber ○

FIGURE 4–2   Comparison of *DARE* Map and Conventional Map of Dialect Variants (from Cassidy 1985:xxix)

The reliance on computer-generated cartographic techniques can go a long way toward eliminating much of the time-consuming and tedious work involved in mapping patterns of geographical distribution by hand, and it is difficult to imagine that future dialectologists would not take full advantage of automatic processing programs in cartographic plotting.

For many regionally diagnostic dialect items, the distribution shows a group-exclusive pattern in which communities in one area use one variant predominantly while those in another region use a different one. For example, in the map of *pail* and *bucket* displayed in Figure 4–1, there is a line of demarcation that sets apart southern and northern regions of Pennsylvania: south of the line *bucket* is used and north of the line *pail* is used. When the distribution shows a fairly clear-cut demarcation, a line called an *isogloss* may be drawn to mark off the limits of the different variants. In addition to the isogloss for *pail* and *bucket* cutting across Pennsylvania, an isogloss may be drawn in which a pocket of eastern New England is set apart from western New England and other northern regions by its use of the term *bucket*.

Isoglosses set apart zones of usage in a very discrete way, but not all patterns of usage are as clear as that delimited for the use of *pail* and *bucket* in the 1930s and 1940s. In many cases, the variants are more interspersed, making it difficult to draw a meaningful isogloss. In the case of *pail* and *bucket*, there are relatively few cases of *pail* south of the isogloss and only a few cases of *bucket* north of it, but distribution patterns are not always this definitive. Sometimes, there are pockets of usage that are more scattered and the pattern resists a single line of demarcation. Furthermore, there are often *transitional zones*, where the variants coexist, so that an individual speaker might use both *pail* and *bucket*. In fact, transitional zones are more typical than the abrupt pattern of distribution implied by isoglosses, especially in more densely populated areas. Isoglosses are certainly useful in indicating the outer boundaries of regional usage patterns, but they cannot be used without important qualifications. In fact, in most cases, isoglosses represent ideal rather than real patterns of delimitation, a "convenient fiction existing in an abstract moment in time" (Carver 1987:13).

In a microscopic view of regional variation, each isogloss plots a different dialect area, but this reduces the definition of regional dialect to a trivial one. When the overall responses to diagnostic forms are considered, different isoglosses may show similar, if not identical, patterns of delimitation. These clusters, or *bundles of isoglosses*, are usually considered significant in determining regional dialect areas. For example, when the isogloss for *pail* and *bucket* is considered along with the lexical differences for *darning needle* versus *dragonfly* and *whiffletree* versus *swingletree*, the isoglosses tend to coincide, as shown in Figure 4–3.

Predictably, major regional areas are typically determined by having larger bundles of isoglosses than minor dialect areas. Using this approach,

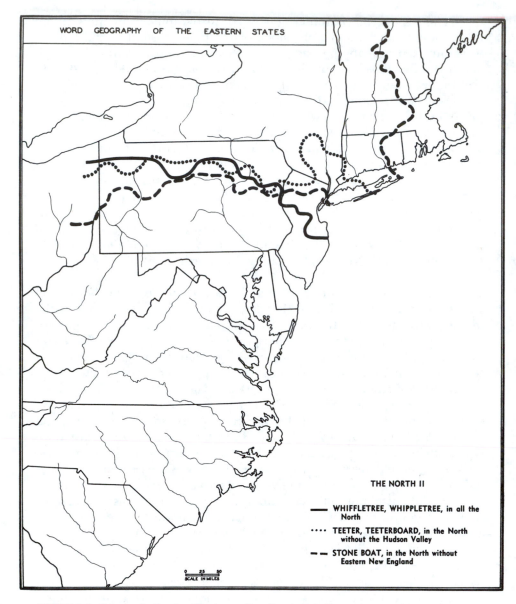

WORD   GEOGRAPHY   OF   THE   EASTERN   STATES

THE NORTH II

—— WHIFFLETREE, WHIPPLETREE, in all the North

···· TEETER, TEETERBOARD, in the North without the Hudson Valley

— — STONE BOAT, in the North without Eastern New England

0   25   50
SCALE IN MILES

FIGURE 4–3   Sample of a Bundle of Isoglosses (from Kurath 1949:Figure 5A)

the initial phase of the *Linguistic Atlas* survey of the eastern United States proposed several major regional dialects and some minor dialect areas. For example, in *Word Geography of the Eastern United States* (1949), Kurath presented a map of major and minor areas which became the standard representation of regional dialects in the East for almost four decades. In this map, three major regional areas were delimited: North, Midland, and South, with a number of subregional dialects for each major area. This map is reprinted as Figure 4–4.

A number of direct quantitative measures have been proposed for determining the relative significance of isogloss bundles. One of the more

FIGURE 4–4 Dialect Areas of the Eastern United States, Based on Linguistic Atlas Isoglosses (from Kurath 1949:Figure 3)

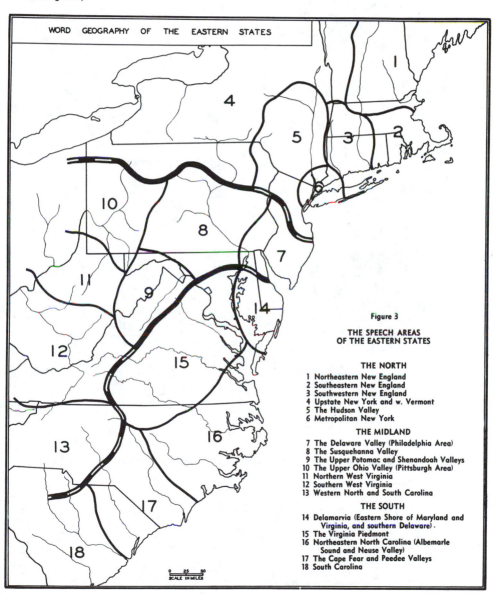

WORD GEOGRAPHY OF THE EASTERN STATES

Figure 3

THE SPEECH AREAS OF THE EASTERN STATES

THE NORTH

1 Northeastern New England
2 Southeastern New England
3 Southwestern New England
4 Upstate New York and w. Vermont
5 The Hudson Valley
6 Metropolitan New York

THE MIDLAND

7 The Delaware Valley (Philadelphia Area)
8 The Susquehanna Valley
9 The Upper Potomac and Shenandoah Valleys
10 The Upper Ohio Valley (Pittsburgh Area)
11 Northern West Virginia
12 Southern West Virginia
13 Western North and South Carolina

THE SOUTH

14 Delamarvia (Eastern Shore of Maryland and Virginia, and southern Delaware).
15 The Virginia Piedmont
16 Northeastern North Carolina (Albemarle Sound and Neuse Valley)
17 The Cape Fear and Peedee Valleys
18 South Carolina

0 25 50
SCALE IN MILES

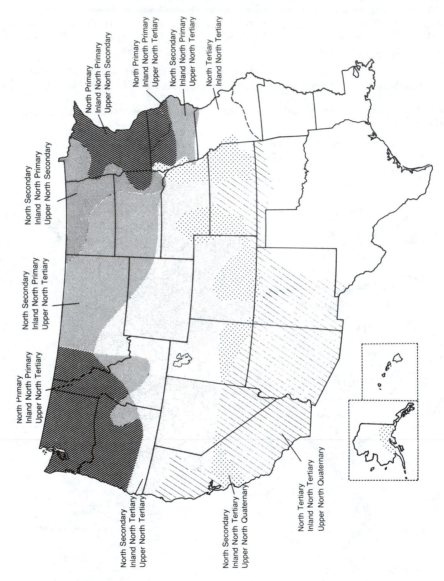

North Primary
Inland North Primary
Upper North Secondary

North Primary
Inland North Primary
Upper North Tertiary

North Secondary
Inland North Primary
Upper North Tertiary

North Tertiary
Inland North Tertiary

North Secondary
Inland North Primary
Upper North Secondary

North Secondary
Inland North Primary
Upper North Tertiary

North Primary
Inland North Primary
Upper North Tertiary

North Secondary
Inland North Tertiary
Upper North Tertiary

North Secondary
Inland North Tertiary
Upper North Quaternary

North Tertiary
Inland North Tertiary
Upper North Quaternary

FIGURE 4–5 An Example of Dialect Layering in the Western United States (from Carver 1987:214)

systematic and comprehensive analyses of regional dialects using isogloss patterning is found in Carver's *American Regional Dialects: A Word Geography* (1987), which is based primarily on lexical data (800 diagnostic lexical items) taken from the files of *DARE*. This analysis uses the notion of *isoglossal layering* to determine major and minor regional varieties. The term *layer*, taken from physical geography, is used to refer to a unique set of areal features, but the importance of this concept lies in the fact that it is used to capture overlap and divergence in regional dialects by examining levels of layering rather than independent sets of isogloss bundles. The most concentrated regional dialect area, where the most dialect features are shared, is the *primary dialect* area. In *secondary* and *tertiary* areas, there is progressively less sharing of dialect variants. For example, the core of the Northeast American English dialect shares 20–24 isoglosses from the inventory of diagnostic lexical dialect items, whereas secondary layers share 15–19 isoglosses, and so forth. While this approach does not eliminate some of the basic problems with isoglosses already pointed out, it captures the hierarchical nature of overlap and divergence in regional varieties. As an example of layering here, Carver's (1987) analysis of the northern dialect extension into the western United States is given in Figure 4–5. The primary area reflects the core of the westward extension of northern dialect features, whereas the secondary and tertiary areas represent less concentrated layers of this extension.

Layering can also be represented hierarchically. For example, Carver's western dialect can be presented in a conventional hierarchical tree, as in Figure 4–6. (Compare this hierarchy with the summary of the West given in Figure 4–12 rather than Figure 4–5, since Figure 4–5 is limited to the extensions of northern-dialect areas into the West.)

FIGURE 4–6   An Example of Dialect Layering in the West, Represented Hierarchically (from Carver 1987:243)

Layer

West (map 7.2)

Regions

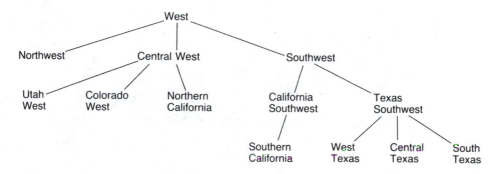

Carver's analysis has led to the redefinition of some traditionally recognized regional varieties while confirming many others. Earlier *Linguistic
Atlas* studies had maintained a major tripartite breakdown into northern,
midland, and southern regional dialects, but Carver's analysis concludes that
the basic distinction is between northern and southern regional dialects. He
also presents the South as a more unified area than previous studies indicated, with secondary and tertiary areas surrounding the southern core (see
Figure 4–12).

The fact that lexical variation is so often used as a primary basis for
regional dialects has been a major source of contention among students of
language variation. For example, Carver's regional analysis is based exclusively on lexical differences. Some linguists have maintained that lexical
differences are among the most superficial types of linguistic structure, and
therefore among the least reliable indicators of dialect areas. However, it
is interesting to note that Carver's lexical boundaries correlate well with
boundaries arrived at independently in cultural geography, including features such as architectural practice, religion, political ideology, and a number
of other culturally significant variables. Thus, lexical items, regardless of
their linguistic status, serve as indicators of more broadly-based cultural and
historical foundations upon which regional dialects rest, and their significance should not be dismissed cavalierly.

Many phonological variables naturally show regional variation in a way
that parallels with, or, in some cases, departs from the patterns shown for
lexical items. In Figure 4–7 the regional distribution of *r*-lessness is displayed.

FIGURE 4–7   An Example of Regional Distribution for *r*-lessness (from Hartman 1985:iix)

Map 1

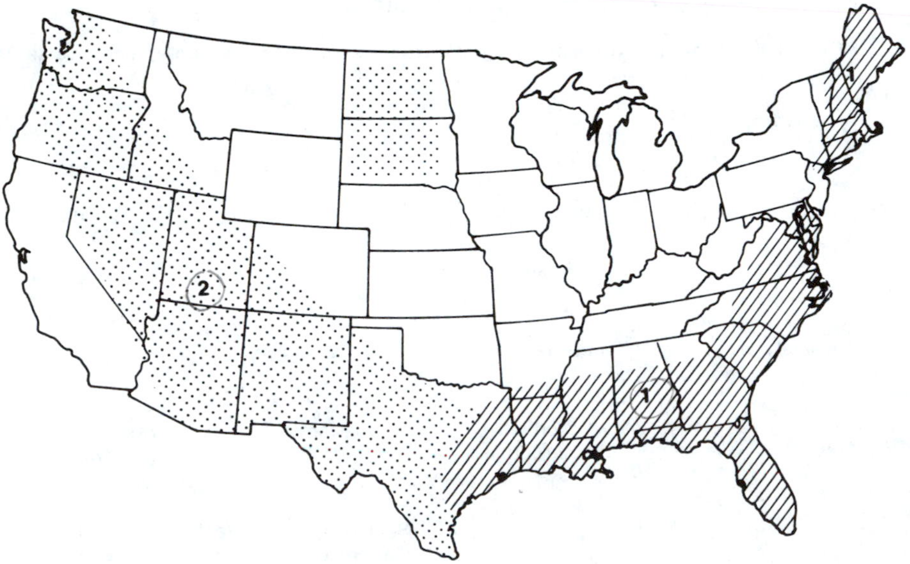

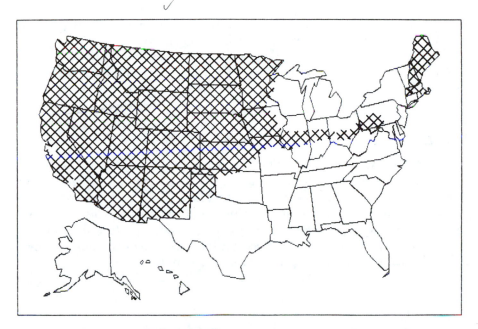

FIGURE 4–8 An Example of Regional Phonological Distribution: The Merger of Open *o* and *a* in *cot* and *caught*

This is a major variable in American English regional variation, which shows intersection with other social variables as well. In Figure 4–7, the area marked *1* represents regions where the postvocalic *r* of *course* or *car* is frequently absent, whereas the area marked *2* has "weakened" or "less retroflexion" of the tongue, according to Hartman (1985:iviii).

In Figure 4–8, there is a similar map of areas where the distinction between the open *o* of words like *cot* and *caught* is merged (i.e., where these words are pronounced the same). The shaded area, where the sounds are merged, is a composite of various *Linguistic Atlas* studies and a survey reported in Labov (forthcoming). As with *r*-lessness, this is a major regional variant of American English, although a comparison of the two maps shows that the two variables exhibit quite different patterns of regional distribution.

As with lexical variables, we may expect a kind of regional isogloss layering for phonological variables. For example, we expect to find a core southern or core northern area, where the highest concentration of shared phonological features is found, and secondary and tertiary zones surrounding these primary areas.

Some of the diagnostic dialect items in phonology involve single items or particular sound units. Ultimately, regional vowel systems are best viewed in terms of various subsets of vowels that work together. The kinds of vowel rotation introduced in Chapter 3 and detailed more extensively later in this chapter are examples where the dialectal pattern affects a subsystem within the overall phonology. Other items, however, may have an independent character, such as the North-South distinction in *greasy* (as [grisi] or [grizi]), or the pronunciation of *aunt* and *ant* as distinct versus homophonous items. We have more to say about regional subsystem differences in vowels later in this chapter.

Exercise 2

Can you think of other examples in which a particular regional pronunciation only seems to affect one word, as with *aunt/ant* and *greasy/greazy*? (Hint: Consider the way natives of a particular city or state may pronounce its name.) There are some linguists who would say that the difference between pronouncing *greasy/greazy* and *aunt/ant* is actually a lexical difference rather than a phonological one, since it affects only one item, not a general phonological rule. Do you agree? Why or why not?

Regional grammatical variation can also be represented in ways similar to the phonological and lexical distributions displayed previously, although these kinds of isoglosses are less commonly found in the dialect literature. In most cases, geographical studies of grammatical variables have been limited to morphological variants, such as the past tense of an irregular verb form (e.g., the past tense of *dive* as *dove* or *dived*) or different prepositional uses (e.g., *sick to/at my stomach*). Most of these cases surveyed in regional dialect studies focus on single forms in grammar rather than general rules. This is not to say that there is no geographical distribution of syntactic patterns, but simply to note that most surveys focus on individual items rather than *rules* of grammar.

As an example of regional distribution in syntax, consider the use of so-called positive *anymore* in sentences such as *They watch a lot of videos anymore.* In these contexts, *anymore* means something like "nowadays." This regionally-based pattern departs from the general English pattern in which *anymore* can only be used with negative sentences such as *They don't watch movies anymore.* The regional distribution of positive *anymore* runs a distinct midland course through central Pennsylvania, Ohio, Indiana, and westward into Missouri, Utah, and other states. Areas to the north and south of this area do not appear to use the form at all.

As we saw in Chapter 3, dialect analysis may focus on the lexicon, phonology, grammar, or language use. While the lexicon and phonology have been investigated from a regional perspective, language use has not. Since the consideration of language use differences is a relatively recent addition to the investigation of language variation, there is no tradition at all for mapping regionally-differentiated pragmatic differences, although there is no reason why this dimension could not be surveyed in a way parallel to the other levels of language organization.

REGIONAL SPREAD

From one perspective, the distribution of regional language features may be viewed as the result of language changes through geographical space over time. A change is initiated at one locale at a given point in time, and spreads outward from that point in progressive stages so that earlier changes reach the outlying areas later. This model of language change is referred to as the *wave model,* as it resembles the rippling-wave effect of a pebble dropped into a pool of water.

We can illustrate this model of language change and geographical spread by looking at a simplified version of a change taking place in the phonetic value of the vowel in words like *bat* and *bad* (phonetically[æ]). We noted in Chapter 3 that there are some locations, particularly large northern cities, where the phonetic value of the vowel is "raised." That is, the tongue position in the production of words like *bat* and *bad* is slightly heightened [æ], so that the vowel is phonetically closer to the vowel of *bet* and *bed*. This change starts in a limited phonetic environment, in this case, when the vowel is followed by a voiced velar sound such as the [g] in *bag* or *rag*. We can call this linguistic environment *a*. In its initial stage, the vowel raising takes place only in this limited phonetic context at a given locale in geographical space. In a second stage, called linguistic environment *b* here, the change expands to another phonological environment, in this case, before voiceless velar sounds such as the [k] in *back* and *tack*. This change first takes place in the geographical locale where the initial vowel raising took place. At this point, the vowel raising would be found (in most cases variably) in environments *a* and *b*, but still not in other kinds of phonological environments. The change would then generalize to another linguistic environment, for example, before an alveolar sound [t] in words like *bat* or *sat*. This is linguistic environment *c*. Again, the change is first found in the locale where the vowel raising was initiated, moving progressively outward from that point. Eventually, the raising would be found in a full range of phonetic environments. At the initiating locale of the change, the *focal area,* a more advanced form of the change would be evidenced, whereas outlying areas, where the change started later, would have an "earlier" stage of the raising when compared to the focal area. For example, when the focal area has vowel raising in linguistic environments *a*, *b*, and *c*, an outlying area might have it only in environment *a*, or in *a* and *b*. From this perspective, the dialect variation revealed by the two areas reflects differences in the stages of development for the vowel raising at the same time it reveals progressive dispersion in geographical space.

A simple representation of the wave spread over time and space might look like that presented in Figure 4–9. The letters *a, b,* and *c* represent the three phonological environments as specified earlier. This is, of course, a very rudimentary version of vowel raising, which is actually much more complex than indicated here.

In the simplistic model of wave spread given in Figure 4–9, the change starts in environment *a* in a given locale, *Time i* in the figure. At this point, surrounding areas do not have vowel raising. As the change progresses to include environment *b* in the locale where it was initiated, it may spread to a surrounding area, but in a more restricted form, for example, environment *a* as shown in *Time ii*. The place of the original change would thus have more advanced versions of the change, whereas outlying areas would have a less advanced version.

There are many qualifications that need to be made with respect to such a model, including the incorporation of variability to be discussed in Chapter 9, but the model is adequate to show how change can spread through space. And, although we are talking about geographical space here, the model is appropriate for explaining language change in social space (for example, changes spreading across social class) and generational space as well.

The pattern of spread presented here rarely works out as neatly or symmetrically as that detailed in Figure 4–9. Because of physical boundaries, migratory movement, and various social factors, the direction of spread can take a variety of configurations. For example, if one were to represent the spread of dialect influence from eastern Massachusetts, one of the early focal areas in the United States, it would look like that in Figure 4–10 rather than the ideal spread given in Figure 4–9.

The major dialect influence from eastern New England historically spread west and north, bounded to a large extent by the Connecticut River. An examination of other early cultural hearths in America (Philadelphia, Tidewater Virginia, Charleston, and New Orleans) would, of course, show important differences in the direction and extent of dialect spread.

FIGURE 4–9 Wave Spread for æ Raising in Three Linguistic Environments

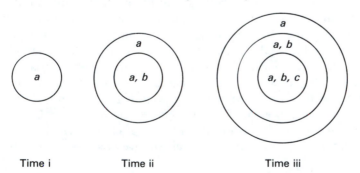

Time i   Time ii   Time iii

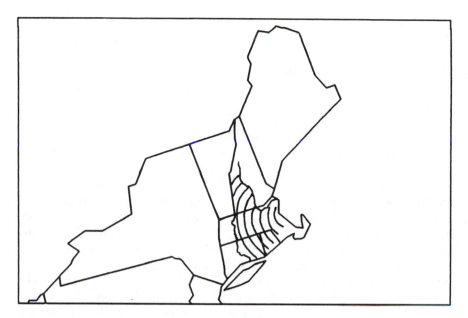

FIGURE 4–10   Dialect Spread in Eastern New England

The focal points for dialect change and spread naturally shift over time, as the society adjusts its cultural centers, migratory patterns, and communication networks. For example, the vowel-raising phenomenon presented earlier is now centered in large northern metropolitan areas such as Rochester, Buffalo, Cleveland, Chicago, and Detroit. Intervening rural areas are not affected, and some inner-city ethnic groups are also unaffected by these changes. The dialectal spread flows outward from these centers of population concentration. In fact, one study (Callary 1975) showed that æ raising correlated with the size of the speaker's community, so that the larger the community, the greater the incidence of raising. Population density, in itself, does not cause vowel raising, but it is symbolic of the current role that metropolitan centers play as focal points for cultural change and the kinds of communication networks in which this change may be facilitated.

Northern metropolitan areas are certainly one focal point for important dialect changes and subsequent spread in American society, but other patterns of spread can also be found. For example, in the midwestern corn-belt, the fronting and raising of the nucleus vowel of *aw* from [aU] towards [æU] (in words like *cow, town,* and so forth), the regional pattern is spreading from a rural setting to the towns (Frazer 1983). In this setting, numbers of subsistence farmers abandoned the rural life altogether, leaving behind a smaller number of farmers whose larger operations meant that the economic and socioeconomic status of these farmers improved. As farmers left the rural areas, they reasserted rural values and rural life, bringing language changes to the towns in the process. The important observation here is that dialect spread cannot be forced into a single, invariant pattern, but that it follows the movement, communication patterns, and social structure of different populations within the United States.

In the spread of regional dialects, it is quite possible for a pattern to pass around an area which is isolated for physical or social reasons. We noted earlier that northern inner-city black populations were largely immune to an overall vowel shift taking place in many of these cities because of social, if not geographical, segregation. In some cases, isolated groups may retain older features by not participating in changes affecting surrounding groups. Areas where these older forms are retained are often referred to as *relic areas*. Prime examples of these populations are found in the relatively isolated, southern mountain ranges of Appalachia and islands along the Atlantic Coast, such as Tangier Island, Smith Island, off the coast of Maryland and Virginia, and the Sea Islands off the coast of South Carolina and Georgia. It is, however, wrong to equate the retention of older, *relic forms* with dialects frozen in time, as in the popular mythology that folks on the eastern shore of Maryland or in Appalachia speak "pure Elizabethan English." Change certainly takes place in these varieties, but the type of and rate of change work in such a way that these groups are often insulated from changes that characterize surrounding dialects.

THE MAJOR REGIONAL DIALECTS OF ENGLISH

As mentioned at the beginning of this chapter, most dialectologists hesitate to specify the exact number of regional dialects in American English. At the same time, there are generally recognized regional dialects which have emerged from various surveys. Several different summary maps, representing varying interpretations and approaches to dialect differentiation, are given here.

The first map, reprinted from Wolfram (1981) as Figure 4–11, represents the kind of summary map that was based on traditional *Linguistic Atlas* surveys. Works such as *The Word Geography of the Eastern United States* (Kurath 1949, see Figure 4–4), *The Pronunciation of English in the Atlantic States* (Kurath and McDavid 1961), and later surveys of other areas conducted under the auspices of the *Linguistic Atlas of the United States and Canada* constitute the basis for the summary. It shows more detail for the eastern and northern regions, giving less detail for the West. It is based on surveys that relied primarily on lexical items and selected pronunciation differences. Classic items characterizing the North are phonological features like the pronunciation of vowels in *morning* and *mourning*, the use of a medial [s] (versus [z]) in *greasy*, and the pronunciation of *roots* with the same vowel as that used in *boot* versus the vowel of *put*, [rut] versus [rUt]; lexical items are

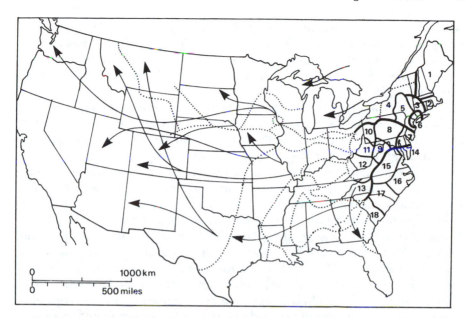

Dialect areas of the USA. Atlantic Seaboard areas (heavy lines) and tentative dialect areas elsewhere (dotted lines). Arrows indicate directions of migrations (adapted from Francis 1958: 580–1)

THE NORTH
1. Northeastern New England
2. Southeastern New England
3. Southwestern New England
4. Inland North (western Vermont, Upstate New York and derivatives)
5. The Hudson Valley
6. Metropolitan New York

THE SOUTH
14. Delmarva (Eastern Shore)
15. The Virginia Piedmont
16. Northeastern North Carolina (Albemarle Sound and Neuse Valley)
17. Cape Fear and Peedee Valleys
18. The South Carolina Low Country (Charleston)

THE MIDLAND
North Midland
7. Delaware Valley (Philadelphia)
8. Susquehanna Valley
10. Upper Ohio Valley (Pittsburgh)
11. Northern West Virginia
South Midland
9. Upper Potomac and Shenandoah
12. Southern West Virginia and Eastern Kentucky
13. Western Carolina and Eastern Tennessee

FIGURE 4–11   A Summary of American Dialects Based on Earlier Dialect Surveys (from Wolfram 1981:50)

of the type specified earlier, *pail* for *bucket, whiffletree* for *whippletree, eaves* (*trough*) for *gutter,* and so forth; grammatical features include items like *dove* as the past tense of *dive,* phrases like *sick to/at the stomach,* and other single item features. Each of the regions has a similar set of features associated with that region.

Three major regional dialect areas are indicated here. The northern dialect runs across the northern part of Pennsylvania, westward through the northern part of Ohio, and the southern border of the Great Lakes. It runs through the Upper Midwest, across Iowa and upward through South Dakota. New England and the far northwestern regions are largely excluded from the northern regions. New England, particularly the eastern region, is generally considered a separate region, as is New York City. The concentration of northern features in the Northwest gradually is diluted. The Midland area, which is generally subdivided into a North Midland and South Midland area, runs across Maryland, taking on a fanning pattern that runs southward along the Appalachian mountain range. Again, there are fairly localized regions within this characterization, such as the Delaware Valley (Philadelphia) and the Ohio Valley area centered around Pittsburgh. The third major area, the South, runs down the eastern coast from the eastern and southern portions of Maryland, spreading westward through the Gulf. Subregional designations include the Virginia Piedmont and eastern shores of Maryland and Virginia. As with other areas specified, the primary indicators of southern dialect lose their force in the westward movement beyond Texas.

The second summary map of American regional dialects in Figure 4–12 is from Carver's *American Regional Dialects: A Word Geography* (1987). Although it is based solely on lexical items taken largely from *DARE,* it is much more representative in its coverage of the entire United States than earlier composite works. It is the first map that gives equal treatment to the western United States, an area largely ignored or minimized in earlier summaries. As we noted before, Carver's method also departs from the traditional isoglossal delimitation by recognizing layers of regional concentration. It is more than a simple update of traditional dialect atlas summaries, although its approach to diagnostic dialect items follows the tradition of the *Linguistic Atlas* surveys.

This map confirms most of the regional varieties traditionally recognized; the major redefinition is the reduction of the tripartite distinction between the North, Midland, and South to a basic North-South regional distinction. The Midland region delimited in earlier surveys is reduced to secondary levels of dialect features concentrated in the southern North and northern South areas. This should be viewed as a significant, but not radical, departure in the delimitation of major regional dialects. For dialect geographers, particularly those concerned with lexical differences, Carver's map is certain to be the standard bearer for years to come.

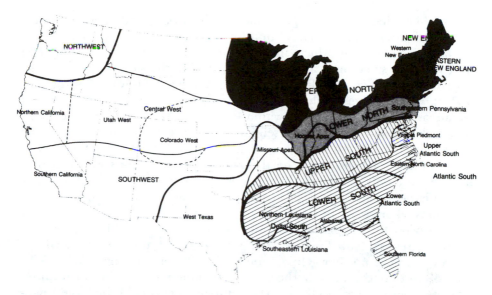

FIGURE 4–12   Summary of Levels of Regional American English Dialects (from Carver 1987:247)

Exercise 3

Examine the summary maps given in Figures 4–11 and 4–12 for differences in regional boundaries. What differences and similarities are observed for the South and West? What are the major kinds of differences in the two maps for the western United States?

A very different approach to determining the major dialects of English is offered in Labov's important article "The Three Dialects of English" (forthcoming). In the first place, his criteria for dialect differentiation are exclusively phonological rather than lexical. Furthermore, his perspective departs radically from the traditional approach in which features are considered on an item-by-item basis. Labov's focus is on overall shifts in subsystems of vowels in English (not only in the United States, but in English as it is spoken worldwide). While traditional views of dialectal phonology have often been content to examine different vowels as independent items, Labov is concerned with overall shifts in the system. Shifts are taking place because of different rotations in the push-pull effect introduced in Chapter 3. Through the careful, instrumental measurement of vowels, Labov has identified two major rotations taking place in English vowels. One rotation is labeled the Northern Cities Shift. In this rotation, the phonetic values of the low long vowels are moving forward and upward and the short vowels are moving downward and backward. For example, the phonetic value of a vowel like the open *o* of *coffee* is moving downward and forward toward the /a/ of *father.* The low vowel in a word like *pop* or *lock,* in turn, moves towards the [æ] of *bat,* which, in turn, moves upward toward the vowel [ɛ] of *bet.* At the same time, another rotation moves the short vowel [I] of *bit* toward the [ɛ] of *bet.* The [ɛ], in turn, moves backward toward the vowel of *but* [^], which is then pushed back (short vowels and long vowels tend to rotate as different subsystems within the overall vowel system). Diagrammatically, the shift may be represented as in Figure 4–13. The conventional vowel chart of English, as presented in Chapter 3, is set up schematically to represent relative tongue height and frontness in the vocal tract. For convenience only, key words in terms of idealized Standard American English phonemes are given. The arrows point to the direction of the phonetic rotations taking place in the vowel shift.

Regionally, the pattern of vowel rotation represented in Figure 4–13 starts in western New England, and goes westward into the northern tier of Pennsylvania, northern Ohio, Indiana, and Illinois, Michigan, Wisconsin, and is more concentrated in the larger metropolitan areas. More advanced stages of this change can be found in younger speakers in the largest metropolitan areas in this northern region, such as Buffalo, Cleveland, Detroit, and Chicago.

Exercise 4

In the following list of words, identify those items that would be involved in the Northern Cities Vowel shift. Is the vowel of the word involved in the low long vowel rotation (e.g., *coffee, bat*) or the short vowel shift (e.g., *bit, but*)? Three answers are possible: (1) the vowel is *not* involved in Northern Cities Shift, (2) the vowel *is* involved in the long low vowel rotation, or (3) the vowel is involved in the *short* vowel rotation.

1.	*beet*	6.	*stack*
2.	*step*	7.	*loft*
3.	*pat*	8.	*top*
4.	*look*	9.	*cut*
5.	*tip*	10.	*rope*

The Southern Vowel Shift as shown in Figure 4–14 is quite different in how the vowels are changing. In this rotation pattern, the short front vowels (the vowels of words like *bed* and *bid*) are moving upward and taking on the gliding character of long vowels. A vowel like the long *e* of *bait* actually consists of a vowel nucleus [e] and an upward glide into a [i], whereas a vowel like the short *e* [ɛ] in *bet* does not have this gliding character, at least

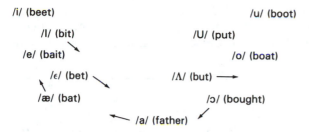

FIGURE 4–13   Vowel Rotation in Northern Cities Shift (adapted from Labov "The Three Dialects of English" forthcoming, p. 25)

not in the idealized standard variety. In the Southern Vowel Shift, the vowel of *bed* takes on a glide, becoming more like *beyd* [bɛId]. Meanwhile, the front long vowels (the vowels of *beet* and *late*) are moving somewhat backward, and the back vowels are moving forward.

Exercise 5

In the following list of words, identify those vowels that would be involved in the Southern Vowel Shift. Is the vowel of the word involved in (1) the short vowel shift (e.g., *bid, bed*), (2) the long vowel shift (e.g., *beet, late*), or (3) the back vowel shift (e.g., *boat, boot*)?

1.	*lid*	6.	*loop*
2.	*rate*	7.	*wrote*
3.	*leap*	8.	*bought*
4.	*red*	9.	*shed*
5.	*keep*	10.	*bid*

A comparison of the Southern Vowel Shift and Northern Cities Shift shows very different rotation patterns, in effect, moving these two varieties of English away from each other. From a regional standpoint, the distri-

FIGURE 4–14   The Rotation of the Southern Vowel Shift (adapted from Labov "The Three Dialects of English" forthcoming, p. 35)

/i/ (beet) ⟍   ⟵ /u/ (boot)
   ↖/ɪ/ (bit)   /U/ (put)
/e/ (bait) ⟍   ⟵ /o/ (boat)
   ↘/ɛ/ (bet)   /ʌ/ (but)
/æ/ (bat)   /ɔ/ (bought)
     /a/ (father)

bution of the Southern Vowel Shift is largely confined to the traditionally-defined South, with differing stages of progression defined in terms of core and secondary areas of the South not unlike that shown for lexical items by Carver (1987).

Exercise 6

Identify whether the vowels in the following words are involved in the Northern Cities Shift or the Southern Vowel Shift. In some cases, the same vowel may be involved in either the Northern Cities Shift or the Southern Vowel Shift, but the rotation is in quite different directions. There are three types of answers: (1) Northern Cities Shift, (2) Southern Vowel Shift, or (3) both the Northern Cities Shift and the Southern Vowel Shift, but rotating in different directions. In cases where the same vowel is subject to either the Northern or Southern Shift, identify the direction of the rotation that differentiates the shift. You might try producing these vowel differences, especially if you know someone who is a good model for the particular shift.

1.	*bed*	6.	*lost*
2.	*cap*	7.	*give*
3.	*pop*	8.	*leap*
4.	*lock*	9.	*kid*
5.	*loop*	10.	*said*

A third major type of phonological region in Labov's delimitation is defined by its lack of participation in the sweeping rotations of either the Northern Cities or Southern Vowel Shift. The vowel /æ/, a pivotal vowel in the Northern Cities Shift, is relatively stable, and there is a merger in the low back vowels of items like *cot* and *caught* or *hawk* and *hock*. Approximate regions of the *Low Back Vowel Merger* area have already been set forth in Figure 4–7. Labov concludes that the merger radiates from two centers, one in eastern New England centered around Boston, extending well to the north but not far to the south, and one centered around Pittsburgh, extending to the northern boundary of the traditional Midland territory. The western extension covers most of the traditional West, with a transitional area running through Wisconsin, Minnesota, Iowa, Kansas, Arkansas, and then southward to the southernmost portions of New Mexico and Arizona. In the West, the Low Back Vowel Merger is not a metropolitan phenomenon, as indicated by the fact that Los Angeles and San Francisco speakers do not typically participate in this merger. Based on these three primary types of vowel systems, the major regional areas actually approximate the traditional classification of North, South, and West. Finally, there are phonological exceptions to these three dialects, such as metropolitan New York, eastern seaboard cities (e.g., Providence, New Haven), Philadelphia, and so forth. A classification of the three major dialect areas and some exceptions, following Labov, might thus look like the summary map given in Figure 4–15. Since some areas have not been surveyed from this perspective, this version must be considered as an approximation rather than a definitive summary.

The classification of regional varieties based on overall vowel systems is an important departure from the analysis of regional distribution based on a set of unrelated items. Labov's treatment also underscores the significance of urbanization in the current system of regional distribution, especially with respect to the Northern Cities Shift and the Low Back Vowel Merger. The former is a metropolitan phenomenon, whereas the latter is largely a nonmetropolitan phenomenon, at least in the West. Analyses of lexical differences relying on traditionally rural items obviously have a dif-

FIGURE 4–15   Dialects of American English, Based on Vowel System

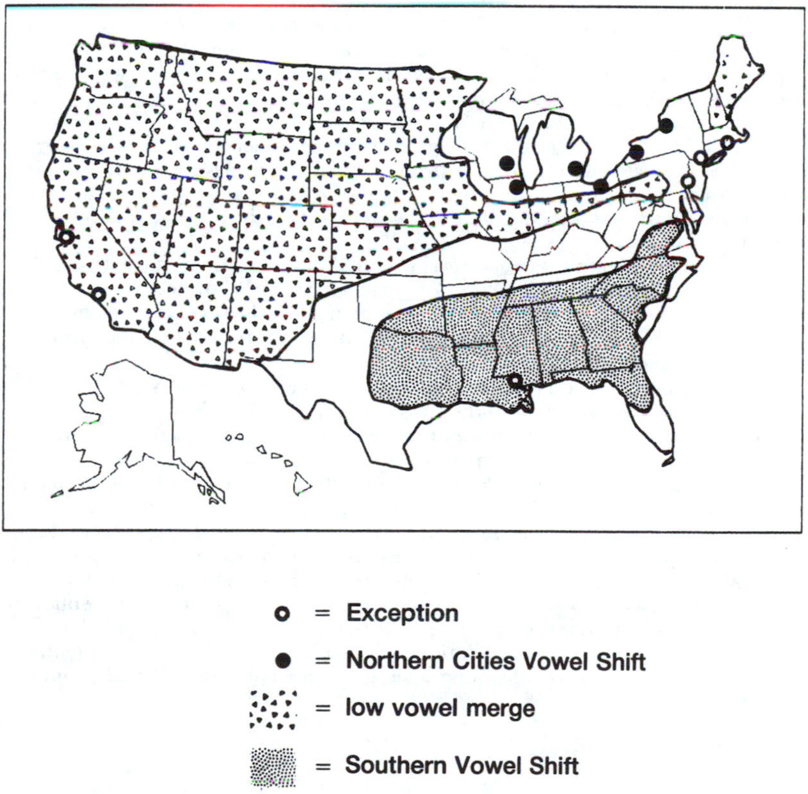

o   =   **Exception**

●   =   **Northern Cities Vowel Shift**

⋮⋮   =   **low vowel merge**

▒   =   **Southern Vowel Shift**

ficult time capturing the current dynamics of the regional flow in American English as depicted in Labov's analysis.

Although there are important differences in data and methods used to define the regional dialects of English, the three summaries given here are, to a surprising degree, supportive of each other. The northern and southern dialect distinction is certainly secure (and, in fact, diverging rather than converging phonologically), and the West still shows a more diffused character. Furthermore, some of the areas which carved out unique regional niches earlier in the settlement history of American English still maintain their peculiar identity. This verification certainly points to the validity of at least the major dialect regions of the United States. With respect to more detailed dialect subdivisions, the disputes will no doubt continue, and most dialectologists will still frame their response to how many dialects of American English there are with considerable qualification.

Further Reading

American Speech. A publication of the American Dialect Society. University, AL: The University of Alabama Press. Articles on various dimensions of regional variation are regularly published in this quarterly journal. Readers may refer to periodically published indices for studies of particular structures and regions.

ALLEN, HAROLD B. AND MICHAEL D. LINN, eds., *Dialect and Language Variation*. New York, NY: Academic Press, 1986. The section on regional dialects in this anthology includes reprints of important articles on linguistic geography; other sections contain a complement of articles on the social dimensions of language variation.

CARVER, CRAIG, *American Regional Dialects: A Word Geography*. Ann Arbor, MI: University of Michigan Press, 1987. This work, based on lexical items taken from the *Dictionary of American Regional English* and from data from *Linguistic Atlas* surveys, offers the most comprehensive mapping of the dialect regions of the United States to date. Its "layered" approach to dialect regions offers a different way of looking at the regional concentration of dialect forms.

CHAMBERS, J. K. AND PETER TRUDGILL, *Dialectology*. New York, NY: Cambridge University Press, 1980. The chapters in the section on spatial variation provide an overview of issues related to boundaries and transitions in regional-based language variation. The chapter on geographical diffusion (Chapter 11) also presents a fresh, systematic approach to the spread of dialect features.

LABOV, WILLIAM, "The Three Dialects of English," in *Quantitative Analysis of Sound Change in Progress*, ed. Penelope Eckert. New York, NY: Academic Press, forthcoming. This work, based solely on phonological shifts within the overall vowel system of English, offers a new perspective on the direction of dialect shift that has resulted in three major types of phonological dialects. Labov's work shows that, with respect to vowels, northern and southern dialects of American English are diverging rather than converging.

PRESTON, DENNIS R., "Five Visions of America," *Language in Society* 15:221–240, (1986). Preston's research on perceptual dialectology focuses on how people in various regions view dialect divisions, as opposed to the typical objective linguistic criteria used by dialectologists in setting dialect boundaries. This perspective shows that dialect perception is generated by linguistic differences, popular culture caricatures, and local identification strategies. Preston provides an informative, complementary perspective on defining dialect boundaries, to be considered along with the traditional dialectological approach to this topic.

CHAPTER FIVE

SOCIAL AND ETHNIC DIALECTS

In many respects, the association of language variation with social status plays a much more significant role in American society than the differentiation of English along regional lines. Regional differences are often interpreted by the American public as matters of quaint curiosity, and may even hold a certain amount of aesthetic charm, but the stakes are much higher when it comes to social status differences in American English. On the basis of status differences, speakers may be judged on capabilities ranging from innate intelligence to employability and on personal attributes ranging from humor to morality.

The social class dimension of dialect has long been recognized in the study of American English, although it was typically assigned a secondary role in large-scale regional surveys. In surveys conducted under the aegis of the *Linguistic Atlas of the United States and Canada,* three social categories of subjects were distinguished, based on the fieldworker's overall impression of the subject. *Type I* subjects were those the fieldworker classified as having "little formal education, little reading and restricted social contacts," *Type II* were those with "better formal education (usually high school) and/or wider reading and social contacts," and *Type III* were those with "superior education (usually college), cultured background, wide reading and/or extensive social contacts" (Kurath 1939:44). Many primary descriptions of regional structures are qualified by phrases such as "used primarily by Type I informant" or "found only among Type III informants," in recognition of the important role of social status in regional variation.

Over the past 25 years, the concern for status differences in language has become a primary rather than secondary focus in many dialect studies, and *social dialectology,* or the study of *sociolects,* is now a recognized subfield of dialectology. The investigation of the social dimensions of language variation over the past several decades has significantly redefined the scope of American dialectology.

DEFINING CLASS

Studies that correlate linguistic behavior with social stratification not only need a clear-cut delimitation of linguistic data, but a valid classification of social strata as well. On an impressionistic level, social status differences seem fairly straightforward. Some people in our society have social prestige, power, and money and others have little of these commodities. At the extremes, few people would disagree about the social status classification of individuals. We would hardly mistake a chief executive officer of a major corporation who resides in a spacious house in a special part of town with an uneducated, unskilled laborer from the "other side of the tracks." The reality of social stratification seems obvious, but identifying the unique set of traits that define these differences in a reliable way is not always that simple. Ultimately, social class distinctions seem based on status and power, where status refers to respect and deference in society and power refers to the social and material resources a person can command and the ability to make decisions and influence events (Guy 1988:39). For the social scientist, the challenge is to reduce these abstract notions to objective, measurable units that can be correlated with linguistic variation. Different kinds of procedures have been used with varying degrees of success in an attempt to capture the construct of social class.

The traditional sociological approach to social status differences isolates a set of objectified socioeconomic characteristics in which individuals are ranked in some way. Typical variables include occupation, level of education, income, and residency, with ranked levels within each variable. For example, occupations may be scaled into categories such as the following:

Rank	Occupation
1	Major professionals
	Executives of large concerns
2	Lesser professionals
	Executives of medium-sized concerns
3	Semi-professionals
	Administrators of small businesses
4	Technicians
	Owners of "petty" businesses
5	Skilled workers
6	Semi-skilled workers
7	Unskilled workers

(From Shuy, Wolfram, and Riley 1968:12)

Similar kinds of scales are set up for other social characteristics and different weightings may be assigned to variables if one trait is considered more significant than another. For example, occupation may be weighted more heavily than education or residency in computing a socioeconomic status score. The overall ranking obtained from combining scores for the different variables is the *socioeconomic status,* usually abbreviated simply as SES. Although this kind of ranking system results in a continuous scale, it is possible to divide the distribution of scores into discrete social status groupings, with attendant labels such as upper-class, middle-class, working-class, and so forth. Groupings may be made on a fairly simple, arbitrary basis (for example, dividing the total range of scores into four social groups), or they may be based on more sophisticated statistical analyses of the clustering of scores distributed on the scale, thus reflecting more natural divisions in the ranking scale.

Exercise 1

Most people can think of individuals who are exceptions to the rule when it comes to the expected correlation between language variation and an objective socioeconomic status index. That is, a person assigned a low SES rating may speak like one typically associated with a high SES rating, or the converse. What kinds of factors may account for such discrepancies? Do such discrepancies discredit the general correlation of language variation with objective SES scores? Why or why not?

As an alternative to the strict objectification of social status differences assigned by an impartial social scientist, it is possible to rely on community members to make judgments about status differences. Ultimately, the real discriminators of social class are the members of the community themselves. From one perspective, social classes are constituted by the community; they have no independent status outside the attitudes and perceptions of the group. Thus, members of a community are rated by other community members in terms of certain imputed status traits. Is a person from the "upper crust" or the "other side of the tracks"? Typically, communities have designations for particular subgroups in terms of the social status hierarchy, and these can be tapped to determine class distinctions. As with externally assigned objective measures, however, there are problems in relying on community members for the assignment of social status differences. Diverse pictures of social class may emerge from different representatives of the system, both on an individual and class level. The lower classes may, for example, perceive social class structure very differently from the upper classes.

Ideally, a valid assessment of social class differences should combine both objective and subjective measurements of many types of behavioral roles and values, but this is often easier said than done. Even if this were possible, such a perspective would not assure a neat fit between social status or class differences and language variation. There are other social variables that intersect with social class, including region, age, and gender; there are also additional factors about community life and relationships that may set apart linguistic variation from other social status considerations. For example, one of the important correlates of linguistic differences relates to the so-called *linguistic marketplace,* in which a person's economic activity, broadly defined, is associated with language variation. People in certain occupations tend to use more standard varieties of the language than their social class counterparts in other occupations. Thus, teachers or receptionists may be more standard in their language than their social status peers in other occupations where they do not have to confront public expectations of standardness. Sankoff and Laberge (1978) show that a person's *linguistic market index,* a ranking assigned to speakers based on descriptions of their socioeconomic life histories, may correlate with standardness in language more closely than traditional social status designations. Another parameter intersecting with strict social class relates to the *social network* (see Chapter 8). Within a given social class or status classification there may be important differences in interactional activity which correlate with language differences. For example, high-density networks, where a person interacts with the same people in a number of spheres of activity (e.g., work, leisure), tend to correlate with a greater concentration of vernacular dialect features. Problems in the neatness of fit between social class and language, then, are not simply problems in the definition of social class, although these problems certainly exist. Instead, many of the difficulties in the correlation of social status with language variation relate to the ways in which different social factors interact with each other in their effect on linguistic variation.

THE PATTERNING OF SOCIAL DIFFERENCES IN LANGUAGE

Not all linguistic structures which correlate with social status differences in a speech community are patterned in the same way. Different linguistic variables may align with given social status groupings in many ways. For example, consider the ways in which two linguistic variables are distributed across four different social strata within the black community of Detroit, third person singular suffix absence (e.g., *She go to the store* for *She goes to the store*) in Figure 5–1 and *r*-lessness (e.g., *bea'* for *bear*) in Figure 5–2.

In Figure 5–1, the linguistic variation correlates with certain discrete social layers. The middle-class groups (UM = upper-middle and LM = lower-middle class) show very little *-s/es* absence, whereas working-class (UW = upper-working and LW = lower-working class) speakers show significant

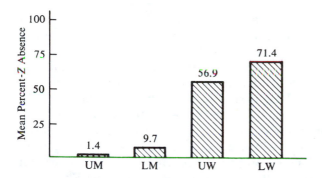

FIGURE 5–1 Third Person Singular *-s/es* Absence: An Example of Sharp Stratification

levels of *-s/-es* absence. The distribution of *-s/es* use shows a wide separation between core middle and working-class groups and is therefore referred to as a case of *sharp stratification.* On the other hand, the distribution of *r*-lessness in Figure 5–2 indicates a pattern of *gradient* or *fine stratification,* in which the relative frequency of *r*-lessness changes gradually from one social class to the adjacent one.

In the examples given in Figures 5–1 and 5–2, sharp stratification is illustrated by a grammatical variable and gradient stratification by a phonological one. Although there are exceptions, grammatical variables are more likely to show sharp stratification than phonological variables. This underscores the fact that grammatical features are more diagnostic of social differences than phonological ones with respect to the standard-nonstandard continuum of English.

Stable linguistic variables defined primarily on the standard-nonstandard continuum of English tend to be sharply stratified, whereas linguistic features undergoing change often exhibit gradient stratification. This is due, in part, to the role of social class in language change within a community. As we discuss shortly, change tends to start in a given social class and spread from that point to other social classes in a diffuse manner. The kind of

FIGURE 5–2 Postvocalic *r* Absence: An Example of Gradient Stratification

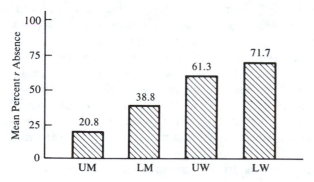

correlation that exists between social status and linguistic variation may thus be a function of both social and linguistic considerations; there is no single pattern that can be applied to this covariation.

Since there are different patterns of correlation between social stratification and linguistic variation, it is sometimes difficult to answer the question of how many social dialects there are in English. On one level, this question is best answered by examining the social stratification of particular linguistic variables. From this perspective, the answer may range from two, for a sharply stratified variable which shows a basic dichotomy between two broadly defined social groups, through six or seven varieties for finely stratified features. For linguistic variation showing a correlation with two basic social groups, the popular dichotomy between a standard and vernacular variety may be matched by the reality of social stratification; however, for other variables, multilayered social dialect differentiation is clearly indicated. It is important to understand that both continuous and discrete patterns of sociolinguistic variation may simultaneously exist within the same population.

THE SOCIAL EVALUATION OF LINGUISTIC FEATURES

Although there is no inherent social value associated with the variants of a linguistic feature, it is not surprising that the social values assigned to certain groups in society will be attached to the linguistic forms used by the members of these groups. It is no accident that standard varieties of a language represent socially favored and dominant classes, and that nonstandard dialects represent socially disfavored, low-status groups. While this general pattern of social evaluation holds, the correlation of particular linguistic variables does not always follow a direct line with social stratification, as sociolinguistic history molds the diagnostic role of language structures in various ways.

The use of particular language variants may be evaluated as socially prestigious or socially stigmatized. *Socially prestigious* variants are those forms that are positively valued through their association with high-status groups as linguistic markers of status, whereas *socially stigmatized* variants carry stigma through their association with low-status groups. In grammar, most prestige forms are related to prescriptive norms of standardness or literary norms, so that the objective form of *who* in *Whom did you see?* or adverbial preposing such as *Never have I seen a more gruesome sight* might be considered prestige variants in some social contexts. Apart from these somewhat special cases, it is difficult to find clear-cut cases of prestige variants on the grammatical level of language, particularly in the grammar of ordinary informal conversation.

Examples of prestige variants are also relatively rare in phonology.

The use of an "unflapped" *t* in words like *better* or *latter* (e.g., [bɛtɚ] as opposed to [bɛDɚ]) as used by a select group of "Brahmin" dialect speakers found in the Boston metropolitan area may be an instance of a prestige variant, as would some other phonological characteristics of this dialect, but this is a fairly isolated, somewhat unusual situation. The model of pronunciation in this restricted prestige dialect is derived more from the Received British pronunciation than from other dialects of American English. The fact that an external norm serves as a model for prestige in this instance is actually a commentary on the relative absence of authentic prestige variants in American English dialects.

The present-day occurrence of postvocalic *r* (i.e., *r* following a vowel as in *bear* or *car*) in New York City, shifting from a prior pattern of *r*-lessness, has been interpreted as a prestige variant (Labov 1966), but it is not entirely clear that this pattern is a simple matter of linguistic prestige. In some regions, where both phonological variants exist, the pronunciation of *either* as [aIðɚ] instead of [iðɚ] or the pronunciation of *vase* as [vaz] versus [vez] may be associated with high status, but these relate to the pronunciation of single lexical items, and are therefore more properly considered lexical rather than phonological variants.

For phonology and grammar, it is clear that the vast majority of socially diagnostic structures exist on the axis of stigmatization rather than the axis of prestige. Classic illustrations include the familiar grammatical cases of multiple negation (e.g., *They didn't do nothing*), irregular verb forms (e.g., *He knowed they were right; She seen that yesterday*), subject-verb agreement (e.g., *We was there*), phonological features such as unstressed *-in'* versus *-ing*, stopping of the interdental fricatives (e.g., [dey] *they* [tInk] *think*), and lexical items like *ain't*. It is relatively easy to come up with examples of stigmatized variants for different levels of linguistic organization, unlike that found for prestigious variants. As we pointed out in Chapter 1, this observation was part of the rationale which led us to conclude that Standard English is more adequately characterized by the absence of negatively-valued, stigmatized items than by the presence of positively-valued, prestige items.

It is essential to understand that stigmatized and prestigious variants do not exist on a single axis in which the alternative to a socially stigmatized variant is a socially prestigious one, or vice versa. The absence of multiple negation, for example, is not particularly prestigious; it is simply *not* stigmatized. Similarly, the nonprestigious variant for *either* [iðɚ] is not necessarily stigmatized; it is simply *not* prestigious. In fact, there are very few cases in English in which the alternate variant of a socially prestigious variant is a socially stigmatized one.

In discussing the social significance of linguistic variants, we must keep in mind that the popular, categorical social evaluation of items usually differs from the way in which linguistic variation actually correlates with status differences. Given two variants for *-ing* pronunciation, [Iŋ] (*swimming*) and

[In] (*swimmin'*), the former may be classified as the standard variant, and the latter classified as the nonstandard variant, but this labeling does not necessarily equate with usage patterns. The actual distribution may show that all social classes use the [In] pronunciation to some extent, but that some groups simply use one variant more frequently. We discuss this notion more fully in Chapter 8.

The discussion of sociolinguistic evaluation up to this point has assumed a particular vantage point about norms of linguistic behavior, namely, the widespread, institutional norms established by higher-status groups. These norms are overtly perpetuated by the agents of standardization in our society—teachers, the media, and other authorities responsible for setting the standards of behavior. There is usually community-wide knowledge of these norms acknowledged across a full range of social classes. Linguistic forms that are assigned their social evaluation on the basis of this widespread recognition of social significance are said to carry *overt prestige*. At the same time, however, there may exist another set of norms which relates primarily to solidarity with more locally-defined social groups, irrespective of their social status position. When forms are positively valued apart from, or even in opposition to, their social significance for the wider society, they are said to have *covert prestige*. In the case of overt prestige, the social evaluation lies in a unified, widely accepted set of social norms, whereas in the case of covert prestige, the positive social significance lies in the local culture of social relations. Thus, it is possible for a socially stigmatized variant in one setting to have covert prestige in another. A local youth who adopts vernacular forms in order to maintain solidarity with a group of friends clearly indicates the covert prestige of these features on a local level even if the same features stigmatize the speaker in a wider, mainstream context such as the school. The notion of covert prestige is important in understanding why vernacular speakers do not rush to become standard dialect speakers, even when these speakers may evaluate the social significance of linguistic variation in a way which superficially matches that of their high-status counterparts. Thus, widely-recognized stigmatized features such as multiple negation, nonstandard subject verb agreement, and different irregular verb paradigms may function at the same time in a positive, covertly prestigious way in terms of local norms.

The social significance of language forms changes over time, just as linguistic structures themselves change. It may be difficult for present-day speakers of English to believe that linguistic shibboleths such as *ain't* and multiple negation were once socially insignificant, but the historical study of the English language certainly supports this conclusion. Furthermore, shifts in social significance may take place from generation to generation. Labov (1966:342–49) has shown that for New York City, the social significance of postvocalic *r* has shifted during the past 50 years. For the older generation, there is very little social class stratification for the use of postvocalic *r*, but the current generation shows a well-defined pattern of social stratification in which the presence of *r* is more highly valued than its absence.

The social significance of linguistic variables may also vary from region to region. As a native Philadelphian, I grew up associating the pronunciation of *aunt* as [ant] with high-status groups—*aunt* and *ant* were homophonous items in my dialect. I was quite shocked to discover in later life that the pronunciation of *aunt* I considered "uppity" was characteristic of some southern dialects regardless of social status, including highly stigmatized vernacular varieties such as Vernacular Black English. In a similar vein, post-vocalic *r*-lessness may be associated with the prestigious Boston Brahmin dialect at the same time it is socially disfavored in other settings, such as present-day New York City English.

Although some socially diagnostic variables have *regionally-restricted social significance*, other variables may have *general social significance* for American English, in that a particular social evaluation holds across regional boundaries. Many of the grammatical variables mentioned earlier have this type of broad-based significance. Virtually every population in the United States which has been studied by social dialectologists shows social stratification for structures like multiple negation, irregular verb forms, and subject-verb agreement patterns. On the whole, phonological variables are more apt to show regionally-restricted social significance than are grammatical variables. No doubt, this is due to the fact that grammatical variables have been ascribed the major symbolic role in differentiating standard from vernacular dialects. Phonological variables show greater flexibility, as they are more likely to be viewed as a normal manifestation of regional diversity in English. As noted earlier, this is particularly true in the case of vowel differences.

There are several different ways in which speakers within the sociolinguistic community may react to socially diagnostic variables. Speakers may treat some features as *social stereotypes,* where they comment overtly on their use. Items such as *ain't*, double negatives, and *dese, dem,* and *dose* are classic features of this type. As with other kinds of behavioral stereotyping, we have to be careful about the nature of the relationship between actual sociolinguistic patterning and the social commentary about such linguistic items. Sociolinguistic stereotypes tend to be overly categorical and are often linguistically naive, although they may derive from a basic sociolinguistic reality. For example, the stereotype that working class speakers *always* use *dese, dem,* and *dose* forms and middle-class speakers *never* do is not supported empirically, although there certainly is a correlation between the relative frequency of the nonstandard variant and social stratification. Furthermore, stereotypes tend to focus on single vocabulary items or selective subsets of items rather than more general phonological and grammatical patterns. The focus on a single lexical item like *ain't* or the restricted pronunciation pattern involving *tomato* and *potato*, where *tomato* as *'mater* [meDɚ] is the stigmatized pronunciation and *tomahto* [tomato] the prestige version are typical of stereotypes. Finally, we have to understand that popular explanations of basic sociolinguistic differences are often rooted in the kind of folk mythology that characterizes other types of behavioral stereotyping, and therefore must be viewed with great caution.

Another type of sociolinguistic role is assumed by the *social marker*. In the case of social markers, variants show clear-cut social stratification, but they do not show the level of conscious awareness found for the social stereotype. Various vowel shifts, such as the Northern Cities Vowel Shift discussed in Chapter 4, seem to function as social markers. There is clear-cut social stratification of the linguistic variants, and participants in the community may even recognize this distribution, but the structure does not evoke the kind of strongly evaluated overt commentary that the social stereotype does. Even if participants don't talk about these features in any direct manner, there are still indications that they are aware of their existence. This awareness is often indicated by shifts in the use of variants across different styles of speaking. Although we take up the notion of style more fully in Chapter 7, we may anticipate our discussion by noting that the incidence of prestigious variants will increase and the use of stigmatized variants will decrease in more formal speech styles.

The third possible sociolinguistic role is called the *social indicator*. Social indicators are linguistic structures that correlate with social stratification without having an effect on listeners' judgment of the social status. Whereas social stereotypes and social markers are sensitive to stylistic variation, social indicators do not exhibit such sensitivity, as shown by the fact that levels of usage remain constant across formal and informal styles. This suggests that the correlation of socially diagnostic variables with social strata differences operates on a more unconscious level than it does for social markers or stereotypes. Although social indicators have been isolated for other communities of English speakers (Trudgill 1974:98), practically all of the socially diagnostic variables in American English qualify as social markers or stereotypes rather than indicators.

SOCIAL CLASS AND LANGUAGE CHANGE

One of the important contributions of the study of social dialectology has do with role that different social classes play in language change. Language change does not take place simultaneously on all different social strata; instead, it originates in particular social classes and then spreads from that point, just as regional dialect change typically starts in a focal area and spreads outward from that point.

What social classes are most likely to originate language change? The popular view seems to be that the upper classes originate change and that other social classes follow their lead. The social model of change showing the elite leading the masses sounds good, but turns out to be largely mistaken. In reality, the lower social classes are much more responsible for language change than they have been given credit for. Furthermore, extremes in the social strata (for example, the highest and the lowest social classes) tend to be peripheral in the origin of change; it is those social classes between the extremes which bear the major responsibility for change. The middle-status groups tend to have the strongest ties to group and local identity so that they are more sensitive to local innovation. According to Guy (1988:58), the highest social groups are not as likely to rely on local solidarity for their identity and the lowest social groups do not have strong local ties or broader community allegiance to serve as a model for change.

In order to understand the role of social class in language change, it is essential to understand the distinction between changes that take place below the level of consciousness, so-called *changes from below,* and those that take place above the level of consciousness, or *changes from above.* Although there is often a social class corollary to the notion of change from above and below in that the lower social classes are more likely to be active in changes from below and the upper classes in changes from above, the distinction refers to the *level of consciousness,* not social class. Many of the phonological changes in American English, particularly those involving the vowel system, are changes from below, or at least start out as changes from below. Changes from above tend to reflect a move away from socially stigmatized features or the influence of external prestige forms that become the model to emulate. For example, the increased use of postvocalic r in New York City in recent years on the basis of dialect models outside of the area is a change from above.

The spread of new forms through the population is only one side of language change. The other side concerns *resistance to change.* Whereas change is certainly natural and inevitable to a certain degree, some social groups may differentiate themselves by withstanding changes taking place in other social groups. As presented in Chapter 2, many changes which take place in language involve very natural extensions of linguistic systems, such as the regularization of irregular grammatical paradigms or the movement of phonological systems toward more natural phonetic productions. For the most part, it is the lower classes that adopt these changes initially and the upper classes that tend to resist them. The regularization of irregular plurals (e.g., *sheeps, oxes*), irregular reflexives (*hisself, theirselves*) and irregular verbs (e.g., *knowed, growed*) in the grammar—attributable to natural pressure from within the grammatical system—are certainly changes in the English language which are witnessed to a greater degree in the lower classes than the upper classes. These changes, along with a number of natural phonological shifts cited by Kroch (1978), have made some headway in the lower classes but are resisted by the upper classes in spite of their linguistic reasonableness.

It is the upper classes who have the most investment in maintaining the language variety the way it is; the lower classes have less investment in maintaining the current state of linguistic structures. Accordingly, more conscious attention by the upper classes is given to withstanding potential changes "offered" by the lower classes, even if they are natural adaptations of the linguistic system. Only a change in the social evaluation of forms can result in the adoption of linguistically natural but socially stigmatized forms by the upper classes.

An important principle of sociolinguistic stratification thus involves the inhibition of natural linguistic changes by high-status groups. By resisting the changes that have taken place in the lower-status groups, the social stratification of linguistic differences is maintained. The bottom line is that higher-status groups do not want to be mistaken for lower-status groups in language any more than they do in other kinds of behavior, but the mechanism by which they do this in language may be somewhat different from other kinds of cultural behavior. With respect to language, high-status groups often suppress natural changes taking place in lower-status groups to keep their sociolinguistic position intact. In many respects, the social differentiation of language in American society is much more typified by the resistance to proposed changes offered by the lower classes by a steadfast upper class than it is typified by the linguistic "flight of the elite" and the "protracted pursuit of the elite by an envious mass" (Fisher 1958:52).

Exercise 2

Some of the changes that typify lower-status groups are also found in a stage of acquisition by the children of high-status parents because they involve such natural linguistic extensions. For example, middle-class children go through a stage of acquisition when they regularize irregular verbs forms (e.g., *growed, knowed*), regularize plurals (e.g., *oxes, sheeps*), use multiple negatives (e.g., *I didn't do nothing, Nobody didn't go*), and so forth. How are these natural tendencies to regularize combatted? Do you recall overt "correction" about these forms? If so, who was responsible for such correction? What might happen if some of these irregular forms were not directly focused on by the parents, teachers, and other language guardians in our society responsible for socializing children into middle-class norms of linguistic behavior?

ETHNICITY

Although the correlation of ethnicity with linguistic variation is indisputable on one level, the precise contribution of ethnic group membership to the overall configuration of dialects is not always simple to isolate. Nominal classification of people into various ethnic categories in our society seems straightforward on the surface, but it is much more difficult to capture the underlying values that ultimately define the cultural notion of ethnicity. From a sociolinguistic perspective, what is popularly identified as ethnicity may be difficult to separate from other social factors such as region and social class. For example, the popular notion of Jewish English has a strong regional association with New York City English; similarly, what is identified as Vernacular Black English is strongly linked to social status within the community as well as southern regional English. Notwithstanding the qualifications that must go into the definition of the ethnicity as a variable in dialect differentiation, Laferriere (1979:603) is correct in observing that "in communities where the local lore acknowledges more than one ethnic group, we would expect ethnicity to be a factor in linguistic variation."

The definition of an ethnic group usually involves the following kinds of parameters (National Council of Social Studies Task Force on Ethnic Studies 1976): (1) origins that precede or are external to the state (e.g., American Indian, immigrant groups) (2) group membership that is involuntary (3) ancestral tradition rooted in a shared sense of peoplehood, (4) distinctive value orientations and behavioral patterns, (5) influence of the group on the lives of its members, and (6) group membership influenced by how members define themselves and how they are defined by others. This is an expansive set of parameters, but even this definition does not always lead to a clear-cut ethnic categorization. In some cases, a subjectively-based self-image turns out to be stronger in determining a person's ethnicity than any of the parameters set forth in the institutional definition.

Notwithstanding the problems involved in teasing out the ethnicity variable, there is ample evidence that ethnicity can contribute to the definition of a dialect in a way similar to other social variables. The literature on American English dialects thus includes descriptions of varieties labeled Italian English, Jewish English, Irish English, German English, Puerto Rican English, Chicano English, American Indian English, Vietnamese English, and, of course, Vernacular Black English. The extent to which ethnicity per se contributes to the definition of dialect in these accounts, however, varies greatly, as does the range of descriptive dialect differences. For example, a survey of research on Jewish English defines this variety on the basis of a restricted set of lexical differences, a small inventory of phonological differences related to vowels and intonation, isolated grammatical features, and several aspects related to conversational style (Gold 1981, Steinmetz 1981). By contrast, there are entire books describing the phonological and grammatical features of Vernacular Black English, and separate books devoted exclusively to the lexicon of black English and language use conventions in the black community.

Ethnic groups tend to form subcultures within the larger culture, and part of this definition may be manifested in linguistic differences, but the distinction between the subculture and the larger culture often exists on a relative scale, depending on the social role of various ethnic groups in American society. We may hypothesize that the greater the isolation of an ethnic group from the mainstream of society, the greater the linguistic diversity will be, but there are so many other intersecting factors and underlying values involved in the definition of language variation that this simple correlation rarely works out as neatly as we might hope.

There are several different kinds of relationships that may exist between ethnicity and language variation. For ethnic groups which maintain a language other than English, there is the potential of language *transfer* from the other language which is "fossilized," stabilized, and perpetuated as a part of the English variety used by members of the ethnic group. For example, Huffines (1984:177) notes that the English of Pennsylvania Germans in southeastern Pennsylvania is characterized by items which seem to be direct translations of German into English, such as the use of *all* (all gone) in *He's going to have the cookies all*, *what for* (what kind of) in *I don't know what for a car you had*, and *sneaky* (finicky about food) in *I'm kind of sneaky when it comes to meat like that*. Similar characteristics can be found in the phonological features, including the "devoicing" of stops, where a voiced sound at the end of a word is replaced by voiceless one (e.g., *bad* [bæd]→ *bat* [bæt], *beg* [bɛg]→ *beck* [bɛk]) and intonational contours of questions having a falling intonation at the end which is characteristic of German rather than the rising intonation characteristic of English questions (Huffines 1986). In a similar way, the use of *no* as a generalized tag question (e.g., *You go to the movies a lot, no?*) in some Hispanic communities in the Southwest may be attributable to transfer from Spanish, as can the merger of *ch* /č/ and *sh* /š/ (e.g., *shoe* as *chew* [ču] *chain* as *Shane* [šen]), the devoicing of /z/ to /s/ (e.g., *doze* as *dose* [dos], *lazy* as *lasy* [lesi]), and the merger of /i/ and /I/ (e.g., *pit* as *peat* [pit], *rip* as *reap* [rip]) in phonology (Peñalosa 1980). In many cases, these linguistic manifestations are directly traceable to transfer from Spanish, but there are also cases where the characteristic extends well beyond the immediate language contact situation.

While certain linguistic characteristics found among ethnic groups may be directly attributable to transfer from another language, others derive from more generalized strategies related to the acquisition of English as a second language rather than specific language structures carried over from another language. It is, for example, not uncommon to find the absence of marked tense forms (e.g., *Yesterday he play at the school*) among a range of English varieties with recent access to another language such as American Indian English and Vietnamese English (Wolfram 1984, 1985).

The tricky question for structures traceable to language contact is determining whether the form is simply a transitional one, which will be eliminated as soon as English becomes the native language of a generation of speakers, or whether the form will be incorporated as a distinct part of the dialect to be carried forth by subsequent generations. Hindsight is ultimately the only way we can answer this question satisfactorily. In some cases, an item traceable to a language contact situation may be retained, but in a redefined form. Our studies of American Indian English in the Southwest (Wolfram 1984) indicate that tense unmarking is maintained by successive generations, but highly limited to cases marking habitual activity (e.g., *Before, we eat at home a lot, but now we don't*). Only the study of the English variety over subsequent generations can ultimately determine which of the characteristics will be integrated as a distinct part of an ethnic variety and which will be cast aside. The current generation of Vietnamese speakers living in various communities in the United States (e.g., Washington, DC, Houston, Los Angeles) may exhibit extensive tense unmarking, but it is still to be determined if this feature will be maintained as part of Vietnamese English. To make this ultimate determination, we must look at future generations of speakers in these communities, particularly those now learning English as a first language.

All transfer from another language is not readily transparent; the effects of an ancestral language in the determination of an ethnically-correlated variation may be more subtle, existing on the substratum of language. Labov thus observes that vowel patterns for the Jewish and Italian communities in New York City do not coincide with that of other New Yorkers, and that this may be due to a *substratum language effect* from the languages spoken by previous generations. Although the vowels of these ethnic group members ultimately may be traced to these ancestral language backgrounds, the route of influence is not nearly as direct as the kind of transfer referred to earlier. This, however, does not diminish the significance of the ethnic variable, as Labov concludes that for the vowel system of these communities "ethnic differentiation is seen to be a more powerful factor than social class differentiation, though both exist in addition to marked stylistic variation" (1966:306).

The restructuring of an item from another language may not only involve linguistic adjustment; it also may involve redefinition in terms of its social and ethnic association. Items like *khutspa* (impudence, guts), *schlepp* (haul, take), and the expression *I need this like a hole in the head* all can be traced to Yiddish, but their social roles and ethnic associations are different. In the case of *khutspa*, its ethnic association is quite strong, and those who are not part of the Jewish community would only use the term as a deliberately borrowed item from that culture. The use of *schlepp* is less embedded in the Jewish community, although it still has an ethnic association; at the same time, it is taking on a much more regional definition as New Yorkese. The expression *I need it like a hole in the head*, directly translated from a Yiddish expression (Gold 1981:288), is the least ethnically identifiable of these items, and is not nearly as regionally restricted as an item like *schlepp*. We thus see that overt ethnic association is often a relative matter and that other social variables obviously intersect in varying degrees.

Finally, we must recognize that ethnically-correlated variation need not be traceable to previous language background at all. Some correlation simply reflects patterns of assimilation and isolation with respect to more widespread regional and social dialects. For example, Laferriere (1979) shows ethnic correlations for Italian, Irish, and Jewish speakers in Boston with reference to the local pronunciation of *-or* in words like *form, short,* and *horse.* The standard Boston pronunciation of the vowel in these items is a vowel like the [ɔ] pronunciation of *dog* or *law* in some other regions, but the vernacular Boston pronunciation involves lowering the tongue more toward the vowel [a] of *father* so that *short* is pronounced more like *shot* [šat] and *corn* more like *con* [kan]. (Remember that this region is largely an *r*-less dialect area to begin with.) Jews most closely follow the standard pattern (i.e., [šɔ(r)t], [kɔ(r)n]), followed by the Irish and then the Italians, who are most apt to use the lower vowel found in the vernacular pattern. These ethnic groups also reflect different stages with respect to the current change taking place in the pronunciation of the vowel. The Jewish community has virtually completed a change toward the Boston standard pronunciation (using the higher vowel [ɔ]), followed by the Irish who are in the middle of the change, and the Italians, who are just beginning a change toward the standard production.

The extent to which ethnic membership correlates with linguistic diversity varies from linguistic variable to linguistic variable. Whereas Italians and Jews do not participate in the typical New York pattern with respect to some vowels, they participate fully in the New York pattern of *r*-lessness. Similarly, the Italian, Irish, and Jewish communities in Boston participate in many of the linguistic characteristics of the regional variety in a way which is indistinguishable from other Bostonians at the same time these ethnic communities distinguish themselves in their realization of a restricted vowel pattern.

THE CASE OF BLACK ENGLISH

The paradigm case for examining the role of ethnicity in dialects is Vernacular Black English. The sociolinguistic scrutiny of this variety dwarfs other ethnic varieties by comparison; as mentioned in Chapter 1, one bibliography of articles and books related to black English contained over 2,000 entries as of 1974 (Brasch and Brasch 1974). There are three major issues related to the description of Vernacular Black English as a dialect of English, including (1) its relation to other vernacular varieties, (2) its historical roots and development, and (3) the nature of language change presently taking place in this variety. These are really the kinds of issues that are involved in any sociolinguistic discussion of ethnicity to a greater or lesser extent, but there are also unique aspects to the consideration of this variety because of the peculiar history and social role traditionally assigned to blacks in American society. Certainly, no ethnic variety is more hotly debated in American society.

In the case of Vernacular Black English, it is still often necessary to start with the disclaimer about language and race. There is no basis for maintaining that there is a genetic basis for the kind of language differentiation evidenced by some black Americans. Hypotheses about the genetic basis for dialect diversity which still surface sometimes in popular discussions are readily rejected anecdotally by citing cases of black Americans raised in a middle-class white context who talk indistinguishably from their white community peers and, conversely, by white Americans socialized linguistically in Vernacular Black English communities who talk no differently from other members of the community. Despite the ready rejection of a genetic basis for dialect differences by dialectologists, myths about the physical basis of Vernacular Black English persist in some circles, so that there is a continuing need to confront and debunk these claims. The following discussion of black-white dialect issues is founded in a cultural definition of black and white ethnicity rather than a genetic definition of race.

WHITE AND BLACK VERNACULARS: SAME OR DIFFERENT

In its simplest form, the issue of black-white dialect relations can be reduced to a question of whether the same or different language structures are exhibited in comparable dialects spoken by whites and blacks. Are there features which are uniquely used in Vernacular Black English when compared with white vernacular varieties? To answer this question, it is necessary to establish what constitutes a "comparable" white vernacular variety. Region and class must be controlled in the comparison; the question can only be answered satisfactorily by examining the speech of low-status white and black groups in the South because of the sociohistorical roots of Vernacular Black English as a southern-based variety. All dialectologists agree that there are many features characterizing Vernacular Black English in a northern urban context that set this dialect apart from the surrounding white varieties in this setting, but the uniqueness of these features in a southern context for comparable socioeconomic black and white groups is much more debatable. Some dialectologists also maintain that social factors other than region and class have to be considered in the comparison of black-white speech relations, such as age, ruralness, and particular region of the South (Bailey and Maynor 1987), but at the very least, region and class are critical dimensions to control.

The issue of black-white speech relations is still not totally resolved after several decades of often polemical debate, but cautious agreement on points of similarity and difference is emerging. At least the issue looked like it was subsiding until the debate over white-black speech relations was renewed in the mid-1980s. In a useful survey of the phonological and grammatical structures of Vernacular Black English in relation to comparable white varieties, Fasold (1981) concluded that there were a limited number of distinctive features in Vernacular Black English, that is, structures not found among white, lower-class Southerners. Based on a careful review of research studies up to that point, Fasold (1981) concluded that the following structures were the best candidates as unique features of Vernacular Black English.

Unique Features of Vernacular Black English

1. devoicing of voiced stops in stressed syllables
   e.g., [bIt] for *bid*
   [bæk] for *bag*
2. present tense, third person *-s/-es* absence
   e.g., *he walk* for *he walks*
   she raise for *she raises*
3. plural *-s/-es* absence on general plurals (as opposed to such absence found on plurals of weights and measures)
   e.g., *four girl* for *four girls*
   some dog for *some dogs*
4. remote time *been* (i.e., an account of something that began a long time ago and is still relevant)
   e.g., *You been paid your dues.*
   I been known him a long time.
5. possessive *-s/-es* absence
   e.g., *man hat* for *man's hat*
   Jack car for *Jack's car*
6. reduction of final consonant clusters when followed by a word beginning with a vowel or when followed by a suffix beginning with a vowel
   e.g., *lif up* for *lift up*
   bussing for *busting*
7. copula and auxiliary absence involving *is* forms (as opposed to more generally deleted *are* forms)
   e.g., *She nice* for *She's nice*
   He in the kitchen for *He's in the kitchen*
8. use of habitual or distributive *be*
   e.g., *Sometimes my ears be itching.*
   She don't be usually be there.

Even with this restricted list of unique features, there are important qualifications to be made. In some cases, it is a particular aspect of the phonological or grammatical pattern which is unique rather than the general pattern. For example, consonant cluster reduction is a very general rule of English, but in many other varieties it only applies when the item is *not* followed by a vowel (e.g., at the end of an utterance or when followed by a word beginning with a consonant, such as *bes' kind* or *lif' packages*). In other cases, the difference between the Vernacular Black English feature and a feature in a comparable white variety may involve a drastic quantitative difference rather than strict group-exclusive usage (i.e., *only* used by a given group). The difference in *-s/-es* third person singular absence (e.g., *she walk*) in black and white vernaculars may thus be based on a substantial difference in percentage of occurrence: some black speakers show levels of absence between 80–95 percent while comparable white speakers show a range of 5–15 percent absence at the most.

Exercise 3

In the actual study of absence of the verb *be* or so-called copula deletion among lower-class whites and blacks in the South (Wolfram 1974), the following conclusions were reached:

> Neither white nor black speakers delete the copula when the form is *am* (e.g., neither group of speakers utters forms like *I nice*).
>
> Both whites and blacks delete the copula frequently when the form is *are* (e.g., *You ugly*), but black speakers have a higher frequency of absence for *are* deletion.
>
> Both whites and blacks delete the copula form *is* when it is followed by the item *gonna* (e.g., *She gonna do it*).
>
> Whites show almost no (less than 5 percent) absence of the copula form *is* with forms other than *gonna,* and blacks show significant frequency levels of *is* deletion (for example, 50 percent).

How do these kinds of observations show the need for considerable descriptive detail in the resolution of the question of black-white speech relations? How would you respond to a person who observed that "copula absence can't be unique to black English because I hear white speakers who say things like 'He gonna do it right now'?"

Despite Fasold's careful review of the present status of Vernacular Black English in relation to other varieties, debate over some of the structures has continued, or in some cases, reemerged. For example, Bailey and Bassett (1986) question whether habitual *be* is as unique to black speakers as set forth in Wolfram (1974), offering documentation that working-class white adults in the South may use this form in a way which matches that found among blacks. At the same time, other investigators have suggested that there are additional forms that may qualify as unique Vernacular Black English forms. For example, Labov (1987) suggests that certain constructions (e.g., *be done* as in *I'll be done put so many holes in it you won't know what happened*) were overlooked in earlier descriptions of Vernacular Black English. Furthermore, studies by Spears (1982) and Baugh (1984) have suggested that there are structures in Vernacular Black English that appear very much like constructions in other dialects of English, but turn out, upon closer inspection, to have uses and meanings that are unique to the variety. These types of structures are called *camouflaged forms,* referring to the fact that the surface similarity of structures to constructions found in other varieties of English may conceal an essential difference in the underlying use of the structure. One of these camouflaged constructions is the form *come* in *She come acting like she was real mad.* This structure looks like a common English use of the motion verb *come* in structures like *She came running,* but actually has a special use as a kind of verb auxiliary indicating indignation on the part of the speaker (Spears 1982). In this use, it is apparently unique to Vernacular Black English. Another example of a camouflaged form is *steady* in *They be steady messing with you,* where *steady* indicates a special progressive aspect indicating intense, consistent, and continuous activity even though it looks on the surface like the familiar English use of *steady* in *Things were holding steady* (Baugh 1984).

Although the debate over black-white speech relations will no doubt continue, it is probably fair to conclude that there is a restricted subset of structures which are unique to Vernacular Black English. At the same time, however, we have to conclude that the inventory of differences is probably much more limited than originally set forth by some social dialectologists studying Vernacular Black English in the 1960s, including myself. If we admit significant quantitative differences of the sort discussed in Chapter

---

Exercise 4

Studies of vernacular dialects of English have documented the use of *ain't* in a broad range of dialects. Typically, *ain't* is used for *have/hasn't* as in *She ain't been there for a while* and forms of *isn't* and *aren't*, such as *She ain't home now.* In Vernacular Black English, we have found *ain't* used for *didn't* as well, as in *She ain't do it yet.* This form is rarely included in discussions of unique features of Vernacular Black English. How does an item like this compare with other kinds of differences cited previously, such as the use of inflectional suffixes or habitual *be*? Is it a major or minor difference? Would you consider it a camouflaged form?

9 to our list of qualitative differences, the distinction between comparable white and black vernaculars can remain fairly extensive.

Although it is certainly possible to compare structures used by white and black speakers on an item-by-item basis, as we have done earlier, the picture that emerges from such an approach does not fully represent the true relationship between black and white vernacular varieties. It appears that the uniqueness of Vernacular Black English lies more in the particular constellation of structures than it does in the restricted set of potentially unique structures. It is the co-occurrence of grammatical structures such as suffixial absence of various types (possessive, third person singular, plural), copula absence, habitual *be,* and so forth, along with a set of phonological characteristics such as cluster reduction, final [f] for *th,* postvocalic *r*-lessness, and so forth (see the Appendix for details) that seems to define the variety rather than the subset of proposed unique features per se. To find that a structure previously thought to be unique to Vernacular Black English is shared by a white vernacular variety, such as Bailey and Bassett (1986) do for the use of habitual *be* in the South, does not seriously challenge the notion of the uniqueness of Vernacular Black English as a distinct dialect. Studies of listener judgments of ethnic identity certainly support the contention that Vernacular Black English is distinct from comparable white vernaculars, as most of these studies (Shuy 1973; Williams 1973) show correct identification of black and white speech samples at a level of 80 percent or higher.

Up to this point, we have discussed Vernacular Black English as if it were a unitary variety in different regions of the United States. We must, however, admit regional variation within Vernacular Black English, just as we have to admit regional variation within other vernacular varieties. Certainly, some of the northern metropolitan versions of Vernacular Black English are distinguishable from some of the southern rural versions, and South Atlantic coastal varieties are different from those found in the Gulf regions. While admitting some of these regional variations, we hasten to point out that one of the most noteworthy aspects of this variety is the common core of features found across different regions. Features such as habitual *be,* copula absence, inflectional *-s/-es* absence, among a number of other grammatical and phonological structures, are found in locations as distant as Los Angeles, New York, Detroit, Meadville, Mississippi, Austin, Texas, and Wilmington, North Carolina. Thus, we recognize regional variation in Vernacular Black English while concluding, at the same time, that the regional differences do not come close to the magnitude of regional differences found in comparable vernacular white varieties in these same regions. The basic core of features in Vernacular Black English, regardless of where it has been studied in the United States so far, attests to the ethnic vitality of this variety.

THE CREOLIST AND ANGLICIST HYPOTHESES:
THE HISTORICAL ISSUE

The major issue concerning the historical development of Vernacular Black English centers around the creole-origin hypothesis. According to this hypothesis, today's Vernacular Black English developed from a *creole language* (a special language developed in language contact situations in which the vocabulary from one primary language is imposed on a specially adapted, restricted grammatical structure) used through a good portion of the New World, including the Plantation South. This creole was fairly widespread during slavery and persisted to some extent in the antebellum South as well. Those who take this position note that this creole was not a unique development which arose in the mainland South, but that it shows continuity with well-known creoles of the African diaspora such as Krio, spoken today along the coast of West Africa (in Sierra Leone) and the English-based creoles of the Caribbean such as Jamaican Creole. Its vestiges in the United States are still found today in Gullah (more popularly called "Geechee"), the creole still spoken by a small number of blacks in the Sea Islands off the coast of South Carolina and Georgia. It is maintained that this creole was fairly widespread among blacks on Southern plantations, but was not spoken to any extent by whites.

Over time, through contact with surrounding dialects, this creole language was modified to become more like other varieties of English including southern standard varieties, in a process referred to as *decreolization*. Since this decreolization process was a gradual one, and not necessarily complete in all its phases, the creole predecessor is cited as the basis for some present-day characteristics of Vernacular Black English, although I am not aware of any serious investigators of Vernacular Black English who would maintain that this variety still qualifies as a genuine creole. For example, copula absence (e.g., *You ugly*) is a well-known trait found in creole languages, so that one might maintain that the present version of copula absence is a vestigial manifestation of the creole origin of Vernacular Black English. Similar arguments have been made for the various types of inflectional -*s* absence in this variety, as well as phonological characteristics such as consonant cluster reduction. Both linguistic traits and social history have been used to argue for the creole origin of Vernacular Black English. J. L. Dillard's book, *Black English: Its History and Usage in the United States* (1972), is still the most complete argument for the creole hypothesis, although there are more careful accounts of particular linguistic and historical details now offered in support of this hypothesis.

The alternative to this hypothesis has been referred to as the *Anglicist hypothesis,* so called because the origin of Vernacular Black English is proposed to be rooted in varieties of English spoken in the British Isles, like white varieties of American English. Briefly put, this position maintains that the language contact situation among blacks in the United States was roughly comparable to other groups of immigrants. In this historical situation, slaves brought with them to North America a number of different African languages. Over the course of a couple of generations, only substratal effects were left from these ancestral languages, as blacks learned the regional and social varieties of the surrounding white speakers. From this perspective, a creole language played no significant part in the history of the vernacular dialect. A widely-recognized creole like Gullah is considered an anomaly among black varieties, which arose through a special set of social and physical circumstances of isolation unique in the Sea Islands.

From the perspective of the Anglicist hypothesis, differences that cannot be explained on the basis of regional and social factors result from the differential preservation of British dialect features brought to North America by colonists. Some of the peculiar features mentioned previously, such as habitual *be* and third person -*s* absence (Schneider 1983, 1989), have been explained on this basis. In this regard, the pursuit of historical evidence is often reduced to the scrutiny of descriptions of earlier English varieties in the British Isles for features similar to those found in Vernacular Black English today. There is, of course, an accompanying search for sociohistorical facts that might place the speakers of the potential donor dialect in a position to make their linguistic contribution to blacks in North America.

As with the current relationship of black and white varieties, the historical issue is not totally resolved, but the evidence offered thus far favors a modified version of the creolist hypothesis, with an understanding that decreolization has been fairly extensive. Nonetheless, there are still vestiges of a creole past. For example, there is no evidence for copula absence in the history of the English of the British Isles; at the same time, there is extensive documentation of this copula absence in creoles which might have been related to Vernacular Black English historically (Wolfram 1974). Similarly, a structure like remote time *been* seems to be best explained as a derivative of the past time use of *been* found in some English-based creoles (e.g., *'im been go* for *he went*), although its use in Vernacular Black English has been redefined to some extent. In phonology, the extensive cluster reduction found in Vernacular Black English seems characteristic of a creole predecessor rather than a particular variety of English found in the British Isles (Fasold 1976). However, since the linguistic line from a creole predecessor to Vernacular Black English was not always direct and straightforward, it is presumptuous to be as dogmatic as some researchers have been about the creole origin of the variety. Certainly, many historical and current social and linguistic factors have blurred the sociolinguistic past.

The issue of the historical development of Vernacular Black English has often been linked with the current-day status of black-white speech relations, but these two issues are not necessarily related. It is, for example, possible to maintain that the creolist position is essentially correct, but that decreolization has been so complete as to eliminate virtually all differences that existed at a prior point in time. Furthermore, it is apparent that sociolinguistic contact among whites and blacks over the generations may have resulted in whites picking up some features historically unique to blacks so that they are no longer different. Certainly, linguistic assimilation has been bilateral rather than unilateral. In fact, my examination of copula absence as used by whites and blacks in the deep South (Wolfram 1974) suggests that whites have picked up this trait from blacks, to the extent that it has been adopted by vernacular English in the South. On the other hand, it is possible to maintain that the Anglicist position is the correct historical one, but that patterns of social and linguistic segregation have led to differences which resulted in a distinct ethnic variety. After all, social and linguistic separation is a well-attested basis for the development of quite distinct dialects. In fact, the next section takes up the hypothesis that current-day Vernacular Black English is actually diverging from other vernacular varieties. At this point, it is adequate to observe that a particular position on the historical development of Vernacular Black English is not intrinsically tied into a position on the status of the current relationship of white and black vernaculars.

BLACK AND WHITE VERNACULARS: DIVERGENCE OR CONVERGENCE

The latest controversy in the study of Vernacular Black English concerns the way it is currently evolving in relation to surrounding vernaculars. Although it commonly has been assumed that Vernacular Black English was gradually converging with other dialects of English, this view was strongly challenged by Labov in the mid-1980s. Based on research conducted by Labov and his colleagues in Philadelphia, Labov concluded that Vernacular Black English actually was diverging from, rather than converging with, surrounding vernaculars. As Labov (1985:1) put it "their [black residents of Philadelphia] speech pattern is developing in its own direction, and becoming more different from the speech of whites in the same communities." The sociological basis for the *divergence hypothesis* is found in the social and economic plight of lower-class blacks—racial isolation brought about by increasing de facto segregation and a widening socioeconomic gap between mainstream American society and lower-class minority groups.

The linguistic basis for divergence is focused on a couple of features, which include the resultative use of *be done* (i.e., a future or hypothetical event which has particular consequences) in sentences such as *I'll be done put so many holes in him he'll wish he wouldna said it* and a special use of -*s* with verbs to mark a lively past time narrative in a way somewhat akin to the historical present found in other varieties of English. This narrative -*s* use is illustrated by the fluctuation of -*s* and non -*s* in the following excerpt (Labov 1987:8):

> . . . they was playin', next thing you know he comed—the li'l boy, he *comes and hit* me right? I *hits* him back now. All the time, my brother and him was hittin' each other an' everything, and he start cryin' . . .

A third candidate for linguistic divergence comes from the research on habitual *be* in the South carried out by Bailey and Maynor (1987). Based on the study of older and younger black speakers in urban and rural contexts, they conclude that this form is developing a unique grammatical function with the -*ing* form of verbs (e.g., *They be messing with me*). The evolution of this use among younger, primarily urban speakers is making one part of the verb-aspect system of Vernacular Black English more different from other vernacular varieties, according to Bailey and Maynor.

At this point, little clear-cut evidence has been presented to support the general conclusion that Vernacular Black English is independently diverging from other vernaculars (*American Speech* Vol 62. No. 1987; Butters 1989). Some of the features cited as evidence for divergence, such as the *be done* construction, remain quite rare and have apparently been a part of the dialect for some time although they have not been described in detail. Other structures, such as the historical narrative forms cited previously, may actually represent an underlying convergence with discourse styles well represented in other vernacular dialects of English (e.g., *I went to the store, I goes in and there before my eyes, I see this guy pull out a gun. . . .*). At the same time, there may be features of Vernacular Black English that are, in fact, developing in a way which makes this dialect more distinct from other vernacular varieties, such as the habitual *be* form already mentioned. To suggest that the *overall* structure of Vernacular Black English is independently developing toward a more divergent dialect does not, however, appear to do justice to the current linguistic status of this variety.

Whereas Labov's assertion that Vernacular Black English grammar is moving away from other varieties seems to be exaggerated, he is more on target when he observes that black residents are not participating in major dialect changes taking place in some areas of the United States (Labov 1987:6). In particular, the vowel systems found in some white varieties may be moving away from Vernacular Black English. For example, blacks in Philadelphia are not involved to any significant extent in the evolution of the unique vowel system described for the Philadelphia white community. Furthermore, there is little evidence that the Northern Cities Vowel Shift discussed in Chapter 4 is spreading to Vernacular Black English varieties spoken in these metropolitan areas. Patterns of social separation for blacks and whites in many regions are still sufficiently strong to inhibit large-scale dialect diffusion across the vernaculars. For the immediate future, it appears that Vernacular Black English will remain a stable and distinct socioethnic dialect of English, with some change but no radical independent restructuring towards or away from other vernaculars. This conclusion is not meant to preclude the divergence or convergence of particular structures as part of the normal dynamics of language change taking place in this dialect, but simply to place the current hypothesis about divergence into proper perspective. Naturally, Vernacular Black English will continue to change, just as any other dialect may be expected to undergo change, but the present evidence does not, in fact, suggest drastic restructuring of this variety.

Further Reading

American Speech 62 (1987), No. 1. University, AL: University of Alabama Press. This entire issue of *American Speech* is devoted to a discussion of the convergence-divergence with respect to Vernacular Black English. Each researcher presents a position statement, followed by a lively panel discussion of the issues raised in the presentations.

BUTTERS, RONALD K.*The Death of Black English: Divergence and Convergence in White and Black Vernaculars*. Frankfurt, Germany: Lang, 1989. This work summarizes the debate on the developmental direction of Vernacular Black English. Butters integrates empirical data from his own studies of the relationship of black and white speech in North Carolina.

FASOLD, RALPH W. "The Relation Between Black and White Speech in the South," *American Speech,* 16:163–189, (1981). Fasold summarizes the major findings on the similarities and differences between white and black vernacular varieties prior to the convergence-divergence debate. It is a useful synthesis based solely on empirically-based research available at the time.

GUY, GREGORY R., "Language and Social Class," in *Linguistics: The Cambridge Survey Vol. IV Language: The Socio-Cultural Context,* ed. Frederick J. Newmeyer. New York, NY: Cambridge University Press, 1988. This overview includes a discussion of essential social constructs relevant to the study of class and language variation, with particular reference to the role of social class in linguistic change.

KROCH, ANTHONY, "Towards a Theory of Social Dialect Variation," *Language in Society*, 7:17–36, (1978). Kroch's article is exceptional for its attempt to explain *why* particular linguistic features are subjected to social evaluation. Most sociolinguistic studies are content to describe patterns of social and linguistic covariation as opposed to trying to explain them.

LABOV, WILLIAM, *Sociolinguistic Patterns*. Philadelphia, PA: The University of Pennsylvania Press, 1972. Several of the most influential studies on the interaction of social and linguistic differentiation are included in this collection of Labov's early research studies. These articles set the stage for much of the social dialect research that has taken place over the past couple of decades.

SCHNEIDER, EDGAR W., *American Earlier Black English: Morphological and Syntactic Variables*. Tuscaloosa, AL: University of Alabama Press, 1989. This translation from German of an earlier (1981) analysis of the linguistic development of Vernacular Black English presents the most extensive rationale for the Anglicist hypothesis to date. Its linguistic analysis is based upon the Slave Narratives collected in the mid-1930s by the Federal Writers' Project, a project which included more than 2,000 interviews with blacks born before emancipation.

CHAPTER SIX

GENDER AND LANGUAGE VARIATION

Few topics in language variation studies have witnessed an explosion of interest as dramatic as that found for language and gender. Just a couple of decades ago, linguists were content to point to several classic studies in other languages where the sex of the speaker or hearer was reflected in the system of grammatical inflections as illustrations of one of the more "exotic" ways in which language codes might reflect social relationships. The role of gender in English was assumed to be minor and relatively uninteresting, despite the fact that third person singular reference required distinguishing masculine, feminine, and neuter pronouns. Today, we find a very different situation. There now exists an extensive collection of studies, anthologies, and books devoted exclusively to issues of language and gender in English and *A Feminist Dictionary* as well (Kramerae and Treichler 1985). Furthermore, most Americans have now confronted the issue of language sexism in spoken and written language. Concerns for sex equity in American society certainly encompass language issues along with other sociopolitical concerns. In the process of investigating gender and language differences from a number of vantage points, we have learned much about the nature of language variation and the linguistic manifestations of social relationships.

In this chapter, we consider several different vantage points on gender and language variation. First, we consider how the demographic variable of sex affects traditionally recognized types of dialect differences. Then, we consider male and female language differences apart from traditional dialect structures in the discussion of so-called "genderlects." Finally, we consider some of the sociopolitical ramifications of gender differences in language, particularly as they relate to the issue of sexism in language.

THE TRADITIONAL DIALECT TREATMENT

Although traditional dialect surveys of American English have not ignored the sex of the speaker in reporting the use of diagnostic dialect forms, this factor rarely has been considered a primary variable in such surveys. In part, this is due to the fact that the focus of these dialect surveys typically has been on geographical or social *distance,* where speakers in one geographical location or in one social class grouping are compared with speakers in another locale or in another social class. Gender differences, however, manifest social *difference* rather than distance, as the variation between males and females within the same regional or social grouping is usually the focus of gender studies.

In the typical treatment of regional and status variation in dialect studies, the sex of the speaker is treated as a moderating variable—a secondary factor that intersects with primary social or regional variables. Thus, male-female differences are plotted in an interacting relationship with other variables to show that being a male or female within a given social group or region correlates with the increased or reduced use of particular linguistic variants. Two fairly typical intersections of this type are given in Figures 6–1 and 6–2. In Figure 6–1 the relative frequency of multiple negation in

FIGURE 6–1 Mean Percentage of Multiple Negation by Social Class Sex of Speaker (from Wolfram and Fasold 1974, p. 93)

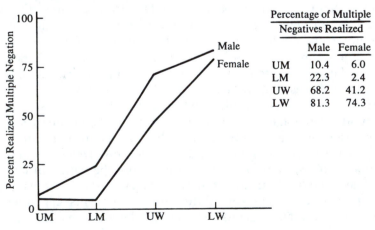

	Percentage of Multiple Negatives Realized	
	Male	Female
UM	10.4	6.0
LM	22.3	2.4
UW	68.2	41.2
LW	81.3	74.3

four different social classes (UM = upper middle class, LM = lower middle class, UW = upper working class, and LW = lower working class) in Detroit is shown for males and females within each social group. In Figure 6–2, selected vowel shifts are shown for male and female speakers in several different social class groupings in Detroit. The three vowels shown in Figure 6–2 participate in the Northern Cities Vowel Shift discussed in Chapter 4.

The diagnostic variable illustrated in Figure 6–1 involves one existing on the standard-vernacular continuum. In this case, the use of multiple negation is stigmatized. As indicated, women tend to have a lower incidence of multiple negation than men, regardless of social class. At the same time, it is clear from Figure 6–1 that the social class of the speaker is more important than the sex of the speaker, as indicated by the drastic difference in the multiple negation scores for middle and working classes compared with the sex of speakers in each group. A number of different social dialect studies have shown similar patterns. By the same token, the study of prestige variants typically shows that women use more prestige forms than their male counterparts in the same social class and region. Some of the more substantive male-female differences in the distribution of socially diagnostic linguistic variables are found among lower middle-class groups, a status group often typified by its upwardly mobile striving to become like the next higher social group. In this social position, women are typically viewed as being more sensitive to prestige norms.

FIGURE 6–2(a)

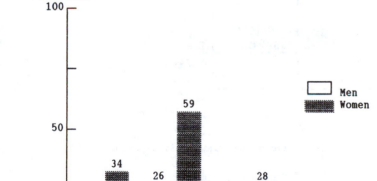

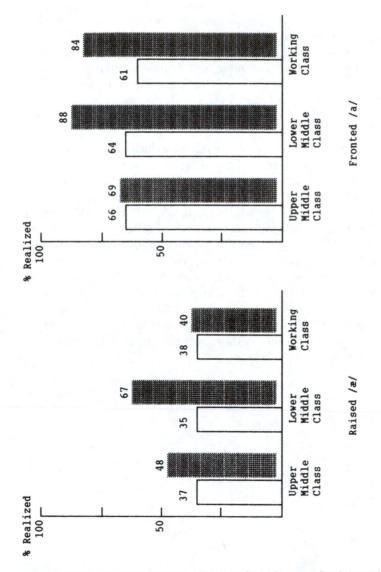

FIGURE 6–2(b) Low Vowel Fronting for Detroit, by Social Class and Sex (adapted from Fasold 1968)

In the case of Figure 6–2, we illustrate a dialect feature undergoing change. The figures here support the contention that women tend to be ahead of men in terms of the vowel changes taking place in The Northern Cities Vowel Shift. Again, this is a pattern that has been found in a number of different settings. Thus, Levine and Crockett, based on the study of speech variation in a Piedmont community in North Carolina, observe that "the community's march toward the national norm was spearheaded by women, young people, short term residents, and those who are near but not quite at the top of the 'white collar' class" (1966:98). In some cases, women have, in fact, been shown to be a generation ahead of men within the same community in terms of advancing change.

In attempting to explain why women would often show more sensitivity to prestige norms in language and why they would be on the forefront of many linguistic changes, Trudgill (1983) cites several sociological reasons. One factor is the traditional involvement of women in the transmission of culture through child rearing, a process which might heighten the awareness for passing on prestige norms. Another reason is the social position of women in our society, which historically has been less secure than men. Given a more insecure social position, women may place more emphasis on signaling social status linguistically. A final reason cited by Trudgill is the differential occupational roles of men and women. Men traditionally have been rated by their occupation—by *what they do*. Women, on the other hand, have often been rated to a greater extent by *how they appear*. For example, women are much more frequently complimented on their appearance than are men, in keeping with a value on "looking good." Linguistically, the "appearance" of language may thus be more important for women than it is for men.

The tendency of males to use more stigmatized variants in their speech than females may also be seen in terms of differential norms and values. For example, nonstandard forms may symbolize virtues of masculinity and toughness for a male. In fact, the notion of "talking like a real man" may include the use of stigmatized forms in a way that is at least covertly prestigious, as we discussed this notion in Chapter 5. This value would foster the maintenance of more socially stigmatized forms in men's speech than in women's speech.

While a general overview of socially diagnostic forms in American English shows that women typically use more prestige variants and men use more stigmatized variants, we have to be careful not to be lulled into the conclusion that this is an inevitable pattern. This pattern results not from the putative attributes of being male or female, but from a set of differential social relationships and sociocultural norms. Different sets of social relationships may result in a configuration of socially diagnostic features different from the "typical" pattern. In fact, Nichols's (1983) study of diagnostic creole language structures for black speakers in coastal South Carolina shows some cases in which women are more progressive and some cases in which they are more conservative than their male counterparts in their use of creole features. Nichols's study focused specifically on three structures that differentiated the creole variety spoken historically in the Sea Islands from the standard variety as follows:

1. infinitive *to* versus *for* (phonetically [fə])
   e.g., I come *for* get my coat.
       I come *to* get my coat.
2. third person singular pronouns *ee* (phonetically [i]) and *em*
   e.g., And *ee* was foggy, and they couldn't see.
       And *it* was foggy, and they couldn't see.
3. predicate locative preposition *to* versus *at*
   e.g., Can we stay *to* the table?
       Can we stay *at* the table?

Her study of two groups of speakers, a mainland group which included those who had moved from the islands to the nearby mainland, and an island group consisting of lifetime island residents, showed important differences. While the younger groups of speakers on both the island and on the mainland showed women to be ahead of men in their use of standard forms such as infinitive *to* versus *for* or pronominal *it* versus *ee* or *em*, Nichols found that older women on the mainland actually used more creole features than their male counterparts. That is, the older women on the mainland were more likely to use forms like *for* for *to* (e.g., *I come for get my coat*) or *ee/em* for *it* (e.g., *And ee was foggy and they couldn't see*) than the older males. These differences are attributed to different occupational and educational experiences for each sex and the communication networks associated with these experiences. For the older mainland group, men had broader-based work experiences and traveled more than the women they lived with; consequently, they had a wider communication network. Given the differential communication networks and life experiences, women in this setting were more likely to preserve older vernacular forms.

Nichols's study raises an important cautionary note for social dialectologists who seem all too eager to conclude that women routinely lead change and use more prestigious variants and less stigmatized variants than men. In the final analysis, it is the life experiences, communication networks, and sociocultural values that dictate where women and men stand in relation to dialect structures. Certainly, there are many situations in American society in which women lead men in dialect change, but it is not an inevitable pattern which can be predicted by simply classifying speakers on the basis of sex demographics. Given some of the social and communication networks that women are involved in, there are also occasions when their speech turns out to be more conservative and just as vernacular as their male counterparts. This pattern may apply to primary regional variants as well as to social status variables. In traditional dialect studies, it is not uncommon to find older women to be more conservative than men in retaining some of the relic forms of regional dialects. Studies of vernacular dialects among younger speakers (Rickford, et al 1988) also indicate that young females may provide excellent examples of these varieties despite the fact that most social dialect studies of adolescents have focused on male speech, based on an assumption that vernacular dialects are maintained and transmitted primarily by adolescent males. This assumption has sometimes overlooked the important role that women may have in transmitting and maintaining vernacular varieties.

GENDERLECTS

Whereas dialectology traditionally considered the sex of the speaker as a secondary factor which intersects with regional and status variables, another perspective treats gender as a primary variable in language variation. In other words, the difference between women's and men's language within a given social and regional community becomes the focus. In most studies of this type, the label gender, as opposed to sex, is used in order to capture the "complex of social, cultural, and psychological phenomena attached to sex" (McConnell-Ginet 1988:76). This definition stands in contrast to the demographic, physiological distinction between male and female. In many studies from this perspective, attention is focused on middle-class, mainstream groups of women rather than women representing different regional or status groups within the United States. This concentration sets these studies apart from traditional dialect studies. In addition, the language structures examined are, for the most part, not the kinds of regionally and socially sensitive items of phonology, grammar, and lexicon that have consumed dialectology; instead, they are structures primarily responsible for displaying, in the words of Lakoff (1986:406), "differences between men's language, or rather the standard language, and women's language." This emphasis has led to a whole new set of diagnostic linguistic items in language variation studies, as well as the uncovering of new relationships for some traditionally recognized diagnostic linguistic items.

Many of the linguistic features scrutinized in the study of gender differences involve variation in language use conventions. Traditional dialect studies have, of course, been much more focused on variation in phonology and vocabulary. Further, studies of genderlect have been particularly concerned with the sociopolitical significance of the language differences. The question of what the differences say about social relationships between men and women and, in particular, what they signify about women's role in American society is often a prime concern in such studies. This consideration is no doubt responsible for the heightened interest in differences in language use conventions, which are more directly indicative of different social roles than, say, phonetic differences in vowels.

What are some of the differences between men's and women's speech that might warrant the label *genderlect*? Some of the major differences found in the literature follow. This list does not include how women and men are spoken about, which we will take up as a separate issue. We also have eliminated from this list the kinds of structures that are primarily regional or status variables as discussed previously. Finally, we should mention that there is also a fairly extensive inventory of nonverbal differences that have been studied, such as eye contact, touching behavior, smiling, and so forth; we do not consider these nonverbal differences here, although they constitute important behavioral differences as well. The list highlights features of women's speech contrasted with men's speech, following the tradition in which men's language is considered as the base for comparing women's language. This perspective is what Lakoff is referring to in the quote cited previously when she equates men's language with "the standard language."

PITCH AND INTONATION

Women tend to use a wider range of pitch than men in speaking. According to Brend (1975), they also use a "polite" pattern of high-rising intonation (e.g., *Yes, yes, I know*) and a wider pitch range of high-low intonation to indicate "unexpectedness" than do men (e.g., *Oh, that's awful!*). Women are also more likely to use question intonation patterns on declarative sentences (e.g., *My new car is white* spoken with the rising intonation at the end which is characteristic of questions such as *Is the new car white?*).

VOICE QUALITIES

Breathiness and higher-pitch ranges tend to be associated with women's speech, whereas lower pitch and "raspiness" are associated with men's speech (Smith 1985:73). Women also tend to indicate lower vocal volume.

SPECIALIZED "HEDGES"

Women are described (Lakoff 1975) as using "hedges" more often than men do. These hedges typically lessen the force of a statement; for example, the use of words such as *well* in *Well, I don't know what to do* or *sorta* and *kinda* in *John is sorta tall* make the statement less forceful than a statement without these qualifiers. According to Lakoff (1975), women are also more likely to preface declarations with phrases such as *I guess, I think,* and *I wonder,* as in *I think I'd like to have soup for lunch.* Hedges may also include the use of tag questions, such as *I guess it will rain, won't it,* but this claim about the more frequent use of tag questions by women has been disputed.

"FROZEN" FORMAL STANDARD GRAMMATICAL FORMS

Formal, prescribed forms, including superstandard forms, are more often used by women than by men. For example, constructions such as *It is I* or *To whom would you like to speak?* are more associated with female speech (see Exercise 3, Chapter 1). This tendency goes along with women's preference for prestige forms as discussed earlier.

SPECIALIZED VOCABULARIES

Women and men tend to have specialized vocabulary in different areas. In certain domains, such as fashion and cooking, women often know and use a broad repertoire of lexical items. One of the classic examples of vocabulary differences is color distinctions, where designations such as *mauve, lavender,* and *fuchsia* are more typically used by women than by men. For men, domains related to athletics, cars, and so forth are more likely to be areas of specialized knowledge.

EXPRESSIVE ADJECTIVES AND INTENSIFIERS

There is a restricted set of expressive items that are most often found in women's speech. These include certain positive adjectives such as *adorable, charming,* or *divine,* as well as intensifiers such as *so* and *such* in sentences like *That is so adorable!* or *It was such a charming play!* It has also been observed that women are more likely to use reduplicated adjectives such as *itsy-bitsy* or *teeny-weeny.*

TABOO ITEMS

Women are more likely to use euphemism when talking about taboo topics such as bodily functions and sexual behavior. Men, particularly in speaking with men, might have to *take a piss* whereas women are more likely to *go to the ladies' room.* The use of expletives by women also tends to be more "modest" (Edelsky 1976). Expletives such as *Fuck!* and *Son of a bitch!* are viewed as male expletives and *My goodness!* and *Oh dear!* are viewed as female expletives. While there are obviously other important social factors that enter into the differential use of these items and various kinds of euphemism, gender is one of the variables that does correlate with such phenomena.

Exercise 1

Based on the items mentioned earlier, make up a list of 10 to 15 sentences which may be associated with women's and men's language differences. For some of the sentences, hypothesize that they will be associated with women's speech, such as *That house was perfectly adorable;* for others, hypothesize that they will be associated with men's speech, such as the taboo items already mentioned or the specialized vocabulary items of sports and cars. A third set of sentences which are neutral with respect to gender association should be included. Ask a group of subjects to identify the sex of the speaker for each sentence (e.g., "Who do you think used the following sentences, a man or a women?"). Be sure to include both male and female subjects in your study. Do the results from your subjects confirm the kinds of gender associations profiled previously? Is there a difference in how male and female respondents classify the sentences?

INDIRECTNESS

More indirectness in speech acts is associated with women's speech. In other words, rather than telling someone to do something directly, women more often "soften" the request by phrasing it differently. For example, a question might be used to make a request (e.g., *Would you like to eat your dinner now?*) rather than a direct command (e.g., *Eat your dinner now!*). Although this trait is often mentioned as a characteristic of women's speech, there is only limited research on this claim; one study (Goodwin 1980) of boys' and girls' play groups showed that boys tended to use imperatives for directives whereas girls were more inclined to use forms like *let's* and *why don't we*. The specialized use of *we* for directives with children and patients in hospitals (e.g., *We're going to take our nap now, right?*) is also more characteristically associated with women, as are a number of other specialized features of the "child talk" register.

CONVERSATIONAL TURN TAKING

In mixed-sex conversations, men tend to take more speaking turns than women; they also "hold the floor" longer than women. Women in mixed-sex conversation tend to have longer periods of silence between turns than men (Zimmerman and West 1975).

INTERRUPTIONS

Men are more likely to interrupt (in the sense that they "violate" a speaker's conversational turn) in a mixed-sex conversation than women (Zimmerman and West 1975; West and Zimmerman 1983). At the same time, men tend to "drop out" of a conversation at a higher rate than women. Women, however, are more likely to contest a male-initiated interruption than the converse.

MAINTAINING CONVERSATION

Women often take responsibility for fostering conversation by using more "backchanneling" devices than men to indicate they are following the remarks of the speaker. Responses such as *uhmhuh, Is that right?*, and so forth, which serve to carry along a conversation, are more frequently used by women than by men, along with certain nonverbal cues (e.g., eye contact) indicating attentive involvement in the conversation.

POLITENESS CONVENTIONS

Although there are a number of qualifications that need to be made in the discussion of politeness (Brown and Levinson 1987), most studies show that women use more polite forms than men. This may range from the use of respectful address forms (e.g., *Mr., Sir,* and so forth) to the use of specific politeness items (e.g., *please, thank you*). Women also offer more apologies and use apology strategies that recognize the rights of their victim more often than men (Holmes 1989). Politeness may also be conveyed by indirectness as already mentioned (e.g., *Could I please ask you to pass the salt?*).

TOPICS OF CONVERSATION

Topics of conversation may also be differentiated along gender lines. For example, Aries (1976) showed that male talk in a university setting centered around competition and teasing, sports, physical aggression, and "doing things." In contrast, talk in a comparable women's group focused more on the categories of self, feelings, affiliation with others, and home and family. In the mixed-sex group setting, some of these themes were modified (e.g., men talked less about physical aggression and women talked less about home and family), although there were still differences. Certain topical differences may actually show fairly dramatic differences, such as the predominance of joke telling by males in mixed-sex groups. Women have also been reported to be more inclined toward self-disclosure in terms of personal and intimate problems, although there are essential qualifications that must be attached to such findings.

Exercise 2

Choose a mixed-sex group (e.g., a class, club meeting) to carry out a simple study of selected language use patterns for men and women. For the purposes of this exercise it might be easiest to tabulate (1) the frequency of verbal comments and (2) interruptions, although you might include other items discussed previously as well. You will need to count how many males and how many females are in the group, since the overall tabulation will have to take into account the proportion of males to females. If the group has a designated leader, do not tabulate the frequency of verbal comments or interruptions by the leader for this observation (although, as a separate item, it would be interesting to observe the leader's patterns of interruption related to the sex of the participant). You can set up a simple coding sheet something like the following, and record male and female participation as it takes place at the scene of the gathering. Be sure to be discreet in recording your tabulation at the scene.

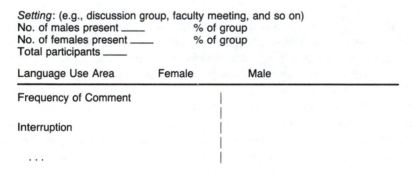

Setting: (e.g., discussion group, faculty meeting, and so on)
No. of males present ＿＿＿   % of group
No. of females present ＿＿＿   % of group
Total participants ＿＿＿

Language Use Area	Female	Male
Frequency of Comment		
Interruption		
. . .		

Does your study support the observations presented in the preceding section? What problems did you encounter in carrying out the project? Are there qualifications about the findings summarized in the previous section that you would make based on your own investigation?

In summarizing differences between men and women's speech as we have done here, it is important to keep in mind a number of qualifications.

In the vast majority of cases, the language differences are a matter of sex-preferential behavior rather than sex-exclusive behavior (Bodine 1975a). That is, there is a tendency for one group to use the form rather than an absolute pattern of usage. Most of the examples also involve quantitative rather than qualitative differences. Thus, women may interrupt less than men in a mixed-sex conversation, but certainly both men and women interrupt; furthermore, there is a good deal of individual variation. In a similar vein, there are certainly men who distinguish color terms more precisely than some women, and women who have more developed sports or car vocabularies than men, but this is not the general pattern. It has also been necessary to modify certain claims originally made about women's language on the basis of empirical investigation. For example, in Robin Lakoff's pioneering treatment of women's speech, *Language and Women's Place* (1975), she reported that women were more apt to use tag questions with declarative functions such as *Dinner will be ready at six o'clock, all right?* The basis for this claim, as well as her other claims about women's language, was personal introspection and informal observation among her acquaintances. Later studies, however, disputed some of the claims based on empirical investigation. Thus, one study of Lakoff's original claim about tag questions (Dubois and Crouch 1976) found this contention to be without empirical support, whereas another study (Crosby and Nyquist 1977) found the claim to be supported in certain kinds of contexts but not in others. Certainly, many of the findings summarized in the inventory of differences presented earlier have important qualifications attached to them. Nonetheless, there remains evidence for some differences in women's and men's language that cannot simply be dismissed.

EXPLAINING GENDERLECTS

What do the linguistic characteristics of women's speech signify about the role of women in our society? Is there particular social meaning with respect to women's role manifested in these language differences? Some of the features may be viewed in terms of their contribution to male-female stereotypes within the society, so that, for example, the greater intonational range exhibited by women may be viewed as contributing to an attitude that women are "more emotional" than men, and more conversational back-channeling by women may be contribute to an image that women are more sympathetic listeners than men. Of course, sorting out the precise contribution that a language difference makes to this image of women can be rather elusive when it is considered as an empirical research question.

Gender differences in language behavior are generally accounted for in terms of broader cultural values and social relationships. One explanation of the differences is based on relationships of *dominance and privilege*. A number of the characteristics of women's speech cited previously can be seen as a reflection of social inequality. Traits such as men interrupting more often and taking longer turns in conversation and women hedging statements and using more indirect speech acts may indicate different relationships of power and dominance.

Are these language characteristics then simply a function of social power and control or are they unique to power relationships between men and women? In attempting to answer this question, O'Barr and Atkins (1980) examined typical features associated with women's speech (for example, hedges, polite forms, hesitation forms) in a criminal courtroom, looking at the distribution of these features for witnesses in the courtroom. In this situation, relationships of power and subordination between witnesses and lawyers and judges are quite clearly delineated. Examining the use of language in this context for male and female witnesses, they found that the incidence of these features was more related to social powerlessness than to sex. Their study concludes that "this style is not simply or even primarily sex-related" (1980:108); instead, it is a general characteristic of "powerless language." From this perspective, the tendency for women to use more powerless language than men is due to the fact that they have traditionally been consigned to relatively powerless social positions. The findings that there are contexts in which men exhibit similar kinds of deferential linguistic behavior is not surprising, but this does not negate the differences between men and women in other contexts where relationships of dominance and control may be more subtle (e.g., male versus female differences in service interactions). Furthermore, not all differences between women's and men's speech can be reduced to a single dimension of social inequality and power. Differential behavioral patterns for men and women may exist apart from relationships of power. Nonetheless, we must concede that some of the differences, particularly those related to the management of linguistic interaction, may be explained reasonably in terms of traditionally consigned roles of privilege and social control.

Other interpretations have relied more heavily on explanations rooted in differential sociocultural behavior than in relationships of power and dominance. McConnell-Ginet (1988), for example, explains many gender language differences in terms of more broadly-based cultural experiences and roles. According to McConnell-Ginet, women are socialized into a cultural experience which recognizes more *social interdependence*. This cultural orientation is somewhat less individualistic than the cultural orientation of men. From this perspective, some of the language traits show that women may pay more attention to conversational intentions with respect to their participants, being "more attuned to the social dimension of her acts of meaning and the attendant potential problems" (McConnell-Ginet 1988:90–91).

Boe (1987) explains genderlect differences from another perspective, which she refers to as the vantage point of "psychological development." This interpretation is founded in social psychology rather than a sociocultural or social interactional model. According to Boe, "language use choices women make are related to their psychological development which favors an 'other' orientation and which can be identified as caring" (1987:271). The "other" orientation is derived from a socialized ability to make and maintain affiliations and relationships, and the "caring" dimension is founded in a sense of cooperation which motivates sensitive, receptive responses to situations and persons. Thus, turn-taking, interrupting, and back-channeling differences may be viewed as supportive concern for another person and hedging, indirectness, and euphemism may be seen as tactful, nonjudgmental empathy. Although this explanation is actually complementary in some ways with the interpretation offered by McConnell-Ginet, it contrasts with explanations derived solely from relationships of power and dominance. Contrastive samples of how selected language items would be viewed from two interpretive models are given in Figure 6–3. One model represents the interactional model based in social dominance and control, whereas the other model represents a sociopsychological model of affiliation and cooperation, as set forth by Boe.

As seen in Figure 6–3, the same linguistic behavior can be interpreted in very different ways. One noteworthy difference in interpretations is the associated evaluation of the linguistic behavior. In the one model, gender differences are viewed in a positive way, as an indication of empathy and cooperation. The other model, however, views the same differences as a manifestation of disadvantaged social position. Boe admits that her proposed developmental psychology model is still just a hypothesis derived primarily from inference, but it nonetheless presents an interesting alternative to the more popular explanation rooted in social dominance.

Exercise 3

Is it necessary to choose between the alternative explanations as presented in Figure 6–3, or are there ways in which these interpretations can be brought together? If so how? If not, why not? Is there a way of determining which of these explanations is more justifiable, or must we be content to speculate about an irresolvable issue?

LANGUAGE SEXISM

Is English a sexist language? Claims and counterclaims to this effect have become a prime topic of conversation in our society. In fact, this issue has affected a sphere of interests and professions that extends far beyond the

1. Linguistic Variations	2. Sociolinguistic Interaction Language, Society, Behavior	3. Developmental Caring, Connectedness
Genesis of language variations	Disadvantaged social position, sexism; Male generated norms—language	Relational caretaking; capacity for caring/empathy/connectedness. Female generated norms—development
I. *Syntactic-Pragmatic* A. *Tag-questions* ♀ ↑ —a declarative statement that becomes a question: "We are ready to go, aren't we?	Deference, leaves choice up to addressee. Non-responsible, manipulative, learned helplessness, indecisive, hesitant style, nonaggressive or forward	Negotiative, nonimposing, mutual empowerment, mutuality
B. *Use of questions* ♀ ↑	Cognitive uncertainty, deference	Communicates interest in other. Facilitates verbal exchange
C. *Hedging* ♀ ↑ —Jane is "kinda" pretty, Your report "wasn't bad" "Maybe we should . . ."	Uncertainty, inconclusiveness Leaves addressee option of deciding how serious to take a statement, deference Yielding a judgment, mitigating a criticism	Nonjudgmental, Softening criticism
D. *Euphemisms* ♀ ↑ —saying something while not really saying it—circumlocutory tactic for sexual, body elimination	Skirting an issue instead of stating it directly; nonconfrontative; certain subjects considered off limits to direct treatment; way of dealing with taboos	Respectful, tactful, nonoffensive. Highly responsive to feeling state of others; Emphatic relator
E. *Compound Requests* ♀ ↑ —"Will you help me with these groceries, please?"	More polite form	Respectful, tactful

II. *Phonological*
   A. *Hypercorrect use of language* — Way of gaining social status, acceptance — "So as to not offend"
   B. *Intonation* ♀ ↑ range — Whining, questioning, helpless patterns / More expressive, cheerful, hesitation pattern — Engaging interaction

III. *Lexical Traits*
   A. *Hyperbole*—intensifies ♀ ↑ — Empty adjectives, dramatic, emotive — Engaging
      —"so" "such" "gorgeous"
   B. *Expletives* ♀ ↑ — Respectful, nonoffensive
      —"oh dear" versus "shit"
   C. *Vocabulary* — Social roles determine word usage — ↑ sensitivity to communicative breaks created with use of jargon

IV. *Paralanguage*
   A. *Interruptions* ♀ interruption ↓, are interrupted more — ♂ deny right to ♀ as equal conversational partners — Learned listening
   B. *Turn taking:* ♀ fewer turns — ♂ control topics — Supportive of continued interaction

FIGURE 6-3 Two Interpretive Models of Genderlect Variation (from Boe 1987:278–279)

study of language variation per se. Most claims about language sexism in English are based on a catalog of differences relating to how men and women are talked to or talked about in English. Some of the major bits of evidence in this discussion follow.

GENERIC NOUN AND PRONOUN REFERENCE

The use of the pronoun *he* and its related forms *his* or *him* to refer to a sex-indefinite antecedent (e.g., *If anybody reads this book he will learn about dialects*) is certainly one of the most often cited cases of sex bias found in English. Use of this form probably correlated with the emergence of the generic use of the noun *man* in structures such as *Man shall not live by bread alone*, according to Smith (1985:50). It is interesting to note that alternatives to the generic male pronoun such as the use of singular *they* (e.g., *If anybody reads this book, they will learn about dialects*) were quite acceptable prior to the nineteenth century (Bodine 1975b), but these alternatives were legislated out of acceptable usage by prescriptive grammarians. This prescriptive norm in formal and written English persists despite the widespread use of generic *they* in informal spoken English, and attempts to use generic *they* in writing continue to meet with steadfast editorial rejection. In fact, to my knowledge no examples of generic *they* usage survived the editing of this book, despite a preliminary attempt to use it for generic reference. Whereas it may be argued that generic *he/man* conventionally dictates a cross-sex reference, experiments (MacKay and Fulkerson 1979; Martyna 1980) show that there is a tendency to associate this form with males even when used generically.

FAMILY NAMES AND ADDRESS

The tradition of family names is another convention that has been cited as a manifestation of linguistic sexism. The traditional adoption of the husband's family name may signify "that women's family names do not count and that there is one more device for making women invisible" (Spender 1980:24). Women's marital status is also distinguished in the traditional address forms *Mrs./Miss,* a distinction unmatched in *Mr.* There have been a number of different interpretations of the sociopolitical significance of this difference, but one of the most prominent is that this pattern is indicative of the definition of women in relation to men.

Other address forms show respect patterns and assumptions of informality that differentiate women from men. Men are more likely to be formally addressed with *sir* than women of comparable status are addressed as *ma'am.* Women are also more frequently addressed informally as *dear, honey,* and *sweetie* in social contexts where men of comparable status would not be addressed in this way.

RELATIONSHIPS OF ASSOCIATION

As noted previously, a number of items suggests relationships in which women are defined in terms of the men with whom they are associated, whereas the converse does not take place. Associations such as *man and wife,* but not *woman and husband,* or the more common use of the designation *Walt's wife* as opposed to *Marge's husband* have been interpreted as an indication of relationship between the owner and the owned (Eakins and Eakins 1978). It has even been noted that the conventional placement of male before female in coordinate constructions (e.g., *husband and wife* but not *wife and husband,* or *host and hostess* but not *hostess and host*) indicates a pattern of male precedence.

Exercise 4

One of the exceptions to the ordering of masculine and feminine coordinate constructions (e.g., *husband and wife*) is in the public address salutation, "Ladies and Gentlemen!". How might you explain this apparent exception to the more general pattern of placing the male first? Can you think of any other exceptions to the male-first pattern in coordinates?

LABELING

There are many instances of differential labeling in English that have been offered as evidence of language sexism in English. These include the scope of semantic reference covered by particular words, the emotive connotations of sex-paired words, and the patterns of derivation in lexical items. The age span typically covered by items such as *boy-girl* and *man-woman* illustrates a case in which the semantic range of analogous items is not comparable for males and females. Older women of comparable status are much more likely to be referred to as *girls* than men are likely to be referred to as *boys*. A person might thus say, "I met this real nice girl" in reference to a 30-year-old female but one would hardly say "I met this nice boy" to refer to a 30-year-old male. In virtually every instance of this type, males are favored. Thus, TV announcers still routinely refer to the NCAA "girls' basketball tournament" while they would hardly refer to the NCAA "boys' basketball tournament," even though both tournaments involve college students roughly between 18 and 22 years of age.

In paired masculine and feminine lexical items, it has been noted that the feminine member of the pair often undergoes "semantic derogation" (Schulz 1975). That is, the feminine member of the pair often acquires a negative or subservient connotation. In pairs such as *mister/mistress, governor/governess*, and *bachelor/spinster*, the feminine counterpart of the masculine item takes on negative or subservient connotations not found for the masculine item. In many cases, the feminine item may also acquire a sexual connotation, as in the case of *mistress*. Even derived feminine items suffer by comparison with their masculine counterparts, as in the diminutive suffix of *bachelorette* or the feminine suffix of *poetess*. In cases where gender is indicated through the addition of a suffix, the burden is typically carried by the feminine item rather than the masculine (e.g., *Carla* is derived from *Carl* or *Paulette* from *Paul*), suggesting a male norm for lexical items. Furthermore, one survey of dictionary items (Nilsen 1977) shows that masculine words outnumber feminine words by a ratio of three to one, and masculine words denoting prestige are six times as frequent as feminine words with prestige.

Finally, there are drastic differences in specialized vocabularies signifying the infamous "double standard" for men and women. For example, Stanley (1978) found only 20 items describing promiscuous men (e.g., *animal, letch*), some of which even carried positive connotations such as *stud* and *Casanova*. By the same token, Stanley stopped counting when she reached 220 labels for promiscuous women (e.g., *whore, slut, tramp*). There are comparable disparities in metaphorical labeling, as women tend to be labeled with reference to consumable items such as foods (e.g., *peach, sugar, cheesecake*).

The linguistic manifestation of inequality and stereotyping based on sex is hardly disputable. So is English therefore a sexist language? One answer might be that language variation simply follows sociocultural patterns; if a society treats women as unequal, then language will simply provide the symbolic mechanism for displaying society's basic discrimination. Changing to alternate forms that are more neutral does not really stop underlying sex stereotyping, as items characteristically undergo semantic derogation when associated with a feminine item. After all, at one point, words like *mistress* and *spinster* were neutral counterparts of their male equivalents *mister* and *bachelor*. So changing language use patterns may simply be a linguistic cosmetic for an underlying problem of social inequality. From this vantage point, language dutifully follows a symbolic course set for it by the established social system; language can hardly be blamed for the more fundamental social inequity to be confronted.

Although it is true that language will invariably find a new way to express underlying social inequality when language forms are censured without changing the corresponding social structure, there is a further point to be made. As Shieffelin and Ochs (1986) point out, there is socialization *through* the use of language as well as socialization in *how* to use language. On the one hand, we may say that the use of generic *he* and *man* simply follows a conventional pattern of usage which is not intended to be sex specific; on the other hand, however, we must concede that English speakers do make associations that link this generic use with a male sex reference. Furthermore, the social disparity symbolically represented in language differences may be used to socialize people into accepting and perpetuating the status quo. At the same time that language mirrors a prevailing social order, the use of language may reinforce the acceptance of these social conditions. There is an interdependence between language as a reflection of social differences and language as an socializing instrument that is hard to deny. Changing language use patterns may thus go hand in hand with changing social conditions. On one level, language reform can, in fact, be an impetus for social change. For this reason, most sociolinguists support guidelines for nondiscriminatory language use with respect to gender reference.

While there remains considerable professional discussion about what constitutes realistic language reform with respect to sex reference in English, there seems to be a consensus on a number of the proposed guidelines (see, for example, "Guidelines for Non-Discriminatory Language Usage" and a "Selected List of Guidelines for Non-Sexist Usage" in Frank and Anshen 1983). I don't think I am being overly optimistic when I say that, in principle, most sociolinguists would take a strong and unified position favoring nondiscriminatory language use.

Exercise 5

A critical word in reforming sex reference in English is the qualification "realistic" guideline. Suggestions for reform have run the spectrum, from proposals to change *history* to *herstory* to changes in address forms (e.g., *Ms.* for women regardless of marital status) and generic noun and pronoun reference (e.g., *people, he/she*). Are there any general guidelines we might follow in determining what constitutes a realistic reform in this area? For example, one principle might apply to a cross-sex item that has primarily masculine association in its current use. In other words, we know that speakers are apt to associate generic *he* with males even in its cross-sex reference, but they may not associate *history* with *his story* (versus *her story*); the principle adopted here therefore would attempt to change the generic pronouns but not advocate changing *history*. What underlying or general principles can you think of to guide nondiscriminatory sex reference? Are there principles based on practical considerations, such as the likelihood that a change will be adopted? As a point of reference, you might consider an actual set of guidelines set forth by a newspaper, a professional organization, or another agency.

Further Reading

BOE, S. KATHRYN, "Language as an Expression of Caring in Women," *Anthropological Linguistics*, 29:271–284, (1987). This presentation offers an alternative interpretation of gender and language differences. The "caring" interpretation offered by Boe sets this discussion apart from the more popular "social dominance" interpretations of genderlects.

FRANK, FRANCINE AND FRANK ANSHEN, *Language and the Sexes*. Albany, NY: State University of New York Press, 1983. As a selective account of language variation and gender, this introduction is quite readable.

LAKOFF, ROBIN, *Language and Women's Place*. New York, NY: Harper & Row, 1975. Although certain conclusions and interpretations found in this presentation have now been challenged, this article stands as a pioneering effort in the history of genderlect studies. Observations initially made by Lakoff served to inspire a generation of empirical research studies on various dimensions of genderlects.

MCCONNELL-GINET, SALLY, "Language and Gender," in *Linguistics: The Cambridge Survey Vol. IV Language: The Socio-Cultural Context*, ed. Frederick J. Newmeyer. New York, NY: Cambridge University Press, 1988, pp. 75–99. This is one of the most thoughtful overviews of language and gender currently available.

SMITH, PHILLIP M., *Language, the Sexes and Society*. New York, NY: Basil Blackwell, 1985. This work includes an extensive review of the literature on language and gender. As a synthesis of research, it is an excellent resource for students interested in the topic.

THORNE, BARRIE, CHERIS KRAMERAE, AND NANCY HENLEY, eds., *Language, Gender, and Society*. Rowley, MA: Newbury House, 1983. This is one of a growing number of anthologies on language and gender. It is an updated version of an earlier collection on the topic, including a number of key studies. A useful, annotated bibliography is included.

CHAPTER SEVEN

DIALECTS AND STYLE

No one speaks the same way on all occasions. People adjust their way of speaking, or *language style,* based on a variety of factors related to the speech event. We certainly don't speak the same way to an intimate family member as we do to an impersonal authority figure, regardless of our native dialect. Some speakers are especially adroit at shifting in and out of different language styles and may use this versatility to great advantage; other speakers seem much more limited, but still show flexibility in varying their speech. I have been impressed with the conscious control shown by certain performers in mimicking particular regional and ethnic dialects as a part of their comic routines, but I am more impressed with the unconscious control exhibited by ordinary speakers in shifting the forms of language in response to a change in the speech situation.

Observing men who "cuss every other word" as they purge their speech of expletives in response to a change in a conversational participant is impressive evidence for the apparent naturalness with which some shifts can be made. At the same time, the observation of speakers of vernacular dialects laboring to shift grammatical forms into a more standard variety in response to a situation calling for the standard dialect suggests that some types of shifts are difficult to control. Thus, stylistic shifting presents a paradox. Certain aspects of language adjustment apparently come easily and naturally, a simple manifestation of the human capability to adapt behavior; at the same time, other aspects of linguistic adjustment seem to be much more difficult, a realistic reflection of the internal habituation of linguistic patterns.

The study of language style has been applied to a broad range of language phenomena, ranging from the comparison of spoken and written language to the analysis of specialized literary genres, and *stylistics* has become an established field of study in its own right. Our interest here does not extend to the more general study of stylistics, but only to those aspects of language variation related to the adjustment of socially and regionally diagnostic language structures in different speech situations.

SHIFTING STYLES

Speakers may shift their language on a horizontal or vertical axis. *Horizontal shifts* refer to adjustments of language within or across dialects without primary reference to social status evaluation and *vertical shifts* refer to shifts which affect the social evaluation of speech in a significant way. A simplistic diagram of this relationship is given in Figure 7–1.

A shift between regionally defined lexical choices such as *submarine* or *hoagie* sandwich would be a horizontal one since there is no particular social evaluation associated with this shift across regional varieties. The choice of *ain't* versus *isn't* has primary social status evaluation so that it involves a vertical shift. Of course, style shifting is much more involved than the simple choice between isolated lexical items and horizontal and vertical variation do not always appear neatly separated. Nonetheless, it is useful to start with this distinction.

Figure 7–1. Diagrammatic Representation of Vertical and Horizontal Shifting

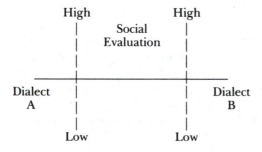

HORIZONTAL SHIFTING

Theoretically, horizontal shifts may take place within or across dialects. Speakers may use forms from other regional or ethnic varieties on an occasional basis, but horizontal shifting of this type is quite restricted for ordinary speakers. There are, however, individual speakers who seem to have extraordinary mimicking or adaptive capabilities with respect to other regional and ethnic varieties. These individuals are usually exceptions, and the vast majority of speakers in a speech community seem incapable of using nonnative regional and ethnic dialect forms other than the occasional stereotyped expression borrowed from these varieties. Speakers with more regular and extended social contact with speakers from a different regional or ethnic variety may be able to make more extensive adjustments, but even then the shift is often more symbolic than real. For example, one study (Ash and Myhill 1986) of Philadelphia speech which examined black and white speakers in different contact situations showed that whites with extensive black contacts typically limited their use of Vernacular Black English to lexical items and some pronunciation features, even though Vernacular Black English may have covert prestige value for some of these whites (particularly white teen-aged males). This situation is, of course, different from one where a white is socialized linguistically in a black community, in which case the speaker would be an authentic Vernacular Black English speaker. Interestingly, Ash and Myhill's study also showed that blacks with extensive white social contacts used white grammatical norms, unlike their white counterparts who did not reveal shifts to Vernacular Black English grammatical structures. This finding probably reflects the differential status of white and black varieties in the broader context of American society and the fact that the pressure is always on socially subordinate groups to adjust to superordinate ones, not the converse. In the final analysis, it may be impossible to consider certain horizontal shifts apart from the vertical social dimension, since different regional and ethnic groups are probably never really considered equal.

In discussing the potential for shifting across regional and social varieties, we have to keep in mind how difficult it is to learn another dialect once a native dialect has been acquired. Although there is not a lot of detailed research on regional dialect shift by speakers who move from one region to another, there have been studies that indicate that the fine details of regional dialects are rarely acquired after adolescence (Payne 1980). On an informal level, it is regularly observed that parents who move to a new locale with young children maintain one regional dialect while their children acquire another. My own children, raised in the Maryland suburbs of Washington, DC, show no traces of the Philadelphia regional dialect that their parents brought to the area and still maintain to a substantial degree. If the fundamental change of a regional dialect is so difficult after adolescence, imagine how much more difficult it would be to maintain authentic shifts between regional varieties on a temporary basis as speech situations and participants are varied. We will return to shifts between different dialect systems, or code switching, in more detail later in the chapter.

The majority of horizontal shifts clearly take place on an *intra*dialectal rather than *inter*dialectal level. One kind of horizontal shift involves the specialized use of language forms for well-defined situations or occasions. These are often referred to as *language registers* to distinguish them from other types of stylistic variation. For example, when a mother says to her baby, "Let Mommy kiss the iddy biddy booboo and make it better," she is using forms that are appropriate only for the parent-baby interaction. The use of the diminutive *iddy biddy* and the reduplicated form of the lexical item *boo boo* outside of the parent-child interaction would invoke rather strange stares. Although, in this instance, there is a relationship between some of the forms found in the adult register and the forms children use in the process of language acquisition (for example, children often use reduplication as a process during their language development), studies of this *baby talk register* show it to be a specialized language style practiced by adults rather than an actual mimicry of baby language. Less exotic kinds of registers may involve specialized uses of language for social occasions which range from the academic language of school to the lexical jargon of a particular field such as computers or sports. This type of shifting may be totally horizontal, or it may involve vertical shifting as well if the field is associated with a particular social status group, as in the case of academic language. Many of the distinct forms of these registers are lexical, but there may also be peculiar syntactic constructions as well. Phonology seems to be the least affected level of language modification in such register shifts.

Exercise 1

One of the language registers that has been examined by sociolinguists is the *math register*—the peculiar uses of language forms associated with the functions of math. In the following items, typical of language use in math, identify the specialized uses of language that might be a part of the math register. What parts of speech seem to be especially affected in this register?

1. Does each real number x have a subtractive inverse?
2. The sum of two integers is 20 and one integer is 8 greater than the other. Find the integers.
3. Find two consecutive *even* integers such that the sum of the first and third is 134.
4. Find three consecutive *odd* integers such that the sum of the last two is 7 less than three times the first.

5. From downtown a suburban phone call costs 15 cents more than a local call. One month Dr. Thorn's phone bill showed 30 local calls and 42 suburban calls, and the total bill was $14.22. What is the cost of one local call?

In a book on dialect differences and math failure, *Twice as Less: Black English and the Performance of Black Students in Mathematics and Science,* Eleanor Wilson Orr (1987) suggests that the roots of the math problem for many working-class black students are found in the grammatical differences that distinguish Vernacular Black English from Standard English. Having examined the typical kinds of languages uses in math in the preceding examples, react to this conclusion. Are there special features of the math register that are common to *all* students studying math? How does the use of language in math differ from "ordinary" language use? Is math language use unique to this field? Do you think there would be special language obstacles for speakers of a vernacular dialect because of dialect differences? Why or why not?

Another type of shift may involve adjusting forms based on a conventionally defined genre, such as writing or public lectures. At least theoretically, these shifts may take place solely on a horizontal plane. For example, within a standard variety, fewer contracted forms, such as contracted negatives (e.g., *can't* versus *cannot*) or auxiliaries (e.g., *Walt'll go* versus *Walt will go*), less syntactic ellipsis (e.g., *What do people want—do they want jobs or do they want unemployment lines?* versus *What do people want—jobs or unemployment lines?*), and more syntactic subordination (e.g., *Returning to our original notion, which concerned the fact that we have dramatic financial overruns . . .* versus *Let's get back to our original notion. That was about our dramatic financial overruns . . .*) would be found in a public address than would be found in a casual social conversation with peers. In this instance, the systematic variation is associated primarily with different versions of a standard variety, although shifts along this dimension may have secondary status associations as well.

VERTICAL SHIFTING

Practically all speakers of English engage in vertical shifting to some extent. At the very least, speakers may vary the relative frequency of socially diagnostic forms in response to different dimensions of the speech situation. This kind of stylistic variation along a basic standard-vernacular continuum has now been studied fairly extensively, starting in the 1960s, and the insights gained from these empirical studies have replaced the popular impression that people simply switch in and out of well-defined social dialects depending on the occasion. The shifting of socially diagnostic features is far more complex than the popular perception.

The typical method used to measure style in dialect studies is based on the tabulation of fluctuating forms in discretely defined social situations of various types. For example, if an analyst is examining the use of postvocalic *r* in *bear* or *board,* each case of "potential" *r* would be tabulated as present or absent in different speech situations. In one of the pioneering studies of style from this perspective, Labov (1966) set up several distinct kinds of stylistic situations within an interview with a single subject. The axis on which these situations was defined was "formality." The first situation, referred to as the "casual" speech situation, was defined by specialized contexts within the interview in which a subject directed speech to a third party outside of the interview or carried on a discussion not in direct response to one of the interview questions. Labov also used a set of paralinguistic channel cues to delimit casual speech—features like changes in speech tempo, pitch, laughter, or breathing. Other kinds of conversational speech in the interview, such as direct answers to questions posed by the interviewer, were classified as "careful" speech. Based on a preliminary classification of interview conversation into "careful" and "casual" contexts, the relative frequency levels of different variants (e.g., the presence or absence of *r* in our example) would then be compared in their different contexts to determine the degree of stylistic shift in the features. Although my own attempts to replicate Labov's distinction between careful and casual speech in a single-subject interview were largely futile (Wolfram 1969), the important insight from Labov's study was the systematic delimitation of particular points in a continuum of formality.

In Labov's original study, a third type of stylistic context in the formality continuum was established by including a connected reading passage as a part of the interview. This reading passage was intended to be more formal than the conversational interview by virtue of the fact that reading is usually associated with more formal occasions than speaking. Finally, the subject was asked to read word lists of words that had no contextual meaning. Some of the words were further set apart by being *minimal word pairs*—words that were phonetically identical except for one sound, such as *bet* and *bat.* These pairs would focus more attention on the pronunciation of a word, and presumably result in an even more formal rendering. These different situations within the single interview were included to represent a continuum of stylistic formality based on an underlying assumption that the more focus on speech in the interview the more formal the style will become. It is probably safe to assume that at least within the context of a one-on-one interview a subject will give more attention to how a word sounds when reading it in isolation than how it sounds when the subject pronounces it in the context of an emotionally involved conversation. Even then, however, shifts may not be solely a matter of a formality, as the recitation of isolated words may bring forth a specialized "citation form register" of pronunciation (i.e., the special pronunciation of a word when spoken in isolation) rather than an extreme point in the continuum of formality.

With respect to socially diagnostic features, we expect that more formal contexts will reveal a lower incidence of socially stigmatized variants or a higher incidence of socially prestigious variants. This kind of correlation can also be combined with the comparison of other variables, such as social status, showing an intersection of style with other social variables. For example, we might expect the distribution indicated in Figure 7–2 for a study of socially stigmatized features in two styles (formal and informal) for two social groups (labeled middle class and working class).

This kind of pattern can be found in many sociolinguistic studies which examine socially diagnostic variables in different stylistic contexts, regardless of how style is defined operationally. A classic example of this type comes from Labov's analysis of the use of a stop consonant ([t] of [tθ]) for the *th* fricative in word like *think* or *thought* in New York City. In Figure 7–3, an index of *th* scores is set up on the vertical line and four different stylistic contexts are set up on the horizontal line. Because the use of the stop [t] instead of the voiceless fricative [θ] is stigmatized, we expect the frequency index for stigmatization to be lower in more formal contexts for all groups, although the relative differences for different social groups are maintained in different contexts.

Labov's study of stylistic variation within a single-subject interview does not replace the need to delimit the set of real-life factors that relate to stylistic variation, but it provides an important simulation of one dimension of stylistic variation that can be tapped in a broad-based dialect survey. Ethnographers of communication such as Hymes (1974) and Gumperz (1982) have been especially concerned with setting forth the kinds of factors that speakers take into consideration in shifting styles. Hymes (1974:54ff), for example, identifies a set of different components which may affect language use, mnemonically grouped under the acronym SPEAKING, where S = setting, P = participants, E = ends (i.e., purposes and goals), A = act sequence, K = key (i.e., tone, manner), I = instrumentalities (i.e., means or agencies of speaking), N = norms of interaction, and G = genres. De-

Figure 7–2

Hypothetical Frequency Pattern for a Stigmatized Variant (adapted from Wolfram and Fasald 1974:85)

SOCIAL CLASS	STYLE	
	Informal	*Formal*
Working Class	High Frequency (80%)	Intermediate Frequency (60%)
Middle Class	Intermediate Frequency (40%)	Low Frequency (20%)

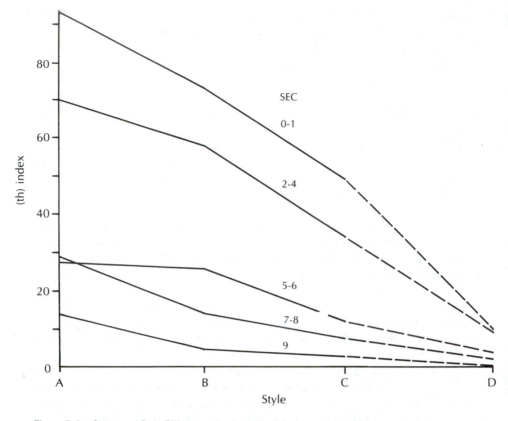

Figure 7–3. Status and Style Differences for the *th* Variable (from Labov 1972b:113)

pending on the fineness of the distinctions, one could come up with a quite
lengthy descriptive list of factors that relate to differences in style in natural
language use (Preston 1986b). Typically included in such inventories are
aspects of the social setting, the addressee(s), the topic, and the purposes
of communication.

EXPLAINING STYLE

Showing that language shifts may take place in response to a number of
social and situational factors and identifying the essential list of factors that
correlate with the shifts is certainly an important aspect of describing stylistic
variation. But it does not explain *why* speakers adjust their speech in response
to these various situational factors. Even if we come up with an exhaustive
list of contextual factors that correlate with variation, we are left with the
question of what it is about these conditions that explains why speakers vary

their language? Are there underlying principles about communication or human behavior that can take us beyond the simple demonstration that language covaries with the set of contextual factors subsumed under the label *style*? Several different proposals have been offered to explain why speakers adjust their speech in various ways—explanations that attempt to take us beyond the simple listing of contextual variables that correlate systematically with language variation.

One of the initial attempts to explain style shift related it to the amount of *attention paid to speech*. As Labov (1972c:208) put it, "Styles can be ranged along a single dimension, measured by the amount of attention paid to speech." According to this principle, the more attention speakers focus on *how* they are talking the more formal and standard will be their speech style. All stylistic variation is thus reduced to the axis of formality. This interpretation was obviously influenced heavily by Labov's concentration on the speaking tasks within a single interview as discussed previously, where the range of speaking was quite controlled in terms of the points of formality incorporated into the interview.

Although it seems reasonable to assume that a person involved in a conversation with a friend would pay less attention to speech per se than a person reading a list of words, it is not very easy to measure attention to speech empirically. Experimentation with aural monitoring of speech (for example, comparing a person's speech with and without "white noise" fed through earphones) suggests that there is covariation of language forms and aural monitoring (for example, standard variants increase with a reduction of white noise), but this conclusion cannot be maintained without important qualifications (Bell 1984). More importantly, there are occasions where increased attention to speech might actually lead to *fewer* standard forms rather than *more*. Imagine, for example, a self-conscious Standard English speaker who wants to be accepted by a group of vernacular speakers. In this context, the speaker might feel a strong need to adjust toward a more informal style in order to accommodate the norms of the vernacular speakers (Baugh forthcoming). Conscious attention to speech might thus result in more rather than fewer vernacular forms, given other considerations. It is not difficult to imagine scenarios in which the social dynamics of a speech situation override simple attention to speech in determining whether speakers become more or less formal. Increased attention to speech, then, might lead to adjustments in quite different directions, given other factors in the social situation. Attention to speech might help explain stylistic variation in a controlled interview situation with a single subject, but it is inadequate as a unitary underlying principle that can account for all stylistic variation.

A more expansive explanation of stylistic variation, referred to as the *speech accommodation model*, has been proposed by the social psychologist Howard Giles and his colleagues (Giles and Powesland 1975; Giles 1984).

In this model, style is explained primarily on the basis of a speaker's social and psychological adjustment to the addressee. The most common pattern of adjustment is *convergence,* in which the speaker's language becomes more like that of the addressee. The tendency to shift speech toward the addressee is summarized as follows:

> People will attempt to converge linguistically toward the speech patterns believed to be characteristic of their recipients when they (a) desire their social approval and the perceived costs of so acting are proportionally lower than the rewards anticipated; and/or (b) desire a high level of communication efficiency, and (c) social norms are not perceived to dictate alternative speech strategies. (Beebe and Giles 1984:8)

Put simply, the model is rooted in the social psychological need of the speaker for social approval by the addressee, but the speaker must weigh the costs and rewards of such behavior in shifting speech to converge with that of the addressee.

The other side of the accommodation model is *divergence,* in which speakers choose to maintain distance from the addressee for one reason or another. Speakers will diverge linguistically from the addressee under the following conditions:

> . . . [when speakers] (a) define the encounter in intergroup terms and desire positive ingroup identity, or (b) wish to dissociate personally from another in an interindividual encounter, or (c) wish to bring another's speech behavior to a personally acceptable level. (Beebe and Giles 1984:8)

As we would expect from a model founded in theories of social psychology, both the motivations of the individual speaker and the social relationships of the speaker are critical to this underlying explanation of stylistic shifting. A number of different experiments by Giles and others (Giles 1984) have shown how speakers converge, and, in some cases, diverge with respect to speech-related phenomena such as the rate of speech, content, pausing, and what is loosely referred to as "accent." Accent is the parameter most closely aligned with our description of dialect variation, but, unfortunately, socially diagnostic linguistic structures as discussed here are not very carefully delimited in most of the studies. Furthermore, the original accommodation model, rooted simply in social approval, has now been subjected to considerable revision as different kinds of data have been examined, so that the original social psychological explanation has so many amendments that it is sometimes difficult to identify the actual underlying principle(s) that "explain" why stylistic variation takes place.

One of the most coherent and encompassing attempts to explain style is Bell's (1984) *audience design model,* which incorporates and extends some of the notions found in the speech accommodation model. This model assumes that speakers adjust their speech primarily on the basis of the attributes of people in the speech audience. The audience, as defined by Bell, may include several different types of participants whose roles are ranked in relation to the speaker. Ranked roles are based on whether the participants are known, ratified (i.e., sanctioned participants), and/or addressed. The main role of the audience is fulfilled by the second person addressee, but secondary roles are filled by third persons present but not directly addressed. These third persons may include known and ratified interlocutors in the audience, called *auditors,* third parties who are known but not ratified, called *overhearers,* and other parties whose presence is unknown and unratified, called *eavesdroppers.* Nonpersonal factors such as topic and setting may come into play in this model, but even these indirectly revert to considerations of the audience. For example, a topic of discussion related to education may correlate with the greater use of standard variants, but this is because such topics project an audience with certain higher-status attributes rather than the nature of the topic per se.

The design of speaking may result from a response to extralinguistic factors, such as the participants who make up the audience, but it may also be initiated by the speaker who uses style as a dynamic force to redefine an existing situation. According to Bell, most initiated style shifts occur in response to certain third person reference groups who are not present but influential upon the speaker's attitudes. Because of the strong evaluation role carried out by these nonpresent parties, they are called *referees.* For example, group reference norms for the standard variety, or, in some cases, for the vernacular variety, may cause speakers to adjust socially diagnostic features in their speech whether or not such parties are present. The various roles and relationships which characterize the audience model of style are diagrammed in Figure 7–4.

Bell has compiled evidence from a wide array of language variation studies to demonstrate the relative roles of addressees, auditors, and overhearers. He admits the significance of different kinds of social relationships between the speaker and audience (e.g., family, peer, employer) but does not detail how these important dimensions of a speaker's social network are integrated into the model. Furthermore, the reduction of stylistic variation to the dimension of audience design can only be as adequate as the delimitation of the crucial attributes of the members of the audience, which are only partially specified even in Bell's elaborate model. Nonetheless, it is a provocative model for explaining style, influenced no doubt by his own extensive research on how radio announcers alter their styles based on projected audiences of listeners.

These are only three of the proposals for explaining style. Most of the recent proposals certainly offer substantial improvement over Labov's original explanation of style on the single dimension of attention to speech, but it is still premature to conclude that we now have a single or simple explanation of why people vary their speech on different occasions. In fact, it

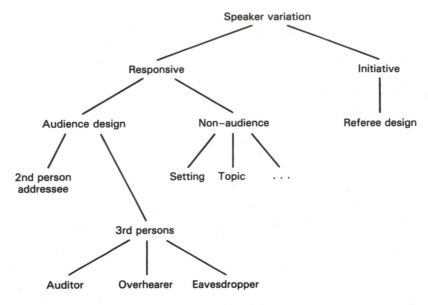

FIGURE 7–4 Style as Audience Design (from Bell 1984:162)

may be unrealistic to expect a unitary explanation. The diverse social and psychological parameters that account for linguistic variation and adaptation may resist a singular explanation, just as other kinds of behavioral variation defy simple explanation. Explaining stylistic variation does, however, seem to be a fruitful area for the convergence of linguistic, ethnographic, sociological, and psychological insight.

DIALECT CODE SWITCHING

One of the issues that often comes up in discussions of style shifting is the question of *dialect code switching.* Do speakers switch dialects in a way analogous to the way bilingual speakers shift between different language systems? It is certainly not uncommon for people to talk about switching between a standard and vernacular dialect as if they were separate codes, and speakers may report that they use a standard variety for some occasions and a "totally different" vernacular dialect for other occasions. Despite popular reference to this kind of vertical switching, speakers' ability to change entire dialect subsystems has not been investigated in any detail. Most studies of code switching have focused on more extreme language differences between systems than those represented by the standard and vernacular dialects of English, such as the switching of bilingual speakers between two languages or, in some cases, the switching of creole and standard language speakers. I have already expressed my skepticism about horizontal dialect switching by ordinary dialect speakers, but the question of vertical switching seems a more open one, given the fact that some speakers of English have disparate sets of social identities and social relationships. In American society, an upwardly mobile rural Appalachian living in a northern metropolitan area or a black resident from a vernacular-speaking community who works in a professional, Standard English setting would be typical cases of people with social identities in two very different dialectal worlds. Not surprisingly, the classic reports of dialect switching come from speakers representing these kinds of community situations.

At first glance, code switching between vernacular and standard dialect systems may seem analogous to the language switch of a Spanish-English speaker, but the issue of dialect switching actually turns out to be somewhat more complex than the typical bilingual situation. Code switching involves changing distinct *sets* of linguistic structures—structures existing in different linguistic systems. Stylistic shifting, on the other hand, takes place by varying forms within a unitary system. This ideal situation is probably overstated to some extent for both switching and stylistic variation, and it seems difficult to determine precisely where stylistic shifting ends and where code switching begins. If it is any consolation, the study of code switching in bilingual situations also turns out to be much more complex than it looks initially, and many actual cases do not match the ideal model of discrete system switches.

As an initial consideration, we need to keep in mind that standard and vernacular varieties of English share the vast majority of their linguistic structures. Certainly, there are many more similarities in the structures of standard and vernacular varieties of English than there are differences. In fact, the dialect differences of English are dwarfed by the overriding commonality of English structures, despite the preoccupation of dialectologists with the differences. We must further recognize that some of the differences between varieties exist on a quantitative rather than qualitative dimension, a point we discuss more extensively in Chapter 9. Thus, speakers of vernacular and standard varieties of English typically differ in the *extent* to which *-in'* is used for *-ing*. That is, both may pronounce *coming* as *comin'* a certain percentage of the time, but the percentages differ. This pattern exists along with group-exclusive patterns such as habitual *be* (e.g., *They always be messing with him*) or completive *done* (e.g., *He done took the garbage out*), which are only found in vernacular dialects. In the case of quantitative differences, the linguistic rule in the standard and vernacular variety is the same; one group simply applies the rule more frequently than the other (e.g., working class uses more of the *-ing* → *in'* rule than the middle class, but both groups have the rule). An authentic dialect switch must thus take into account the configuration of relationships diagrammed in Figure 7–5.

In Figure 7–5, features 1 and 2 represent group-exclusive patterns,

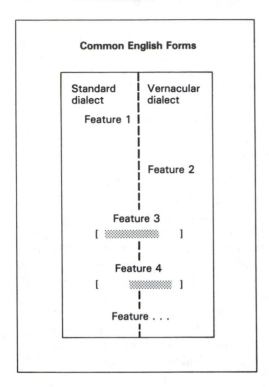

FIGURE 7–5 Diagrammatic Relationship between Dialects of English

one for the standard variety (1) and one for the vernacular variety (2), whereas features 3 and 4 represent shared linguistic patterns with differing degrees of application. In feature 3, one variant (the nonstigmatized one) is more frequently found in the standard variety and in feature 4, one variant (the stigmatized one) is more frequently found in the vernacular variety. As we see in Chapter 9, the patterns found in features 3 and 4 are quite common among English dialects. Given this variable dimension of linguistic structures, it can be very difficult to pin down true cases of switching distinct subsystems, especially when we underscore the fact that switching should in principle involve an entire set of vernacular or standard structures.

It is easier to find cases in which selected structures associated with one dialect or another are clustered together at a given point in a conversation. For example, consider the following excerpt from a single interview with 59-year-old man from West Virginia. In the course of a descriptive narrative, he used four consecutive *a-* prefixed forms in the following context:

> . . . and I just stood there a minute and here came a big mule with his ears *a-floppin'*, and a man *a-leadin'* it and somebody on the saddle. And it was a

fellow that went in there *a-coon huntin'* that night, said he was goin' *a-coon huntin'* . . . (Wolfram 1988:251)

The speaker only used one other *a-* prefixed form during the rest of the one-hour interview, although there were more than 50 structural opportunities for this form to occur. This type of clustering of the *a-* prefix is not the typical pattern of distribution found for varying structures (see Chapter 9), which tend to be much more evenly distributed throughout an interview. When this concentrated use of *a-* prefix is considered in light of its occurrence at a particularly dramatic and vivid point in the narrative discourse, it seems reasonable to consider this cluster of *a-* prefix forms as a case of a systematic switch to a vernacular form. But the *a-* prefix switch in the previous example was not accompanied by dramatic shifts in other linguistic structures; the phonology, as well as other grammatical structures, remained relatively stable at the point of the *a-* prefix clustering. This kind of evidence, although admittedly anecdotal, suggests that speakers tend to switch selected structures rather than entire grammatical systems. At this point, there is little hard evidence that speakers can control entire dialect subsystems. Available evidence (Mims and Camden 1986) suggests that the vast majority of speakers has trouble controlling both a standard and vernacular dialect grammar.

Exercise 2

Gumperz (1982) has observed that switches in a conversation typically carry out special conversational functions. For example, a switch may be used to set apart a quotation or reported speech, such as *So the man said, "I ain't goin' do nut'n for you* or *Den the man say, "I really don't want you to do anything."* Following are other types of conversational functions that such switches might fill, according to Gumperz. For each instance, imagine a reasonable scenario that might involve switching into a vernacular or standard dialect.

1. addressee specification (directing a message to one of several possible addressees)
2. interjections (marking an interjection or sentence filler)
3. reiteration (repeating the same form in a different dialect code to clarify, amplify, or emphasize)
4. personalization versus objectification (degree of speaker involvement, dramatic description)

Obviously, different speakers may indicate varying capabilities in switching, just as some speakers have much more stylistic flexibility within a dialect than others. We would certainly expect those speakers with more disparate social identities and relationships to be capable of manipulating a broader range of structures than those who function in a relatively homogeneous dialect world.

Although most speakers may not be able to switch readily into and out of overall vernacular and standard dialects, this does not mean that speakers cannot reconcile disparate social relationships and identities through language. However, it appears that the sociopsychological effect of shifting group identities does not come from switching systems per se, but through other symbolic linguistic means, such as specialized language use conventions (e.g., greetings, conversational exchange formats) and selective lexical choices. For example, the examination of speeches given by Martin Luther King, Jr. to quite diverse audiences (e.g., southern rural black church congregation versus an official government event attended by majority culture dignitaries) shows distinct differences in his speaking style, but the actual switching of standard and nonstandard forms as described here is limited and restricted. The primary adjustment in King's speeches to different audiences is found in the manipulation of language use conventions, along with changes in prosody (e.g., intonation, timing, stress), it is not found in the manipulation of distinct grammatical subsystems. There is certainly phonological and grammatical variation, but the shifts are not as drastic as those typifying disparate social dialects. Generally speaking, differences in the stylistic variation within a given class dialect are not as great as those found across different class dialects. In other words, the difference in the variation between a formal and informal style indicated for a middle-class speaker would not be as great as that found for a middle-class speaker when compared with a working-class speaker in the same style.

Exercise 3

Based on an audio recording of speeches to diverse audiences, examine the stylistic differences of a person well known for the ability to bridge different cultures (e.g, Jesse Jackson or Martin Luther King, Jr.). Compare a speech to an indigenous community audience and a speech to a majority culture audience. Are there any qualitative differences in linguistic form (e.g., phonology, grammar)? What kinds of differences are there in language use conventions to the different audiences (e.g., speaker-audience interplay, salutations)? Are there particular socially diagnostic features that the speaker might be manipulating (e.g., multiple negation)? What kinds of socially diagnostic features do *not* appear to be manipulated? For example, are socially diagnostic irregular verbs shifted?

HYPERCORRECTION

One of the phenomena that may result from shifting language forms along the standard-vernacular continuum is linguistic behavior that goes too far in terms of the target linguistic group. This kind of linguistic behavior is not unlike the situation in which people try so hard to "act like the Joneses" that they become more like the Joneses than the Joneses themselves. When this kind of behavior affects the forms of language, it is referred to as *hypercorrection*. The notion of hypercorrection as a technical term in language variation studies has both a linguistic and social side. Linguistically, it refers to the fact that a form has been extended beyond its regular linguistic boundaries in some way, either by analogy or by generalization, as discussed in Chapter 2. However, hypercorrection is more than simply a linguistic notion, since analogy and generalization per se are fairly widespread linguistic processes found in many language situations, including language acquisition and change. What sets hypercorrection apart from these other natural linguistic extensions is its sociopsychological side. Typically, this behavior is manifested in social settings in which the speaker feels a need to use more standard or "correct" forms, hence the label *hypercorrection*. The social side of hypercorrection is, in fact, the reason we discuss this notion in this chapter on style rather than in another chapter.

There are a couple types of hypercorrection that need to be recognized. Furthermore, its linguistic manifestations may take quite different forms, depending on the level of language organization involved. One major type of hypercorrection is *structural hypercorrection*, where the boundaries of linguistic patterns are extended. For example, when speakers extend the objective case ending of the relative pronoun to subjective function of this form as in *Whom is it?*, they are extending objective case marking beyond its regular linguistic boundaries. In a similar way, a speaker attempting to use "precise pronunciation" might add a [t] to words which end in [s], so that *synthesis* may be pronounced as *synthesist*. Although we have to be careful in speculating about what is exactly taking place in the mind of the speaker when linguistic structures are extended in this way, we might conjecture about a scenario in which a speaker feels social pressure to produce the standard form for an item that the speaker is unsure about. The speaker may fight off a natural linguistic urge to use what might be judged a nonstandard form by overapplying or misapplying the standard one. The source of hypercorrection is *linguistic insecurity*, as speakers uncertain of the "correct" form overcompensate linguistically. Of course, over time, hypercorrect forms can become thoroughly habituated so that their use is no longer restricted to social occasions where the speaker feels extraordinary sociolinguistic pressure to be standard.

In phonology, structural hypercorrection usually results in the substitution or addition of sounds. For example, a speaker of vernacular dialect

who normally uses the [f] pronunciation for the Standard English *th* forms
in items like *bath* [f] or *ath[f]letic* might overcompensate for this tendency
by using the [θ] pronunciation for an [f] sound. With an unfamiliar lexical
item like *slough*, normally produced with a final [f] in the standard dialect,
the speaker might overcompensate by producing it with a [θ]. For reasons
I won't detail here, this [θ] for [f] hypercorrection actually doesn't take place
very often for speakers of Vernacular Black English, the dialect most often
associated with the θ/f correspondence in American English, but it does
occasionally occur with more unfamiliar words. More frequently, hypercorrection involves the addition of sounds, such as the *synthesist* for *synthesis*
pronunciation already mentioned. Thus, a friend of mine by the name of
Wes [wɛs] was referred to as *West* [wɛst] by a vernacular speaker on occasions
when she tried to produce his name "precisely." On other occasions, she
was content to pronounce his name simply as *Wes*. This addition of sounds
would occur at the end of words ending in an [s] as an overcompensation
for the natural tendency found in some vernacular dialects to reduce final
consonant clusters.

   Spelling pronunciations, where an item is pronounced following its
spelling as opposed to how it is normally produced in spoken language may
also be a type of hypercorrection. A classic example of this is the spelling
pronunciation of *often* with a [t], which now takes place so frequently that
it may no longer be considered as simple hypercorrection by those attempting to be precise and correct. Similarly, the pronunciation of words like
singer with a [g] instead of a single velar nasal sound [ŋ] (e.g., [sIŋgɚ] for
[sIŋɚ]) may be a spelling pronunciation if it results because the speaker is
attempting to follow the spelling "exactly."

Exercise 4

Certainly, not all "spelling pronunciations" can be considered hypercorrection as we have discussed this term here. For example, consider the case
of a foreign language learner who has never heard the word *island* in spoken
language before and therefore pronounces it as [Island]. What is the basic
difference between this type of spelling pronunciation and the kind of
spelling pronunciation which might be classified as hypercorrection?

   Studies of stylistic shifts in phonological variation also have led to the
recognition of another type of hypercorrection, which we refer to as *statistical
hypercorrection*. In statistical hypercorrection, the structural placement of
forms follows a common, shared rule, but the relative frequency of the
forms quantitatively exceeds the norms of the target group. A classic example
of this kind of hypercorrection again comes from Labov's study of social

and stylistic variation in New York City (1966). When the relative frequency of postvocalic *r* use in items like *guard* and *floor* is tabulated for different social status groups of New Yorkers in different styles, the display shown in Figure 7–6 is found.

As shown in Figure 7–6, all social groups increase the relative use of *r* as the style becomes more formal. The most interesting part of the figure, however, is the "crossover" pattern shown by the lower middle class when compared with the upper middle class in the more formal styles, in particular, the word lists and minimal word pairs. In the less formal styles, the lower middle class uses less *r* than the upper middle class, but in the more formal styles, the frequency of *r* presence is greater for the lower middle class than the upper middle class.

In attempting to understand why this pattern would occur, we must recognize that the upper middle class already "has it made," and therefore can afford to be linguistically secure in more formal contexts. The lower middle class, on the other hand, constantly strives to emulate the upper middle class in their effort to attain equal status. Being close to but not equal to the upper middle class makes speakers in this group "try harder."

FIGURE 7–6 Class and Style Stratification for Postvocalic *r* (from Labov 1972b:114)

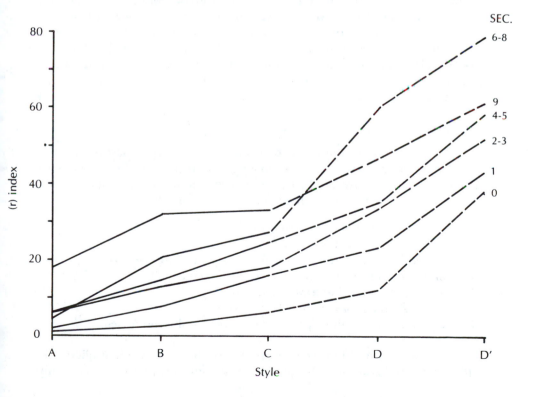

When speech itself is most in focus, as it is in the word lists, the more linguistically insecure lower middle class outdoes the more prestigious group at its own linguistic game.

Grammatical hypercorrection, which is typically structural rather than statistical, can take a variety of forms, but classic examples of grammatical overcompensation involve case marking. We already mentioned the case of objective forms of *whom*. In this instance, we may note that the objective form of the relative pronoun has been disappearing from English for some time now, and is now largely obsolete. This situation leaves speakers unsure of what form to use when formal occasions call for attention to the prescribed form. Uncertain as to where the subjective and objective forms are to be distinguished, the speaker overcompensates by using the objective case with subjective functions, as in *Whom is it?*

Another common type of grammatical hypercorrection involves the case marking of pronouns in coordinate constructions such as *you* and *I*. In this instance, subjective case markings are overextended into objective functions, resulting in forms such as *The woman gave it to you and I.* In this case, speakers are usually trying to avoid the nonstandard construction in which objective forms may fill a coordinate subject slot, as in the vernacular pattern *Me and you can go to the movies tomorrow.* Protecting against the nonstandard use of an objective pronoun form, speakers overcompensate by extending the subjective case forms to objective functions, producing constructions like *He cheated you and I* or *The argument is between she and I.* The attempt to use older, disappearing forms that are still prestigious and the desire to avoid developing forms that are still stigmatized are two tokens of the classic situation which leads to grammatical hypercorrection.

Exercise 5

One of the common grammatical forms affected by hypercorrection is the reflexive pronoun. Based on the following examples, identify the reflexive pronoun form most affected by hypercorrection and the types of constructions in which hypercorrect reflexive forms are typically used.

1. Donna and myself often work together.
2. Please give the ticket to myself.
3. Between Marge and myself, we should be able to raise the kids.
4. This book was really written by the students and myself.
5. I arranged for myself to leave early.
6. He brought the project to myself for review.
7. The students often give a party for the other faculty and myself.

Although the notion of hypercorrection has traditionally been applied only to phonology and grammar, the general sociolinguistic phenomena certainly can be extended to other levels of language organization as well, particularly if we adjust slightly our notion of linguistic boundary. For example, if we assume that part of "knowing a word" involves knowledge about its use in particular social settings, we may say that one type of lexical hypercorrection involves the use of words set aside for more formal occasions in more informal settings. Just as slang items are restricted to informal occasions (see Chapter 3), there are items that are restricted to formal uses. Latinate synonyms such as *bifurcating* for *branching* or *vendible* for *sale*, for example, appear to markedly formal. When speakers tend to use "big" words in less formal occasions, deliberately seeming to avoid a more common synonym, we may have a kind of *lexical hypercorrection*. I sometimes call this the "thesaurus syndrome," in reference to the tendency of students in composition classes to use dictionaries of synonyms to avoid a more common and ordinary vocabulary item in their writing.

Admittedly, there is sometimes a thin line between precision in selecting an appropriate descriptive word and lexical hypercorrection, so that the intention of the speaker and the social context play an especially critical role in determining when the choice of a particular word is overdone. In part, lexical hypercorrection of this type may be determined by the expectations of the audience. There are certainly sociolinguistic situations where a word may call attention to itself as being too formal for the occasion, just as slang items flout an informal lexical choice. When an acquaintance of mine, in an informal gathering, described a talk she had with her teenage son by saying, "He and I discoursed about that particular matter," my immediate reaction was to wonder why she was trying to sound fancy by using "discourse" when she meant "talk." In these cases, the words may be used with appropriate semantic reference, but the item is extended beyond its conventional boundary with respect to formality.

This kind of lexical hypercorrection should not be confused with other types of lexical choice, such as "lexical avoidance" or euphemism. For example, *bureaucratese*, a language style associated with government statements that resort to euphemism and technical jargon to describe common events, may strike people as "lexically overdone." However, many of these cases derive from a deliberate attempt to speak about a topic indirectly for one reason or another rather than an attempt by the speaker to simply use more educated and "fancy" words, although the end result to listeners may seem the same. For example, terms like *fiscal stress* to describe a big budget problem and *offensive initiative* to describe starting a war are not used simply to sound educated and fancy. Instead, these choices are made to deflect the strong emotive connotations of words like *debt* and *war*.

Some types of lexical extension, commonly referred to as *malapropism*, involve the mistaken semantic reference of a word. Many cases of malapropism involve words which sound somewhat similar, so that *amnesty* may be confused with *amnesia* in a sentence like *I think the draftees who went to*

Canada should be given amnesia or *sedate* may be confused with *seduce* as in
He was heavily seduced in the hospital because of the pain. If the confusion results
because a speaker tries to use a bigger, more intelligent-sounding word,
these instances can legitimately be considered a kind of lexical hypercorrection. But not all malapropism can properly be called hypercorrection,
since some cases may result simply from the false association of items that
takes place in the normal acquisition of new vocabulary items.

In the natural course of learning new vocabulary items, a word is
learned through repeated association of the semantic reference with a phonological form. This association takes place in simple trial and error fashion
as language learners attempt to internalize new associations between form
and meaning. In the process, some false associations between labels and
semantic references may arise, particularly if one word shares a number of
sounds in sequence with another item. For example, children often confuse
ammonia and *pneumonia*. When this false association results as a function of
normal vocabulary expansion, as it often does with young children, it can
hardly be called hypercorrection, but when it occurs in a social context
where the speaker stretches to use less familiar but more erudite words,
then it is appropriately viewed as a kind of hypercorrection. In a sense,
then, the diagnosis of particular vocabulary choices as hypercorrection depends on the intention of the speaker and it is not always clear why speakers
choose particular words. Since our traditional sense of social propriety
doesn't permit us to ask a speaker why the word *discourse* was used instead
of *talk*, we are left with considerable speculation about what word choices
constitute genuine cases of hypercorrection. At the same time, most of us
have pretty good sociolinguistic intuitions as to when people are simply
trying to impress us with their vocabulary and when they choose a word
because it conveys exactly what they wanted to say. In fact, some communities
have terms for a speech style which is defined, among other characteristics,
by lexical extensions of the type described here. Certain types of "fancy talk"
and "talking proper" in the black community include lexical hypercorrection
as described here. In other communities, "talking uppity" may convey this
notion.

By analogy with other types of hypercorrection, we should recognize
cases of hypercorrection on the level of language use as well as other linguistic
levels. It is not difficult to imagine a speaker being more polite or more
indirect than the situation calls for in an effort to compensate for a tendency
to be "too direct" or "too familiar." I have observed, for example, students,
unsure of their rightful access to me as their teacher, "overapologize" for
interrupting me during regularly scheduled office hours—a time set aside
solely for student assistance. From one perspective, this behavior may be
seen as overcompensation due to the students' uncertainty about our status
relationship. Of course, it may also be due to the fact that students do not

interpret faculty offers of assistance as a sincere invitations to discuss their work.

On a somewhat different level, a male attempting to avoid all appearances of sexist language, might refer to teen-age girls as "women" while referring to teen-age males as "boys"—an overcompensation borne, no doubt, of the historical tendency to refer to older women as *girls*. A policy of generic pronoun reference that one of my colleagues sometimes uses, in which female pronouns are used for generic reference instead of the traditional generic male pronoun (e.g., *When a speaker tries too hard, she often ends up hypercorrecting*) strikes me as a kind of hypercorrection, although in this case it is premeditated and intentional.

It should be observed that the notion of hypercorrection presented here is somewhat broader than the one which defines linguistic boundaries in a very strict sense. It is also broader than the traditional limitation of hypercorrection to the dimension of status and the standard-vernacular continuum of linguistic variation. The general sociolinguistic phenomena strikes me as one which has a much broader sociolinguistic base than the one set out for it in social dialectology. Linguistically insecure lower middle-class groups are not the only ones who can be found to engage in sociolinguistic overcompensation. Indeed, the conditions of linguistic insecurity and uncertainty which result in hypercorrection on various levels of language seem appropriately applied to a wide range of intergroup situations which include ethnicity, gender, and region, as well as social status.

Exercise 6

Based on the preceding discussion, think of other examples of hypercorrection which pertain to interethnic, intergender, and interregional overcompensation. With respect to these types of hypercorrection, think of particular linguistic forms that might be overdone. For example, might a Northerner moving to the South overdo a southern speech form like *y'all*? Why or why not? What types of forms are most likely to be overdone in interethnic and intergender communication? Why?

Finally, we should mention the possibility of overdoing a vernacular variety, just as it is possible to overcorrect the standard variety. For example, if a nonnative speaker of a vernacular variety attempts to speak this variety, the speaker may overuse or extend the boundaries of the form. Thus, a nonnative speaker of Vernacular Black English might overextend the structural contexts of habitual *be*, using it in both habitual (*My ears usually be itching*) and nonhabitual contexts (*My ears be itching right now*). The latter context would, of course, be an extension of the nonstandard grammatical pattern just as the use of *you and I* in an objective uses would be an over-extension of the standard pattern. This type of situation, which seems to be a fairly common phenomenon found among standard speakers trying to speak a vernacular dialect, has been referred to as *hypocorrection* (Baugh forthcoming).

Further Reading

BELL, ALLAN, "Language Style as Audience Design," *Language in Society*, 13:145–204, (1984). This article is one of the most encompassing attempts to explain the dynamics of stylistic shifting. As indicated in the title, the model gives primacy to the speaker's audience in its account of stylistic variation.

GILES, HOWARD, ed., "The Dynamics of Speech Accommodation," *International Journal of the Sociology of Language*, No. 46, (1984). This issue of the journal is devoted to articles on the major themes of accommodation theory, one of the most popular explanations of stylistic variation. Its explanation is rooted in social psychology.

GUMPERZ, JOHN J., *Discourse Strategies*. New York, NY: Cambridge University Press, 1982. Chapter 4, on conversational code switching, offers a readable account of some of the major variables that effect code switching in a discourse. Although the examples are taken primarily from bilingual situations, the principles apply to many bidialectal situations as well.

LABOV, WILLIAM, *Sociolinguistic Patterns*. Philadelphia, PA: University of Pennsylvania Press, 1972. Chapter 2 in this collection describes a classic department store experiment carried out in New York City in which "casual" stylistic responses are contrasted with "empathic" ones. It is worth reading for the ingenuity of the field technique. Chapter 3 reports one of the earliest attempts to incorporate stylistic variation into the study of social dialectology. The approach to stylistic variation set forth in this chapter has heavily influenced dialectologists' approach to stylistic variation, although it now has been replaced by more comprehensive models.

POPLACK, SHANA AND DAVID SANKOFF, "A Formal Grammar for Code-Switching," *Papers in Linguistics*, 14:3–46, (1981). A reasoned account of the parameters of code switching in terms of the linguistic system. Again, the data come from different languages rather than dialects, so that the applicability of the data to bidialectal situations is largely by inference.

CHAPTER EIGHT

GATHERING DIALECT DATA

Any casual observer of language differences is a potential collector of data on dialects. In reality, there is no restriction as to who may collect information about dialects and the circumstances under which it can be gathered. As long as people from different groups speak to each other, there is equal access to the dialect laboratory, and the most interesting dialect forms have been known to turn up in rather unusual places. Many fascinating dialect curiosities can be observed by simply keeping your ears attuned to conversations taking place around you, but reliance on this procedure also reduces data collection to the luck of the conversation. Most surveys of dialects cannot depend solely on such fortuitous circumstances to collect data, and therefore rely on a more structured approach to gathering data.

In the following sections, we describe techniques for collecting data, including both traditional approaches to conducting dialect surveys and more recent sociolinguistic strategies developed over the past several decades. As we discuss the various methods, we note the advantages and disadvantages of particular procedures. At the outset, however, we should observe that various methods for collecting data on dialects should, in many ways, be viewed as complementary rather than competitive with one another. There are advantages and disadvantages associated with each technique, so that these techniques can only be evaluated in terms of the goals of the study they are applied to.

THE TRADITIONAL QUESTIONNAIRE

Over the past half century of systematic surveys of American English dialects, the most widely used questionnaire format has been the one associated with the areal studies undertaken under the auspices of the *Linguistic Atlas of the United States and Canada*. This series of surveys began in the 1930s and, in one form or another, is still taking place in various sections of the United States. In this format, a predetermined set of dialectally sensitive items is chosen for direct elicitation, and the task of the fieldworker is to get the subject to offer the variant that is most commonly used in the community.

Traditional questionnaires can be quite exhaustive, and take hours to administer as each possible dialect form is probed directly. For example, the questionnaire used for the *Dictionary of American Regional English* contains over 1,800 questions in all. The actual questions used to elicit forms may vary, depending on the item. Some typical elicitation frames are given below:

1. Labeling Based on Description of Item
    e.g., *What do you call a small amount of food that's eaten between meals?*
    What do you call the heavy metal pan that's used to fry foods?
2. Labeling an Item Present at the Scene
    e.g., *What do you call that piece of furniture you're sitting on?*
    What time is it in this picture?
3. Completing Incomplete Phrases or Sentences
    e.g., *When your skin and eyeballs turn yellow, you're getting* _____.
    When a pond or lake becomes entirely covered with ice, you say it's _____.
4. Listing Topical Inventories of Items
    e.g., *What kinds of wild flowers do you have around here?*
    What kinds of squirrels do you have around here?

The underlying procedural principle simply is to get subjects to offer the appropriate dialect variant without biasing their choice by suggesting a variant of the item in the elicitation frame. Basically, this is a kind of variation on the popular Password game. Occasionally, however, a commonly known variant may be used in the stimulus (e.g., "What is your word for *harmonica*?"), but this procedure raises suspicions about the authenticity of the response, so that it is not generally recommended. For particular items, a fieldworker may also follow up an initial response by asking directly about other variants, to see if there is more than one variant with which the subject is familiar and to determine if variants have any special connotations. However, such probes must always be set apart from the subject's response to an elicitation frame.

A fieldworker's notes may thus include the variant offered by the subject in response to a particular question frame, appropriate notes about reactions to forms, familiarity with alternative forms, and any other relevant observations. In Figure 8–1, we have excerpts from the fieldnotes of a leading American dialectologist, Raven McDavid. The interview was conducted in

FIGURE 8–1 Samples from a Dialect Atlas Worksheet (Data provided by the editorial staff of the *Linguistic Atlas of the Middle and South Atlantic States*, University of South Carolina) (from Wolfram "Varieties in American English," in *Language in the USA*, 1981:47–48)

Pronunciation

What are the two parts of an egg? One is the white; the other is
Variants: *yok, yelk, yulk, yilk, yoke*
Response: *yulk*; "heard": *yelk*
What color would you say the yolk of the egg is?
Variants: *yellow, yallow, yillow, yollow, yeller*
Response: *yellow*; heard from grandmother, old fashioned": *yillow, yollow*: "new way": *yallow*
When your skin and eyeballs turn yellow, you're getting
Variants: *yellow jaundice, janders, yellow janders, jaundice*
Response: *jaundice, jandice,* "I say either"

Grammar

I wanted to hang something out in the barn, so I just took a nail and
Variants: *drive, druv, driv, drove, droove*
Response: *drove a nail*
The nail didn't get in far enough; you'd say, "It's got to be _____.
Variants: *drive, drove, droven, driven*
Response: *driven*
A schoolboy might say of a scolding teacher, "Why is she blaming me, I _____ wrong."
Variants: *ain't done nothing wrong, haven't done anything wrong.*
Response: *I haven't done anything wrong.* [Fieldworker noted subject never used double negatives except quotatively, e.g., "I never had no head for machinery."]

Vocabulary

Where did you keep your hogs and pigs? Did you have a shelter or was it open?
Variants: *hog pen, pig pen, hog lot, hog crawl, cattle crawl*
Response: *hog pen, pig pen*; "old-fashioned or obsolete": *crawl, hog crawl, cattle crawl*
harmonica (with reeds and blown, as distinct from a "Jews' harp)
The thing you put in your mouth and work back and forth and blow on it. Do you remember any other names for it?
Variants: *harp, breath harp, French harp, mouth organ, mouth harp, harmonica*
Response: *mouth organ*

1946 in Charleston, South Carolina, with a white female, age 69, who was an artist and author, and a member of the highest social class in the community.

The excerpt in Figure 8–1 includes sample questions designed to elicit pronunciation, grammar, and lexical forms as contained in the fieldwork manual used by each fieldworker in the survey. Listed below each question are possible variants for the item, also provided in the manual for the fieldworker's reference. The response in this instance not only includes the actual item given, but also variants that the subject listed as "heard," extraneous comments volunteered during the course of the interview, and observations by the fieldworker from other portions of the interview which related to the item. Before the widespread use of high-fidelity recording equipment, all of this information, including the detailed phonetic transcription of items, had to be written on the spot. Some fieldworkers developed rather remarkable skills at recording fine phonetic detail, in addition to making copious notes about items.

It should be apparent that the construction of a traditional dialect survey questionnaire must be based on a considerable amount of preknowledge about the linguistic culture of a community. Decisions about what to include and what to exclude in the elicitation frames can be a painstaking chore. In most cases, however, dialect studies based on this type of questionnaire format build on previous surveys, deleting and adding relevant items for a particular study. Given the many surveys conducted under the aegis of the *Linguistic Atlas of the United States and Canada*, along with the extensive study conducted by *DARE*, an extensive list of dialectally sensitive items already exists, including conventional protocols for eliciting these items. The existence of an established dialect survey questionnaire format also provides a convenient basis for comparing dialect surveys in different communities and in the same community at different points in time. For example, in *The Regional Dialects of English* (1987), Carver compares a set of common items elicited in *DARE* and the *Linguistic Atlas of New England* survey conducted thirty years earlier, along with a new set of items to conclude that "despite enormous changes in the distribution and currency of the regional vocabulary during the middle third of the twentieth century, these subregions [of New England] and their particular dimensions have remained intact" (1987:51).

Exercise 1

Following are some dialect variants, including pronunciation, grammar, and vocabulary items. For each of the items, construct reasonable question frames that would directly elicit the items without using the item in the question. Try your questions on subjects and evaluate the relative success of your frames. What kinds of items seem the easiest to elicit, and what items the most difficult? Why?

Pronunciation

1. The production of the vowel in *ten* and *tin*.
2. The production of first vowel in *ferry, fairy,* and *furry*.
3. The production of the vowels in *caught* and *cot*.

Grammar

1. The plural form of *deer*.
2. The past tense and participle form (e.g., *has* _____) of *creep*.
3. The use of indefinite forms in a negative sentence (e.g., *He didn't go anywhere/ nowhere*).

Lexical

1. The use of the term *frying pan, skillet, spider,* and so on.
2. The use of *dresser, chest of drawers, bureau*.
3. Distinctions between different shades of *purple* in the color spectrum.

The traditional survey questionnaire can lead to much informative data about dialects, but it is essential to understand its limitations. To begin with, the construction of this kind of questionnaire requires a great amount of preknowledge about the culture of a community and the kinds of dialect forms that might be expected. Although previous survey questionnaires can guide a researcher to some extent, more recent manifestations of dialect differences are particularly susceptible to oversight unless the researcher is well versed about the current culture of the community. One of the common complaints about these traditional questionnaires is that they are too focused on the older forms used mainly by older lifetime residents of rural areas. This focus severely limits their usefulness in arriving at contemporary dialect profiles, although it certainly provides essential data in terms of historically oriented dialect goals.

Another limitation concerns the formality of the interview situation. Unless subjects are very secure about their use of language, there is strong tendency for subjects to offer more standard or more formal forms, whether or not these forms are used in everyday speech. For example, if the past tense of *see* is elicited by a completion frame such as *I see a lot of accidents and yesterday I* _____ *one*, there is a chance that the subject may offer *saw* even though *seen* might be the dominant form used in everyday conversation. The tendency to elicit more standard forms is particularly evident in grammatical structure, but there may also be a shift towards more formal pronunciations or more general vocabulary words when these alternates are available. Thus, a subject who frequently pronounces *seven* something like *sebm* [sɛbm] in informal conversation might pronounce it as [sevIn] when directly elicited. Or, the subject might offer the more general lexical term *attic* rather than *garret* when both are in use in the area. The focused attention on dialect variants in direct elicitation can sometimes shift responses in irregular ways, typically towards more formal usage but also, on occasion, towards more vernacular forms. This kind of problem is captured in the *principle of subordinate language shift*: "When speakers of a subordinate dialect are asked direct questions about their language, their answers will shift in an irregular manner toward [or away from] the superordinate dialect" (Labov 1972c:111). The authenticity of a particular form simply cannot be guaranteed when it is elicited apart from its everyday, ordinary uses.

It is also important to recognize that there are limitations in analyzing data from a traditional questionnaire from the standpoint of linguistic description. In the typical questionnaire, a single instance of a form is elicited, which means that the linguistic context of an item is very restricted. An important part of understanding how items pattern linguistically, however, is determining the range of linguistic structures in which they occur. In effect, a *linguistic rule* is a precise statement of the structural contexts in which a form can occur; the way the rule is set up should also indicate where the form may *not* occur by setting up linguistic boundaries for the rule. The information necessary for the specification of a linguistic rule cannot be provided by the elicitation of an item in a limited linguistic context. For example, suppose a dialect questionnaire is concerned with eliciting the *a-* prefix that is found with *-ing* forms in items such as *He was a-huntin' and a-fishin'*, a form we have discussed at a number of points in the previous chapters. For a linguistic description of this structure it is important to understand the range of structures to which the *a-* form may be attached. A more extended analysis of the *a-* prefix shows that it may attach to forms such as *He goes a-huntin'*, *He makes money a-huntin'*, and *He kept a-huntin'*; at the same time the prefix may *not* attach to *-ing* structures such as **He likes a-huntin'*, **The movie was a-shockin'*, and **He was a-discoverin' a cave*. Thus, there are some *-ing* forms to which *a-* may be attached and others where it is prohibited. (Following the standard convention in linguistic description these nonpermissible, or "ungrammatical," structures are indicated by an asterisk*.) In describing the linguistic patterning of *a-* prefixing, it is critical to determine precisely where the *a-* prefix can and cannot occur, so that the concise boundaries for the linguistic rule can be set up. If we want to formulate a linguistic rule for a given dialect, then we need information about how forms pattern in a representative range of linguistic structures. But the direct elicitation of a form in a single structure cannot provide this kind of information. From the viewpoint of the linguistic description of dialect forms, the single-frame elicitation simply does not provide information necessary for analysis.

Finally, there is the matter of inherent variation in language. For some linguistic structures, dialects are differentiated not so much by the existence or nonexistence of a form, but by the relative frequency with which it is used. We have pointed out this trait at various points in the previous chapters and take it up more extensively in Chapter 9. As we have mentioned already, virtually all dialects of English produce [n] as the final segment in unstressed *-ing* forms (e.g., *swimmin'* for *swimming*, *runnin'* for *running*), but socially stigmatized, vernacular dialects of English tend to apply this process much more frequently than their nonstigmatized counterparts. The major difference between these dialects is thus based on the relative frequency with which the *-in'* form is used by different social groups of speakers. In order to determine meaningful quantitative figures, however, it is necessary to gather a substantial number of cases where the fluctuation between *-ing* and *-in'* might occur. This can hardly be done by a direct elicitation questionnaire which limits itself to a single elicitation frame for each item, or, at best, a couple of frames per item. For the study of social dialects in particular, where many of the differences are quantitative rather than qualitative, this type of questionnaire is particularly limiting.

Direct elicitation questionnaires are more useful for gathering data about lexical items than they are for grammatical structures and phonological structures, and most survey questionnaires of this type now supplement them with a "spontaneous conversation" section to obtain more "naturalistic" detail on phonology and grammar. It should also be remembered that the history of these kinds of questionnaires predates the era of reliable audio and video recording, when the fieldworker was limited to what could be obtained on the spot. Furthermore, many of these kinds of dialect surveys were considered a kind of linguistic geography related to an historical goal rather than linguistic studies per se. Most major areal studies of American English still rely on some form of direct elicitation questionnaire to determine the regional varieties of English, despite its limitations for other purposes. The format remains particularly useful in ensuring that information on lexical forms is gathered and in ensuring comparability with surveys of American English in other regions.

THE CONVERSATIONAL INTERVIEW

Most studies of dialects since the 1960s have gathered data on language variation through the use of the conversational interview. For studies focused on regional variation, with primary attention given to lexical items, a spontaneous or natural conversation may serve as an important supplement to the direct elicitation of particular items. For studies of social dialects, with primary focus on phonological and grammatical structures, a conversational interview has become the primary basis for collecting data, with direct elicitation techniques sometimes providing supplementary data. The role of conversational data is dependent to a large extent on the goals of the study, but it is difficult to envision an adequate, present-day dialect study that does not at least include a conversational component of some type. Certainly, the collection of a sample of conversational speech is necessary to overcome some of the limitations of direct elicitation raised previously.

Even in a conversational interview focused on relatively neutral topics of discussion, the fact that a person is being interviewed and tape recorded is a formidable obstacle to obtaining ordinary, everyday speech—the kind of speech that is so central to most studies of dialect variation. This problem has become known in sociolinguistics as the *observer's paradox* : "to obtain the data most important for linguistic theory, we have to observe how people speak when they are not being observed" (Labov 1972c:113). A lot of attention in social dialect studies has been given to developing strategies for overcoming the inherent constraints of a tape-recorded interview, ranging from concern with the personal characteristics of interviewers to the best physical locations for conducting these interviews, and the kinds of questions to be asked in the interview.

The underlying goal of most conversational interviews is quite straightforward: to get as much naturalistic speech as possible by the subject, that is, speech that represents how the subject speaks in ordinary, everyday conversation when language is not directly under examination. This is sometimes easier said than done, but various dialect studies have used rather ingenious strategies to bring this about. Over the years, a fairly good range of "safe" topics for discussion by fieldworkers has emerged, and most social dialect surveys now start with a traditional set of conversational questions, and modify the topics based on cultural and social differences in the community under study. Quite typically, the interview includes questions about childhood games (e.g., "Tell me about the kinds of games you played as a kid"), leisure activities such as TV and movies (e.g., "Tell me about some of your favorite TV programs or movies"), peer group activities (e.g., "What kinds of things do you do with your friends?"), descriptions of life experiences (e.g., "Have you ever been in a situation where you thought you were going to die?"), and other items of personal interest that might produce extended conversation. In the typical situation, cues about items of interest are picked up by the fieldworker and pursued with a series of follow-up questions that will encourage the subject to develop themes of interest into a comfortable conversation focused on the topic of the conversation rather than the kind of speech the subject is producing.

One of the overriding considerations in the conversational interview is the need to avoid questions that might arouse suspicions about hidden intentions in interviewing. Subjects often find it hard to believe that an interviewer is interested in finding out about culture and language, simply for the sake of knowing such information, and they often are on guard for a disguised motive. Questions about social conditions and politics from an interviewer often can arouse these suspicions, even when they arise from a topic introduced by the subject rather than the fieldworker. Over the years, I have had to dissuade subjects from thinking that I was a tape recorder salesman, truant officer, and FBI investigator, among other presumed identities.

Many surveys of vernacular dialects now employ fieldworkers from the community itself, and some of the richest sources of data we have collected over the years come from interviews conducted by indigenous fieldworkers. Of course, there are a number of personal characteristics that go into the profile of a good fieldworker which are not necessarily unique to community members, and an empathetic, nonthreatening interactional style can often turn out to be more important than classic social variables such as status, race, age, and sex of the interviewer. Other things being equal, however, indigenous interviewers certainly possess the highest potential for tapping the natural use of vernacular forms, and there are some sociolinguists who feel that the deepest, most authentic forms of a vernacular variety are truly accessible only through the use of community fieldworkers. The attributes of good fieldworkers are unrelated to the characteristics of good language analysts once the data are collected, although an ideal format for data collection and analysis might hope to combine the insights of both perspectives in a dialect study. The qualities of rapport and empathy in conversational interviews may be discussed at length, but ultimately they cannot be programmed. Nonetheless, good fieldworkers are invaluable to any significant dialect study, and it seems advisable that community members be involved in this process.

Although a fieldworker cannot control the elicitation of particular diagnostic forms when the focus of the interview is simply on obtaining reasonable amounts of conversation, it is possible to include certain kinds of questions which raise the potential for targeted structures to occur. Thus, interview questions about past time events, such as the narration of movies, TV programs, or past experiences, are likely to result in a considerable number of past tense verb forms. Similarly, descriptions of different attributes (e.g., "What does he look like?") may raise the potential for predicate adjective constructions to occur (e.g., *He's tall and he's kinda thin . . .*).

The kinds of questions that promote the potential for certain structures are, of course, determined only after pilot trials with various formats, and in some cases only after the analysis has begun. For example, in our early studies of Detroit speech (Wolfram 1969), we found that many of the occurrences of habitual *be* (e.g, *They be tagging somebody when they catch them*) among children occurred during their descriptions of traditional game activities, situations which called for the description of a regularly occurring, or habitual activity. Such information not only aided us in the analysis of the invariant form of *be* (Fasold 1969), it also helped future studies of this form structure questions that might bring out the use of *be* (Bailey and

Maynor 1987). Care may therefore be given in a conversational interview to the kinds of questions that might elicit sufficient data for analysis, the kinds of linguistic structures that certain questions are likely to call forth, and the cultural topics that are relevant to the community of speakers. When these considerations are taken into account, the demands for conversational interviews may present a significant challenge. These concerns also point to the need for extensive pilot testing before wide-scale surveys are conducted. The success of particular topics in eliciting conversation varies considerably from community to community and from subject to subject, since the actual interview sometimes strays considerably from the structured topics as the fieldworker follows the subject's interests.

Exercise 2

Suppose that you are interested in examining the use of third person, singular present tense forms in a study of a dialect (e.g., *She goes to the store*). Think of conversational questions that might produce these forms. Try out these questions in a brief, tape-recorded interview with a subject. When finished with your interview, review the recording and count the number of times a third person singular verb form was used by the subject. Was your questioning strategy successful in producing cases of this type? If not, why not?

Through structuring the kinds of questions in the conversational interview, it also is possible to get a range of styles in the interview. So direct discussion questions about language use or mainstream educational values might be included to elicit a more formal language style, while other questions might be designed to get the subject to sublimate the attention being given to speech as opposed to the content of the conversation. In most cases, however, styles are more systematically manipulated by including reading passages or word lists and comparing this formal style with conversational style focused on a topic of natural interest, since reading invariably involves a more formal speech style than spontaneous conversation.

It is difficult to say how much conversation is necessary for meaningful analysis of dialect data, since this is subject to the kinds of structures that are being considered and the type of analysis being undertaken. For frequently occurring units in the phonology, a limited interview of 15 minutes might provide adequate tokens of the sound unit for analysis, while for grammatical structures, considerably more conversation typically is required. Most studies relying on individual conversation interviews set minimal time limits of between 45 minutes and one hour, although there is certainly no hard and fast rule.

There are limitations to the single-subject conversational interview, just as there are limitations to other data elicitation formats. Although this technique provides access to a kind of naturalistic language data, it is not always successful in overcoming the observer's paradox, as speakers still may be conscious that their speech is being "examined." In most cases, there are interludes where the attention to speech is sublimated, but it is never far away from the subject's consciousness. These kinds of interviews typically provide casual, but somewhat careful conversational style.

The single-subject conversational interview also tends to be restricted in terms of the kinds of conversational discourses it elicits. For example, an interviewer may be able to elicit a narrative account of a past time event, but it will typically not be the kind of "performed narrative" that the subject might recount for a group of listeners. Thus, linguistic structures that might occur in animated, lively narrative recounting usually would not be found among the discourses of the interview. In a similar way, subjects' use of question forms within a conversation tend to be underrepresented, since the interviewer typically asks most of the questions.

Given the underlying concern with obtaining sufficient amounts of conversation, there is no assurance that certain forms will be included as a part of the interview, even with considerable forethought to the kinds of structures that certain questions might encourage. As noted earlier, this problem is more acute for grammatical and lexical structures. Unfortunately, there are instances where the most critical structures for resolving a point in the descriptive analysis focus on structures that occur quite infrequently. For lexical differences, the situation is even more drastic, given the hundreds of possible dialect items. In fact, it is difficult to conceive of any significant study of lexical differences that relies exclusively on conversational interviews of approximately an hour per subject. For dialect studies focused on the lexicon, the conversational interview is virtually always considered supplemental to more direct probes about lexical forms and uses.

Finally, there is the issue of comparability. It is difficult to ensure comparability in language structures even when subjects talk about similar topics for approximately the same length of time. For example, I have tabulated potential multiple negative usage (i.e., negative sentences with indefinites such as *She didn't go no/anywhere*) for speakers with similar quantities of conversation only to find that one speaker had over 50 instances of potential multiple negation and another speaker had less than five instances. Given the flexibility that must be built into a meaningful conversational interview, it is difficult to ensure comparability for different subjects in a given study, to say nothing of comparability with other studies. Unfortunately, we cannot be sure that particular structures were absent from an interview simply because they didn't have an occasion to occur, or because they were legitimately not part of the speaker's linguistic system.

Obviously, there are many advantages found in gathering dialect data through the use of a conversational interview, but significant limitations exist as well. As with other types of data collection techniques, these limitations must be kept in mind as the researcher coordinates data collection with the goals of a particular dialect study.

THE GROUP INTERVIEW

In the group interview, subjects who form a natural social set are tape recorded in conversation with each other. The topic of conversation may be left up to the participants rather than the fieldworker, but initial guidance in offering natural topics of conversation is often called for. The simple instruction to "talk about anything you want to talk about" tends to lead to difficulty in selecting topics for conversation in an obviously contrived situation, so that it is generally recommended that topics for conversation be offered in line with the group's interests (e.g., "What did you think of that game on TV last night?" "What do you think about planting according to the signs?"). Once the organizer of a group session has arranged for the details of the interview and offered a couple of lead-in questions, the situation calls for the interviewer to take a background role in the group dynamics. In the ideal situation, a natural peer group will follow its own structure in carrying forth a conversation, and the fieldworker may even find a "convenient" excuse to leave the scene for a period during the interview.

The greatest advantage of the group interview is the fact that it provides a context most conducive to collecting data on the structure of natural conversational interaction—data unobtainable through the classic technique of conversation between the fieldworker and a single subject. This kind of interactional style may be necessary to provide data on particular forms and uses of language forms. For example, studies of single-subject interviews reveal few instances of the historical present in narratives (e.g., *I went down to the store, and I see this guy, and he looks like he's dying, so I say to him . . .*), a type of discourse not at all uncommon in some communities when a speaker performs a narrative for a natural group of listeners. Similarly, Labov (1972) found early in his studies of the speech of black urban youth that data on certain kinds of ritualistic insults (e.g., "playing the dozens," sounding, or signifying) could only be tapped through the group interview. Group interviews may prove to be invaluable in accessing the range of language forms and uses found in a given dialect, in addition to raising the potential for the most casual speech styles.

In setting up group interviews, there are important technical considerations to keep in mind. For most kinds of detailed language analysis, each speaker must be recorded on a different track, since adequate fidelity typically cannot be maintained when a single track is used. Furthermore, it is difficult to identify individual speakers when each member of the group is not recorded on a different track. From a practical standpoint, it must be recognized that some speakers will dominate group sessions and others will have very little to say, due to the natural dynamics of the interactional patterns. It is therefore difficult to guarantee adequate amounts of data for individual speakers on the basis of a group recording.

As with other kinds of conversational interviews, it is possible to build situational variables into a group interview. Thus, one recent study of black vernacular speech (Edwards 1986) segmented the interview into five different segments in order to examine intersituational variation in dialect forms: (1) a formal interview with a white investigator, (2) a formal interview with a black interviewer, (3) a racially mixed conversation with a research team member sharing a number of informal attributes with the subjects, (4) a black peer group conversation without an interviewer present, and (5) informal conversation with a black interviewer. The systematic manipulation of different variables within a conversational interview can provide important information about the breadth of dialect forms used by subjects and the kinds of stylistic adjustment of dialect forms that takes place in response to attributes of the fieldworker and conversational situation.

Exercise 3

Choose a naturally determined social group for an interview (e.g., family members, peer cohorts, and so on). Choose topics that may be relevant to the group, and conduct a tape-recorded interview. (For this exercise, you will probably have to ignore the advice to use multitrack recording equipment.) What kinds of practical problems arise in carrying out the interview? What role did you have to assume as the facilitator of the group interview?

STRUCTURAL ELICITATION

Notwithstanding all the ingenuity and refinement that has taken place recently in the methods for collecting spontaneous data, there are occasions in the collection of dialect forms which may call for more direct probing of linguistic structure. One problem that may arise concerns infrequently occurring forms. For one reason or another, some items may turn up very infrequently in spontaneous conversation. Unfortunately, some of these forms may be critical to the resolution of problematic points in the analysis. For most vernacular dialects of English, there remains a core of structures which has not been analyzed in detail simply because these structures occur too infrequently in the spontaneous speech data collected to date. There are also occasions where obtaining more direct speaker reactions or "intuitions" about forms can confirm or disconfirm emerging hypotheses about how particular rules work for a given dialect. We have to remember here that the real basis for language rules resides in the minds of the speakers, and that any way we can get closer to the cognitive imprint of language patterning can only aid our analysis. In fact, in modern syntactic theory, the most commonly offered kinds of data for analysis come from native speakers tapping their intuitions about what kinds of sentences are well formed (technically *grammatical*) and what kinds of structures are not well formed (technically *ungrammatical*).

For standard dialects, linguists often (and somewhat naively) access speakers' intuitions like an acceptable English sentence. In return, the native speaker responds to the direct inquiry by saying that a particular sentence is or is not a well-formed English sentence. Thus, a native speaker of English would not hesitate in saying that a sentence such as *The package will arrive tomorrow* is a well-formed, or "grammatical," English sentence and *Package the will arrive tomorrow* is ill formed, or "ungrammatical." There are limitations to direct probing for any kind of linguistic analysis, but direct questioning of this type is particularly problematical when it comes to vernacular dialect forms. This special problem is due to the confusion of social acceptability and linguistic "well-formedness." The social context in which these forms exist makes it difficult to get reliable responses when questions of grammatical structure are probed directly. For example, experimental attempts to get speakers of Vernacular Black English to respond on a purely linguistic basis to uses of *be* in sentences such as *Sometimes my ears be itching* or *He be practicing a lot* provided us with many anecdotes about how our linguistic intentions could be misinterpreted, but gave little reliable information about the linguistic well-formedness of various sentences with *be* in this dialect. Because of the special problems involved in obtaining valid responses from vernacular speakers about socially stigmatized forms, some researchers have retrenched to a position in which they will include only data from everyday language use. However, this position does not take into account some of the limitations of data we mentioned previously. A comprehensive approach to dialect data therefore may call for direct probing, but such elicitation needs to be tightly controlled and the data gathered in this way need to be viewed as supplemental to and complementary with data collected from conversational speech.

We have already mentioned that one of the limitations of the conversational interview is that a restricted range of structures may occur, particularly for some kinds of grammatical forms. Given such a limitation, it may be difficult to arrive at a descriptive linguistic rule which accounts for all but only the range of linguistic contexts in which the form may occur— the cornerstone of any linguistic "rule." Even if it is possible to collect a wide range of items, there may be questions about the boundaries of a rule, particularly in terms of separating the grammatical from the ungrammatical linguistic contexts. For example, in my initial investigation of the *a-* prefix forms in constructions such as *He was a-huntin' and a-fishin'* (Wolfram 1980), I had collected a number of different constructions in which the *a-* form occurred. Among them were the following sentence types:

Progressives

1. She was *a-lookin'* for the kids.

Starting and Continuing Verbs with -in' Complements

2. She started *a-shootin'* at the target.

Movement Verbs with -in' Complements

3. They went *a-huntin'* for bears.

Adverbial Participles

4. He makes money *a-buildin'* houses.

The preceding examples give a good indication about the range of forms with which the *a-* prefix can occur, but it leaves unanswered questions about the precise parameters of the *a-* attachment rule. I observed initially that certain kinds of structures with *a-* prefix were notably absent from my data. Was this absence due to the limited data, or an indication of linguistic structures where the *a-* rule could not apply? For example, to formulate an explicit rule for *a-* attachment, I needed to know if *a-* prefix could be added to a nominal (e.g., *She likes a-fishin'*) and adjectival (e.g., *The movie was a-shockin'*) participle. And could it be used with adverbial complements that occurred with a preposition (e.g., *He makes money by a-buildin' houses*)? I also noticed that *a-* prefix did not occur on certain verbs when the first syllable was unstressed (e.g., *He was a-discoverin' a cave*) even though these constructions seemed grammatically well formed. Information on these structures was critical to the formulation of a rule for *a-* prefix attachment that was descriptively precise. In order to check out my hypothesis about the *a-* prefix attachment rule, I therefore designed a "forced choice" sentence pair test in which two sentences were given and the subject was forced to choose one as the correct sentence for *a-* attachment. Following are the simple instructions and some sample sentence pairs in the task.

> Some dialects of English put an *a-* sound before words that end in *-ing*, so that you hear phrases like *a-huntin'* we will go. There's some question about how this form is used, so we'd like to get your reactions to it. I'm going to give you two sentences and you choose which sentence the *a-* form should go with. Only choose one, and if you're not sure, make your best guess.

1. a. John likes sailin'.
   b. John went sailin'.

2. a. The woman was comin' down the stairs.
    b. The movie was shockin'.
3. a. He makes money buildin' houses.
    b. He makes money by buildin' houses.
4. a. Sam was followin' the trail.
    b. Sam was discoverin' the cave.

The subjects made choices between sentences that I had hypothesized were well formed and those that were not well formed in the dialect, as they used their linguistic intuitions to determine the appropriate sentence for *a-* prefix attachment. For example, sentence pair 1 contrasts *-in'* with a movement verb (b) with nominal *-in'* (a), sentence pair 2 progressive *-in'* (a) with adjectival *-in'* (b) form, sentence pair 3 the prepositional (b) versus nonprepositional adverbial *-in'* (a), and sentence pair 4 the contrast between an unstressed syllable (b) versus stressed syllable (a) following a-. All of these dimensions were essential to the formulation of the rule for *a-* prefix attachment. The results obtained by giving this task to a set of native speakers clearly confirmed that the absence of *a-* from certain structures was not simply accidental, and provided essential information about the precise parameters of the rule for *a-* prefix attachment.

Exercise 4

Give the preceding sentence pairs to a group of English speakers. Before doing this, however, add another sample sentence pair for each contrast type. For example, make up another example which contrasts a progressive *-ing* form with an adjective (sentence pair 2), another with a stressed and unstressed initial syllable contrast (sentence pair 4), and so forth. Now give this task to at least five different speakers to see if the response pattern matches the distribution for *a-* prefix described earlier. It is not important that the speakers you choose for this experiment be native speakers of an *a-* prefix dialect in this case, since research has shown that virtually all native speakers of English show the same response pattern (Wolfram 1982).

Native speakers have more to tell us about their language than their overt performance. Such information may prove critical to our understanding of dialect rules, but these cannot be accessed simply by asking direct questions about language rules. Various creative tasks have to be used to gain access to the inner knowledge dialect speakers have about their rules to complement the information obtained from observing ordinary language usage. When focusing on dialect forms, the major challenge is to overcome the speaker's natural sociolinguistic inclination to respond on the basis of social acceptability rather than linguistic well-formedness. In the preceding illustrative case, we attempted to do this by a forced-choice task, but there are other ways that this may be done as well.

One relatively simple type of structural elicitation uses a variant of the direct elicitation strategy discussed under the traditional questionnaire, in which the subject simply fills in the blank, or completes an incomplete sentence or phrase. For example, in our own research, we elicited items for the analysis of word-final consonant clusters (e.g., *test fact*) by employing a technique originally used by Berko (1958) for the investigation of plural forms in language acquisition. In the exercise, we wanted to find out how plurals were formed depending on the shape of the form of the final consonant. Pairs of illustrative cards were designed; one of the cards had a single item illustrated and the other card had several of the same item. Some of the words were real English words and others were nonsense words, so that we could examine the productive rule the subject was using apart from particular English words. For example, we may use a word like *desk* and its plural counterpart, illustrated in two cards in Figure 8–2a. Similarly, we may illustrate a contrived form and label it with a nonsense word such as *wust* in Figure 8–2b. The subjects are given the sample item and told, "This is a *wust*." Then the plural card is shown and the subject is told, "If this is a wust, then a whole bunch of them would be called: _____." On the basis of the subjects' responses (e.g., [wUsIz], [wUs:], [wUsts]), we were able to gather important information about the pluralization rule for some vernacular dialects of English.

FIGURE 8–2 Sample Cards for the Elicitation of Plurals

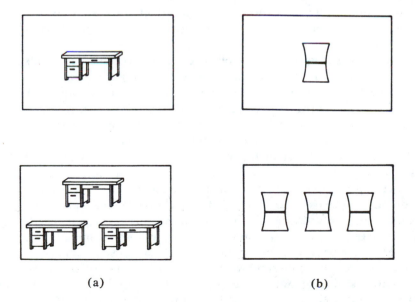

(a)   (b)

In another kind of structural elicitation, a stimulus frame is set up and the subject responds by converting it into a related structure. For example, a subject may convert a present tense form into a past tense form or a subject may change a positive sentence into a negative one. In one study of the relationship of black and white vernacular speech in the deep South (Wolfram 1974), we used a simple positive-to-negative conversion task in order to examine the different uses of *be*. Subjects were told that they would be given positive sentences and that they should convert them into their negative counterparts. Along with a number of other sentences that helped set up the task response frame were the following sentences:

1. He *be* in in a few minutes.
2. Sometime Joseph *be* up there.
3. Sometime his ears *be* itching.

These sentences were included in order to examine what kinds of auxiliary forms were used with the negative forms of *be*, since this information gave important insight into how *be* was being used. For sentence 1, there was no significant difference in the use of the auxiliary by white and black vernacular dialect speakers; both groups of subjects formed the negative predominantly as *He won't be in in a few minutes*. The responses to sentences 2 and 3, however, showed significant differences for the two groups, with the majority of the Vernacular Black English speakers negating the forms with a form of *do* (e.g., *Sometime Joseph don't be up there*; *Sometime his ears don't be itching*). White vernacular speakers, on the other hand, used forms other than *do* (e.g., *Sometime Joseph won't be up there*; *Sometime Joseph isn't/ain't up there*). Data from this elicitation task supported the observation derived from examining spontaneous conversation from these subjects that white and black vernacular speakers were using the form *be* in different ways.

In the preceding paragraphs, we briefly presented three different kinds of structural elicitation formats, including a *completion task*, *conversion task*, and *forced-choice selection task*. Some researchers have used these and other formats to considerable advantage in dialect research. However, we must reiterate that the use of such techniques with vernacular dialect speakers can be somewhat precarious because of the tendency to sublimate natural linguistic choices in favor of socially favored forms. Tasks which can control this tendency in some way (such as a forced-choice exercise) have a better chance of providing authentic data than open-ended formats. Furthermore, these tasks do not relieve us from the challenge to overcome the "observer's paradox" and obtain good conversational data. In the illustrative cases cited, the structural elicitation tasks were initiated only after close examination of many hours of conversation representing a broad sample of vernacular speakers. When there are conflicts between language use and introspective judgments, patterns of language usage should take precedence over experimental tasks. Furthermore, in directly eliciting particular structures, traditional concerns of validity and reliability must be taken into account, and the results of the study must be interpreted with the kinds of cautions that go along with careful experimentation. These cautions, however, are not meant to diminish the essential data that can come from structural elicitation tasks—data that sometimes can prove indispensable for analysis of a given dialect and our understanding of language structure.

SELECTING DIALECT SPEAKERS

From time to time, one of my friends will enthusiastically proclaim that they have met the perfect speaker for my studies of dialect. Naturally, this ideal subject is someone who represents a dialect markedly different from my friend's own dialect. The popular view of who is an ideal subject for dialect study is clearly tied in with the folk notion that dialects are spoken by people in other regions, and that the more different the variety is from others, the more worthy it is of dialect study. Although dialectologists have sometimes been more influenced by the popular obsession with "exotic" dialects than they would like to admit, the consideration of subjects for a dialect study starts with the fundamental understanding that there is no universal definition of the ideal dialect subject. Likewise, there is no one method for selecting these subjects in a research study. In the final analysis, the selection of subjects for a dialect study cannot be divorced from the goals of a study. Given the objectives of a particular study, one study's ideal speaker may be another study's inappropriate selection. For example, a study of the historical dialect of a particular locale might be focused on older, lifetime residents of the area, but a study of geographical mobility and dialect adaptation would have to systematically select people who represented, at the very least, different age levels at the time of arrival and different lengths of residency in the area.

The relationship between the selection of subjects and the goals of a dialect study has not always been fully appreciated by those in disciplines traditionally concerned with sampling procedures, so that dialectologists have sometimes been censured for their methods of subject selection. Traditional *Linguistic Atlas* surveys have, for example, been harshly criticized by survey sociologists (Pickford 1956) for focusing on older, distinctly local, lifetime rural residents when the United States was a largely mobile society culturally centered around its metropolitan areas. But such a criticism does not take into account a primary objective of these surveys—to give an historical account of settlement patterns within the United States. For example, consider the following rationale for subject selection in the earliest *Linguistic Atlas* survey, which focused on New England.

> It was regarded as important to record this old-fashioned and most definitely local type in every community, in order that the earlier regional pattern might

be accurately delineated and the oldest living forms of speech preserved as fully as possible for the historian of New England speech. (Kurath 1939:41)

Obviously, focus on subjects of this type has certain built-in limitations. We could not claim that the *Linguistic Atlas* surveys represent a cross section of American society and the current mobility of the general population. The study is, however, true to its goal of capturing the dialect manifestations of the settlement history of particular regions of the United States. The question of subject selection boils down to the appropriateness of the choice of subjects in terms of the goals of a particular dialect study.

METHODS OF SUBJECT SELECTION

Before selecting subjects for a dialect study, it is essential to determine the *population* of potential speakers. Is this population defined by locale, class, ethnicity, or some combination of these variables? While there is no inherent reason why we can't define our population on a broadly-based variable, such as a general geographical region or a particular metropolitan area, there are usually a number of restrictions which make such generic designations less than ideal for most dialect studies. A study advertised as a dialect survey of Detroit, Michigan, or any other area, usually has important built-in restrictions that need to be noted. For example, our study of Detroit speech (Shuy, Wolfram, and Riley 1968) actually was restricted to those who resided in Michigan a specified number of years, had children registered in local schools, were native speakers of English, were willing to be interviewed, and so forth. This sample is biased as a representation of Detroit in that it excludes entire segments of the Detroit population such as childless couples, more recent in-migrants, and those whose native language is not English. For the practical purposes of our dialect description, this may be an adequate delimitation of the population, but we cannot claim it is representative of the *total* population of Detroit. Most areal and social dialect studies are at least this restricted in terms of their definition of population, although these limitations often get lost in referring to particular dialect surveys.

Once a population has been determined, it is possible to select a sample of speakers from the population in a number of different ways. One may, for example, follow a *strictly random selection* procedure, in which each member of the population has an equal statistical chance of being selected. This is typically done by assigning each subject in the population a number and then referring to a table of random numbers for the selection of subjects. (Most elementary statistics texts include such tables.) Dialect studies which have attempted to follow such a procedure usually plug into sociological surveys already established for the area, but even then various adaptations are necessary for the study of dialect. For example, a speaker with an obvious speech and language pathology is not useable for a dialect survey, nor is a person who does not respond to questions by the interviewer. Furthermore, the number of subjects needed to attain statistical representativeness in random sampling surveys is not realistic for most dialect surveys. At the same time, it may be argued that there is an underlying homogeneity in language variation which makes less rigorous demands for large samples of subjects to achieve representativeness for a population. Various studies of dialects have indicated that as few as five speakers per cell (e.g., upper-class, middle-aged females in a given locale) may be an adequate sample of speakers to represent a given social variable.

In one of the most extensive surveys of a metropolitan area undertaken in the United States, the Detroit Dialect Study (Shuy, Wolfram, and Riley 1968), over 700 residents of Detroit were interviewed, but practical limitation made it impossible to work with such a large number of subjects in analyzing the conversational section of the interview. In most cases, the analysis of linguistic variables had to be limited to well under 100 subjects from the original sample of speakers. At the same time, the sampling procedure did not even provide enough speakers for the analysis of certain social and ethnic variables in the social dialect analysis. For example, the original sample did not provide enough upper-class black speakers to undertake an analysis of status differences in the Detroit black community (Wolfram 1969). For most dialect studies, sole reliance on the strict random sampling procedures is not particularly feasible, nor even desirable given the goals of these studies.

An alternative to a strict random sample is a *quota sample*, in which specified numbers of subjects are selected to represent predetermined social variables. Subjects selected to represent these social variables may, of course, be chosen on a random basis. Thus, we may specify that the sample is going to include ten speakers in two different ethnic groups and four different social status groups. This type of sample avoids the problem of over- and underrepresentation of speakers in certain social categories for language analysis, but the number of categories, or *cells*, in the sample can proliferate rapidly with the expansion of social variables. For example, a sample of ten speakers in each of four different social classes, two ethnic groups, and both sexes would mean that 160 subjects would be have to be included if there were to be 10 upper-class white females, 10 upper-class white males, 10 upper-class black males, and so forth. The number of cells in the sample is the sum of the number of divisions in each variable multiplied by each other. In other words, 4 social classes multiplied by 2 ethnic groups, multiplied by 2 sexes, equals 16 cells ($4 \times 2 \times 2 = 16$); when this is multiplied by 10 subjects per cell (10×16), we have 160 subjects. For dialect studies typically more concerned with the representation of particular social categories than proportional representation of a population, this sampling technique is preferable to strict random sampling, but the sample can easily expand beyond reasonable working limits unless different social categories can be combined for some aspects of the analysis.

The most typical sample used for dialect surveys is the *judgment sample*. In this technique, the researcher identifies the types of speakers to be sampled and then selects a quota of speakers who fits the particular category types. Even dialect studies based on more rigorous random selection techniques often end up making judgments about the representativeness of speakers which guide the final choice of subjects for dialect analysis. This is the case for both Labov's *The Social Stratification of English in New York City* (1966) and Shuy, Wolfram, and Riley's (1968) survey of Detroit speech, well-known urban dialect studies which attempted to follow techniques of random subject selection. When it came to the actual analysis of linguistic data for speakers in the sample, a strong dose of judgment selection vitiated the rigorous sampling procedure used in the original determination of subjects. A judgment sample should not, of course, be confused with a *convenience sample*, where subjects are chosen simply on the basis of their availability at the time of the survey. The typical TV survey of people on the street uses a convenience sample, but such a technique has very limited usefulness for most dialect studies.

Although judgment sampling may be looked at critically by researchers in some disciplines, the special concerns of dialect studies have led some to the conclusion that "it may be more realistic for researchers conducting . . . an urban dialect survey to judgement sample *on the basis of specifiable and defensible principles* than to aim for true representativeness" (Milroy 1987:28). The challenge for dialect researchers is to demonstrate that their judgment is rational and well motivated in terms of the goals of the study. In our study of Appalachian English (Wolfram and Christian 1976) we focused on a survey of vernacular structures found in this variety, not on a general survey of speech in Appalachia. From this vantage point, we started selecting subjects by using indigenous fieldworkers to establish an informal network of subjects who qualified as rural, working-class lifetime residents of Appalachia—the type of subject most likely to use vernacular dialect forms. This network led to interviews with approximately 150 different male and female subjects divided into different age groups (7–11, 12–14, 15–18, 20–40, over 40). Since the original sample was too large for the kind of detailed linguistic analysis we wished to undertake, a smaller set of subjects was selected—five male and five female subjects for each of the age levels. The selection of subjects to represent each cell was made on the basis of several different criteria, including the independent, subjective assessment of speaker vernacularness by the principal investigators, the relative amount of conversation in the interview, an assessment of the relative naturalness of the conversation, and the fidelity of the tape-recorded interview (Wolfram and Christian 1976:13). This systematic selection is certainly limited in terms of the representing the broad-based distribution of dialects in Appalachia, but it does provide the kind of data base necessary to describe many of the vernacular linguistic structures found in Appalachia, which was the goal of the project.

SOCIAL NETWORKS

In the types of subject selection just described, individuals are chosen to represent broad-based social categories such as region, social class, age, and so forth. It is, however, possible to start with a preexisting social group which is defined by a network of relationships between people in the group. For certain types of language analysis, this network of personal social relations will be more revealing of patterns of language variation than the description of a subject in terms of more abstract demographic attributes. For example, suppose a researcher wants to analyze how peer group interaction affects the rise and spread of slang in a college fraternity. In this instance, the social group to be considered is predetermined (the college fraternity), and the essential dimension necessary to figure out the pattern of slang acquisition rests in determining the social relationships that exist between the members of the fraternity. Since language variation may be tied in with dimensions of personal group identity and solidarity, it stands to reason that many aspects of language variation may be closely correlated with networks of social relationships.

There are, of course, many different types of interpersonal relationships that might be linked to language variation, but we just mention two of them here. One is a type of primary peer group relationship found for adolescent and teen-aged hang-out groups in Harlem street culture as described by Labov (1972a). To plot relationships between members of the street hang-out group called the Jets, Labov used a *sociogram*, a sociometric chart showing the structure of interpersonal relations in group situations. This common sociological technique was used to determine the relative peer status of these youths in relation to each other. Basic questions used to chart relations were "Is there a bunch of cats [the study took place in the 1960s, hence the term *cats*] you hang with?" and "Of all the cats you hang with, who's the leader?" The main relations are indicated by reciprocal namings. Based on the number and types of reciprocal naming patterns, members could be broken down into core, secondary, peripheral, and lame (those not considered members) subgroups.

An analysis of the street group terms of their peer relations provides a basis for explaining important kinds of linguistic variation. For example, lames, showing marginal membership roles, showed a lower incidence of symbolic Vernacular Black English structures than the core members of the group; the lames also show higher levels of reading achievement, showing an important relationship between peer group status and school success. In a traditional abstract demographic classification of speakers, these important correlations between social relations and linguistic variation would more than likely be completely overlooked.

Exercise 5

You have decided to study the patterns of teen-age slang or jargon use found in a suburban shopping mall. You want to know what the lexical items are, who uses them the most, and how innovations take place within the group. Given this concern, what types of social relationships among those who hang out at the mall might be important to understand? Select three questions about social relationships among the participants that you are going to ask in plotting a sociogram of the hang-out group. What type of additional background demographic information might be important in understanding the particular use of shopping mall slang by teen-agers?

A different analysis of social relationships is offered by Milroy (1980, 1987), who defines a social network in terms of who a person associates with under what conditions. One aspect of this relationship is referred to as density, the extent to which individuals in a person's network are in contact with each other in independent activities. If the members of a person's network of social relations are in contact with each other independently, the network has *high density*; if not, it has *low density*. The two network types are displayed in Figure 8–3, where the individual being studied is indicated by the asterisk, the other people in the network by dots, and the contact between them by a line.

Networks may also be *multiplex*, where there are a number of different spheres of activity in which individuals interact, for example, work, the neighborhood, and leisure time activities. Or they may be *uniplex*, where the interaction with various people is restricted to a particular sphere of activity. A person's network might be relatively close-knit in the sense that the ties with others are dense and multiplex or it may be less dense and uniplex if a person's social contacts extend to different groups of people who have varied sets of social contacts. Milroy (1980:141–142) even provides a basis for calculating a person's *network score* as follows:

1. Membership of a high-density, territorially based cluster.
2. Having substantial ties of kinship in the neighborhood (More than one household, in addition to his own nuclear family.).
3. Working at the same place as at least two others from the same area.
4. The same place of work as at least two others of the same sex from the area.
5. Voluntary association with workmates in leisure hours. This applies in practice only when conditions three and four are satisfied.

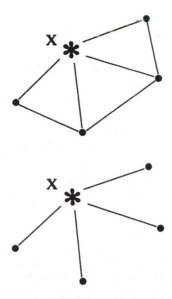

FIGURE 8–3   High- and Low-Density Network Structure (reprinted from Milroy 1987:20)

In this index, scores may range from 0, for someone who fulfills none of the conditions, to 5, for someone who fulfills all of them. The overall network score may independently correlate with language variation, or it may interact with other social variables such as gender and age to account for language variation. Since personal social relationships may exert considerable influence on language, an understanding of social networks may help provide insight into the fundamental principles of dialect maintenance and change.

Social network studies may be adapted for different kinds of sociolinguistic studies, but the framework must be sensitive to the social dynamics of the particular community. For example, Walter Edwards (1986), in formulating a Vernacular Culture Index for the Detroit Eastside black community, set up a scale which took into account the following: (1) daily interaction patterns with neighbors, (2) the extent of kinship ties in Eastside Detroit, (3) kinship ties in the immediate surrounding area, (4) the desire to remain in the general Eastside neighborhood, (5) the desire to stay in the specific immediate neighborhood, and (6) participation in street culture.

Studies of the social relationships of groups usually require the extended association of a fieldworker with the social group, so that there is an additional benefit for obtaining good vernacular dialect data. In order to get at the most authentic use of vernacular dialect forms, the focus of study must be on the naturalistic everyday conversation of people interacting with their peers; following social networks of one type or another is thus the technique most likely to lead to this sociolinguistic context. For this reason, a number of more recent studies of vernacular dialects have turned to social network analysis to get at the most authentic version of the vernacular.

Social network analysis is particularly advantageous for studying small, self-contained groups, or groups of speakers for whom the concept of social class is difficult to apply, such as minority ethnic groups, migrants, and isolated rural groups of speakers. However, this technique is of limited usefulness in large-scale areal surveys unless particular subgroups of speakers within the population are chosen for more concentrated study. We thus return to the observation we made at the beginning of our discussion of the selection of subjects—the choice of subjects in the study of dialect and the kind of information about social relationships and demographics important for examination are tied in with the objectives of the study.

Further Reading

CASSIDY, FREDERIC G., general editor, *Dictionary of American Regional English, Volume 1: Introduction and A–C.* Cambridge, MA: The Belknap Press of Harvard University Press, 1985. The introduction including the text of the questionnaire used to collect data indicate the extensive set of considerations that go into planning, implementing, analyzing, and publishing the results of a dialect survey.

DAVIS, LAWRENCE M., *English Dialectology: An Introduction.* Tuscaloosa, AL: University of Alabama Press, 1983. Davis discusses the research design of some of the major studies of social dialectology as well as traditional dialect studies. An introduction to statistical considerations in the collection of quantitative data is included.

EDWARDS, VIV, *Language in a Black Community.* San Diego, CA: College-Hill Press, 1986. Chapters 4 through 7 of this book demonstrate how fieldwork methods need to be designed in direct response to the underlying research questions that guide the study of language variation. While the methods detailed in this study are not all directly applicable to the language contact situation in the United States (the study took place in a West Indian community in the United Kingdom), some of the creative procedures systematically incorporated into the collection of data in this study are instructive for any prospective fieldworker.

FRANCIS, W. NELSON, *Dialectology: An Introduction.* New York, NY: Longmans, 1983. Chapters 3 through 5 provide an excellent overview of typical methods used in dialectology. These include sampling the language, sampling the speakers, and collecting the data. Francis also includes some of the methodological contributions of social dialectology.

LABOV, WILLIAM, "Some Principles of Linguistic Methodology," *Language in Society*, 1:97–120, (1972). Labov discusses some of the underlying principles that may guide subjects to react in different ways to various kinds of linguistic probing. The "observer's paradox," an essential consideration in virtually all kinds of fieldwork situations, was originally set forth in this article.

MILROY, LESLEY, *Language and Social Network*, 2nd ed. Baltimore, MD: University Park Press, 1987. By focusing on the type of social networks subjects are involved in rather than their background social demographics, Milroy demonstrates that the consideration of social relationships is critical for the analysis of linguistic variation. The social network index presents an important systematic alternative for classifying the social position of dialect speakers. This work has had an important impact on procedures for subject selection in studies of language variation.

MILROY, LESLEY, *Observing and Analyzing Natural Language: A Critical Account of Sociolinguistic Method.* New York, NY: Basil Blackwell, 1987. This book is devoted to a discussion of the problems and principles of studying language in its social context. Both theoretical and practical implications of particular methodological choices are considered.

CHAPTER NINE

THE PATTERNING OF DIALECT

According to popular beliefs, dialect patterns are quite simple: all members of one group invariably use a particular dialectal form while members of a different group categorically use another one. Thus, the caricature of the Pittsburgh speech community may assume that *all* speakers from Pittsburgh pluralize *you* as *youns* and use the lexical term *gumband* for *rubberband*. Similarly, the popular view holds that vernacular dialect speakers always pronounce *swimming* as *swimmin'* and always use multiple negatives such as *they didn't do nothing* while speakers of a standard variety never use these forms. As we have seen already at various points in the previous chapters, this "all or nothing" perspective often veils a number of different ways in which dialect forms may be manifested. Some of these patterns are quite transparent, but many of them are distributed in more subtle and complex ways. In this chapter, we examine in more detail some of the distributional patterns that dialectally diagnostic forms may take among different groups of speakers. As used here, the term *dialectally diagnostic* refers to any form that has the potential to differentiate social groups of various types, whether defined on the basis of region, status, ethnicity, gender, age, or some other social variable.

THE SOCIAL DISTRIBUTION OF DIALECT FORMS

The pattern of dialect distribution which most closely matches the popular perception of dialect differences is referred to as *group-exclusive usage*, where one community of speakers uses a form, but another community never does. In its ideal interpretation, group-exclusive usage means that *all* members of a particular community of speakers would use the dialect form, whereas *no* members of other groups would ever use it. This ideal pattern is rarely, if ever, manifested in American English dialects. The kinds of social grouping that take place in American society are jsut too complex for this pattern to work out so neatly. In some cases, distinctions between groups exist on a continuum rather than in discrete sets. Furthermore, the definition of a social group usually involves a constellation of characteristics rather than a single dimension, making the simple correlation of a linguistic form with social structure more complex. And, as we have seen, dialects are dynamic not static systems, so that they are constantly undergoing change—change which is distributed disproportionately even within tightly-defined speech communities. Thus, when considering the native Pittsburgh resident who might use *youns* and *gumband*, we have to take into account a number of different objective social dimensions that we discussed in the previous chapters. The best we can do is come up with a profile of the kind of Pittsburgh resident most likely to use these forms.

Notwithstanding the qualifications that have to be made when talking about group-exclusive dialect features, there are items that are not shared across groups of speakers. The essential aspect of these dialect forms, however, seems to be the fact that speakers from other groups do *not* use these forms rather than the fact that all the members of a particular group use them. Not all native speakers from Pittsburgh use *youns* and *gumgand*, but it is a safe bet that a native speaker from San Francisco or Seattle would *not* use these forms. Group-exclusive usage is therefore easier to define negatively than positively. Viewed in this way, there are many dialect features of all levels of language organization which show group-exclusive distribution. On a phonological level, many of the regional vowel productions we discussed in previous chapters (e.g., the "open o" of *coffee, caught*, the productions of diphthongs of *time, buy*, and so on) show group-exclusive distribution across regions. There are similar examples in morphology (e.g., the absence of -*s* plural on nouns of weights and measures as in *four acre, five pound*, the pluralization of *you* as *youse, y'all, youns*), syntax (e.g., positive *anymore* as in *They go to the movies a lot anymore*, verbal complements as *The kitchen needs remodeled, The dog wants out*, and so on), and lexical distribution as well (e.g., *gumband/rubberband, garrett/attic*, and so on).

According to Smith (1985), group-exclusive patterns of dialect distribution may be *saturated* or *unsaturated*. Saturated patterns refer to those that typify the vast majority of speakers within a particular social group or speech community and unsaturated patterns refer to those that are less pervasive, but still group exclusive. For example, among younger working-class black Americans, the habitual *be* form with *verb + ing* as in *They usually be going to the movies* might be considered a saturated form since the majority of speakers in this group use this form at one time or another. Note that the definition of the group in this case must include at least ethnicity, status, and age. By the same token, speakers of other varieties of English do not typically use this construction. In contrast, the use of *be done* as in *The chicken be done jumped out the pen* as found within the same population of working-class black speakers might be considered an unsaturated, group-exclusive form. Only speakers of this variety have been found to use this construction.

Descriptive qualifications such as *saturated* and *unsaturated* group-exclusive usage are useful approximative labels, but they have not yet been defined with any rigor. That is, the classification of a form as saturated or unsaturated is not determined on the basis of a specific proportion of speakers sampled within a given population (e.g., more than 75 percent of the speakers in a representative sample use the form in saturated usage and less than 20 percent of the speakers use the form in unsaturated usage). Thus, these designations are imprecise and limited, although admittedly convenient as informal characterizations of dialect patterns.

Group-exclusive dialect forms may be taken for granted in one dialect while, at the same time, they are quite obtrusive to speakers from other dialect areas. Speakers from other regions may thus be quick to comment on how strange forms like *youns*, *The house needs painted*, and *gumband* seem to them when visiting Pittsburgh, much to the surprise of the lifetime resident of Pittsburgh who has assumed that these were in common use. With increased interaction across dialect groups, however, speakers may become aware of their own group-exclusive uses. As the consciousness about these forms is raised, some of them may take on symbolic significance in identifying people from a given locale or social group. And, from these features come the stereotypes of particular regional and ethnic dialects found in popular caricatures. However, it is important to remember that the stereotypical, symbolic caricatures by outsiders and, sometimes even by insiders, are often not linguistically faithful to the actual use of the form by speakers from the particular speech community.

In contrast to group-exclusive forms, *group-preferential* forms are distributed across different groups or communities of speakers, but members of one group simply are more likely to use the form than members of another group. For example, narrowly defined color terms (e.g., *mauve*, *plum*, and so on) are often associated with females, but there are certainly males who make similar distinctions, and, of course, there are females who do not make such refined color designations. The association of a narrowly defined color spectrum is thus statistically based, as more women make these distinctions than men. We thus refer to this narrowly defined color spectrum as a group-preferential pattern rather than a group-exclusive one. We would not expect the symbolic effect of a group-preferential pattern to be as socially marked as a group-exclusive marking, although popular stereotypes of group-preferential dialect patterns sometimes treat them symbolically as if they were group exclusive. The popular characterization of vernacular dialects as saying *dese*, *dem*, and *dose* is such an instance where the stereotype of group-exclusive behavior actually betrays a fairly complex pattern which is really group preferential and also highly variable.

Exercise 1

Suppose your approach to dialect patterning started with the classification of speakers on the basis of linguistic distribution rather than social classification. In other words, you started your analysis of *youns* by separating everyone who used this form into one group and those who did not use it into another group. What would be the implication of this approach for the notions of group-exclusive and group-preferential distributional patterns as discussed previously?

LINGUISTIC VARIABILITY

Up to this point, we have looked only at dialect distribution in terms of *interspeaker* dialect representation, that is, the use of dialect forms by speakers representing a variety of social and/or regional groups. This level of dialect distribution is certainly important, but it is also limited in the insight it can offer us about the nature of dialect differences. As we have already noted in previous chapters, the careful examination of dialect forms shows that dialects may also be differentiated on the basis of how frequently particular forms are used by speakers. In other words, individual speakers may fluctuate in their use of forms, sometimes using one form and other times using an alternate, and the quantitative differences in fluctuating forms are important in the determination of dialects. For example, consider the following excerpt showing the fluctuation of *-ing* (representing [Iŋ] phonetically) and *-in'* (representing [In] phonetically) within the speech of a single speaker in a stable social situation.

> We were walk*in'* down the street and we saw this car go*ing* out of control. The driver looked like was sleep*ing* at the wheel or someth*in'*. The next thing I knew the car was turn*in'* around and just spinn*ing* around. I thought the car

was com*in'* right at me and I started runn*in'* like crazy. I was so scared, thin*king* the car was gonna hit me or som*ething'* . . .

In the ten examples of the form *-ing* in this passage, four cases end in *-ing* and six in *-in'*. According to the linguistic rule describing this process, a rule in which *-ing* might have been realized as *in'*, yet only six of them occur as *in'*. This kind of variation within a single speaker is reffered to as *inherent variability*, where a speaker sometimes produces one variant and sometimes an alternate one. The term *inherent variability* reflects the fact that this fluctuation is an internal part of a single linguistic system, or dialect, and should not be considered an importation from another dialect. In other words, there is no evidence that the speaker fluctuating between *-ing* and *in'* is switching between two dialects, one exclusively using *-ing* and another exclusively using *-in'*. Instead, a single dialect system simply possesses two phonological variants of this ending, and the speaker sometimes uses one form and sometimes another. This kind of fluctuation has long been recognized within linguistics, where certain rules are considered optional because they may or may not be applied. For example, in Standard English, there is an optional rule which permits a speaker to move the particle *up* to a position after a noun phrase, so that *She looked up the number* may alternately be realized as *She looked the number up*. We would not say that the sentences with and without the particle movement belong to distinctly different dialects, and that a speaker switches between the dialects. Instead, we would say that both of these sentences are options within a singular system. Similarly, we may say that *in'* and *ing* forms are alternating variants within one dialect system for most English speakers. The notion of inherent variability is just an extension of a commonly recognized pattern of fluctuation between variants within a system.

One of the important discoveries to emerge from the detailed study of dialects (in particular, social dialects) was that dialects were sometimes differentiated not by the discrete, or categorical use or nonuse of forms, but by the *relative frequency* with which different variants of a form occurred. We noted earlier that the popular view of standard and vernacular speech holds that vernacular dialects will always use *-in'* in unstressed syllables and standard dialects will always use *-ing*. The actual facts do not support this perception. In a number of phonological and grammatical cases, it can be shown that dialects are more typically differentiated by the extent to which a particular rule applies, its relative frequency, rather than its qualitative absence or presence.

Table 9–1 displays the frequency levels of *in'* for *-ing*, a phonological variable, of pronominal apposition (e.g., *My mother, she's coming to school* as opposed to *My mother's coming to school*) in four different social status groups of Detroit speakers (adapted from Shuy, Wolfram, and Riley 1967). Although the figures represent the mean scores for each social group, *all of*

Table 9–1

Relative Frequency of a Variable Phonological and Grammatical Feature in Four Social Groups in Detroit (based on Shuy, Wolfram, and Riley 1967 *Linguistic Correlates of Social Stratification in Detroit Speech*)

	Upper Middle Class	Lower Middle Class	Upper Working Class	Lower Working Class
Mean Percentage of *-in'* Forms	19.4	39.1	50.5	78.9
Mean Percentage of Pronominal Apposition	4.5	13.6	25.4	23.8

the individual speakers also exhibit variability between *-ing* and *in'*, and *my mother, she* . . . and *my mother*. . . . Frequency levels were computed for individual speakers by first noting all those cases where a form like *-in'* (namely, an unstressed syllable) *might have* occurred, followed by determining the number of cases in which *-in' actually* occurred. For example, in the sample passage just given, there are ten cases where *-in'* could have occurred, but only six of them (60 percent) were actually produced with the *-in'* form. This tabulation procedure follows a fairly standard format for determining frequency levels of dialect forms, which can be indicated in the simple formula:

$$\frac{\text{Number of Cases Where a Given Form Occurs}}{\text{Number of Cases Where the Form Might Have Occurred}} \times 100$$

In other words, we calculate the proportion of actual cases out of potential cases (i.e., .6) and multiply by 100 to arrive at a percentage score (60 percent).

The fact that there is fluctuation between forms such as *-ing* and *in'* does not mean that the fluctuation is random or haphazard. Although we cannot predict which variant might be used in a given instance, there are factors that can increase or decrease the likelihood that certain variants will occur. These factors are known technically as *constraints on variability*. The constraints are of two major types. First, there are various social factors, such as social class in Table 9–1, which systematically increase or decrease the likelihood that a particular variant will occur. In other words, looking at Table 9–1, we can say that a speaker from the lower working class is more likely to use both *-in'* for *-ing* and pronominal apposition than speakers from other classes.

Not all of the systematic effects on variability, however, can be accounted for simply by appealing to various social factors. There are also aspects of the linguistic system itself that may affect the variability of particular forms. Particular kinds of linguistic contexts, such as the kinds of surrounding forms or the type of construction in which the form occurs, may also influence the relative frequency with which these forms occur. Because the linguistic influences on variation operate apart from the social factors that correlate with variability, these are sometimes referred to as *independent linguistic constraints* on variability. Linguistic constraints on variability are discussed in further detail in the following section. Our discussion of social variables in previous chapters has already set forth some of the social constraints on variability.

LINGUISTIC CONSTRAINTS ON VARIABILITY

The systematic effect of linguistic factors on the relative frequency of particular forms can best be understood by way of an actual case from phonology. Consider the example of word-final consonant cluster reduction as it affects sound sequences such as *st, nd, ld, kt,* and so forth. In this rule, items such as *west, wind, cold,* and *act* may be reduced to *wes', win', col',* and *ac',* respectively. The incidence of reduction is quite variable, but certain linguistic factors systematically favor or inhibit the operation of the reduction process. The linguistic factors, or constraints, include whether the following word begins with a consonant, as opposed to a vowel (more precisely, a nonconsonant), and the way in which the cluster is formed.

  With respect to the phonological environment that follows the cluster, the likelihood of reduction is increased when the cluster is followed by a word beginning with a consonant. This means that cluster reduction is more frequent in contexts such as *west coast* or *cold cuts* than in contexts like *west end* or *cold apple.* An individual speaker might, for example, reveal consonant cluster reduction in 75 percent of all cases when the cluster is followed by a word beginning with consonant (as in *west coast*) but only 25 percent in all cases where the cluster is followed by a nonconsonant (as in *west end*). The important observation is that reduction may take place in both kinds of linguistic contexts, but it is consistently *favored* in those contexts where the word following the cluster begins with a consonant.

Exercise 2

In the following passage, tabulate the incidence of cluster reduction for all the italicized word-final clusters (technically, clusters that end in a stop consonant and share the feature of voicing or voicelessness with the preceding consonant). Observe whether the cluster is reduced or not, as indicated by the phonetic content indicated in the brackets following the underlined item (e.g., gue*st*[s] would indicate a reduced item since the final [t] has been omitted, and gue*st*[st] would not). For the time being, ignore consonant clusters that are not italicized. Tabulate the items by setting up two columns, one for clusters followed by a consonant and one for clusters *not* followed by a consonant. (Items at the end of a sentence should be considered as nonconsonant.) For each cluster, first determine whether it is followed by a consonant or nonconsonant and then enter it under the relevant category and denote in some way whether it is reduced or non-reduced. After extracting the first couple of items, your tabulation sheet might look like the following:

Clusters Followed by a Consonant	Clusters Followed by Nonconsonant
0 e.g., be*st*[st] movie	*0* e.g., mo*st*[st] of
1 e.g., la*st*[s] year	*1* e.g., coa*st*[s]. It
...	...

1 = reduced cluster
0 = unreduced cluster

After you are finished entering all the items under the appropriate category, calculate the percentage of cluster reduction for each category by dividing the total number of clusters in the category into the number of clusters that are actually reduced. This will give you a reduction percentage for clusters followed by a consonant and clusters NOT followed by a consonant. What can you say about the influence of the following context based on this calculation?

PASSAGE FOR WORD-FINAL CLUSTER REDUCTION TABULATION

La*st* [s] year I saw the be*st* [st] movie. It seemed silly but it was serious too. It was about this detective who lived in California, but he travelled up and down mo*st*[st] of the coa*st*[s]. It seemed like he was always one step ahead of the cops and one step behi*nd*[n] the bad guys at the same time. Nobody really liked him, and it seemed like he was almo*st*[s] killed every time he left the house. Mo*st*[s] of the time, he was running from both the criminals and the police. In fa*ct*[kt] both sides were totally confused by him.

One time, the police set up a scam bu*st*[s] by pretending to smuggle in some drugs off the coa*st* [st]. When they smuggled the stuff inla*nd*[n] they wanted to sell it to the dealers. But the detective wasn't told so he thought it was a chance for a real bu*st*[st] on the dealers. Ju*st*[s] as he jumped in to make an arre*st*[s] a couple of dealers showed up, and he had to a*ct*[k] like he was one of them. So the police thought he was part of the dealers and the dealers thought he was part of the police. Both sides jumped in and he was trying to a*ct*[k] as if he was with the other side. He told a policeman

to go along with him 'cause he was making a bus*t*[st] and he told a drug
dealer to go along with him and he would get the drugs. Both sides were
so confused by him they ju*st*[s] went along with the ac*t*[kt] and followed his
lead. As it turned out, some of the police had gone undergrou*nd*[n] and
some of the dealers had turned evidence to the police. He was so confused
himself he didn't know who to arre*st*[st]. Finally, he just left both groups
shooting at each other. He ju*st*[s] couldn't figure out who was bad and who
was good.

As mentioned earlier, cluster reduction is also influenced by the way
in which the cluster is formed. Clusters that are a part of an inherent word
base, such as *wind* or *guest*, are more likely to undergo reduction than clusters
that are formed through the addition of an -*ed* suffix, such as *guessed* (which
ends in [st] phonetically, [gɛst]) and *wined* (which ends in [nd] phonetically,
[waInd]). Again, fluctuation takes place in both types of clusters, but reduction takes place more frequently when the cluster is an inherent part
of a word rather than the result of the -ed suffix addition.

Exercise 3

Using the passage of Exercise 2 again tabulate the incidence of final-con-
sonant cluster reduction for clusters formed through the addition of the -
ed suffix. As with Exercise 2, the clusters formed through the addition of
-*ed* are italicized and the phonetic content indicated within the phonetic
brackets that follow the italicized item. In order to control for the influence
of the linguistic environments we already tabulated in Exercise 2, the tabulation will need to separate those -*ed* clusters that are followed by a consonant (e.g., *They guessed five*) from those that are not followed by a nonconsonant (e.g., *They guessed at the answer*). Along with your figures from
Exercise 2, you should now have figures for the incidence of cluster reduction
in four different categories: (1) base word cluster followed by a consonant,
(2) base word cluster followed by a nonconsonant, (3) -*ed* cluster followed
by a consonant, and (4) -*ed* cluster followed by a nonconsonant. This table
should look something like the following:

base word followed by consonant	base word followed by nonconsonant	-*ed* cluster followed by consonant	-*ed* cluster followed by nonconsonant
best[st] movie	most[st] of	seemed[m] silly	lived[vd] in
0	*0*	*1*	*0*
...	...	...	...

0 = unreduced cluster
1 = reduced cluster

Last year I saw the best movie. It see*med*[m] silly but it was serious too. It was about this detective who li*ved*[vd] in California, but he travelled[l] up and down most of the coast. It see*med*[m] like he was always one step ahead of the cops and one step behind the bad guys at the same time. Nobody really li*ked*[kt] him, and it see*med*[m] like he was almost kil*led*[ld] every time he le*ft*[f] the house. Most of the time, he was running from both the criminals and the police. In fact both sides were totally confu*sed*[z] by him.

One time, the police set up a scam bust by pretending to smuggle in some drugs off the coast. When they smug*gled*[l] the stuff inland they wanted to sell it to the dealers. But the detective wasn't to*ld*[ld] so he thought it was a chance for a real bust on the dealers. Just as he jum*ped*[pt] in to make an arrest a couple of dealers showed up, and he had to act like he was one of them. So the police thought he was part of the dealers and the dealers thought he was part of the police. Both sides jum*ped*[pt] in and he was trying to act as if he was with the other side. He to*ld*[ld] a policeman to go along with him 'cause he was making a bust and he to*ld*[l] a drug dealer to go along with him and he would get the drugs. Both sides were so confu*sed*[z] by him they just went along with the act and followed his lead. As it tur*ned*[n] out, some of the police had gone underground and some of the dealers had tur*ned*[nd] evidence to the police. He was so confu*sed*[zd] himself he didn't know who to arrest. Finally, he just le*ft*[f] both groups shooting at each other. He just couldn't figure out who was bad and who was good.

When we compare the relative effect of linguistic constraints on the pattern, we find that certain linguistic factors have a greater influence on variability than others. Thus, in some dialects of English, the influence of the following segment (the consonant versus nonconsonant) is more important than the cluster formation type (e.g., non-*ed* versus -*ed* clusters). When this situation occurs, the most influential constraint is referred to as the *first-order constraint*, the next most important, the *second-order constraint*, and so forth. The ordering of constraints may be likened to the relative effect of different social factors, where social status, age, and gender may all influence the relative incidence of cluster reduction, but not in equal proportions.

In many cases, linguistic constraints on variability can be ordered differently across varieties of English. Table 9–2 presents a comparison of word-final cluster reduction for different dialects of English, based on a sample of speakers in each population. As seen in Table 9–2, all of the varieties of English represented here show clusters to be systematically influenced by the following phonological context and the cluster formation type, although the proportional differences and the relationship between the linguistic constraints is not always the same. In some cases, such as Standard English and Appalachian Vernacular English, the influence of the

Table 9-2

Comparison of Consonant Cluster Reduction in Representative Vernacular Dialects of English

LANGUAGE VARIETY	Followed by Consonant		Followed by Vowel	
	Not -ed % Red.	-ed % Red.	Not -ed % Red.	-ed % Red.
Standard English	66	36	12	3
Northern White Working Class	67	23	19	3
Southern White Working Class	56	16	25	10
Appalachian Working Class	74	67	17	5
Northern Black Working Class	97	76	72	34
Southern Black Working Class	88	50	72	36
Chicano Working Class	91	61	66	22
Puerto Rican Working Class	93	78	63	23
Italian Working Class	67	39	14	10
American Indian Puebloan English	98	92	88	81
Vietnamese English	98	93	75	60

(from Wolfram 1986)

following consonant is more important than the cluster type, whereas in other cases, such as Southern White Working Class and Southern Black Working Class samples, the influence of the cluster type is a more important constraint than the following phonological context.

Exercise 4

As noted previously, the influence of the following consonant (i.e., a following word that begins with a consonant versus one that does not) is more important than the influence of the cluster type (i.e., base word versus -ed) for Standard English and Appalachian Vernacular English. At the same time, we observed that for Southern White Working Class and Southern Black Working Class varieties, the cluster type is more important than the following consonant. The ordering of constraints in relation to each other can be determined through a rather simple procedure. First, the scores in all the logical combinations of relevant linguistic contexts are listed in progressively descending (or ascending order) with the cross section of environments labeled in the row along side the frequency levels. For example, for Standard English and Appalachian Vernacular English, we find the following arrangement.

		Standard English	Appalachian Vernacular English
Followed by C,	not -*ed*	66 (high score)	74
Followed by C,	-*ed*	36	67
Not Followed by C, not -*ed*		12	17
Not Followed by C, -*ed*		3 (low score)	5

In labeling the progressive scores according to the combinations of linguistic subtypes, the consecutively listed linguistic category will be the higher-order constraint. For example, *followed by C* and *Not followed by C* are consecutively listed; therefore, the following consonant is the first-order constraint. If we apply this procedure to the cases of Southern White Working Class and Southern Black Working Class varieties represented here, we get the following progression.

		Southern White Working Class	Southern Black Working Class
Followed by C,	not -*ed*	56	88
Not Followed by C,	not -*ed*	25	72
Followed by C, -*ed*		16	50
Not Followed by C, -*ed*		10	36

Notice that in this listing, it is the "not -*ed*" factor that is consecutively listed rather than the following consonant; hence, this is the more important constraint.

Using the figures given in Table 9–2, apply this procedure to determine which linguistic constraint is more important for the following varieties: (1) Puerto Rican Working Class, (2) Chicano Working Class, and (3) Italian Working Class. Is the following consonant or non-*ed* (i.e., base word cluster) more important?

The analysis of linguistic constraints on variability can get much more sophisticated than the simple kinds of "raw" frequency tabulations and comparisons introduced here, as there now exist computerized programs for determining probabilistic figures of rule application for different kinds of linguistic constraints. These programs can take the analyst considerably beyond the level of statistical sophistication available through raw tabulations. While extended discussion of these software programs for calculating probabilistic figures is beyond the scope of this overview, the serious investigator interested in variation studies is obligated to learn such programs. For our purposes here, it is sufficient to recognize several fundamental insights about linguistic variation that have been derived from such an approach to systematic variation.

First, dialect differences are in large part reflected in the patterning of variability and quantitative differences. As a result, their characterizations must refer to this quantitative dimension. We must also recognize that there are important constraints on relative levels of frequency based on linguistic structure. The actual frequency levels associated with linguistic constraints are not as crucial as the relative effect that they have in favoring or inhibiting the operation of variable linguistic rules. Finally, our studies show that not all linguistic constraints are of equal value, as their effect may be *ordered* with respect to each other. In other words, some are more important than others in their effect on the fluctuation of forms. In the typical case of systematic linguistic variation, there are only a couple of major linguistic constraints on variability. More extensive analysis may reveal finer constraints, but the effect seems to be much diminished as these constraints become more detailed. The analysis of word-final consonant clusters we presented previously has been extended to include other linguistic constraints as well as following environment and cluster type discussed here (e.g., more detailed characteristics of the cluster), but these additional constraints tend to be much less significant by comparison with the effects isolated here. The investigation of linguistic constraints on variability reveals one of the subtle and complex ways in which dialect differences are systematically structured—a far cry from the casual observation that dialect speakers randomly "drop consonants" when they speak.

Before concluding our discussion of inherent variability, we should note that variability may combine with invariant forms in the delimitation of dialect patterning. Forms that fluctuate in one linguistic environment may become invariant, or categorical, in another one. In order to get a true picture of dialect distribution, it is important to understand this coexistence of variability and invariance. For example, there are many speakers of vernacular dialects who *always*, or categorically, use the singular forms *was/is* with plurals when the subject is the existential form *there*, as in *There's five people in the store*. At the same time, these speakers may fluctuate between singular and plural forms in other constructions, so that they may fluctuate between *was* and *were* in other constructions, such as *The men was in the room* and *The men were in the room*. In a similar way, *-in'* and *-ing* may fluctuate for some words in a person's dialect while *-ing* is categorically used with one set of words and *-in'* is used categorically with still another set of lexical items. Thus, a speaker may use only *-ing* with certain formal words (e.g., *reciting, pursuing*); the same speaker may use only *in'* with certain other informal words (e.g., somethin'). For a third set of words, the speaker would show fluctuation between *in'* and *-ing* as set forth earlier. Particular linguistic environments or even particular words may show an invariant pattern at the same time that other environments show true variability. An authentic description of dialect patterning must therefore separate special conditions of invariance from regular fluctuation influenced by linguistic and social constraints.

IMPLICATIONAL RELATIONSHIPS

The quantitative analysis of systematic variation is not the only way in which the orderly relationships of dialects can be viewed. Another way of looking at the relationship between varieties is through the combinations of language structures. The forms which differentiate one variety from another are often not distributed randomly throughout the system; instead, there may be *implicational relations* that hold within dialects.

An implicational relation in language holds when the presence of a particular characteristic of language implies the presence of another characteristic. When form *B* is always present whenever form *A* is present, we say that "*A* implies *B*." However, in an implicational relationship, the converse is not true, so that *B* may exist with or without the presence of *A*. This parallels the logical formula "if *A*, then *B*."

As an example of an implicational relation, consider the case of so-called copula deletion (i.e., the absence of the verb *be* in the present tense of forms such as *You ugly* (cf. *You're ugly*) or *He reading the book* (cf. *He's reading the book*). Varieties of American English not only differ in the existence and extent of copula deletion they show; they also may exhibit a systematic implicational relationship between copula deletion involving the forms *is* and *are*. Copula deletion of *is* necessarily implies the deletion of *are* but the converse is not true. In other words, if a variety of English shows the absence of *is* in sentences such as *He ugly*, it will also show absence in sentences with *are*, such as *You ugly*. However, a variety may have sentences such as *You ugly* without having sentences such as *He ugly*. An implicational array for this characteristic, displayed in both Vernacular Black English and Vernacular White Southern speech, is found in Table 9–3, where "*1*" stands for the presence of the characteristic (in this case, the operation of the copula deletion rule), and "*0*" the absence of the characteristic. The implicational relationship is indicated in Table 9–3 by setting up the table in such a way to read that the value "*1*" in a column implies the presence of "*1*" in columns to the right of it. Thus, a *1* in the *is* deletion column implies a *1* in the *are* deletion column to the right of it as well. In the table, each row represents a different variety of English in terms of the implicational relationships, including a variety of Vernacular Black English, Vernacular Southern White English, and Standard English, which has neither *is* nor *are* deletion.

Table 9–3

Implicational Relationship Between *IS* and *ARE* Deletion

Language Variety	IS Deletion	ARE Deletion
Standard English	0	0
Vernacular Southern White English	0	1
Vernacular Black English	1	1

The display in Table 9–3 shows that there are varieties of English which have neither *is* nor *are* deletion (many Standard English varieties), that there are varieties that have both *is* and *are* deletion (Vernacular Black English), and that there are still other varieties (some Southern White varieties) which have *are* deletion but not *is* deletion. There are, however, no varieties that have *is* deletion but not *are* deletion, as indicated by the way the "*1*s" and "*0*s" are set up in the table.

The implicational relationships that hold between structures in the dialects of American English can sometimes be much more complex than the simple case presented in Table 9–3, and may also incorporate a variable dimension. To give a slightly more extended case, we can look at the implicational relations that hold among different kinds of multiple negation. As it turns out, there are several different types of structures which can involve multiple negation. For our purposes here, we will identify three types: (a) the realization of the negative on indefinites following the verb phrase (e.g., In *They didn't go nowhere because they were too tired*, the indefinite *nowhere* comes after the verb phrase with *didn't*), (b) the realization of the negative on an indefinite before the verb phrase and placement of a negative within the verb phrase, as in *Nobody can't do it 'cause it's too hard*, and (c) inversion of a negative of the verb phrase and an indefinite before the phrase as in *Can't nobody do it 'cause it's too hard.*

In Table 9–4, three values are given with respect to the use of multiple negation, including categorical presence, categorical absence, and variation between presence and absence. This three-valued classification incorporates the variable dimension we discussed earlier. In the table, *1* means that multiple negation is used wherever it may be used, that is, it is *categorically present*; *0* means that it is never used, or *categorically absent*; *X* is added here to refer to variable application. *X*s may also have an implicational relationship with other *X*s in that an *X* in a column may be used to imply that a higher frequency level of the variant will be indicated in those *X*s to the right of the column. Various dialects of American English are delimited in terms of the combinations of rule applications, as indicated in the rows in Table 9–4.

Table 9–4

Implicational Array for Different Types of Multiple Negation in Selected Varieties of English

	Multiple Negation Type		
English Variety	*c*	*b*	*a*
Standard English	0	0	0
Some Northern White Vernacular Varieties	0	0	X
Other Northern White Vernacular Varieties	0	X	X
Some Vernacular Southern White and Black English	X	X	X
Other Varieties of Vernacular Black English	X	X	1

If a variety has type *c* multiple negation, then it will have type *b* and if a variety has type *b*, it will also have type *a*. However, the converse does not hold, so that *a* does not imply the existence of *b*, nor does *b* imply *c*.

Exercise 5

There are many types of regularization of subject-verb agreement patterns in English that show implicational relations. For example, if a dialect has (*a*) regularization of present tense *be* forms as in *We is here*, it will also have (*b*) regularization in past tense *be* forms, as in *We was here*. Furthermore, if a variety has past tense *be* regularization, it will have (*c*) regularization with the existential *there* as in *There's five of them*. (For convenience here, just label these types *a*, *b*, and *c*, as we did earlier.) However, the converse is not true, as it is possible for a dialect to have regularization of the existential (e.g., *There's five of them*) but not regularization with past tense (e.g., *We was here*), and so forth. Show this implicational relationship by setting up in a table as we have done previously. For the sake of this exercise, consider only the value *1* for this regularization pattern and *0* for the absence of this regularization pattern.

Several observations should be made about the application of implicational analysis to dialect patterning. First, we should note that not all speakers in a given speech community will conform to the ideal pattern. The fit between the ideal implicational pattern and the actual cases of language patterning is referred to as the *scalability*, or reproducibility of the implicational array. In the most simple computation (and some analysts think this is too simplistic to be useful), scalability is determined by dividing the number of nondeviant cells by the total number of filled cells in order to arrive at a percentage score. Each point of intersection between the rows and columns in the matrix is a cell so that Table 9–4, for example, has 15 cells. If there are 90 nondeviant cells out of 100 filled cases for a given group of speakers, the scalability score would be 90 percent. A score above 85 percent or 90 percent scalability is usually considered a reasonable level for establishing a valid implicational relationship.

Second, it is observed that implicational relationships among dialect structures are more systematic when the constellation of items represents subcategories within linguistically related structures rather than totally unrelated ones. Thus, subcategories of copula deletion show implicational relationships with each other and subtypes of multiple negation show implicational relationships with each other, but copula deletion may not show any real implicational relationship with multiple negation, as these represent unrelated structural sets.

Despite some limitations, the consideration of implicational relationships provides several important insights about dialect patterning. First, this model establishes a systematic basis for looking at the orderly relationships that exist among different dialects of English. This includes a basis for looking at how closely related dialects are to one another and the progression of language change. For example, our illustration of copula deletion shows a couple of steps in the orderly differentiation of Standard English, Vernacular Southern White English, and Vernacular Black English. Given these progressive steps, we may get a systematic indication of the relative distance between dialects. For example, we see in Table 9–3 that Vernacular Black English is closer to Vernacular Southern White English than it is to Standard English in its use of copula deletion, but that Vernacular Southern White English is closer to Standard English than Vernacular Black English.

The second insight relates to language change. As we have mentioned at various points in the previous chapters, language change is an ongoing, dynamic process that usually takes place in orderly stages. One way of observing various stages in the process of change is to look at implicational relationships. Typically, the implicational array captures the systematic sequencing of stages in the change, so that we can observe what steps may have preceded or what steps are likely to follow in the progression of the change. For example, consider the case of *h* in words such as *hit* [hIt] for *it* [It] and *hain't* [hent] for *ain't* [ent], forms still found to some extent in isolated regions of the United States such as Appalachia, the Ozarks, and some eastern coastal islands. At one point, *h* was invariantly found in these items when it occurred as the stressed syllable (e.g., *Hit's the one I like*) or the unstressed syllable (e.g., *I like hit*). The occurrence of *h* in these items then began to fluctuate (sometimes *h* occurred and sometimes it didn't) in unstressed syllables while it was still retained categorically in stressed syllables. Next, the *h* was variably lost in both unstressed and stressed syllables, but it was more frequently lost in unstressed syllables, where the change first started. Through time, the *h* was completely lost in unstressed syllables while maintained variably in stressed syllables. And finally, *h* was lost in both stressed and unstressed syllables categorically. The stages of this change are summarized in Table 9–5, using *1* to indicate the categorical presence of *h*, *X* to indicate variable presence, and *0* to indicate categorical absence. The implicational relationships between a column and columns to its right hold as we have presented them in our other implicational arrays.

Among American English dialects today, stages *3* and *4* are still represented in various isolated vernacular varieties and stage *5* is Standard English usage, where the loss of *h* is complete. As found in this example, aspects of dialect differences may represent ongoing change at different stages in its progression. Although this is a simplified picture, given other social and linguistic complexities, it provides a model of the progressive steps that typically characterize language change.

Table 9–5

Stages for Language Change in the Loss of *h* in (*h*)*it* and (*h*)*ain't* in American English

Stage of Change		*Unstressed Syllables*	*Stressed Syllables*
Stage 1	Earliest stage of English, before undergoing change	1	1
Stage 2	Earlier stage of English, at start of *h* loss	X	1
Stage 3	Change in full progress, still exhibited by some older speakers of isolated dialect areas	X	X
Stage 4	Change progressing towards completion exhibited by some current speakers in isolated dialect areas	0	X
Stage 5	Completed change, exhibited by most English dialects outside of isolated regions	0	0

Our survey of systematic patterning in dialects has been brief and, believe it or not, relatively nontechnical. It is sufficient, however, to demonstrate that dialect patterning within and across dialects can ultimately be very systematic and often rather intricate. Simplistic, categorical characterizations cannot come close to capturing the organizational detail that accounts for the constellation of structures making up the dialects of American English.

Further Reading

CHAMBERS, J. K. AND PETER TRUDGILL, *Dialectology*. New York, NY: Cambridge University Press, 1980. The section on "Mechanisms of Variation" reviews implicational scales and variable rules in a quite readable format. Chambers and Trudgill also consider the mechanisms of language change in more detail than that included in this chapter.

FASOLD, RALPH W., "Two Models of Socially Significant Linguistic Variation," *Language*, 46:55–563, (1970). This article was an early attempt to reconcile implicational analysis and variable rules as models for describing systematic variation in language. It remains one of the more reasonable discussions of these models.

HORVATH, BARBARA M., *Variation in Australian English: The Sociolects of Sydney*. Cambridge, England: Cambridge University Press, 1985. The chapter on analytical methodology in this description (Chapter 5) gives a brief programmatic overview of the steps in analyzing data on linguistic variation, as well as a description of principal components analysis, a statistical procedure for grouping speakers on the basis of linguistic similarity.

LABOV, WILLIAM, "Contraction, Deletion and Inherent Variability of the English Copula," *Language*, 45:715–762, (1969). As the initial presentation of variable rules, this article is historically significant in its launching of variation theory, although many of the original details of this formulation have been revised substantially over the years. The article is also reprinted as Chapter 3 in Labov's *Language in the Inner City* (1972a).

ROMAINE, SUZANNE, *Socio-Historical Linguistics: Its Status and Methodology*. Cambridge, England: Cambridge University Press, 1982. This book presents and critiques a number of the essential tenets of variation theory. It is a useful treatment for serious, more advanced students of language variation.

SANKOFF, DAVID, ed., *Linguistic Variation: Models and Methods*. New York, NY: Academic Press, 1978. Several of the articles in this collection deal with underlying issues related to the description of systematic variation in language. The regularly published articles from the annual *New Ways of Analyzing Variation* conference offer a convenient updating of continuing developments in variation theory, as does the journal *Language Variation and Change*, published by Cambridge University Press.

CHAPTER TEN

STANDARD ENGLISH AND EDUCATION

In the previous chapters we discussed important parameters related to the description of dialect variation in American society. For some dialectologists, this is a sufficient reason for studying dialects. Because dialects are highly fascinating, many dialectologists are content to spend their lives collecting and cataloguing examples of dialect forms. However valid this reason for studying dialects may be, many people still ask a basic utilitarian question: "What good is all this information on dialects anyhow?" I hope that this question already has been answered to some extent. If nothing else, an authentic respect for the integrity of language diversity and an appreciation for the complexity of the social role of language variation should have been developed by this point. But there is more. Educators may, for example, still want to know what value such information may have in an educational setting. Or parents may want to know how this information is relevant to their children's welfare. It is not even exaggerated to think that leaders in various levels of American society may want to know how such information bears on sociopolitical issues related to language.

In the final three chapters, we take up several different areas of *applied dialectology*. First, we return to the issue of spoken Standard English. This time, however, we examine this notion as an educational concern in our schools and society. Following that, we take up the critical question of dialects and language assessment; this is a pressing issue, given the role that testing plays in our lives. In the final chapter, we examine the role of dialect in language arts. We discuss the impact of dialects not only on the development of particular skills such as reading and writing, but also in terms of its potential as a resource to be tapped in enhancing language arts instruction.

STANDARDS AND ENGLISH

The discussion of standards of usage in the English language usually can be counted on to stir up a good debate. Most people have an opinion about the present state of Standard English and what should be done about it. Writers, teachers, and critics often lament the alleged demise of standards as if the state of Standard English were a symbolic indicator of a deeper moral issue in our society. More than once, someone has earnestly asked me if the "decline" of Standard English is not simply a reflection of declining morals in American society. To put this discussion in proper perspective, we must realize that this worry is hardly unique to present-day society. In fact, there is ample evidence that "authorities" complained about the supposed demise of English at least as far back as the fifteenth century. Concern for standards of usage in English has been with us a long time, and, in one form or another, is bound to remain with us.

To begin with, we need to understand that much of the popular discussion of dialects in American society actually stems from an underlying concern for the sovereignty of Standard English. Not surprisingly, media presentations typically focus on the educational obstacles posed by the use of vernacular dialects, and this coverage is often reduced to headline pronouncements such as "Black Kids Need Standard English" (William Raspberry, *The Washington Post*, October 1, 1986). In many educational circles, the basic reason for studying vernacular dialects is based on an assumption that knowledge about these dialect structures will lead to more effective instruction in the standard variety.

There are several different dimensions that make the topic of spoken Standard English controversial, and in some respects, also make it an elusive educational issue. One major issue involves the practical definition of spoken Standard English. What precisely is Standard English in a given community context, and who speaks it? Another area of concern is the status of vernacular dialects in relation to the standard variety. What happens to vernacular dialects when they confront the standard variety in different settings? Can a delicate balance between the appropriate uses of a vernacular and standard dialect coexist? Finally, there is the matter of methodology in teaching Standard English. Can Standard English really be taught effectively in an educational setting? Where and how is the standard variety best learned? Given the nature of the issues surrounding Standard English, it is not surprising that discussions of this topic can become quite heated. Unfortunately, these popular discussions are often filled with sociolinguistic misconceptions about the nature and significance of dialect differences. In the following sections, we discuss the major dimensions involved in teaching and learning spoken Standard English, and set forth the sociolinguistic context in which these issues exist.

WHAT STANDARD?

We already noted in Chapter 1 that the notion of Standard English operates on both a formal and informal level. The formal standard is codified, prescriptive, and relatively homogeneous whereas the informal standard is more subjective, somewhat flexible, and tends to exist on a continuum. Obviously, the formal standard is easier to define than the informal one, since we may simply appeal to established sources such as usage guides and established authorities on the English language for specific guidance. Even though there is no single central authority for the formal standard variety, there are not that many items over which there are persistent quibbles about the standard convention. The relevance of the formal standard, however, is relatively restricted, largely confined to writing and specialized public presentations. On the other hand, the informal standard is more widely applicable, and relevant to the vast majority of everyday language interactions. Furthermore, it is the informal standard, rather than the formal one, that most consistently governs people's everyday evaluation of the social significance of dialect differences.

Given the real-world heterogeneity of the spoken standard, we may ask if there is any way we can unify this notion, at least for instructional purposes. In an effort to unify the notion of spoken Standard English, the British linguist Peter Strevens, in the article "Standards and the Standard Language" (1985), separates *accent*, which refers to features of phonology, from other levels of dialect. He notes that accent is highly localized and variant, whereas other components of a language, particularly grammar, are less localized and less variant in terms of social norms of standardness. Once accent is eliminated from the definition of the standard language, he maintains that there is one standard which may be paired with any local accent. According to this definition, Standard English has no local base, and is the "only dialect which is neither localized in its currency nor paired solely with its local accent" (Strevens 1985:6).

There is certainly some merit to the separation of phonology from other aspects of dialect when talking about Standard English, but Strevens's proposal oversimplifies the issues. For one, there are aspects of pronunciation alone which may mark a person as a vernacular speaker, such as the frequent use of *d* for voiced *th* (the stereotypical *dese, dem*, and *dose* pattern), and the *t* for voiceless *th*, as in *trow* for *throw* or *tink* for *think*. In fact, we have cases where speakers are classified as nonstandard on the basis of phonology alone. By the same token, one locale's normative grammar may sometimes be considered nonstandard in another context. A grammatical construction such as the southeastern Pennsylvania's structure *I didn't know what for a car you had* or central Ohioans *The house needs painted* may be rated as nonstandard when used in other regions, even though they are part of the normative dialect within the local area. So we see that phonology is not always excused in the definition of the spoken standard, nor is grammar always generally applicable in judging standards across different regions. On the whole, however, grammar is less flexible than phonology in defining the standard, but it is a matter of degree rather than kind.

A couple of terms often used in reference to spoken Standard English in the United States are *Standard American English* (SAE) and *Network Standard*. The designation SAE is often used in comparison with other Englishes used throughout the world, such as Standard British English (the so-called Received Pronunciation, or RP), Australian English, and so forth. It is the variety strived for in teaching American English to speakers of other languages, and is the ideal model most often used as the basis for teaching standard varieties to vernacular speakers. The Network Standard simply seems to be a concrete example of SAE; it is the model aimed for by TV and radio announcers whose audiences are national in scope, in much the same way that BBC English is an instantiation of the RP pronunciation in the British Isles.

What exactly do people mean when they refer to SAE and Network Standard? Although these notions are difficult to pin down precisely, they typically refer to a variety of English devoid of both general and local socially stigmatized features, as well as regionally obtrusive phonological and grammatical features. This does not eliminate dialect choices altogether, however, as we have repeatedly noted that it is impossible to speak English without speaking some dialect of English. In those cases where dialect choices have to be made, the guiding principle calls for the selection of a form that will be least likely to call attention to itself for the majority of speakers outside of the area because of its dialect uniqueness. Items that have distinct regional connotations are therefore to be avoided in striving for SAE. Of course, the determination of what features are least likely to call dialect attention to themselves is somewhat subjective and tends to be a relative rather than absolute matter.

For example, the SAE pronunciation of the open *o* [ɔ] vowel in items like *caught* or *fought* would typically avoid a raised vowel quality (something closer to the [U] of *put*) or a lowered quality (something like the [a] of *father*), since these are likely to be dialectally marked. Interestingly, in actual network announcing, the latter pronunciation is apparently becoming more acceptable, as the low vowel merger of *caught* and *cot* spreads among American dialects. Whatever the case, the choice of the short *o* pronunciation is hardly dialect free. However, given the alternative pronunciations, the [ɔ] pronunciation is the least likely to call attention to regionality; hence, it is most dialectally unmarked. In this framework, some entire dialect areas will be considered more marked than others, so that entire regions may be singled out as dialects to be avoided in striving for the SAE ideal. The following is a fairly typical, somewhat stereotypical treatment of those dialects to be avoided in the pronunciation of SAE.

> In the U.S., three areas are traditionally singled out as being markedly different with regard to pronunciation both from each other and from the rest of the country. These three areas are Eastern New England, New York City, and the South. The rest of the country is surprisingly uniform with respect to major features of pronunciation. It is the pronunciation prevalent in this vast area that our description is aimed at . . . (Bauer, et al. 1984:2)

In reality, of course, many other regional and local vowel pronunciations have to be added to this inventory of avoided pronunciations in attaining SAE, such as the broad *a* of Philadelphia (e.g., *bad, pass*), the diphthong of *out* and *about* in many parts of the United States, and so on.

Regionally diagnostic grammatical features also have to be added to the list of excluded features in the production of SAE, so that items like positive *anymore* (e.g., *Anymore, we go to the movies a lot*), -ed complement with *need* (e.g., *The house needs painted*) might be avoided, even though they are certainly used by middle-class, educated speakers within particular regions. To the extent that it is possible, then, SAE strives to become the American dialect "from nowhere" in particular.

The attempt to deregionalize speech in SAE or Network Standard is, of course, easier said than done, and most speakers considered representatives of SAE still retain vestiges of their regional dialect. A comparison of nightly news programs will reveal that some network announcers are better than others at camouflaging their native regional dialect heritage; however, discerning dialectologists can usually still identify regional traces in pronunciation and lexical choice. In many cases, those who aspire to acquire this ideal standard have worked very hard to eliminate the most regionally obtrusive features. Manuals of instruction and so-called "accent reduction" training is available to help attain this goal, but in most instances, success in the SAE ideal remains a matter of degree rather than kind.

Contrary to popular opinion, the notion of SAE is fairly limited in terms of the occasions and professions that call for its usage; it is also quite restricted in terms of who routinely uses it. On most speaking occasions,

Regional Standard English is more pertinent than SAE, although this notion certainly receives much less public attention. Regional Standard English refers to the fact that, in a given locale, there exists a variety which is recognized as standard for the speakers of that community. This variety may contain regional features, particularly in pronunciation and vocabulary, but also some features of grammar and language use. At the same time, this standard differs from the regional vernacular in that it avoids both general and local socially stigmatized features of English. Most typically, it is associated with middle-class, educated native speakers of the region. In the local context, these speakers would be rated as Standard English speakers by community members from different social strata within the community.

In a Mid-South setting such as Memphis, Tennessee, this standard variety may include a number of southern regionalisms, such as the lack of contrast between [I] and [ɛ] before nasals in *pin* and *pen*, vowel diphthong ungliding in *time* or *Hi*, southern plural *y'all*, personal dative pronouns in *I got me a new outfit*, and so forth. The standard Philadelphia variety would not, of course, have any of these features, but might include the local broad *a* pronunciation (i.e., [ɛə] or even [Iə] in items like *bad* and *pass*, the vowel [i] in *-itude* items such as *att*[i]*tude* versus *att*[ə]*tude*, *magn*[i]*tude* versus *magn*[ə]*tude*), positive *anymore* (e.g., *Anymore we watch videos rather than go to the movies*), and pronoun absence in personal *with* phrases (e.g., *Are you coming with?*), among others. In both locales, the standard dialects would share the avoidance of a general set of socially stigmatized features such as multiple negatives and different irregular verb classes (e.g., *They seen it, They brang it to the picnic*), and so forth.

Regional standards are not necessarily transferable, so that the standard dialect for Memphis might not be considered standard in the context of Philadelphia and vice versa. To a large extent, the acceptance of a regional standard outside of its indigenous locale is tied in with attitudes and stereotypical views of the region by speakers from other areas. The difficulty in transferring regional standards from one area to another has sometimes concerned educators who wish to teach a Standard English, and, as mentioned earlier, there are privately available instructional programs specifically geared towards teaching SAE as a replacement for a regional standard. These programs may work with individuals or with small, select groups, but it is doubtful whether SAE can be taught to replace a regional standard on a broad-based scale. On a large-scale basis, such as a school system, this problem would be compounded by the fact that the majority of the instructors themselves probably would model in their speech the regional standard rather than SAE. We have more to say about the conflict between the regional standard and SAE when we discuss the practical considerations for instructional programs in Standard English. At this point, it is sufficient to understand the types of Standard English relevant to the discussion of spoken language standards in an educational context.

Exercise 1

From your personal background, can you think of standard features in your region that might be considered nonstandard outside of the area? What makes you think these features are considered nonstandard by speakers in other regions? In the context of your region, can you think of any advantages to using a regional standard as opposed to SAE?

APPROACHES TO STANDARD ENGLISH

In the late 1960s and 1970s an intense educational debate took place about the teaching of Standard English. This debate occurred in conjunction with the introduction of instructional materials specifically designed to teach Standard American English to vernacular dialect speakers, typically Vernacular Black English speakers. In the late 1970s, the debate subsided somewhat, as the initial phase of experimentation died down. In the mid-1980s, a revival of interest in materials to teach spoken Standard English again raised some of the same issues introduced a decade earlier. Although the new wave of materials is being introduced with somewhat less controversy, the issues initially raised a decade earlier have not gone away. In fact, in some ways, the recession of the debate is discomforting, for there remain critical issues about language education and cultural and linguistic diversity that need to be confronted honestly in any program designed to teach spoken Standard English to vernacular dialect speakers.

There are basically three different philosophical positions on the teaching of Standard English. One position maintains that Standard English should be taught as a *replacive* dialect, supplanting the dialect of vernacular-speaking students. This position, sometimes referred to as *eradicationism*, is the one manifested by educators who "correct" the nonstandard dialect forms of their students. Traditionally, much of the motivation for this position has been based on the conviction that vernacular dialects are simply linguistic corruptions of Standard English, following the popular mythology we discussed in Chapter 1. A more enlightened sociolinguistic viewpoint, however, still might maintain that the realities of present-day American society confer social stigma on speakers of a vernacular dialect in the mainstream marketplace, so even if a vernacular dialect is linguistically equal, it is not socially equal. Therefore, the vernacular variety should be replaced with the more socially acceptable, mainstream Standard English variety.

Another position on teaching Standard English maintains that Standard English should be taught as an *additive* dialect rather than a replacive one. This position is referred to as *bidialectalism*, by analogy with bilingualism, in which two separate languages are maintained. An educational curriculum with this goal is geared toward maintaining both the standard and vernacular variety for use in different social situations. For many community contexts, where the vernacular serves essential solidarity functions, the vernacular would be available. For more formal, mainstream marketplace functions, the nonstigmatized standard variety would be available. Like the eradicationist position, the bidialectal position recognizes the social stigmatization of vernacular dialects, but it rejects the notion that the vernacular dialect is an inferior linguistic system that needs to be replaced. Instead, it advocates the use of two different systems for different purposes within and outside the local community.

A more extreme position rejects the obligation to learn spoken Standard English at all, maintaining that both the eradicationist and bidialectal positions stand too ready to accommodate the dialect prejudices of American society. Rather than teach Standard English as a replacive or additive notion, the *dialect rights* position devotes attention to attacking the underlying ethnocentrism and prejudice that are at the heart of dialect intolerance. A subdivision of the nation's largest and most influential organization of English teachers, the National Council of Teachers of English (NCTE), adopted in 1974 a strong position on students' dialect rights, as follows:

> We affirm the students' right to their own patterns and varieties of the language—the dialects of their nurture or whatever dialects in which they find their own identity and style. Language scholars long ago denied that the myth of a standard American dialect has any validity. The claim that any one dialect is unacceptable amounts to an attempt of one social group to exert its dominance over another. Such a claim leads to false advice for speakers and writers, and immoral advice for humans. A nation proud of its diverse heritage and its cultural and racial variety will preserve its heritage of dialects. We affirm strongly that teachers must have the experiences and training that will enable them to respect diversity and uphold the right of the students to their own language. (College Composition and Communication, *Students' Rights of Language*, 1974, pp. 2–3)

Predictably, such a forceful position statement turned out to be quite controversial. It also proved to be vague in terms of its implications for teaching Standard English. A number of discussions from within and outside NCTE have attacked this position, and subsequent discussion has attempted to modify it and clarify the meaning of critical phrases such as "the rights of students to their own language."

While the dialect rights position may seem overstated and unrealistic to some, it rightly points to the unequal burden placed on vernacular speakers. The need for linguistic adjustment is placed squarely on vernacular speakers, when there should be an equally strong moral responsibility placed on the mainstream population to alter its prejudices and respect dialect differences for what they are—a natural manifestation of cultural and linguistic diversity. The dialect rights position may be morally right, but there is another issue to be confronted. Whether we like it or not, some type of language standardization seems inevitable. This conclusion comes not just from examining the situation in the United States or in English-speaking areas, but from surveying language situations throughout the world (see, for example, Fasold 1984). Given the fact that some kind of language standardization is bound to take place in English, as in other languages, the crux of the Standard English debate ultimately seems to involve balancing the inevitability of dialect diversity and standardization with the sociopolitical realities that confer the status of nonstandardness on nonmainstream, vernacular speaking groups.

PROSPECTS FOR SUCCESS

The previous discussion ignored a practical but essential factor in the consideration of teaching Standard English—the prospects for success. Is it really possible to teach spoken Standard English on a broad-based scale? So far, the evidence has not been very encouraging. No one denies individual cases of students from vernacular-speaking backgrounds who learn Standard English, but there is no indication that this is happening for large groups of speakers in our schools. Furthermore, it may be questioned whether the majority of the individual success stories can be attributed to specific instructional programs. We have to remember that, in one form or another, the educational system has been attempting to impart Standard English to its students for a long time, without apparent wide-scale success.

   Why is it that so many students from vernacular-speaking backgrounds obviously resist efforts to teach them Standard English? Although this question cannot be answered definitively, a couple of reasons for this resistance can be offered. Probably the most essential explanation is a sociopsychological one, in that dialect is such a strong indicator of social identity. Despite mainstream values stigmatizing vernacular dialects, there are positive values, often covert but sometimes not even that covert, which favor the vernacular dialect. The acquisition of spoken Standard English simply cannot be isolated from its social connotations, as some other academic subjects may be. There is an important difference in learning a set of facts about math or science, for example, and learning a Standard English language structure. When peer influences dictate vernacular dialect use to symbolize solidarity and identity, Standard English may become involved in an identity crisis. Notwithstanding the different contexts in which the respective varieties may be appropriate, students are still called on to choose symbolically between one or the other. And some of these occasions may take place right in the classroom. For many students, group reference norms simply overrule the values of the mainstream-oriented classroom. To use Standard English in the context of a roomful of vernacular-speaking peers may be an open invitation to ridicule by other students; I have collected many personal anecdotes about students being put down by their peers for using the standard variety, even in the context of a classroom.

There is also a dimension of language learning to consider in explaining why Standard English forms may be difficult even for motivated students who want to learn the standard variety. When two systems are highly similar, with minor differences, it is sometimes difficult to keep the systems apart. In these cases of wide-scale overlap, more careful attention to the small differences is required, especially if one way of speaking has been thoroughly habituated. In some ways, systems that are drastically different may be more easily confronted, since the temptation to merge overlapping systems and ignore relatively minor differences is not as great. Naturally, dialectologists tend to emphasize differences rather than similarities between dialects, but from an overall linguistic standpoint, standard and vernacular dialects show minor differences, and these differences may be difficult to overcome for a learner.

Once a linguistic structure is entrenched, it is difficult to break out of the pattern without paying careful, special attention to the details of the pattern. The special attention needed to do this, referred to as *monitoring*, is actually somewhat unnatural, given the fact that we do not ordinarily have to think about the structures of language in order to speak a language. In fact, excessive monitoring has its own set of problems; for example, too much monitoring can be disruptive to the normal fluency of relatively unmonitored speech, where we focus on what we are talking about rather than the structures we are using.

To remind impatient teachers of Standard English how difficult it is to reprogram a habituated linguistic pattern, I often relate my personal experience in attempting to rid myself of male pronoun forms for generic reference (i.e., the use of *he*/him in sentences such as *When a person studies dialects, he learns to appreciate the rich heritage of linguistic diversity in the United States*). It has now been over a decade since I resolved to eliminate this generic *he* pronoun from my speech, but careful observers of my speech still remind me that I have been far from successful in this seemingly simple language reprogramming endeavor. And this is just one linguistic structure! If we compound this task for the vernacular dialect speaker confronted by a number of structures to be monitored simultaneously, we can begin to understand the true linguistic challenge involved in learning Standard English. I can appreciate the frustration of one vernacular-speaking student who was highly motivated to learn Standard English, when she despaired, "It's just so hard to keep track of everything when you're just trying to talk!" This linguistic complication stands apart from the social significance of dialect choice, which is a sufficient factor in its own right.

The previous discussion is not meant to discourage efforts to teach or acquire Standard English if this is what a speaker desires, since I personally believe that students have a right to this variety just as they may have a right to their vernacular varieties. On this score, I agree with the linguist James Sledd, who has sometimes been singled out as opposing the teaching of Standard English because he wrote several polemical articles in the early 1970s in which he questioned the motives of "linguists for bidialectalism."

> Bureaucratic pretenses to the contrary notwithstanding, nobody has in fact opposed, or in any reason could oppose, the teaching of standard English, for the good ends and by good means, to students of any age who want to learn it. The question whether or not it should be taught is thus a spurious one . . . (Sledd 1976:236)

It may well be that the major issue surrounding Standard English instruction is not whether it should be offered or not, but what Sledd refers to as "the good ends and good means" which underlie its teaching. Notice also that Sledd qualifies his endorsement by limiting instruction to "students of any age *who want to learn it*." In the next section, we try to specify attributes that might typify a sociolinguistically and pedagogically sound instructional program.

CONDITIONS FOR TEACHING STANDARD ENGLISH

As concluded previously, the major issue in teaching Standard English seems to involve the appropriate conditions and means of instruction rather than the question of whether or not it should be taught. These conditions should offer a reasonable chance of succeeding at the same time they remain respectfully faithful to fundamental sociolinguistic premises underlying dialect diversity.

As a preliminary consideration, the *teaching of Standard English must take into account the group-reference factor*. The available evidence on second-language and second-dialect learning suggests a strong dependency on the sociopsychological factor of group reference for success. Speakers who desire to belong to a particular social group will typically learn the language of that desired group, whereas those with no group reference can be stubbornly resistant to change. Thus, vernacular speakers will best achieve success in learning Standard English if their social orientation is geared toward a Standard English-speaking group.

The group-reference dimension may be the most essential of all the factors affecting the learning of Standard English, but it is also the most difficult to program into pedagogical materials. Social network values and aspirations are typically not under the control of the educational system, and efforts to motivate students in terms of future, vague employment opportunities are often illusory and pretentious. Remember that the positive values of the standard dialect in mainstream culture are countered with a competing set of values for the vernacular—values that are often a lot more compelling for an adolescent than the pronouncements made by a classroom teacher. Any Standard English program with a realistic hope of success has to mold peer and indigenous community influence into a constructive force endorsing the standard variety. This is, of course, easier said than done, but there may be situations within the everyday lives of an indigenous peer group advantageous for the use of Standard English, and these must be exploited in the construction of a rationale for the standard variety.

At the very least, an instructional program in Standard English should involve an honest, open discussion of the values of both the vernacular and standard varieties of American English and relevant, concrete scenarios that might underscore the utility of both a vernacular and standard variety. The key here is the "immediate" need for Standard English in terms that are meaningful to the members of an appropriate reference group. This may seem like a preliminary activity to actual instruction, but students must feel within themselves, and reinforce in one another, that Standard English serves a useful purpose in their life. The reasons for learning Standard English must be examined closely from the honest perspective of the student, and, in some cases, such instruction can be offered as an optional program for those who see a need for it.

Exercise 2

Think of reasons why a junior high school student might want to know Standard English, *apart from the traditional educational values*. Try to imagine this from the perspective of a junior high school student who is not really thinking about future educational success and distant employment opportunity. What might it do for the students right now, in terms of people they interact with? Looking at it from such a vantage point, what do you conclude about the utility of Standard English at this point in their lives?

Once a program in Standard English is adopted, *the goals for teaching Standard English should be clearly recognized in the instructional program*. There are obviously quite different goals that might be incorporated into a Standard English program, ranging from the unidirectional establishment of Standard English in a restricted real-world context (for example, receptionist interactions, service encounters, and so forth) to the bidirectional maintenance of Standard English and vernacular English for a full set of social relations. The goals of a particular program should be transparent in the materials, and the pedagogical strategies should be consistent with these goals. Thus, if the stated goal of a program is functional bidialectalism in which both the standard and vernacular are maintained to serve different social purposes, then the materials should integrate this perspective pedagogically in a meaningful way. The program should incorporate language scenarios which start with the vernacular and move to the standard variety, and others that start with the standard and move to the vernacular as well. In this regard, it is interesting to note that many current instructional programs articulate the goal of bidialectalism as an educational ideal, but never support the notion with truly bidialectal instructional materials. Just as there are social contexts in which Standard English may be more appropriate, there are contexts in which vernacular dialects are more appropriate, and these differential social contexts must be squarely faced and evidenced in the materials if they are to capture the real-life significance of dialects in students' lives. How this is manifested is open to the creativity of materials and instructors in encouraging students to act out role playing or to engage in real-life scenarios that show this dialectal versatility. The bottom line consideration, however, is a program in which underlying educational goals and pedagogical strategy are in harmony.

Another principle that must be considered in teaching Standard English is *the need to couple information about the nature of dialect diversity in American society with pedagogical instruction in Standard English.* Given the level of misinformation and dialect prejudice existing in our society, there is a strong need to incorporate basic sociolinguistic information into instructional materials. This should include a basic understanding of how natural dialect diversity is, as well as an introduction to the sociolinguistic premises that lead to the development of dialects. Students should know that the reason they are learning Standard English is not related to the inherent inadequacy of their linguistic system or their presumed failure to learn "the English language." In all fairness, they have a right to understand that their own vernacular dialect is systematic and patterned—a linguistic if not social equal. Students have a right to know that all dialects are highly patterned and that the dialects of English differ from each other in systematic ways. Furthermore, they should be exposed to interesting sociolinguistic developments that have resulted in the present-day patchwork of dialects.

An understanding of basic sociolinguistic principles related to dialect differences can do two things for a student. First of all, it can provide a proper perspective on dialect diversity to counteract the popular misconceptions that presently abound. The obligation to present such adequate information seems no less than the educational obligation to present students with accurate information about chemistry and biology in the face of erroneous myths surrounding these subject areas. Students can never gain genuine linguistic self-respect unless they realize the sociopolitical basis of dialect inequality rather than simply assuming that the basis for dialect differences lies in an inherent linguistic deficiency. Furthermore, there is now an indication that students who feel more positive and confident about their vernacular dialect are more successful in learning the standard one. So there is also a pedagogical reason for presenting to students an accurate perspective on their own dialect. A second reason for incorporating information about the nature of dialect diversity is related to its high interest level. Learning about dialect differences piques a natural curiosity about cultural differences; presented properly, it is a fascinating subject in its own right. Whether or not students choose to learn Standard English, they deserve the opportunity to learn about English dialects as a part of general education. It is not a frivolous or tangential study, but one which presents a unique laboratory for scientific inquiry as well as social science and humanities study. We discuss this more in Chapter 12.

The incorporation of basic information about dialect differences into an instructional program in Standard English also gives it wider applicability, since this information is relevant to all students, not only those who speak vernacular dialects.

Exercise 3

Consider the following quotation, taken from an editorial by William Raspberry in the *Washington Post*, October 1, 1986. The article, entitled "Black Kids Need Standard English" takes the unequivocable position that vernacular-speaking students should be taught Standard English.

> And how could teachers help them [i.e. Vernacular Black English speakers] to acquire standard English without eroding their innate pride in Black culture?
> One retired teacher of my acquaintance used to do it by explaining that so-called Black English is nothing more than the language slaves learned from their ignorant white overseers.

How does this reasoning jibe with the facts of dialect diversity? What potential pitfalls do you see in such reasoning as a motivation for learning Standard English?

Another consideration in teaching Standard English is the *focus on systematic differences between the standard and nonstandard English forms*. Teaching Standard English is not identical to teaching a foreign language, where a speaker starts with no knowledge of the language. We have already noted that the similarities between the dialects of English far outnumber the differences, and this fact cannot be ignored in instructional materials on Standard English. Given the similarities and differences, it seems reasonable to organize materials which will highlight this systematic relationship between standard and nonstandard forms. Students do not need to learn the "English language"; they need to learn Standard English correspondences for particular socially stigmatized forms. Materials should take into consideration the systematic differences between standard and nonstandard correspondences, including the nature of the linguistic rule differences, the relative social significance of differences, and even how frequently particular stigmatizing forms might be expected to occur. In other words, the program should take advantage of current descriptions of vernacular dialects. This contrastive base must be taken into account regardless of the type of instructional method used to teach Standard English.

Although dialectologists tend to focus on the structural linguistic differences between standard and vernacular varieties, the teaching of Standard English cannot be limited to grammatical and phonological structures. *Functional uses of language also enter into the consideration of Standard English, and such dimensions must be incorporated into an effective program of instruction in Standard English.* In fact, many of the concerns about language expressed by those in the workplace turn out to be focused on *how* language is used rather than *what* particular nonstandard English linguistic structures are used. How people answer the telephone or engage in service encounters in the workplace is a vital concern to employers, and these often become central issues in cross-cultural and cross-regional interactions. The different regional and social group conventions for communicative encounters tend to be more responsible for interpersonal conflict than linguistic structures per se, so these conventions have to be included along with the incorporation of more narrowly defined linguistic structures. Conventional language routines such as greetings, leave taking, turn taking, and so forth, as well as particular speech acts such as denial, refusal, and so forth have to be considered as important components of the program. To underscore the significance of these conventions in the workplace, I often ask educators and employers which is preferable—a person who responds about the boss's whereabouts by saying *"She's not here. What do you want?"* or a person who replies with *"I'm sorry, she not in now. She be back this afternoon."* In practically every case, people prefer a person who comes across as "polite, but vernacular" to one who uses Standard English forms without adopting the appropriate conventions for carrying out various mainstream language functions.

Whether we like it or not, a program for teaching Standard English probably cannot be very successful without considering the broader conventions of language use and behavior. Such a program may move closer to a prescription of "appropriate" appearance and attire than most sociolinguists, including myself, feel comfortable with, but the overall context in which Standard English forms exist cannot naively disregard a full set of behavioral complements, including norms for carrying out various communicative functions.

Exercise 4

Suppose you were asked to design a broadly-defined Standard English program specifically for receptionists whose primary responsibility is to answer the telephone and take messages. What particular functionally-based routines and specialized language use conventions have to be included in this program? Are there any particular structural features that you might anticipate occurring fairly regularly in such a situation? In order to answer these questions, you will have to envision the kinds of interactions that ordinarily occur in this situation. Better yet, try observing actual telephone conversations that fit this description in order to accumulate real data.

In determining Standard English norms, it is important to point out that *the standard variety taught in an instructional program should be realistic in terms of the language norms of the community*. Repeatedly, I have pointed out that the definition of spoken standard English is a flexible one, sensitive to regional variation, stylistic range, and other social and ethnic variables. The reality of general Standard American English is not going to prove very useful to a classroom of students who speak a Gulf South or Eastern New England dialect in varying stages of nonstandardness, particularly if this class is likely to be instructed by a local teacher speaking a standard version of the local regional variety. It's ironic that instructors in the South should attempt to get a classroom of school children to make the distinction between [I] and [ɛ] in *pin* and *pen* when the instructor, a standard southern dialect speaker, does not maintain the distinction. Similarly, I have witnessed a New England speaker pontificating about the need to "put in your *r*'s" while pronouncing the word letter *r* without the postvocalic *r* (i.e., [az] for *r's*). Apart from the difficulty instructors may have in teaching dialect uses they do not maintain themselves in their regional standard, it seems futile to attempt to rid vernacular speakers of local standards on a wide-scale basis. There is very little realistic hope of success if a program in Charleston, South Carolina sets out to make Standard English speakers sound like they now come from the Midwest. I noted earlier that there are individual cases in which this external standard norm is attained, but they seem to be restricted and idiosyncratic. Besides, these speakers run the risk of coming across as pretentious and "phony" in their native region.

The admission of local standard norms in a program of instruction does not necessarily rule out generally applicable materials, since there are many aspects of social differentiation in grammar that cut across regional varieties. This concern does, however, imply that items selected for direct instruction should represent the broadest-based socially stigmatized items at the same time the instructional program allows for regional flexibility.

This flexibility will naturally be greatest with respect to pronunciation, but may include dimensions of grammar, vocabulary, and language use as well.

Finally, current materials in Standard English instruction *should take into account our current understanding of how a second dialect is acquired.* At this point, there is considerable debate about how a second dialect is acquired, and the extent to which an alternate dialect can actually be mastered once the native dialect has been acquired. Our knowledge about acquiring a second language is much more advanced than our knowledge of second-dialect acquisition, so that we might turn to studies of second-language acquisition for models of development. In doing so, however, keep in mind the clear-cut differences in second-language and second-dialect acquisition. Programs for teaching a standard dialect have been heavily influenced by second-language instructional models and methods in recent decades, but most Standard English materials have not kept up to date with the rapid development of second-language acquisition models in more recent years.

One of the early adaptations of second-language techniques found in second-dialect materials is the use of *contrastive drills.* A typical contrastive approach relies heavily on five different kinds of drills, which tend to be sequenced as follows:

1. *Discrimination drill.* In this drill a standard structure is contrasted with a non-standard one in order for students to clearly detect the difference between a standard and nonstandard variant. Sentence pairs are given, and subjects are asked simply to identify the sentences as the same or different. A typical drill for *-s* third person would look something like the following:

Stimulus Pair	Subject Response
She works hard.	different
She work hard.	
She play after school.	same
She play after school.	
She comes home late.	same
She comes home late.	

2. *Identification drill.* In an identification drill, labels are given to the standard and vernacular varieties, usually euphemisms such as "formal" and "informal" or "school" and "home," and the subjects are asked to identify the standard and nonstandard version of the same sentence, as follows:

Stimulus	Response
She works hard.	formal
She work hard.	informal

3. *Translation drill.* In this drill, a stimulus is given in one dialect and the subject responds by giving the corresponding sentence in the other variety. In a truly

bidialectal program, this translation task goes from the nonstandard to standard, and conversely, from the standard to nonstandard dialect.

Stimulus	Response
She work hard.	She works hard.
She works hard.	She work hard.

4. *Substitution drills.* In substitution drills, a structure in the stimulus is systematically exchanged with one in a responsive reply, while holding constant the standard or nonstandard version of the original sentence.

Stimulus	Response
Wanda work hard.	She work hard.
Wanda works hard.	She works hard.

5. *Response drills.* The various types of response drills require a subject to change the format of the sentence in the response, while again matching the standard or nonstandard version given in the stimulus. For example, one version of this drill may use a positive stimulus with a negative response, as follows:

Stimulus	Response
Wanda works hard.	No she doesn't.
Wanda work hard.	No she don't.

Exercise 5

Using the structure of -*s* plural absence on nouns of weights and measures (e.g., *We have four acre/We have four acres*), construct a set of drills that typifies each of the types given previously. Give a couple of sentences illustrating each type.

Many standard dialect materials have depended on these or similar kinds of drills as a central component in the instructional program. The advantage of such drills is their direct, contrastive focus on those items that systematically differ in the standard and vernacular variety. For a motivated student, this kind of drill certainly raises the level of consciousness about the structural differences of the standard and nonstandard variants. There are, however, practical and theoretical concerns that have to be raised about these kinds of drills. On a practical level, they can be very boring and students lose interest rapidly unless they are highly motivated to begin with. Certainly, the level of self-motivation this kind of activity must assume precludes its usage in a regular classroom situation. Even when complemented with higher-interest activities, the routine of the drills can become tiresome in a hurry. In most cases, then, the practical limitations of these drills are quite severe.

Developing research in second-language acquisition also casts doubt on the role of direct contrastive drills as an effective language learning strategy. In second-language acquisition studies as they have developed over the last decade (Krashen 1982; Krashen et. al. 1982), an important distinction is made between language acquisition and language learning. *Language acquisition* involves tacit or implicit knowledge of language rules and tends to come forth automatically, whereas *language learning* is the explicit knowledge of rules, which tends to come forth under certain conditions involving increased awareness of speech (so-called monitoring). Acquisition, rather than learning, is responsible for fluency in a second language, and too much explicit learning of language rules can even interfere with second-language fluency, as a speaker may tend to overmonitor speech. This hypothesis would seem to have important implications for second-dialect acquisition. Contrastive drills tend to rely on explicit learning rather than the tacit rule knowledge characteristic of acquisition. This approach may serve a person adequately when speech is being heavily monitored, as in language testing or deliberative writing, but it may break down in less monitored, more natural situations. Thus, a heavy dose of more naturalistic uses of language with Standard English forms might prove to be more effective in the acquisition of Standard English than reliance on the kind of explicit learning that takes place in structural drills. Of course, we cannot assume that acquiring a second dialect is identical to acquiring a second language, and it may well be that the overwhelming similarities of two dialect systems leave little alternative but to focus on the finer points of differentiation that are targeted through these kinds of drills.

Unfortunately, we do not have exhaustive research data on the ideal conditions under which a standard variety is acquired as a second dialect. Case studies of native vernacular speakers who have acquired a standard variety, however, underscore the motivational factor rather than pedagogical technique. The set of strategies used for successful acquisition includes "immersion" in a Standard English speaking context, mimicry of personal and impersonal Standard English models, explicit drill techniques, and even traditional prescriptive "correction." A guaranteed pedagogical strategy has not yet emerged in teaching Standard English. We would, however, expect a reasonable instructional approach, at the very least, to be consistent with fundamental sociolinguistic premises.

AGE OF ACQUISITION

In the preceding discussion, we did not mention the optimal age for second-dialect acquisition. This is often a primary consideration for educators. Some programs, taking a cue from the apparent naturalness of second-language acquisition during the preadolescent period, feel that the optimal program should focus on children in their early years of schooling. Certainly, there is evidence that native-like control of a language, particularly with respect to phonology, is realistically only achieved prior to the "critical period" of development, the prepubescent period. The study of second-dialect acquisition (Payne 1980) also shows a similar cut-off period for dialect shift, although some adjustment apparently takes place after this period. At the same time, there is evidence that Standard English grammar certainly can be acquired after this period, and selective changes in socially stigmatized phonological features can also take place. Thus, the "critical age hypothesis" about language acquisition is not nearly as imposing for acquiring Standard English as it is for acquiring another regional variety of English. This is particularly true if we admit regional Standard English pronunciation as a reasonable goal of the instructional program. Remember here that this case may require considerable adjustment of the system, but it does not call for a complete overhaul.

A strong argument against teaching Standard English in the earliest years of a child's education comes from the sociopsychological considerations stressed so much in this chapter. Children may learn Standard English forms when presented in primary education, but will these forms persist in the face of strong peer pressure as these children move into adolescence? Will these structures remain when they are assaulted by the vernacular dialect spoken by their peers? There is a good chance that the speech of a student's peers will preempt other considerations in the formative adolescent and teen-aged years of dialect development, regardless of what took place in school prior to that time. I still recall my son's comment when I casually asked about a marked change in his speech toward a more vernacular dialect in his teen-aged years. His spontaneous remark could not have been more candidly indicative of the emerging significance of his "jock" peer speech model, as he said, "Dad, I can't stand talking proper! You sound like such a sissy."

Due to the severity of the sociopsychological factors, some sociolinguists feel that success in teaching spoken Standard English will only come if and when a person realizes the utility of this dialect on a very personal level. In most cases, this heightened, personal awareness of the uses of Standard English in the broader marketplace does not take place until early adulthood. After years of informal and formal programs to teach spoken Standard English, there is still no evidence that it can really be imposed against a student's will. However, where there's a will, there are probably a number of different ways to attain this dialect goal. Thus, the role of instructional programs is best viewed as facilitating this process for motivated students by providing systematic and relevant opportunities to move toward the desired Standard English goal. This observation is not meant to denigrate the many well-intended programs that currently exist, but simply to place them in their proper sociolinguistic perspective. Sometimes the truth hurts! But an honest acknowledgment of what we are up against in teaching Standard English must set the stage for establishing any sociolinguistically meaningful educational program in the standard variety.

Further Reading

BRANDES, PAUL D. AND JEUTONNE BREWER, *Dialect Clash in America: Issues and Answers*. Metuchen, NJ: The Scarecrow Press, 1977. Part 2 ("Possible Solutions to the Dialect Clash") and Part 3 ("Suggested Solutions to Specific Problems Caused by Dialect Clash") of this book deal with the practical ramifications of dialect diversity in an educational setting. A case study approach is used to highlight the practical nature of the dialect "clash."

FASOLD, RALPH, *The Sociolinguistics of Language*. Oxford, England: Basil Blackwell, 1989. The final chapter of this book, "Some Applications of the Sociolinguistics of Language," covers a number of educational implications that result from the consideration of language variation. The approach to the application of sociolinguistic knowledge is quite similar to that found in this treatment.

MILROY, JAMES AND LESLEY MILROY, *Authority in Language: Investigating Language Prescription and Standardization*. London: Routledge & Kegan Paul, 1985. This book offers an historical and contemporary commentary on the problem of prescription and "correctness" in English. The presentation shows how the notion of standard language has affected a wide range of practical issues in society.

STREVENS, PETER, "Standards and the Standard Language," *English Today No. 2* (April 1985), pp. 5–8. This brief article offers a fresh perspective on language standards and Standard English. The journal *English Today*, published in the United Kingdom, often contains articles on standards of English from varying vantage points.

TAYLOR, ORLANDO L., "Standard English as a Second Dialect," *English Today No. 2* (April 1985), pp. 9–12. In this article, Taylor overviews the framework for teaching Standard English in a school setting. It provides a philosophical and procedural skeleton for implementing a program to introduce Standard English.

WOLFRAM, WALT AND DONNA CHRISTIAN, *Dialects and Education: Issues and Answers*. Englewood Cliffs, NJ: Prentice Hall, 1989. This work directly deals with the most common educational questions about dialects and standards in a question-answer format. It is intended primarily for practitioners who confront the practical manifestations of dialect divergence in an educational context.

CHAPTER ELEVEN

DIALECT AND TESTING

The importance that mainstream American society places on testing is fairly obvious to anyone with the slightest sense of recall. In fact, standardized testing probably could be added to the small list of inevitables in our society, such as taxes and death. Before we entered elementary school, we were given a battery of tests to determine our readiness for school, including a speech and language screening test to measure if our language was developing normally. Throughout our elementary and secondary education, standardized achievement tests were administered at regular intervals. Among the academic areas measured in these tests was the area of "language usage," which determined our progress in the recognition of "correct" English. Our preparedness for college was further evaluated on the basis of the Scholastic Aptitude Test, in which one major score was computed for "verbal skills" and another score computed for the "Test of Written Standard English."

Many standardized tests directly tap dimensions of language form and use, but language issues with respect to testing extend considerably beyond test items focused on language per se. The language in which directions are given, the language register used to tap information in other content areas, and even the language used in the interaction between test administrators and test takers establish an essential sociolinguistic dimension for tests regardless of the subject area. No area of testing is really safe from considerations of language.

There are, of course, many different vantage points for scrutinizing the validity and reliability of testing instruments, but we limit ourselves here to issues related to dialect diversity and the sociolinguistic context of testing. A sociolinguistic perspective informs us about three critical dimensions of testing: (1) the definition of "correctness," or the normative linguistic behavior that serves as a basis for evaluating responses to test items, (2) the peculiar way in which language is used as a medium to tap different kinds of behavior in a test, and (3) the sociolinguistic situation in which testing takes place. The first area involves an understanding of dialect differences since the focus is on norms taken from some dialect of English, usually the standard dialect. The second area more typically involves an understanding of specialized language uses, as the focus is on language as a medium to access data. The third area involves more broadly-based issues of language socialization and underlying sociolinguistic values. In the overall effect on test performance, all three dimensions may play a significant role, although differences in structural form tend to be the most transparent when it comes to dialect and testing.

CORRECTNESS AND DIALECT

The identification of a *correct* or *normative* response is essential to success in most types of standardized tests. In some cases, this definition of linguistic correctness is based on response data collected from sample populations used to standardize testing instruments—typically middle-class majority populations which use a variety of Standard English. In other cases, the definition of correctness is not based on data obtained from sample populations at all, but is based instead on the opinions of prescriptive language authorities who determine what the ideal standard form is to be—usually Formal Standard English in our earlier definition. There is considerable latitude in classifying "incorrect" responses, but the traditional notion of correctness historically used in standardized testing instruments has usually been restricted to items characterizing the standard dialect in its real or ideal state.

LANGUAGE ACHIEVEMENT

One of the clearest examples of the impact of dialect differences on standardized test instruments comes from the kinds of achievement tests given to students at regular intervals in their educational progress. For example, consider how the notion of correctness is defined in several examples taken from a language use section of an achievement test. The examples in this case come from a version of the California Achievement Test given to lower-level elementary school students. The directions for choosing a response simply instruct the student to identify one of the items in the brackets that "you think is correct."

1. Beth $\begin{Bmatrix} \text{come} \\ \text{came} \end{Bmatrix}$ home and cried.

2. Can you $\begin{Bmatrix} \text{went} \\ \text{go} \end{Bmatrix}$ out now?

3. When $\begin{Bmatrix} \text{can} \\ \text{may} \end{Bmatrix}$ I come again?

In each of these three cases, the "correct" form is the standard one. The incorrect choice, however, includes several different kinds of "distractors." In sentence 1, the choice is between a standard dialect variant and a vernacular dialect variant. The use of the bare root form *come* as an irregular past tense form is quite common in a number of vernacular dialects (e.g., *Beth come home and cried*), whereas *came* is the standard dialect past tense form. In this sentence, incorrect is simply defined as a vernacular dialect form.

In sentence 2, the choice is between a form acceptable in *both* standard and vernacular dialects and one unacceptable in these varieties. In other words *Can you go out now?* is a well-formed standard and vernacular dialect form and *Can you went out now?* is unacceptable in both varieties. In this case, the choice is between a linguistically well-formed, or *grammatical* sentence as defined in Chapter 9, and a linguistically ill-formed sentence, or *ungrammatical* sentence, regardless of the dialect.

The differentiation between a correct and incorrect response in sentence 3, unlike 1 and 2, seizes upon the distinction between a formal standard variant and an informal standard one. In informal spoken Standard English, most speakers would say *When can I come again?* (reflecting a natural semantic expansion of the model *can* to include both capability and permissibility). In the case of sentence 3, the contrast is therefore between an ideal prescriptive Standard English form (*may*) and an informal spoken language standard one.

What do these different notions of correctness and incorrectness mean for speakers of different dialects, in particular, for the vernacular and standard dialect speaker respectively? For sentence 1, vernacular speakers relying on knowledge of their language rules would choose the incorrect response, whereas a standard speaker relying on this same knowledge would make the correct choice. In this regard, the linguistic knowledge of the rules of vernacular dialects found in the Appendix can be used to understand why vernacular speakers might systematically select "incorrect" answers. In order to make the correct choice for this sentence, the vernacular speaker must make a counterintuitive linguistic choice and select a *socially acceptable* Standard English structure instead of a *linguistically well-formed* vernacular structure. In this respect, we see that there may be very different tasks involved in responding to this item for a native vernacular dialect speaker and a native Standard English speaker. Perhaps more importantly, the confusion between linguistic acceptability and social acceptability brings us back to the erroneous assumption about vernacular dialects widely held in some educational circles: forms that do not agree with rules of Standard English violate basic rules of grammar, that is, they are "ungrammatical." We see that this mythology about the nature of dialect differences, discussed originally in Chapter 1, has worked its way into the definition of correctness built into a standardized language achievement test.

For sentence 2, reliance on knowledge of language rules should result in a correct response for both the vernacular and standard speaker, other things being equal, since the incorrect item is linguistically unacceptable across dialects. For sentence 3, however, reliance on such knowledge would lead to an incorrect response by both a vernacular and standard speaker, since the item tests a prescribed formal structure not typically an integral part of the standard or vernacular variety. In this case, both standard and vernacular test takers would have to resort to explicitly learned knowledge about formal Standard English to obtain the correct response.

A survey of representative language achievement tests given to students in early schooling shows that many of the test items focus on the first notion of correctness—the simple distinction between vernacular and standard dialect forms. In the California Achievement Test from which the preceding examples were taken, 14 out of 25 total sentences in the section entitled Language Usage focus exclusively on this distinction. The distinction between formal and informal standard (as in sentence 3) is not so critical in early achievement testing, but it becomes much more prominent as students proceed to the higher levels of education; it is rampant in tests such as the Scholastic Aptitude Test.

Exercise 1

Following are additional items from an achievement test. Identify the focus of each item in terms of the three dimensions of correctness discussed earlier: (1) standard versus vernacular sentence structure, (2) grammatical versus ungrammatical structure regardless of the dialect, and (3) formal Standard English versus informal Standard English sentence structure.

1. My sister $\left\{ \begin{array}{c} \text{am} \\ \text{is} \end{array} \right\}$ six years old.

2. She will give me $\left\{ \begin{array}{c} \text{them} \\ \text{these} \end{array} \right\}$ dolls.

3. I $\left\{ \begin{array}{c} \text{shall} \\ \text{will} \end{array} \right\}$ go there tomorrow.

4. I $\left\{ \begin{array}{c} \text{am} \\ \text{are} \end{array} \right\}$ a good pupil.

5. There $\left\{ \begin{array}{c} \text{was} \\ \text{were} \end{array} \right\}$ no ducks on the lake.

6. Is George going to eat with $\left\{ \begin{array}{c} \text{us} \\ \text{we} \end{array} \right\}$?

7. Father and $\left\{ \begin{array}{c} \text{they} \\ \text{them} \end{array} \right\}$ are going on a trip.

The examination of standardized language achievement tests clearly shows that such tests are often obsessed with recognizing Standard English forms. Assessing whether or not a student can recognize Standard English is not, in itself, a problem, especially if an educational system incorporates the systematic introduction of the standard dialect into its educational curriculum. It is, however, problematic as an overall measure of achievement, since it may measure different things for different groups of speakers. For a standard speaker, an achievement test may measure what the student, for the most part, already brings to school from the home community—inner language knowledge of the standard dialect. For a student from a vernacular dialect introduced to the standard dialect, it actually may measure an aspect of achievement—the ability to recognize standard dialect forms after the student has been introduced to Standard English forms. The underlying problem, then, is in the comparison of standard and vernacular speakers as if both groups started from the same linguistic baseline.

One of the recurring questions that surfaces with language tests of all types centers on the matter of *content validity*: Does the testing instrument measure the content area it claims to measure? As we have seen, a test might measure quite different language capabilities for different dialect groups. Thus, vernacular speakers who have learned to recognize some forms in the standard dialect may have made significant educational progress, yet still score well below Standard English speakers who get credit for achievement when they are simply resorting to language knowledge they brought to school to begin with. Those who construct such tests and those who interpret the scores of these tests must be careful to determine what the test actually measures in relation to what it claims to measure, particularly since language usage tests so often emphasize the standard-vernacular distinction.

SPEECH AND LANGUAGE DEVELOPMENT TESTS

As children develop, they are routinely assessed in a number of areas of behavior, including "speech and language." The purpose of such testing is fairly straightforward—to determine if children are acquiring their language at a normal rate of development. Virtually all children are screened initially for speech and language development before entering school for the first time, and, on that basis, they are recommended for more extensive diagnosis and subsequent classification as "normal" or "disordered." If they are judged as disordered, they are typically enrolled in a speech and language therapy program, so that the consequences of the diagnostic procedure can be quite significant. Because of such wide-scale assessment of children for speech and language, there are many formal standardized instruments which have been developed to measure the normalcy of linguistic development. Unfortunately, the definition of normal development traditionally has been based on the norms of the Standard English speaking population, as middle-class samples of children typically have been used to arrive at developmental norms.

The definition of normative responses exclusively in terms of Standard English structures holds considerable potential for *dialect discrimination*, where a normative response in a non-Standard English dialect is erroneously classified as an unacquired Standard English form. For example, a testing instrument frequently used to measure language development is the Grammatic Closure subtest of the Illinois Test of Psycholinguistic Abilities (ITPA). This test claims to assess "the child's ability to make use of the redundancies of oral language in acquiring automatic habits for handling syntax and grammatic inflections" (ITPA 1968:7), but many of the items actually focus on differences between standard and vernacular dialect forms. In this assessment procedure, the examiner points to appropriate pictures while reading a statement, stopping at the point where the child is to fill in the missing word(s). For example, the child may be shown two picture frames, one with one bed and another with two beds, while the examiner says, "Here is a bed, and here are two _____." The child then completes the utterance, with a correct response in this case being the plural form *beds*. In scoring the test according to the procedures set forth in the test manual, only Standard English forms are considered as "correct" responses. For example, consider several of the items from the test; the response scored as correct is given in italics and all other responses are considered incorrect, or "not acquired."

Item 3. Each child has a ball. This is hers and this is *his*.
Item 6. The boy is opening the gate. Here the gate has been *opened*.
Item 14. He wanted another cookie, but there weren't *any/anymore*.

As with the achievement tests discussed previously, an understanding of dialect differences reveals that many of the forms scored as "incorrect" constitute linguistically well-formed structures in terms of vernacular dialect norms. For example, item 3 might legitimately be rendered as *hisn* by an Appalachian English speaker, item 6 might be rendered as *open* by a Vernacular Black English speaker who applies the consonant cluster reduction rule, and item 14 might be given as *none* or *no more* by speakers representing a broad range of vernacular dialects. All of these alternate responses meet the norms of adult vernacular-speaking communities, yet they are considered nonnormative, and therefore "incorrect" answers according to the standard scoring procedures.

Exercise 2

Following are five more items from the ITPA Grammatic Closure subtest. Based on the kinds of dialect rules found in the Appendix, predict which of these items might have legitimate dialect alternates. What are the variant dialect forms? Refer to the dialect rules in the Appendix in your response. The response considered correct according to the manual is given in italics.

Item 9. The boy is writing something. This is what he *wrote/has written/did write*.
Item 15. This horse is not big. This horse is big. This horse is *bigger*.
Item 19. This is soap, and these are *soap/bars of soap/more soap*.
Item 22. Here is a foot. Here are two *feet*.
Item 29. The boy has two bananas. He gave one away and he kept one for *himself*.

In some cases, the effects of imposing standard norms of development on vernacular speakers can be quite severe. For example, in the case of the Grammatic Closure subtest, over 20 of the 33 items have legitimate dialect variants. If the test is scored at face value, a normally developing child who uses dialect variants where possible would look like a linguistically delayed Standard English speaker. A normally developing 10-year-old vernacular speaker may, in fact, be assessed as having the linguistic development of a child less than five years of age. On the basis of such a discrepancy between chronological and "psycholinguistic" age, vernacular-speaking children commonly have been enrolled in therapy, even though they are developing quite normally in terms of their community dialect.

PREDICTING DIALECT INTERFERENCE

The model of language analysis typically used to determine the points at which a test may be affected by dialect diversity generally follows the procedures set up in contrastive linguistics. In its most simple version, *contrastive linguistics* places the rules of language variety X and language variety Y side by side, and on the basis of comparing similarities and differences in the systems, points out areas of potential conflict for a speaker of X confronted with the norms of Y. This is the procedure we employed earlier when we compared the correct responses of a test normed on Standard English speakers with the rules of vernacular varieties, and determined where alternate responses might be expected due to differences between systems. Over the past two decades, a number of major language assessment instruments have been examined from this perspective. However, it is necessary to balance ideal predictions of dialect interference with actual studies of a speaker's performance. In this type of empirically-based *error analysis*, some of the predicted structures show up much more frequently than others. Furthermore, there are other "incorrect" responses that may be attributed to dialect differences, but not in a direct way. And there may be items that turn up that are not predictable based on a simple side-by-side comparison of language varieties.

There are a couple of reasons why not all predicted dialect variants may occur in the assessment procedure. Many of the predicted dialect alternates may be variable structures, as discussed in Chapter 9, rather than categorical ones. For example, we might predict plural -*s* absence for a Vernacular Black English speaker in a formal test, but vernacular speakers typically show plural absence levels of between 10 percent to 20 percent when actual levels of absence are tabulated in relation to those cases where a plural form might be absent. Certainly, we would expect this inherent variability to have an effect on the response; presumably, a low-frequency dialect item will have a lower probability of occurring as an alternate than a high-frequency one. It is also possible that the formality of the testing situation may bring forth responses not directly predictable, as speakers may shift away from their native forms in sometimes erratic ways. For example, a test taker sensitive to the social stigmatization of a vernacular verb agreement pattern such as *We was there* might compensate by extending *were* usage beyond its specified limits using a form such as *I were there*. This form follows neither the standard nor vernacular dialect rule, as the vernacular dialect rule generalizes *was* to cover both *was* and *were*, not *were* for *was* and *were*. This is a special kind of hypercorrection as discussed in Chapter 7, due no doubt to the special formality related to the testing situation. Indirectly, we may attribute this usage to the dialect, but not as a case of simple transfer of a vernacular dialect form in place of a standard dialect one.

Although all predicted dialect forms will not occur in an actual test, studies of the incidence of dialect forms in relation to predicted forms indicate that these dialect variants may still account for a significant portion of "incorrect" responses. In several empirical studies, over 50 percent of predicted dialect alternates have been found to occur (King 1972).

TESTING LANGUAGE

The concern for dialect differences in language testing actually raises deeper questions about the conventional instruments used to assess language capability. Most standardized language assessment instruments focus on restricted domains or levels of language, raising the question of content validity mentioned earlier. In the case of tests constructed to assess language development, we may ask if the selective language capability measured by the instrument adequately represents the language content it proposes to measure. For example, consider how a traditional assessment instrument like the Peabody Picture Vocabulary Test (PPVT) measures "word knowledge" in relation to the linguistic definition of this concept. In the PPVT, "knowing a word" is defined by the test taker's ability to associate a word label given by a test examiner with a pictorial representation of the object or activity, given a multiple choice of pictures (e.g., "Show me *toboggan*"). This notion of word knowledge involves a passive recognition task limited to items that are sometimes culturally specific and dialectally restricted. From a broader linguistic perspective, however, knowing a word involves at least the following: (1) syntactic constraints—knowing appropriate sentence structures for the word, (2) semantic constraints—knowing appropriate ideas for its usage and how it relates to associated ideas, (3) stylistic constraints—knowing appropriate settings and styles of speaking for using the item, (4) morphological information—knowing what words the item is related to and how it attaches to other forms, (5) pragmatic constraints—knowing what the word entails, presupposes, and implies, and (6) phonological information—knowing how it is produced. Compared to the expansive linguistic nature of word knowledge, the PPVT measures a very restricted aspect of knowledge.

Many language assessment instruments focus on the more superficial aspects of language rather than the underlying categories and relationships that constitute the deeper basis of language organization. Word inflections (e.g., plural suffixes, possessive suffixes) and transparent grammatical structures (e.g., the *be* copula verb, negative indefinite forms) are often examined rather than the deeper conceptual basis of language capability such as the underlying categories of negation, possession, and identity. The limitations of traditional tests in this regard have led to reservations about using such instruments for *any* speaker, but their impact is even more significant given the ways in which the dialects of English typically differ from each other. Most comparisons of vernacular and standard varieties of English indicate that the majority of differences are found on the more superficial levels of language organization. The deeper the language level, the more similar the different dialects of English are apt to be. Unfortunately, it is the level of maximum differentiation among dialects, the "surface level," that is most often the focus of traditional standardized testing instruments. We therefore offer the following hypothesis about language testing and dialect differences: *The more superficial and limited the scope of language capability tapped in a testing instrument, the greater the likelihood that the instrument will be inappropriate for speakers beyond the immediate population upon which it was normed.*

In a discussion of language development assessment tools, Vaughn-Cooke (1980) sets forth a number of useful linguistic and sociolinguistic guidelines on which these instruments may be evaluated. The chart of guidelines, along with the evaluation of prominent language assessment tools in the field of speech and language pathology, is reprinted in Table 11-1. In addition to traditional instruments, several procedures that go beyond formal tests are included in the evaluation (for example, Bloom and Lahey's 1978 "content, form, and use" analysis).

It is apparent that a number of popular assessment instruments do not meet reasonable linguistic and sociolinguistic guidelines. Although none of the instruments surveyed by Vaughn-Cooke has been constructed to deal with dialect diversity per se, those designed to tap deeper levels of language organization have an inherent advantage over those limited to more superficial aspects of language which, at the very least, would require special adaptation procedures to accommodate dialect diversity.

USING LANGUAGE TO TAP KNOWLEDGE

Although differences in linguistic form are the most transparent dimension of dialect differentiation in test instruments, sociolinguistic differences are certainly not limited to structural variants under direct examination. Considerations in testing must also include how language, as a medium of presentation, is used to obtain information. These language-based tasks cover test directions and strategies used in the test to obtain data. Since language is used as a medium for tapping data in such a broad range of content areas, sociolinguistic differences may affect the results of tests which, at first glance, have very little to do with language.

Test directions call for the establishment of a common frame of reference for test takers. Obviously, the desired goal of directions is clarity—the unambiguous understanding of what behavior is to be performed by all test takers. The negotiated meaning of the directions cannot be assumed, however, despite the fact that methods of standardization can sometimes

Table 11-1

An Evaluation of Representative Language Assessment Instruments According to Linguistic Guidelines

Proposed Guidelines	Language Assessment Tools						
	UTLD	HTLD	PPVT	BLST	GCS	DSS	CFUA
(1) The procedure can account for language variation.	–	–	–	+	+	⊕	⊕
(2) The assumptions about language which underlie the procedure are valid.	–	–	–	– +	+	+	+
(3) The procedure includes an analysis of a spontaneous speech sample (when an oral system is used to communicate).	–	–	–	–	–	+	+
(4) The procedure reliably indicates whether a system is developing normally.	–	–	–	–	–	+	+ –
(5) The results of the procedure provide principled guidelines for language intervention.	–	–	–	–	–	– +	+
(6) The procedure can provide an adequate description of some aspect of the child's knowledge of language.	–	–	–	–	+	+	+

UTLD: Utah Test of Language Development
HTLD: Houston Test of Language Development
BLST: Bankson Language Screening Test
PPVT: Peabody Picture Vocabulary Test
DSS: Developmental Sentence Scoring
CFUA: Content, Form and Use Analysis
GCS: Grammatic Closure Subtest of the Illinois Test of Psycholinguistic Abilities
+ –   Some aspects of the test can meet the guideline, others do not
⊕   The procedure can be adapted to meet this guideline
–   The procedure cannot meet the guideline
+   The procedure can meet the guideline
(from Vaughn-Cooke "Evaluating the Language of Black English Speakers: Implications of the Ann Arbor Decision" 1980:41)

be quite elaborate. Even the most "simple" and "obvious" directions may be laden with the potential for misinterpretation. This misinterpretation may involve a particular item or the presentation format for the discourse of directions. For example, our observation of a simple instruction to "repeat" a sentence shows the word *repeat* to have different possible interpretations. In some communities, we have found that this simple direction may be interpreted as a paraphrasing task rather than a verbatim repetition task. We found that some children would "dress up" a stimulus sentence such as *The car is in the garage* by paraphrasing it so that the original sentence might be rendered as *That little old car just sitting in the garage*. Obviously, such children were attempting to succeed at the task, but their creative paraphrase in this instance would only lead to lower scores since the way to succeed assumed that *repeat* would be interpreted as verbatim repetition.

There are many ways of getting at the subject matter incorporated into a test, but most standardized tests rely on special language uses to access the information. In fact, close scrutiny of the language used in testing tasks suggests that there is a special language register that guides those who write test items. In part, the language of test items is derived from a version of formal written language, but it is often more than that. For example, a "question" may be defined as an incomplete declarative statement, as in the following: "To prevent scum from forming in a partly-used can of paint, one should _____" (from Arco, *Practice for the Armed Forces Tests* p. 23). In addition to the specialized definition of a question as a completion task, the impersonal pronoun *one* and the infinitive at the beginning of the sentence set apart the sentence from everyday language usage. Note how this sentence differs from a common everyday question such as "What do you do if you want to keep scum [i.e., *skin* in some dialects] from forming in a can of paint that's been opened?"

Exercise 3

Consider the following questions, taken from training manuals for the Armed Forces Vocational Aptitude Battery and the Scholastic Aptitude Test. First translate these items into ordinary spoken language style. How would a person ask this question in everyday spoken language? Compare your spoken language version with the formal test version of the question and note the kinds of differences between the two types of language use. What differences may be attributable to the conventional distinction between spoken and written language and what usage patterns seem peculiar to the way language is used in test questions?

1. When measuring an unknown voltage with a voltmeter, the proper precaution to take is to start with the . . .

2. When a certain pitcher contains 3 cups of water, the pitcher contains half its capacity.
3. It can be inferred from the passage that all of the following are characteristic of the author's grandmother EXCEPT . . .
4. Unlike a patient with Wernicke's aphasia, a patient with Broca's aphasia can do which of the following?

In some cases, the language register of testing may even use sentence structures that are ungrammatical in ordinary conversation. For example, the specialized use of verb + *-ing* forms in a frame such as *"Show me digging!"* (from the PPVT) is not a grammatical sentence in spoken or written Standard English. The construction would have to be formed something like *"Show me [a picture of] somebody [who is] digging!"* in its grammatical form. Examples of unique testing formats for asking questions accumulate fairly rapidly when actual language usage in formal testing instruments is examined.

At this point, we need to observe that many specialized uses of language in testing do not separate neatly on the basis of dialect diversity. Certainly, these specialized uses are different from the everyday language of *all* test takers to some extent. Nonetheless, the Standard English speaker is likely to be closer to the formal Standard English variety from which most language use in testing is originally derived than the vernacular speaker. We hypothesize the following: *The more distant a person's everyday speaking style is from the language used in testing, the greater the potential for task interference from the language register of the test.* We must also remember that specialized styles of language use will favor those who are especially socialized into test taking, a factor historically favoring middle-class groups.

Along with the specialized registers of language used in testng, it is important to understand that many tests rely on peculiar *metalinguistic tasks,* that is, special ways of organizing and talking about language apart from its ordinary uses for communication. These peculiar ways of using and referring to language may be critical to obtaining the relevant data for measurement. For example, specialized notions like *synonymy* and *antonymy* may become the metalinguistic process through which word definition is accessed, but these tasks involve peculiar relationships involving word replaceability and opposition. There is certainly ample indication that all individuals can give approximate definitions or uses of words, but this does not necessarily involve word replaceability or opposition. These are peculiar tasks which are extracted from natural language usage, where the meaning of a word is likely to be defined through a story example or context which uses the word appropriately (Meier 1973:10). For example, the notion of antonymy may legitimately be interpreted as "very different from" rather than a single dimension of opposition, so that *tall* and *far* might be considered opposites just as readily as *tall* and *short*.

In a similar way, the special use of rhyming or miminal word pairs (i.e., where the words sound alike except for one sound difference, such as *pit* and *pet*) to tap a person's ability to decode letters in reading or spelling involves skills that has little or nothing to do with decoding per se. Yet, it is common for reading and spelling tests in the early grades to use such tasks to measure decoding capability, as in "Find the word that rhymes with *sad*" or "Find the word that sounds the same as *too.*" Minimal word pairs and rhymes, of course may be different across dialects. We have already seen that *pin* and *pen* are homophonous rather than a minimal word pair in southern dialects; *fine* and *mind* rhyme in some dialects, and in my native Philadelphia dialect, *bad* rhymes with *mad*, but not with *sad*. The particular metalinguistic tasks used to determine decoding capability may turn out to be just as significant, and in some cases, a more significant stumbling block in testing than transparent structural dialect differences, although this type of effect on the results of a test may be more subtle and indirect.

THE TESTING SITUATION

Although the broader-based social situation might seen somewhat removed from the discussion of dialect structures in testing, we must remember that dialects are ultimately embedded in sociocultural differences. Tests do not take place in a contextually neutral social setting with a noncontextual orientation, although many tests implicitly make this assumption, or at least assume that it is possible to control the social situation so tightly that unwanted background factors do not influence performance in a significant way.

Testing calls for the test taker to enter the experimental frame created by the test constructor and administrator. If the test taker is unable or unwilling to "play the experimental game," the measurements resulting from the administration of the test cannot be valid. Values and assumptions about language use are a part of the definition of this experimental frame, so that different cultural orientations may guide how language is used by the test taker. For example, language usage may be guided by the status relationship between the test administrator and test taker. One ethnograhic study of a rural black southern community concludes that "experience in interacting with adults has taught him [the child] the values of silence and withdrawal" (Ward 1971:88), commonly expressed in the working-class dictum that "children should be seen, not heard." This cultural orientation about language interaction with adults may influence how a child responds to an adult administrator; it may also determine a child's willingness to ask questions about directions when confused. Culturally-determined response and interaction patterns may ultimately end up affecting some of the measurement indices, although this influence is considerably more difficult to pin down specifically than structural dialect differences. The experimental frame of testing may assume and indeed demand that participants divorce themselves from cultural orientations about status relationships, interactional norms, and the role of language use just for the sake of the test.

Labov (1976) has pointed out that some of the most innocuous-appearing procedures for eliciting data (for example, eliciting spontaneous conversation) may be fraught with sociolinguistic values. For example, a friendly invitation by an adult to a child to "tell me everything you can about the fire engine on the table" is laden with values about verbosity (the more you tell the better), obvious information (describe the object even though you know the adult knows all about it), and consequences about information sharing (what a child tells the adult will not be held against the child). Values about language use, however, are particularly difficult to reorient upon entering an experimental frame. There may be quite different socialization processes that go along with community values to make it very difficult for a test taker to enter into the experimental frame. For example, Heath (1983) reports that "labeling" obvious information objects and activities (e.g., "What is this?" or "What are they doing?" when the questioner already knows the answer) is a sociolinguistic routine quite common in some communities but not in others. Thus, speakers from different communities might relate to this common "teacher routine," sometimes used in informal language assessment procedures, in quite different ways.

There is a peculiar socialization that defines the testing situation, and this socialization assumes particular experiences with language, testtaking, and orientation about the experimental frame of formalized testing. In this situation, the local sociolinguistic context must be suspended, since there is nothing quite comparable to it outside of this occasion. In the jargon of current educational psychologists, the experimental framework of testing calls for relatively *context-independent text*, in the sense that text is not embedded in the local context or practice. Some groups not oriented to the social occasion of testing are more prone to use more *context-dependent text*, in the sense that it is more embedded in the local context and assumed knowledge of the context (Bernstein 1981). While the distinction between context-dependent and context-independent text may be oversimplified, there is little doubt that some cultural groups are more socialized than others in terms of entering into the testing game of context-independent text.

Exercise 4

Following are hints for taking a test, found in a U.S. Department of Labor guide on tests. Examine these hints in terms of the social situation of testing. What kinds of factors might affect the outcome of the test? What do these factors have to do with the capability being tapped in a test? Do any of the hints deal with underlying assumptions about language?

1. Get ready for the test by taking other tests on your own.
2. Don't let the thought of taking a test throw you, but being a little nervous won't hurt you.
3. Arrive early, rested and prepared to take the test.
4. Ask questions until you understand what you are supposed to do.
5. Some parts of the test may be easier than others. Don't let the hard parts keep you from doing well on the easier parts.
6. Keep time limits in mind when you take a test.
7. Don't be afraid to answer when you aren't sure you are right, but don't guess wildly.
8. Work as fast as you can but try not to make mistakes. Some tests have short time limits.

Exercise 5

Due to the potential effects of testing socialization on test performance, some educators have advocated the teaching of test taking as a special topic in the educational curriculum. What are the advantages and disadvantages of including such a topic? Do you think this curriculum would skew the interpretation of test results for students? What aspects of language use might have to be included in this curriculum?

RESOLVING THE ASSESSMENT DILEMMA

Given the potential bias that many assessment instruments have for non-mainstream groups, it is not surprising that a number of alternatives have been offered for reducing sociolinguistic bias in testing. Vaughn-Cooke (1983:29) has identified seven alternative proposals for resolving the dilemma of test bias for nonmainstream dialect groups.

1. Standardize existing tests on nonmainstream English speakers.
2. Include a small percentage of minorities in the standardization sample when developing a test.
3. Modify or revise existing tests in ways that will make them appropriate for nonmainstream speakers.
4. Utilize a language sample when assessing the language of nonmainstream speakers.

5. Utilize criterion-referenced measures when assessing the language of non-mainstream speakers.

6. Refrain from using all standardized tests that have not been corrected for test bias when assessing the language of nonmainstream speakers.

7. Develop a new test which can provide a more appropriate assessment of the language of nonmainstream English speakers.

Although research has been undertaken on each of the alternatives, the choice of unbiased instruments, according to Vaughn-Cooke (1983:33), still "reveals a rather dismal picture." This conclusion seems especially warranted when the overall sociolinguistic context of assessment is considered. A strategy of assessment which gives vernacular dialect speakers credit for acquiring a vernacular dialect form in a formal development test may neutralize one type of dialect discrimination, but it does not resolve the issue of how this information is most equitably tapped for speakers representing a wide range of cultural and sociolinguistic backgrounds. By the same token, the use of nontraditional procedures to obtain language data may improve the possibility of obtaining valid data, but this alternative does not meet the criteria necessary for the standardization process. Meanwhile, formal testing continues to flourish in American society and there is little realistic hope of systematically dismantling the testing bureaucracy in the name of sociolinguistic equality. Even if the cry of those calling for a testing moratorium were heeded, it would not dissipate the need for accurate knowledge about language development and capability for different groups of speakers.

After a couple decades of confronting testing from a sociolinguistic perspective, it has become clear that there is no "quick fix" solution. Each of the alternatives previously cited has both advantages and disadvantages. Given this situation, the best we can offer is some realistic ways of coping with the need for adequate assessment in a context which is heavily favored toward middle-class, Standard English-speaking groups. There are two sets of recommendations we can make, one for those vested with the responsibility for assessing language capability and one for those practitioners who are primarily consumers of information from formal testing.

THE LANGUAGE DIAGNOSTICIAN

Specialists such as speech and language pathologists and English/language arts teachers often have little alternative but to assess the langauge capabilities of their clients or sutdents. How can these professionals arrive at an authentic picture of the language of those who do not come from Standard English-speaking communities? The answer to this question involves acquiring a knowledge base founded in descriptive sociolinguistics and applying this information to a language diagnostic in a practical way. As a starting point, such *professionals must know the descriptive linguistic characteristics of the local communities they serve.* A language specialist in southern rural Appalachia must know the linguistic structures characterizing this community, just as a language specialist in a northern black urban context should know the dialect characteristics of this community. However, such knowledge must extend beyond the structural language details. Rules for communication interaction and values about language use governing both in-group and out-group communication must also be part of this background sociolinguistic knowledge that a specialist brings to the assessment context. This perspective is not narrowly structural, but extends into language use as it is embedded in different cultures and subcultures. While descriptive sociolinguistic profiles of different communities are certainly not complete, there are now a number of dialect overviews available to specialists. In most cases, however, these general descriptions still need to be balanced with active observation about the sociolinguistic peculiarities of local communities. The serious language diagnostician really needs to become an observer of community language behavior as well as a reader of available sociolinguistic profiles.

In cases where the selection of formal test instruments is outside the diagnostician's control, there is a critical need to bring sociolinguistic information to bear on subjects' responses. More than once, specialists have bemoaned the fact that they thought a particular language assessment test was unfair to vernacular dialect speakers, but that they have no choice in its administration. In these situations, *it is necessary to be able to identify those particular linguistic responses that might be attributable to dialect differences and how these responses might affect the score.* Of course, this kind of analysis can only be conducted when item-by-item responses are made available to the language specialist.

Where possible, *language specialists should also experiment with the administration of required standardized tests in a nontraditional or nonstandardized manner.* A test can be given in a standardized approach first, then given in a way which might provide the client or student an opportunity to perform at a maximum level. Instructions can be reworded, additional time for responding can be given, and additional props can be used, among other nonstandard administration options. Where possible, it is also important to *ask test takers why particular responses were chosen.* Practitioners who do this may find the explanations quite insightful, often revealing different kinds of sociolinguistic processing. Some "wrong" answers turn out to be quite reasonable when the test taker explains how the answer was obtained.

When tests are given in a nonstandardized manner, this must be reported for the record, so that both a standard and alternative score have to be included in any report of the test, along with an explanation of how the scores were obtained. Nonetheless, this procedure may provide important information on how different sociolinguistic tasks are interfering with the valid interpretation of the test data.

In reality, an accurate picture of language capability can only go so far on the basis of formalized assessment instruments, since so many of these tests measure limited, superficial aspects of language. *Formal measures of language must be complemented with assessment strategies more focused on underlying language capabilities in realistic communicative contexts.* In some professions, such as speech and language pathology, there is increasing emphasis on the use of a language sample in assessment. As defined in this discipline, a *language sample* is language data collected through a natural conversational interview instead of a technique in which language items are directly elicited. This interview is typically conducted by the diagnostician, but there is no reason why it couldn't be conducted just as effectively by a community member (e.g., parent, peer, or some other meaningfully-defined community participant). A reasonable profile of the language capability should also move away from the more superficial aspects of language form, focusing instead on underlying aspects of the communicative message. As mentioned previously, such an approach is less likely to penalize the vernacular dialect speaker, since the vast majority of structural dialect differences involve the "surface" level of grammar and phonology. In their extensive study of children acquiring Vernacular Black English, Stockman, Vaughn-Cooke, and Reveron (Stockman 1986) have found very few differences from Standard English speakers when the focus is on underlying semantic content categories and relationships (following Bloom and Lahey's approach, 1978) rather than surface grammatical form. This model neutralizes the effect of dialect in the assessment of language capability; it also provides a baseline for distinguishing those normally developing Vernacular Black English speakers from the small percentage of speakers who are genuinely disordered in their language development in terms of community language norms.

Finally, *it is essential to complement the assessment of language capabilities with ethnographic information about language use in a natural setting.* How is language used in a natural setting with peers, family members, and other community participants? To some extent, such information may be obtained by questioning relevant community participants. Since it is the community context which sets norms, the community perspective on a person's speech may be critical for obtaining a true profile of language capability. But more than simple questioning of community members is involved if a true picture of language is to emerge. There is a sense in which the diagnostician must become an active observer of how language is used in its representative social settings—on the playground, in the bus, in the local community, and in the classroom with teachers and other students. How does the student use language to communicate and interact socially? Whereas an ethnographic perspective may take a language diagnostician considerably beyond the clinic or classroom setting, it is imperative to extend the context of langauge observation if an accurate picture of language capability is to emerge. The insight from such an ethnographic perspective may not be as readily quantifiable as data obtained from standardized formal instruments, but it is invaluable for a true picture of language capability.

THE CONSUMER OF TEST RESULTS

Language diagnosticians may have a special responsibility for knowledge in conducting assessments, but all educational practitioners need to develop a critical, discerning sociolinguistic perspective on testing. The requisite knowledge of a consumer of test information may not be as demanding as that of the diagnostician, but there are still essential guidelines that should temper practitioners' interpretation of the test score results.

One of the initial questions that has to be asked relates to the purpose of a test. The consumer must ask *what the test claims to be testing in relation to what it actually tests*. This is particularly important with respect to language since so many language tests measure something different from what is claimed in the test manual. This question is relevant for any test taker, but it can be particularly sensitive for the speaker of a dialect different from that assumed in the test. In our previous discussion, we saw several clear-cut cases in which the stated purpose of the test was quite different from what the test actually measured. It is also possible that a test may measure something different for a test taker from a standard dialect than it does for a vernacular dialect speaker, as we saw with respect to the language usage section of an achievement test. In this regard, any limitations of the test in connection with its primary purpose must be noted, and scores must be interpreted with these limitations in mind. In some cases, the test manual itself may state that the test is limited to Standard English speakers, but this restriction is often ignored in its actual administration. Such limitations cannot be ignored, however, if the test information is to be valid.

It is also essential to ask *what kinds of assumptions about language may underlie the test*. Some of these assumptions may not be readily transparent, but a careful analysis of the targeted content area should reveal the underlying notions of language which have guided the test constructor. Thus, a proclaimed language usage test that measures a limited domain of language, such as receptive vocabulary recognition, is guided by an assumption that language is little more than labeling. It is also essential to ask *what kinds of language-related tasks may be necessary to participate in the test*. Does participation in the test require that the test taker be able to read, to understand special test-taking formats, or to respond through the use of peculiar metalinguistic skills? If so, what might be the outcome if the test taker cannot participate in these assumed tasks? We need to be aware of how assumptions about language-related tasks may impact on getting at information in areas that, on the face of it, have nothing to do with language.

It is also important to *know demographic information about the groups on which the test was standardized.* The region, sociocultural background, ethnicity, age, and gender of the population on which the test was standardized may give an important indication of its sociolinguistic restrictions. Based on such introductory information, we can often infer how generalizable the information might be, particularly in relation to the norms established for the test scores. Background information of this type is more than boring, irrelevant introductory material for the practitioner concerned with the validity of the test scores for different sociolinguistic communities.

Although it might be idealistic to expect a practitioner to know what kinds of responses produced by speakers of vernacular dialects might be attributable to dialect differences, it is important to understand that systematic differences in responses to test items by different sociocultural groups might give a clue to relevant sociolinguistic differences. The non-language specialist who has concerns about different groups of speakers in a classroom thus has a need to be able to retrieve item-by-item information. Such information may give valuable insight into possible sociolinguistic interference in the assessment process.

Ultimately, the consumer of test information must ask *how the results of the test must be interpreted for different sociolinguistic groups.* Can the results of the test be qualified or adjusted in some way to account for systematic dialect differences, or must the results be taken as given? We must ask what the results of the test mean from a much more informed sociolinguistic vantage point. Admittedly, the kinds of principles explicated here make demands that go beyond the traditional training of educators and other consumers of test information. But the persistence of the testing dilemma, along with the continued significance assigned to test scores in our society, give us little alternative but to advocate much greater consumer awareness about the sociolinguistics of testing, particularly as it affects vernacular dialect speakers.

Further Reading

LABOV, WILLIAM, "Systematically Misleading Data from Test Questions," *Urban Review*, 9:146–169 (1976). Labov's article on the general question of language assessment and cultural and linguistic divergence examines the broad sociolinguistic context of interviewing and interpreting test data.

TERRELL, SANDRA L., ed. *Nonbiased Assessment of Language Differences: Topics in Language Disorders* 3, No. 3, Rockville, MD: Aspen, 1983. This special issue of the periodical *Language Disorders* is devoted to the question of assessing the language capabilities of linguistically diverse populations in a nonbiased manner. The articles are of most immediate concern to speech and language pathologists involved in assessing vernacular dialect speakers but also have broader application.

VAUGHN-COOKE, ANNA FAY, "Improving Language Assessment in Minority Children," *Asha* 25:29–34, (1983). Vaughn-Cooke discusses the strategies that have been offered in an effort to neutralize the traditional bias of standardized testing instruments toward vernacular-speaking children. It is an insightful, concise overview.

WOLFRAM, WALT AND DONNA CHRISTIAN, "On the Application of Sociolinguistic Information: Test Evaluation and Dialect Differences in Appalachia," in *Standards and Dialects*, eds. Timothy Shopen and Joseph M. Williams. New York, NY: Winthrop, 1980. Using data from Appalachian English, the authors take the reader through the procedures for applying descriptive information about dialects to actual test items.

CHAPTER TWELVE

DIALECTS AND LANGUAGE ARTS

What effect do dialect differences have on basic educational skills? Certainly, educational problems are more prevalent among students who speak vernacular varieties of English than they are among their standard dialect counterparts. Although there is an obvious correlation between educational failure and speaking a vernacular dialect, a more basic question is whether language variation contributes to educational problems in a significant way. Are dialect differences a symptom or are they a primary cause of educational problems? We have already seen that sociolinguistic differences can have an important effect on the assessment of students when the evaluation instruments are normed on Standard English-speaking populations. Do dialect differences have a comparable effect on the attainment of basic educational skills such as reading and writing?

In this chapter, we consider the effect of language variation on the fundamental skills of reading and writing. This is a central area of application for sociolinguistic knowledge and educators deserve informed, honest answers to their questions about dialects and literacy skills. But there is more to dialects in language arts than the examination of how dialect differences may create obstacles for the attainment of reading and writing skills. These issues are critical for education, but it is shortsighted to limit the examination of dialects in education to this vantage point. There is another side that is much more positive and upbeat. In their own right, dialects offer a rich resource for enhancing students' knowledge about language and society. Introducing students to this side of dialects can do a great deal to alleviate the fundamental misunderstandings about dialects that persist in our society. The final section of this chapter thus proposes a program of study on dialects for students in our schools. Such a program is an exciting prospect because, once implemented, it offers a systematic basis for developing an understanding of language and dialects that is essential for changing popular misconceptions and stereotypes about this topic.

DIALECTS AND READING ACHIEVEMENT

Certainly there are many factors that correlate with reading failure, ranging from students' nutritional problems to the number of books in the home of the student. Among these factors is the spoken dialect of the reader. Given this correlation between vernacular speech and reading failure, it is important to understand how language variation affects the reading process so we can determine whether or not dialect in its own right may cause reading difficulties. In this section, we consider ways in which language variation may affect the reading process.

One process in reading which may be affected by dialect is *decoding*. By decoding, we mean the process whereby the written symbols are related to the sounds of the language. In English, of course, this process refers to the ways in which the letters of the alphabet, or orthography, are systematically related to the English sound system (or, in a few cases, to the English morphemic system). Whereas different approaches to reading rely on decoding skills to varying degrees, and many current approaches deemphasize a basic decoding model of reading, the systematic "sounding out of letters" referred to as the *phonics approach* to reading has been popular for over half a century. As students proceed in the acquisition of reading skills, the significance of decoding may be diminished drastically, but it still is a rudimentary skill that plays a significant role in the beginning stages of many reading programs.

A reading teacher engaged in decoding tasks with students must recognize that there are systematic differences in the symbol-sound relationships from dialect to dialect. For example, consider how a reader of a vernacular dialect might decode orally the passage "There won't be anything to do until he finds out if he can go without taking John's brother." A modified orthography is used here to indicate the pronunciation differences for the vernacular speaker.

An Example of Vernacular Dialect Decoding

Deuh won't be anything to do until he fin' out if he can go wi/out takin' John bro*vuh*.

Systematic decoding differences may affect a number of symbol-sound relationships in the example, such as the final consonant of *find*, the *th* of *without*, the *th* and final *r* of *brother*, and so forth. These differences are no more severe than variant regional decodings of the vowel *au* of *caught* (e.g., [ɔ] or [a]) or the *s* of *greasy* (e.g., [s] or [z]), except that they involve a couple of heavily stigmatized variants. The variant decoding becomes a problem only if an instructor does not recognize dialectally appropriate sound-symbol relationships and classifies these differences as errors in decoding. Imagine the confusion that might be created for a dialect speaker if an accurate dialect decoding such as *th* → [f] in *without* or *the* → [v] in *brother* is treated as a problem comparable to the miscoding of *b* as [d] or *sh* as [s]. To avoid this confusion and potential misdiagnosis of reading problems, reading instructors need to be able to separate dialect differences from actual reading disabilities. The potential impact of dialects on the decoding process can be minimized if reading instructors have this information.

An Example of Grammatical Mismatch in Written Text and Spoken Vernacular Dialect

It won't be *nothing* to do till he find out *can he* go without taking John brother.

The use of existential *it* for *there*, multiple negation, the absence of inflectional *-s*, and the inverted question order of *can he go* are all instances of mismatch between the spoken vernacular variety and the written word. By comparison, the passage is relatively close to the spoken grammatical form of Standard English, so that the mismatch between spoken and written language is greater for a vernacular speaker than it is for a standard dialect speaker.

From the standpoint of simple linguistic processing, it is reasonable to hypothesize that the greater the mismatch between the spoken and written word, the greater the likelihood of processing difficulties in reading. But the real issue is whether dialect differences are great enough to become a significant barrier to linguistic processing. At this point, there are no carefully designed experimental studies that have examined this important research question in detail, but several observations are germane to this issue. First of all, there is an indication that vernacular dialect speakers do have receptive capability to process most spoken Standard English utterances whether or not they use this variety productively. Although receptive and productive capability in language may not transfer to the reading process in the same way, we would certainly expect considerable carryover from this receptive capability in spoken Standard English to the reading process, which in itself a receptive language activity.

It is also erroneous to assume that Standard English speakers confront written language that is identical to the way they speak and vernacular speakers do not. In reality, all readers encounter written text that differs from spoken language to some extent. Even in early reading, sentences with an adverbial complement moved to the beginning of the sentence, such as *Over and over rolled the ball* and *Up the hill he ran*, represent a written genre that differentiates written from spoken language for *all* speakers. So the problem of mismatch between written and spoken language is a matter of degree rather than kind.

Admittedly, the gap between written language and spoken language will be greater for vernacular dialect speakers than it is for speakers of standard varieties. But is this gap wide enough to cause problems on the basis of linguistic differences alone? Again, carefully controlled experimentation of this issue is lacking, although I am reminded of the fact that there are situations in the world where the gap between spoken dialect and written text is quite extensive, without resulting in significant reading problems. In northern Switzerland, for example, texts are written in standard German although much of the population speaks Swiss German, yet the Swiss population does not reveal significant reading failure. Although it is difficult to measure "degree of dialect difference" in a precise way, Swiss German is certainly as different from standard written German as many vernacular dialects of English are from standard written English. Pointing to linguistic mismatch as the basis for reading failure among vernacular speakers thus seems suspect. Differences in the written and spoken language may have to be taken into account by an aware reading instructor, but it is doubtful that the neutralization of these differences in reading material would alleviate the reading problems associated with various vernacular-speaking populations.

Another area of language variation to consider in the reading process involves the broader sociolinguistic base of language, including background cultural differences. In most current models of the reading process, the application of background knowledge is essential for comprehension. Readers need such background in order to derive meaning by inference; they may also need to apply knowledge about the world in order to process some of the literal content. For example, imagine the differences in how a third grader from California and one from New York City might interpret the following passage on the age of giant redwood trees. Incidently, this item appeared in the Metropolitan Achievement Test designed for third graders.

> They are so big that roads are built through their trunks. By counting the rings inside the tree trunk, one can tell the age of the tree. (from Meier 1970)

Meier (1970:15) reports that some children in New York City conjured up fairy-tale interpretations of this passage that included, among other things, pictures of golden rings lying inside trees. The fairy-tale interpretation was certainly fostered by images of cars driving though giant holes in trees. On the other hand, children who live near the Redwood Forest in California would interpret the passage quite differently, since its literal content would match their knowledge of the world. There is certainly the potential for students to expand their range of experience through reading, but background information is critical for comprehension. As a result, different community language and culture experiences may actually affect reading comprehension in subtle but important ways.

Finally, we need to remember that dialect differences may have an effect on the assessment of reading skills. Early-level reading tests are particularly susceptible to the impact of dialect because they often rely on metalinguistic tasks that are sensitive to dialect-specific decoding differences. For example, as discussed in Chapter 11, the use of minimal word pair tasks or rhyming tasks to measure decoding skills might result in misclassifying cases of dialect-appropriate symbol-sound relationships as incorrect responses. Consider test items (taken from an actual reading achievement test) that include the following word pairs as part of an attempt to determine early readers' specific decoding abilities.

Choose the words that sound the same:

pin/pen
reef/wreath
find/fine
their/there
here/hear

For speakers of some vernacular varieties, all of these items might legitimately sound the same. The "correct" response, however, would be limited to *there/their* and *hear/here*, based upon the northern standard dialect norm. An informed perspective on language variation must therefore consider the ways in which reading skills are measured in testing, along with other dimensions of the reading process.

DIALECT READERS

At one stage in the consideration of dialects and education, it was proposed that "dialect readers" be used in teaching vernacular-speaking children to read. A *dialect reader* is a text that incorporates the nonstandard grammatical forms typical of a vernacular-speaking community. As a brief illustration of how a dialect reader might look, we may compare two versions of the same text, one in Standard English and one in the vernacular dialect (from Wolfram and Fasold 1974:198).

Standard English Version

"Look down here," said Suzy.
"I can see a girl in here.
That girl looks like me.
Come here and look, David!
Can you see that girl?" . . .

Vernacular Black English Version

Susan say, "Hey, you-all, look down here!"
"I could see a girl in here.
That girl, she look like me.
Come here and look, David!
Could you see the girl?" . . .

The second passage is a deliberate attempt to incorporate the presumed features of children's vernacular dialect into a basal reader. The aim of dialect readers, which typically use a Standard English orthography rather than a modified, dialect spelling, is not to develop a dualistic reading system, but to use a familiar language system in the initial step in the reading process. This beginning phase is then followed by a transition stage which leads a reader into materials written in the standard written variety. Although the use of dialect readers may seem like a radical departure from traditional approaches and materials in reading, this is not the only example of specially adapted reading materials designed for the incipient stages of developmental reading. The use of a special, invariant phonetic alphabet such as the Initial Teaching Alphabet for teaching initial decoding skills and the so-called "language experience approach," in which children dictate stories which are written down and then given back to them to read, certainly depart to some extent from traditional reading primers.

Other kinds of alternative strategies in teaching reading may engender debate, but the controversy over dialect readers stands in a class of its own. There seem to be two major reasons for this controversy. One reason involves the deliberate use of socially stigmatized language forms in written material. This tactic is viewed by some as a reinforcement of nonstandard dialect patterns, thus flying in the face of traditional mainstream, insitutional values endorsing standard dialects. The other reason concerns the fact that this approach singles out particular groups of readers for special materials, namely, those who speak vernacular dialects. This selective process may be viewed as patronizing, and ultimately, racist and classist educational differentiation.

From a sociolinguistic vantage point, the use of dialect readers seems to be based on three assumptions: (1) that there is a sufficient mismatch between the child's system and the Standard English textbook to warrant distinct materials, (2) that the benefits from reading success will outweigh any negative connotations associated with the use of a socially stigmatized variety, and (3) that the use of vernacular dialects in reading will promote reading success. We have already considered whether the mismatch of spoken and written language is a significant problem; at this point, there simply is no good evidence for this strong position. Given children's socialization into mainstream attitudes and values about dialects at an early age, there is also little reason to assume that the sociopsychological benefits of using a vernacular dialect would outweigh the disadvantages. In fact, the opposite seems to be the case, as children reject nonstandard forms in reading and parents and community leaders rail against their use in dialect readers. A positive relationship between reading success and the use of vernacular-dialect readers also has not been firmly established. Some initial investigation of dialect readers reported slight gains for children given these materials (Leaverton 1973), but substantive research in favor of dialect readers is lacking. Due to the continuing controversy surrounding the use of dialect primers, this alternative now has been largely abandoned.

Perhaps the most developed curriculum using a version of dialect readers is found in *Bridge: A Cross-Cultural Reading Program* (Simpkins, Simpkins, and Holt 1977). This program is not designed for beginning readers but for older junior high and high school students who have experienced reading difficulty. The program limits the dialect text to passages representative of students' cultural background experiences so that the use of vernacular is placed in an appropriate community context. It also makes a sincere effort to provide positive motivation and successful reading experiences for students. While this program has hardly been free of controversy, its limitation of dialect passages to culturally appropriate contexts has made it less offensive than other approaches which use dialect passages without regard for their culturally appropriate setting. In many respects, the use of dialect passages in the *Bridge* program falls in line with a well-established tradition of representing dialect in literature. In this instance, the intent is to seize upon this literary tradition of dialect representation for the benefit of a reader who may identify with the dialect rather than the representation of a dialect assumed to be different from that of the reader. Rigorous measurement of the outcomes of this program has not been undertaken, but it has been acclaimed in some circles as an approach to reading that capitalizes in a more positive, appropriate way on the use of vernacular dialect.

Although there are essential ways in which dialect may affect reading, most current approaches play down simple linguistic differences as a primary factor in accounting for the high levels of reading failure found among vernacular-speaking populations. Instead, cultural values about reading, the process of socialization into the social activity of reading, and the mismatch between students' interests and the content of reading material have been considered more essential factors in accounting for high failure rates among nonmainstream populations. Focus on these other variables does not, however, excuse reading instructors from understanding the ways in which dialects may affect reading and from taking these factors into consideration in the teaching process.

Exercise 1

It has been noted that mature readers often make "miscues" in their oral rendition of reading which reflect that they are actually processing the passage based on an underlying knowledge of *their* language. In fact, there is an approach to reading evaluation that examines closely these kinds of miscues to determine reading comprehension (Goodman 1973). Based on your understanding of vernacular dialect features in phonology and grammar, predict what kinds of miscues might be found in an oral rendition of the following passage by a vernacular dialect speaker. Consider both symbol-sound relationships and changes in morphology and syntax that might take place. Refer to the Appendix for more detailed information about particular structures in vernacular dialects.

> There were five players who missed a chance to play in the game. It wasn't anything that they did, but there was a rule that kept students from playing in a game if they didn't attend all their classes the day of the game. The players knew the rule, but they didn't follow it, so they missed a chance to play in the most important game of the season.

DIALECT INFLUENCE IN WRITTEN LANGUAGE

When a rural schoolboy in southeastern Pennsylvania writes a sentence like *Cow feed don't have jagers* or a phrase like *the corn got all*, attention is drawn to the fact that such writing may reflect some aspect of the student's spoken language. In this case, a term like *jagers* (perhaps spelled better as *jaggers*) is a common label for thorns and other objects capable of causing scratches, the use of *don't* with a third person singular subject is a common vernacular agreement pattern, and the use of *got all* is a regional expression traceable to the influence of Pennsylvania German (Wolfram and Fasold 1974:205). Obviously, spoken language can have influence on written language. However, the relationship between spoken and written language is not always as simple and direct as examples of this type might lead us to believe. Writing, after all, is more than a simple reflection of spoken language, and very few people actually write exactly as they talk. With respect to dialects, the important question is how language variation may be manifested in written language style. Educators usually are much more concerned with dialect structures which exist along the standard-vernacular axis than they are about those that might reflect a regional dimension. A teacher would be much more likely to be concerned with the use of *don't* than the regional word choice *jagger* in our illustrative phrase given previously.

It is not particularly difficult to document cases of spoken language influence in writing such as those already cited, regardless of the vernacular dialect under review (e.g., Wolfram and Whiteman 1971; Farr-Whiteman 1981; Wolfram and Hatfield 1984). What is of more interest than the simple cataloguing of examples is the determination of patterns of influence. As it turns out, dialect features are not reflective of spoken language in a simple one-to-one relationship. As we shall see later, we need to appeal to general principles of writing as well as knowledge about dialects in order to explain the patterns of nonstandard writing that have been found.

One of the interesting findings about dialect structures in writing relates to the relative frequency with which certain nonstandard forms occur. For example, Farr-Whiteman (1981) identifies nonstandard structures that occur relatively frequently in writing and others that occur infrequently, at least at certain stages in the writing process. Among those forms frequently found in a sample of writing by eighth grade students are the following: (1) verbal -s absence (e.g., *She go*), (2) plural -s absence (e.g., *four mile*), (3) possessive -s absence (e.g., *John hat*), (4) consonant cluster -ed absence (e.g., *Yesterday they miss*) and copula *is/are* absence (e.g., *We going to the game*). On the other side of the ledger are nonstandard structures which appear relatively infrequently, including multiple negation, the use of *ain't*, and habitual *be*. In spelling, the phonological reflection of *f* for *th* and postvocalic *r* absence were also relatively rare in writing compared with their incidence in speech.

A partial explanation of the different frequency levels in writing may relate to the social evaluation of forms. Items that are highly stigmatized and that affect relatively small sets of items would probably be the first to be corrected in the traditional focus on Standard English writing within the schools. By the time students are in eighth grade, as they were in the Farr-Whiteman study, shibboleths of nonstandard usage such as *ain't* may have been purged from writing. There is, then, a dimension of social evaluation that enters into the explanation as to why some nonstandard structures would be more susceptible to reflection in writing than others. But there is certainly more to the explanation than simple social evaluation.

One of the most revealing aspects of spoken and written language relationships in Farr-Whiteman's study comes from her comparison of the relative frequency of nonstandard forms in speech and writing, tabulated for both vernacular white and vernacular black dialect speakers. In Figure 12–1, the incidence of verbal -s and plural -s absence in spoken (S) and written (W) language is summarized for 32 white and black eighth graders in southern Maryland.

Figure 12–1 indicates relationships between spoken and written language that go beyond a simple *direct transfer model*. In this transfer model, the occurrence of a form in writing which is matched by one in the spoken dialect is interpreted as a direct carryover from a spoken language pattern to written language. That is, there is a straightforward causal relationship between spoken and written language variation. The figures in Figure 12–1 do not support a simple version of this model. For example, whites have a higher frequency of verbal and plural -s absence in their written language than they do in their spoken language. This pattern would hardly be predicted on the basis of their spoken language, since the white speakers do not have appreciable levels of suffix -s absence in their speech. Furthermore,

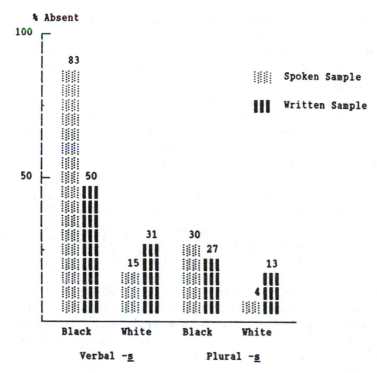

% Absent

Spoken Sample

Written Sample

Black   White   Black   White

Verbal -s   Plural -s

Figure 12–1 Percentage of -s Suffix Absence in the Speech and Writing for Whites and Blacks (adapted from Farr-Whiteman 1981:158)

we would normally expect a lower incidence of a socially stigmatized feature in the formal context of a written school essay than in spoken language.

Differences in the relative occurrence of suffixes in spoken and written language are also shown for the black population of writers. Plural absence is relatively infrequent compared to verb -s absence in spoken Vernacular Black English, yet both types of suffix absence are relatively high in writing. This pattern is confirmed on the basis of a much more extensive examination of writing taken from the writing samples collected for the National Educational Assessment Profile (Whiteman 1976).

The pattern of suffix absence in writing is further confirmed by a pattern found for final consonant cluster reduction. In writing, cluster reduction affecting -ed forms (e.g., *miss* for *missed*) is much more frequent than it is for clusters that are part of the same morpheme (e.g., *mis* for *mist*), quite the reverse of what it is for spoken language (see Chapter 9). As Farr-Whiteman (1981:160) puts it, "these features (plural -s, verbal -s, and consonant -ed) seem to be omitted in writing at least partly *because* they are inflectional suffixes." In this regard, we note that inflectional suffixes are typically redundant markings, and that most words may stand as independent items apart from the suffix. In other words, *miss* alone is a whole word whether or not the *-ed* is added; *mis* for *mist*, however, cannot stand alone in this way. All writers of English, regardless of their native dialect, seem to reveal instances of suffix omission in the process of learning the written form of the language.

While generalized strategies relating to the developmental writing process may affect all writers to some extent, this does not nullify the effect of dialect on writing. Some forms may still be directly attributable to the spoken dialect; other spoken language forms, however, combine with different principles of writing to account for nonstandard written language forms. Inflectional *-s* absence may be revealed as part of the natural process of learning how to write regardless of the spoken dialect, but speakers of a dialect with substantial levels of suffix absence still tend to show a higher incidence of suffix omission in writing than that found for writers of other dialects. The point that needs to be emphasized here is that dialect definitely can influence writing, but it is not solely responsible for the occurrence of nonstandard forms.

Writing failure, like reading failure, is a complex issue that goes far deeper than the surface differences of dialect forms. Nonetheless, a writing instructor who is aware of the way in which dialect may surface in writing is certainly in a better position to improve writing skills than one who has no awareness of potential spoken language influences on the written medium.

Exercise 2

In the following sample composition, there are two types of digression from standard written English. First, there is a set of errors related to the mechanical conventions of written language. These include various arbitrary punctuation conventions and some types of spelling errors (e.g., *to* versus *too*, *fair* versus *fare*). The second set of nonstandard writing forms may reflect the influence of spoken language by a speaker of a vernacular dialect. Based on your knowledge of vernacular dialect features, differentiate the error types, labeling mechanical problems as *Type I* errors and spoken language influence as *Type II*. In the case of those forms classified as *Type II*, indicate what vernacular dialect feature may be the source of the spoken language influence. You may need to consult the Appendix of dialect structures for this exercise.

> I tel you bout me and my fren basebal team. wen we together we do all kinds of things he play basketball and I play basebal. Las yere I seen the basketbal teme play and it look like I didnt have a chanc of making it. Im a pretty good baseball player tho and the coch knowed it. James the best player we miss him when he couldnt play last weak.

Before concluding our discussion of dialect influence on writing, we should mention the potential role of hypercorrection. Given the formality of many writing occasions, especially in an educational setting, hypercorrection often surfaces as students try hard to produce "correct" written English. We already discussed in Chapter 7 some of the lexical hypercorrection that may go along with the formal context of written classroom essays. There may also be peculiar cases in grammar that extend the boundaries of hypercorrection beyond what is typically found in spoken language. For example, sentences such as *one of my cow were missing* or *my grandfather's got a big stick* are not typical of spoken language hypercorrection. In the former case, an agreement pattern is extended, whereas in the latter case a possessive suffix is added. In both instances, the forms are extended beyond the grammatical boundaries revealed even in extreme cases of spoken language hypercorrection.

WRITING DIALECT FOR LITERARY PURPOSES

In the previous section, we discussed how spoken dialect forms unintentionally may be manifested in writing by a vernacular dialect speaker. There is another side of dialect in writing, in which dialect is deliberately represented in literature. There is a well-developed tradition in which writers attempt to portray characters through dialect, extending from the popular cartoons found in the daily comic strips of most newspapers to respected literary works going back as far as Chaucer. In American literature, this dialect representation developed largely in the nineteenth century and is now quite common in modern literature depicting different regional, status, and ethnic characters.

There are a number of reasons why an author would want to represent intentionally some aspect of dialect in a literary work. In one tradition, dialects have been used for comic effect, to poke fun at a character which the author feels superior to because of the character's lack of cultural sophistication or education. This tradition is well documented in various cartoon characterizations of "hillbilly" speech. In another tradition, the development of a character calls for the representation of a person's speech that is appropriate in terms of a particular regional and social background. It would be incongruous for Mark Twain's Huckleberry Finn to speak like a citified Midwest Standard English-speaking adult when the viewpoint being developed is that of a rural south midland adolescent. Part of the development of a folkway may come from the portrayal of a nonmainstream, regional dialect.

Dialect writing may even be used as a kind of dramatic statement of identity on the part of a writer. The poet Paul Laurence Dunbar, writing at the turn of the century, wrote about one fourth of all his poems in a vernacular dialect, in an apparent attempt to portray realistically the conditions of black life in America. From a somewhat different perspective, we find the text of Geneva Smitherman's *Talkin' and Testifyin'* (1977), a book about Black English which strongly endorses its usefulness as a communicative system in the black community, deliberately sprinkled with doses of a written Vernacular Black English. The written code switching into Vernacular Black English at various points emphasizes important perspectives on this dialect in a way that underscores the effectiveness and legitimacy of the variety. Different authors obviously use dialect for purposes which range from gross stereotyping to essential character development, so that the justification of dialect in a literary work has to be evaluated in terms of what the writer is trying to accomplish through the representation of dialect rather than the use of literary dialect per se.

The representation of literary dialect is actually quite tricky from the perspective of a dialectologist, since a tender balance must be maintained between presenting a credible version of a dialect and holding the reader's attention. My own introduction to literary dialects as a high school student was not a very happy one; I found these written versions of dialect overwhelming and confusing, so I simply skipped or skimmed such passages. It was not until I started studying dialects myself that I realized that most literary representations of dialects were actually quite selective and conventionalized, and that there was much more that could have been done in an authentic written portrayal of dialect.

There are, of course, different levels of language variation that may be captured in a literary dialect, but the most inherently difficult level to represent is phonology, as it must be reflected through spelling modifications. Given the inherent obstacles of representing dialect phonology through spelling, most writers have resorted to a tradition which relies heavily on a selective and largely arbitrary set of spelling changes.

One of the traditional ways of representing dialect in spelling is through *eye dialect*. Eye dialect typically consists of set of spelling errors that bear no resemblance to the phonological differences of real dialects. In fact, the reason it is called eye dialect is because its appeal is solely to the eye of the reader, as opposed to an attempt to capture genuine phonological differences. The spellings of *was* as *wuz*, *does* as *duz*, *excusable* as *exkusable*, *maybe* as *mebbe*, or *wunce* for *once* do not represent any known aspect of phonological variation; these changes are just a different way of spelling a common word to convey dialect to the eye of the reader.

Certain changes in spelling conventions may, on the other hand, be used to portray real phonological variation, in most cases going from a standard dialect to a nonmainstream variety. A writer who spells *them* as *dem*, *fellow* as *feller*, *first* as *fust*, or *itch* as *eetch* is attempting to convey a phonological difference in which a sound is changed (*them* → *dem*, *itch* → *eetch*), a sound is added (*fellow* → *feller*), or a sound is lost (*first* → *fust*) in a nonmainstream variety. Consonant changes are relatively easy to portray in this convention, but vowels are difficult, given the small phonetic details often involved in differentiating dialects. Furthermore, symbol-sound correspondences tend to be more varied for vowels than they are for most consonants. Nonetheless, using the spelling *ee* for *eetch* would symbolize the phonetic value of [i] rather than the value of [I] usually associated with the *i* spelling, based on the predominant correspondence of *ee* for [i], as in *beet*, and *i* for [I], as in *bit*. Certain changes of this type have become fairly traditional in literary representations, seizing upon frequent patterns of sound-symbol representation (e.g., *u* to symbolize a central vowel in *tuck*). Other cases exemplify specially created conventions for dialect writing. For example, an apostrophe is usually used in dialect writing to indicate that a sound or a syllable has been "lost" in the dialect by comparison with the standard variety, so that *mo'* for *more*, *ac'* for *act*, *'cause* for *because*, and *'cept* for *except* would all indicate an "absent" sound or syllable.

Of course, literary spelling conventions do not always differentiate clearly between eye dialect and real dialect differences, sometimes combining both traditions within the same word. Dialect spellings such as *wunst* for *once* and *'nuff* for *enough* combine eye dialect (*wu* . . . of *wunst* and the . . . *uff* of *'nuff*) with a genuine pronunciation difference, namely, the intrusive *t* of *once* and the deleted word initial syllable of *enough*. For descriptive and practical reasons, it is virtually impossible to be faithful to dialect pronunciation in writing, although there are certainly different degrees of accuracy that distinguish writers.

In principle, the literary representation of dialect grammar and vocabulary should be easier, and some authors choose to represent dialect by ignoring phonology and concentrating on peculiar grammatical and vocabulary structures. As it turns out, however, dialect accuracy in grammar and vocabulary also is a matter of degree, since it requires detailed descriptive familiarity with the dialects in focus to be dialectally faithful. Many writers resort to selective grammatical and lexical features of dialects rather than attempt to use a comprehensive set of structures based on descriptive dialectology. Consequently, many writers often lapse into stereotypes based on a mixture of personal experience with people and a conventional set of structures taken from other authors' literary representations of dialect. Even for writers quite familiar with the representative dialects, it is virtually impossible to be completely faithful to a dialect in writing. This is especially true when we consider the variable dimension of dialects as discussed in Chapter 9.

Based on descriptive accounts of various dialects, it is quite possible for a dialectologist to evaluate how accurately different varieties are represented in literary works. For example, it is possible to evaluate the literary representation of regional dialects found in *The Adventures of Huckleberry Finn* (Rulon 1971), based on descriptive knowledge of the dialects Twain intended to represent in his characters. It is also possible to compare how different writers represent the same dialect, as Weaver (1970) has done for the literary representations of Vernacular Black English in several different works. Detailed tabulations of dialect features which include both a qualitative and quantitative dimension show considerable variation and degrees of faithfulness among authors. Some authors are obviously more skilled at portraying dialect details than others. For example, although Claude Brown's (1965) portrayal of Vernacular Black English in *Manchild in the Promised Land* shows discrepancies between his literary representation and the dialect as it is typically used in northern urban communities, the author manipulates the relative frequency of nonstandard structures in the character's passage from adolescence to adulthood and in shifting between different speaking styles in a subtle, but effective way, according to Weaver's (1970) sociolinguistic analysis.

Exercise 3

Examine the following passage from Richard Wright's *Native Son* (1961). The passage portrays the vernacular dialect of a black preacher. Answer the following questions, based on the passage, which is taken from page 263 of a 1961 publication of this work. The original work was published in 1941.

1. What forms seem to be simple examples of eye dialect?
2. What cases of spelling changes represent actual phonological differences?
3. What kinds of grammatical details are included in the passage?
4. Are there phonological and grammatical differences that you might expect but do not appear in the passage?

   fergit ever'thing but yo' soul, son. Take yo' mind off ever'thing but eternal life. fergit what the newspaper say. Fergit yuh's black. Gawd looks past yo' skin 'n inter yo' soul, son. He's lookin' at the only parta yuh tha's *His*. He wants yuh 'n' He loves yuh. Give yo'se'f t' 'Im, son. Lissen, lemme tell yuh why yuh's here; lemme tell yuh a story tha'll make yo' heart glad. . . .

IMPLICATIONS FOR THE LANGUAGE ARTS PRACTITIONER

Given the ways in which the indigenous language patterns of students may impact various educational skills, it seems essential that language arts specialists become familiar with the kinds of community dialect patterns students bring with them. The significance of such dialect knowledge for teachers was perhaps best underscored by the Ann Arbor Decision (1979), a case of litigation in which 11 black plaintiff children in Ann Arbor, Michigan filed suit against the Ann Arbor School Board District for the failure of their teachers to take into account their home community dialect in teaching them how to read. The judge ruled in favor of the children, ordering the defendant school district to devise a plan to accomplish the following:

> (1) to help the teachers of the plaintiff children at King school to identify children speaking "black English" and the language spoken as a home or community language, and (2) to use the knowledge in teaching such students how to read standard English. (Charles W. Joiner, United States District Judge, 1979, p. 11)

A court-ordered, in-service training program to educate teachers is probably not the most conducive atmosphere for encouraging an understanding of dialects, but at least it emphasizes the need for practitioners to have some knowledge.

What are types of knowledge about dialects that are critical for practitioners? Probably the most important dimension involves an informed perspective on dialects. As an underlying, attitudinal approach to dialects, it is essential that practitioners *appreciate the complexity and naturalness of community language patterns*. We have mentioned repeatedly that the conflict in the linguistic patterns of the community and school is not related to the inherent nature of the linguistic system, but to the relative social position of different communities in our society. This understanding should serve as the basis for developing a nonpatronizing respect of community language and should stimulate the natural curiosity about language that might be expected on the part of language arts educators. Unfortunately, genuine respect for and appreciation of linguistic diversity cannot be legislated by a court order.

Knowledge of community language must, of course, extend beyond respect for the naturalness and complexity of community language systems. It should also involve *knowledge of the structural details of the community language system*. It seems reasonable to expect that a language arts practitioner serving a rural southern white community or a practitioner serving an urban northern black community know what the major pronunciation and grammar rules of these respective varieties are, especially where these rules contrast with the language norms presumed in classroom. Knowledge of the structural language details of the community language system serves as the basis for understanding how these language differences may influence basic educational skills such as writing and reading. It may further serve as a basis for understanding the differences in the standardized testing of language arts skills as well. As mentioned previously, there are now available linguistic descriptions of the major regional and social/ethnic language systems which comprise these community language systems. However, available summaries of varieties broadly defined as Vernacular Black English or Appalachian English focus on shared characteristics across communities, so that it is necessary to complement available descriptions with community-specific information.

Insight into particular language forms found in various communities is not the exclusive domain of the linguist or dialectologist. As observers of language behavior, language arts specialists are in an excellent position to contribute to our understanding of such differences. This does not mean that language arts specialists need to know the technical formulas for rules as used by linguists, but it does obligate them to know what language forms are commonly used in the community they serve. A person who pays close attention to language and is willing to spend time where ordinary language is used—on the playground, in shops, and in other natural community contexts—is in a good position to make observations about community language and to apply this knowledge by examining how these language patterns may carry over to specific language skills in the context of the school.

Knowledge of community language must also involve *an understanding of community conventions for language use*. These conventions may dictate how students from different communities will participate in classroom situations, ranging from students' turn-taking styles to students' direct and indirect use of language in discussing particular topics. On one level, such knowledge provides a perspective for understanding student language behavior. On another level, this information may provide an important contrastive basis for the eventual socialization of students into the norms of language behavior expected in a classroom context. Knowledge of language use conventions must also include information about community values and beliefs with respect to language use. What kinds of language styles are positively and negatively valued in the community, and how is school language valued in the community by comparison? How is learning Standard English viewed in the community? Is it associated with "acting white," as found in some working-class black communities? Is it associated with acting "uppity," as it may be in some working-class white communities? Understanding values about the relative social significance of community language and school language is not a frivolous adjunct for the language arts or English teacher; information of this type may impact the language arts curriculum in a fundamental way and determine how students respond in very practical ways to the English language objectives set forth in the classroom.

Knowledge of language use must further consider community-specific language interactional styles as they may relate to the learning process. Is the community model for language interaction between a speaker and audience the one which follows a participatory, "call-response" pattern or is it one which calls for single, recognized-turn response as expected in many classroom situations? These considerations may lead to defining the notion of interruption in a classroom context very differently for various communities, and must be understood by the language arts practitioner if the classroom and community are to come together in the educational process.

Finally, language arts specialists should *become aware of community re-sources in the language arts.* Are there community language uses that dovetail with important language arts skills to be taught in the classroom? Are there exceptional storytellers or recognized styles of creative language use that can bring together the community and classroom? If so, students can build on community language strengths. Furthermore, teachers and students to-gether can turn to the community as a natural resource. Language arts specialists may choose to reject giving the community language a role in the classroom, feeling that their task is to ensure that the acquisition of school-related language conventions takes place, but such an approach may simply force students to make a language choice between school and com-munity language. The history of such choices does not bode well for students from nonmainstream communities. A more reasonable alternative is to start with a fundamental understanding and recognition of the significance of the community language and build on it wherever possible. We take up this matter more extensively in the next section, as we discuss incorporating the study of dialects into the educational curriculum.

INCORPORATING DIALECT STUDY INTO THE EDUCATIONAL CURRICULUM

We have now seen that there are a number of reasons why educators should obtain fundamental knowledge about dialects. It is easy to argue that ed-ucators who deal with dialectally diverse groups of students have a respon-sibility to know something about the dialects of their students. But what about such knowledge for the students themselves? Is the study of dialects a subject area that should be included in the educational curriculum, so that students too may learn about the nature of dialect diversity? I would argue strongly that this should be the case, that a curriculum unit on dialects in American English is appropriate and, in fact, necessary for language arts and English studies in our schools. I realize that there are presently not many school systems which have implemented this type of program, and that most educational systems still would consider it somewhat of a luxury. To me, this is a short-sighted perspective. Informative, highly relevant units on dialects hold appeal for levels of education ranging from elementary school to postsecondary levels.

A RATIONALE FOR STUDYING DIALECTS

Why should students be given a unit of study on dialects when they are already engaged in the study of some aspect of language arts or English at every grade level of their compulsory education? There are several reasons for such a unit which include both philosophical and practical aspects of education. Most educational systems hold dear a fundamental search for truth—the truth about laws of nature and matter. When it comes to dialects, however, there is an educational tolerance of misinformation and folklore that is matched in few subject areas. Remember, from our original presentation in Chapter 1, that there is an entrenched mythology about dialects that pervades our understanding of this topic, particularly with respect to the nature of standard and vernacular varieties. In its own way, the popular understanding of dialects is probably akin to a position in modern geophysics maintaining that the planet Earth is flat. That may seem like an exaggerated analogy offered by an alarmist linguist, but when we consider the facts about dialects in comparison with the popular mythology, it is not far-fetched. And the factual misinformation is not all innocent folklore, as we saw in our discussion of dialects and testing. At times, this misinformation has a significant impact on students' lives. At the very least, then, the American educational system should assume responsibility for replacing the entrenched mythology about dialects with factual information.

The issue of educational equity is also tied in with the need for accurate information about dialects. Operating on erroneous assumptions about language differences, it is easy for students to fall prey to the perpetuation of unjustified stereotypes about language as it relates to class, race, and region. Equity in education is hardly limited to how educators view students. It also affects how students feel about other students and themselves. Students who speak mainstream varieties may view their vernacular-speaking peers as linguistically deficient, just as the broader-based educational system often does. Worse yet, the students themselves may accept this viewpoint about their dialect. It is no accident that the Speech and Hearing Clinic which I am associated with at the University of the District of Columbia routinely receives requests from students for therapy when they are perfectly normal speakers of a vernacular variety. And in most cases, these students describe their problem as "not being able to talk right." So the stereotypes that evolve from the mythology about dialects obviously affect how people are viewed and how they view themselves.

The equity issue with respect to dialect does not stop with perceptions and attitudes; the failure to recognize dialect differences may lead to a kind of discrimination that is as onerous as other types of discrimination based upon race, ethnicity, or class. As Milroy and Milroy (1985) note:

> Although public discrimination on the grounds of race, religion and social class is not now publically acceptable, it appears that discrimination on linguistic grounds is publically acceptable, even though linguistic differences may themselves be associated with ethnic, religious and class differences. (Milroy and Milroy 1985:3)

Dialect discrimination cannot be taken more lightly than any other case of potential discrimination, and there is now a precedent for litigation based on such discrimination. An educational system that takes as its responsibility the obligation to educate students concerning the truth about racial and social differences and the effects of discrimination based on these differences in other areas should feel obligated to extend this discussion to language as well. Students need to understand the natural sociolinguistic principles that lead to the development and maintenance of *all* dialects, and they need to understand that a dialect difference is not a linguistic or cognitive deficit. Only then can we expect to start seeing some change in the current practice of discrimination on the basis of dialect.

From a humanistic standpoint, the reasons given thus far are probably a sufficient rationale for introducing the study of dialects into the educational curriculum. There is, however, another rationale related to the nature of intellectual inquiry. The study of dialects affords students a fascinating window through which they can see how *language* works. In its present form, the English language curriculum exposes students to the study of language organization through the rather laborious study of the "parts of speech," sentence parsing, and other related metalinguistic exercises. Certainly, an important aspect of understanding about language in general, and the English language in particular, is the development of an appreciation for how it develops over time and space into its various dialects. Studying dialects offers a rich laboratory for examining the dynamic nature of language. Given the inherent public interest in dialects, this study has great potential for piquing students' interest in how language works. The unique organizational base of language is just as readily observed in examining the ways of dialects as it is through exclusive study of a single standard variety.

The study of dialects offers another enticement. Language, including dialects, involves a unique form of knowledge in that speakers know a language simply by virtue of the fact that they speak it. Much of this knowledge is not on a conscious level, but it is still open to systematic investigation. Looking at dialect differences provides a natural laboratory for making generalizations drawn from carefully described sets of data. We can hypothesize about certain forms of language and then check them out on the basis of actual usage patterns. This, of course, is a type of scientific inquiry. Such a rationale for studying dialects may seem a bit esoteric at first glance, but it really is quite within the grasp of a well-conceived study of language. In fact, I have actually led classes of students in the middle elementary grades through the steps of hypothesis formation and testing in very practical exercises using particular dialect forms as examples. In the next section, I demonstrate a simple example of how this can be done.

Finally, there is a practical reason for studying dialects. Information about dialects should prove helpful to students as they work to develop the language skills required as a part of the educational process, including the use of the standard variety. Vernacular dialect speakers may, for example, apply knowledge about dialect features to composing and editing skills in writing as a by-product of their study of dialects. I have personally witnessed students who studied about -*s* third person absence in a course on dialects transfer this knowledge to their writing when called upon to write Standard English. Studying about various dialects hardly endangers the sovereignty of Standard English in the classroom; in fact, it seems to enhance learning the standard variety through the heightened sensitivity to language variation. The study of dialects provides an informed background from which knowledge can be applied by the student as well as the teacher.

A CURRICULUM ON DIALECTS

What would a curriculum on dialects actually look like, given the rationale developed in the previous section? Although it is beyond the scope of this book to present actual lesson plans, it is reasonable to introduce the major themes in this curriculum, especially since dialect study is a relatively novel idea at the elementary and secondary levels of education. Following are some of the proposed units appropriate for such a curriculum. They are intended for secondary level, but similar units can be designed for an upper-level elementary language arts curriculum as well.

UNIT ONE: THE NATURALNESS OF AMERICAN ENGLISH DIALECTS

In an initial unit, students need to confront stereotypes and misconceptions about dialects. This is probably best done inductively. An easy method of doing this involves having students listen to representative speech samples of regional, class, and ethnic varieties. Students need to hear how native Standard English speakers in New England, the rural South, and urban North compare to appreciate the reality of diverse regional spoken standards, just as they need to recognize different vernacular varieties in these regions. And students in the Midwest need to consider the features of their own dialect as it compares with others in order to understand that everyone really does speak a dialect. Although most tape-recorded collections of dialect samples are personal ones that are not commercially available, the video production *American Tongues* (Alvarez and Kolker 1987) can be used to provide an entertaining introduction to dialects while, at the same time, exposing basic prejudices and myths about language differences.

It is important for students to contribute examples of dialect variation from their own community in this introductory unit, as a basis for seeing how natural and inevitable dialects are. For starters, students should at least be able to offer regional names for short-order, over-the-counter foods (e.g., *sub/hoagie/hero*, and so on) and drinks (e.g., *soda/pop*, and so forth). In phonology, they can start with a simple exercise focused on how they produce sets of vowels in a limited context, such as the vowel(s) before -*r* in words like *Mary, merry, marry*, and *Murray*. The straightforward goal of this introductory unit is to get students to acknowledge that they, too, speak a dialect. Of course, we need to recognize that dealing with the students' underlying attitudes about dialects is a formidable challenge, equal in magnitude to confronting any other prejudice students bring with them to the classroom.

UNIT TWO: LANGUAGE RULES AND DIALECTS

One of the most fundamental notions for students to master about dialects, or about language for that matter, is that language patterns or "rules" have their reality in the minds of speakers. The popular stereotype is that various dialects, particularly vernacular varieties, are simply imperfect attempts to speak the standard variety. In addition, students tend to think of "grammar rules" as prescriptive dictums that take on life through their written specification in grammar books. An inductive exercise on the systematic nature of dialects can go a long way towards dispelling this notion. It also can set the stage for generating a nonpatronizing respect for the complexity of systematic differences among dialects.

Incorporated into Exercise 4 is a sample exercise of this type, based on the placement of the *a*- prefix in structures like *He was a-huntin'* (see the Appendix for specific structural details about its placement). The idea behind this exercise is simply to demonstrate that students can make systematic judgments about the linguistic contexts for *a*- attachment—judgments that correspond to its patterned distribution as a "linguistic rule" in a vernacular dialect. The advantage of this particular example is that it involves a form for which the intuitions of native and nonnative *a*- prefix speakers are alike (Wolfram 1982). This fact makes the exercise appropriate for students regardless of their native dialect.

Exercise 4

Work through the following student exercise as a student might work through it. What insights about language structure does it provide for a student? How do the insights from such an exercise counter existing notions of "linguistic rules"?

A- Prefix: An Exercise in Dialect Patterning

Some dialects of Appalachia and other rural parts of the United States put an *a-* type sound before words that end in *-ing*, as in *They went a-hunting*. It appears that this *a-* may occur with some *-ing* forms but not with others. In the following pairs of sentences, choose one of the sentences that "sounds right" for the placement of the *a-*. Choose only one sentence for each pair. If you're not sure of the answer, simply make your best guess. Do not look at the answers given below until you have made all of your selections.

1. a. John likes sailing.
    b. John went sailing.
2. a. The woman was coming down the stairs.
    b. The movie was shocking.
3. a. He was charming.
    b. He was running to the store.
4. a. They kept hunting for a snake.
    b. They thought hunting was great fun.
5. a. Sarah was following the trail.
    b. Sarah was discovering the cave.
6. a. The dog was eating the food.
    b. The dog was drinking the water.
7. a. The man was repeating the chant.
    b. The man was hollering at the dog.
8. a. Raymond kept asking the question.
    b. Raymond kept telling the answer.

Questions

1. One observer of the English language wrote that "in popular speech almost every word ending in *-ing* has a sort of prefix, *a-*." Based on your reaction to the sentence pairs, do you agree with him? Are there some sentences where the use of *a-* "feels" right and others where it doesn't? Check the choices you made above with the following correct answers for this dialect pattern: (1) *b* (2) *a* (3) *b* (4) *a* (5) *a* (6) *b* (7) *b* (8) *b*.

2. The language pattern, or "rule," that explains the use of the *a-* turns out to be very complicated and detailed. Few people can say exactly how the rule works, yet practically everyone makes the correct choices for the placement of the *a-* prefix. Based on this observation, what can we say about the nature of language rules? Are language patterns based on written "grammar" books or are they based on an inner system of patterning that governs how we use language?

3. You are involved in a conversation with a person about dialects, and the person says, "Dialects don't have rules; they're just deviations from real English." Based on this exercise, how would you respond to this statement?

An exercise of this type is an effective way of confronting the myth that dialects have no rules of their own; at the same time, it effectively demonstrates the underlying cognitive basis for all language patterning.

UNIT THREE: LEVELS OF DIALECT PATTERNING

One of the fundamental notions for students to understand about language is its organization on several different levels. As we presented originally in Chapter 3, language variation may be manifested on each of the levels of language organization. The study of dialects can be a basis for probing the various levels of language organization at the same time that it presents exemplary cases of dialect diversity. It is, of course, possible to present students simply with some of the dialect rules found on different levels, but it is more effective for students to work with dialect data to arrive at these dialect rules on their own. Working with data of this type also introduces students to the methods of dialectologists as they formulate hypotheses about language patterns and then check them out with actual language data. For example, consider the sample exercise incorporated into Exercise 5.

Exercise 5

Work through the following exercise. What might a student learn about phonological rules from this exercise? Does this exercise involve a critical thinking skill? If so, what type of skill does it represent?

A Southern Vowel Pronunciation

In some southern dialects of English, words like *pin* and *pen* are pronounced the same. Usually, both words are pronounced as *pin*. This pattern of pronunciation is found in other words as well. Following is a list of some of the words in which the *i* and *e* would be pronounced the *same* in these dialects.

1. a. *tin* and *ten*
   b. *kin* and *Ken*
   c. *Lin* and *Len*
   d. *tinder* and *tender*
   e. *sinned* and *send*

Although *i* and *e* would be pronounced the same in the preceding word pairs, there are other words in which *i* and *e* are pronounced differently.

Following are some of these word pairs in which the vowels are pronounced *differently*.

2. a. *lit* and *let*
    b. *pick* and *peck*
    c. *pig* and *peg*
    d. *rip* and *rep*
    e. *litter* and *letter*

Is there a pattern that can explain the similar pronunciation of *i* and *e* for the words in list *1* and the different pronunciation of *i* and *e* in list 2? To answer this question, you have to look at the sounds that are next to the vowels, in particular those that come after the vowel. What common sound is found next to the vowel in all of the examples given in the list *1*? *Based on the pattern you discovered, which of the following word pairs would you expect to be pronounced the same* in this southern dialect and which would you expect to be pronounced *differently*?

3. a. *Rick* and *wrech*
    b. *bit* and *bet*
    c. *bin* and *Ben*
    d. *Nick* and *neck*
    e. *din* and *den*

State the southern pronunciation rule that explains the identical pronunciation of *pin* and *pen*.

The advantage of these types of exercises should be obvious, as students learn how linguists collect and organize data to formulate rules. It also provides a protocol for students to apply to data that they might collect from their own community. In the best-case scenario, students may record language data, extract particular examples from the data, and formulate linguistic rules themselves. In this way, students may learn firsthand about examining language in a scientific way.

Exercise 6

Write an exercise for the southern rural dialect rule in which the final, unstressed syllable spelled *-ow/oe/o* (phonetically [o]) of words like *hollow*, *tomato*, and *yellow* is produced with an *r*, as in *holler*, *tomater*, and *yeller*, respectively. You will need to contrast a list of words which may take a final *r* with a list of words that cannot be produced with an *r* in order to get students to see that how the rule operates. For example, words like *toe*, *flow*, *below*, and *bestow*, with a final [o], are *not* produced with an *r* because they occur in a stressed syllable. As a final part of the exercise, have students choose words that may and may not be produced with the *r*, as we did for the *i/e* exercise previously.

UNIT FOUR: INDEPENDENT RESEARCH ON DIALECTS

In addition to seeing dialect study as a kind of scientific investigation of language, students should be encouraged to see how dialect study merges with the social sciences and humanities. This study can be viewed from the perspective of geography, history, or sociology; it also can be linked with ethnic or gender studies. In this far-reaching role, the examination of dialect differences offers great potential for students to probe the linguistic manifestations of other types of sociocultural differences. A student, or group of students, interested in history may thus carry out independent research to determine the contributions of various historical groups to a particular locale by researching the migratory routes of the original settlers of the area, and showing how this is reflected in the dialect. Similarly, a group of students interested in sociology may examine status differences in a community as manifested in language. Or, a group of students may probe the linguistic manifestations of in-group behavior by examining the way new vocabulary items are formed in some special-interest group. The way in which new words are formed, as discussed in Chapter 3, can be examined through the investigation of the jargon of an athletic specialization (e.g., playground basketball) or through the investigation of slang as used by peer cohorts who hang out at the mall just as readily as it can through the study of how mainstream words have developed. Students can even create a new slang term and follow its spread among their peers to observe the social dynamics of language.

While it is possible to develop specific lessons on this research phase of dialect study, its true value is realized by allowing groups of students to examine complementary topics and by having the groups share their investigation with other class members. The underlying objective in introducing students to the way in which language differences reflect deeper sociocultural variation can obviously be tapped in a number of creative and interesting activities for students.

UNIT FIVE: THE CONSEQUENCES OF DIALECT

Part of understanding about the nature of dialects ultimately entails comprehension of the consequences of using standard and vernacular varieties. To a large extent, students are already aware of the respective roles that such varieties may play, but this often exists on an implicit rather than explicit level. Students should, however, profit from an investigation of how standard and vernacular varieties develop, and the relative roles they play in society. It is important that this phase of instruction on dialects be realistic so that students fully understand the relative advantages and disadvantages of both standard and vernacular varieties in different social situations. There is no reason why students cannot even be involved in active debate about teaching Standard English in the schools. In fact, some of the best debates I have witnessed on this topic were conducted by students who were asked, simply for the sake of argument, to defend a particular position on the need for Standard English. The discussion of Standard English by students can be as active and lively as any topic in the study of dialects, as long as their opinions are self-generated and open. This discussion may also allow students to confront the Standard English question for themselves, instead of simply being preached at by the teacher about the marketplace value of the standard variety.

Exercise 7

Make a list of questions about the usefulness of Standard English which you might want a class of high school students to consider in a debate on Standard English. For each question, what positions might be taken?

THE EDUCATIONAL OUTCOMES

There are a number of positive results that might derive from a unit of study on dialects. If students simply replace the current stereotyped mythology about dialects with informed knowledge, the curriculum is probably justified, given the far-reaching effects of dialect prejudice in our society. Along with this perspective, students should develop a positive understanding of the complexity and naturalness of dialects.

One of the greatest attributes of a curriculum on dialects is its potential for tapping the language resources of students' indigenous communities. In addition to classroom lessons, students can learn by going into the community to collect live dialect data. In most cases, the language characteristics of a local language community should make dialects come alive in a way that is unmatched by textbook knowledge. Educational models that treat the local community as a resource to be tapped rather than a liability to be overcome have been shown to be quite effective in other areas of language arts education, as demonstrated by the success of Wigginton's Foxfire experiment in Rabun Gap, Georgia (Wigginton 1986). There is no reason why this model cannot be applied in an analogous fashion to the study of community dialects. A model that builds on community strengths in language, even when different from the norms of the mainstream educational system, seems to hold much greater potential for success than one that focuses exclusively on language conflicts between the community and school. In fact, the community dialect may just turn out to contain an educational lodestone for the study of language arts. The study of dialects can, indeed, become a vibrant, relevant topic of study for all students, not just for those who choose to take an optional course on this topic at a postsecondary level of education.

Further Reading

BROOKS, CHARLOTTE K., ed., *Tapping Potential: English and Language Arts for the Black Learner*. Urbana, IL: National Council of Teachers of English, 1985. This collection of articles offers approaches and methods in language arts that may be appropriate for minority students, including those who speak vernacular dialects. Subsections include articles on language, reading, writing, and literature. In a number of the articles, the background of students is constructively used as support for the educational process.

FARR, MARCIA AND HARVEY DANIELS, *Language Diversity and Writing Instruction*. Urbana, IL: National Council of Teachers of English, 1986. This reasoned treatment offers a theoretical framework, along with practical suggestions for educators who wish to improve the writing skills of students from vernacular-speaking communities.

GLOWKA, WAYNE AND DONALD LANCE, eds., *Ideas for Teaching About Language Variation: American English and Related Topics*. New York, NY: Modern Language Association, forthcoming. This collection of essays is devoted to the discussion of practical methods for presenting notions about language variation to students. Some of the articles offer helpful aids for getting students involved in the study of language variation.

WILLIAMSON, JUANITA V. AND VIRGINIA M. BURKE, eds., *A Various Language: Perspectives on American Dialects*. New York, NY: Holt, Rinehart and Winston, 1971. This is one of the few anthologies of dialect articles that includes a separate section devoted to literary representations of American English dialects. Seven articles on literary dialects are included, including a couple of widely cited ones by Sumner Ives.

WOLFRAM, WALT, "Sociolinguistic Alternatives for Teaching Reading to Speakers of Non-Standard English," *The Reading Research Quarterly*, 6:9–33, (1970). Although this was one of the earlier sociolinguistic critiques of alternative strategies in teaching reading to vernacular dialect speakers, the advantages and disadvantages of each approach as set forth here are still applicable.

APPENDIX

A SELECTIVE INVENTORY OF SOCIALLY DIAGNOSTIC STRUCTURES

The following inventory summarizes many of the structures mentioned in the text; it also introduces structures not covered in the preceding chapters. It is limited to phonological and grammatical structures. For each of the structures, a brief general comment is given about the linguistic patterning of the structure, as well as a statement about its dialect distribution. The focus is on items that are socially significant in terms of the standard-vernacular continuum rather than regional variation, although some regional features are included. For more detail on regional pronunciation, see the introduction by Hartman in the *Dictionary of American Regional English* (Cassidy 1985). To the extent possible, traditional orthography is used in representing forms, but this is not possible in all cases.

PHONOLOGICAL STRUCTURES

Consonants

FINAL CLUSTER REDUCTION

Word-final consonant clusters ending in a stop can be reduced when both members of the cluster are either voiced (e.g., *find*, *cold*) or voiceless (*act*, *test*). This rule affects both clusters which are a part of the base word (e.g., *find*, *act*) and those clusters formed through the addition of an -*ed* suffix (e.g., *guessed*, *liked*). In Standard English, this rule may operate when the following word begins in a consonant (e.g., *best kind*), but in vernacular dialects, it is extended to include following words beginning in a vowel as well (e.g., *best apple*).

This pattern is quite prominent in Vernacular Black English and in dialects of English that retain influence from another language, such as Chicano English and Vietnamese English. It is not particularly obtrusive in most Anglo-based dialects, such as Vernacular Southern and Northern White varieties.

PLURALS FOLLOWING CLUSTERS

Words ending in -*sp* (e.g, *wasp*), -*sk* (e.g., *desk*), and -*st* (e.g., *test*) may take the -*es* (*phonetically* [Iz]) *plural* (e.g., *tesses*, *desses*) in many of these vernacular varieties. In such cases, the regular English plural simply operates after the application of the cluster reduction rule, since -*es* is the form that regularly occurs following *s*-like sounds (i.e., sibilants).

In Vernacular Appalachian English, an intrusive stop may occur, resulting in items such as *postes* and *deskes*. Such forms are considerably more rare in Vernacular Black English, and seem to be a function of hypercorrection or "overlearning" Standard English plural forms.

INTRUSIVE T

A small set of items, typically ending in *s* and *f* in the standard variety, may be produced with a final *t*. This results in a final consonant cluster. Typical items affected by this process are *oncet*, *twicet*, *clifft*, and *acrosst*. This is found typically in Appalachian varieties and those other rural varieties retaining more relic forms.

A quite different kind of intrusive *t* involves the "doubling" of an -*ed* form. In this instance, a verb which has already added an -*ed* in the phonetic form of [t] (e.g., [lUkt] for *looked*), adds another *ed*, treating the word as if it ended in [t]. Thus, a form such as *looked* [lUkt] may be produced as *lookted* [lUktId] and *attacked* [ətæk] as *attackted* [ətæktId]. These forms arise as a kind of "false analysis" of the base form and tend to be limited to particular verbs.

TH SOUNDS

There are a number of different processes that affect the *th* sounds. The phonetic production is typically sensitive to the position of *th* in the word and the sounds adjacent to it. At the beginning of the word, *th* tends to be produced as a corresponding stop, such as *dey* for *they* ([d] for [ð]) and *ting* for *thing* ([t] for [θ]). These productions are fairly typical of a wide range of vernaculars, although there are differences in the distribution of the voiceless and voiced *th*. The *t* for *thing* tends to be most characteristic of selected Anglo and second-language influenced varieties, whereas the *d* for *they* is spread across the full spectrum of vernacular varieties.

Before nasals, *th* participates in a rule in which a range of fricatives, including *z*, *th*, and *v*, may also become stops. This results in forms such as *aritmetic* for *arithmetic* or *headn* for *heathen*, as well as *wadn't* for *wasn't*, *idn't* for *isn't*, and *sebm* for *seven*. This pattern is typically found in southern-based vernacular varieties, including Southern White and Black English.

In word-final and intervocalic position within a word, *th* may be produced as *f* or *v*, as in *efer* for *ether*, *toof* for *tooth*, *brover* for *brother*, and *smoov* for *smooth*. This production is typical of Vernacular Black English, with the *v* for voiced *th* [ð] production more typical of eastern varieties of the vernacular. There are scattered Anglo dialects, as well as varieties influenced by other languages in the recent past, such as Chicano English, that also show limited evidence of the *f* production in *tooth*.

Some restricted Anglo varieties use a stop *d* for intervocalic voiced *th* as in *oder* for *other* or *broder* for *brother*, but this pattern is much less common than the word-initial stop for *th*.

R AND L

There are a number of different linguistic contexts in which *r* and *l* may be lost or reduced to a vowel-like vestige. After a vowel, as in *sister* or *steal*, the *r* and *l* may be reduced or lost. This feature intersects strongly with a regional dimension, and is quite typical of southern-based and New England varieties.

Intervocalically, an *r* also may be lost, as in *Ca'ol* for *Carol* or *sto'y* for *story*. This intervocalic *r* loss is more socially stigmatized than the simple postvocalic version of the rule cited earlier, and is found in rural, southern-based vernaculars.

Following a consonant, the *r* may be lost if it precedes a round vowel such as *u* or *o*. This results in pronunciations of *thru* as *thu* and *throw* as *tho*. Postconsonantal *r* loss may also be found if it occurs in an unstressed syllable, such as *p'ofessor* for *professor* or *sec'etary* for *secretary*. This *r*-lessness also has a strong intersection with a regional southern variable.

Before a labial sound, *l* may be lost completely, giving *woof* for *wolf* or *hep* for *help*. Again, this is only characteristic of southern-based varieties.

Some vocabulary items also have been affected by *r*-lessness, so that *they* for *their* as in *theyself* or *they book* apparently has been derived historically from the process of *r*-lessness.

There are occasional instances in which an intrusive *r* may occur, so that items such as *wash* may be pronounced as *warsh* and *idea* as *idear*. For the most part, these are limited to particular lexical items and are regionally restricted.

INITIAL W REDUCTION

In unstressed positions within the sentence, an initial *w* may be lost in items such as *was* and *one*. This results in items such as *he's* [*hiz*] *here yesterday* for *he was here yesterday* and *young 'uns* for *young ones*. This appears to be a generalization of the restricted process affecting the initial sounds of the modals *will* and *would* in standard varieties of English (e.g., *he will* → *he'll*; *he would* → *he'd*). This process is found in southern-based vernaculars.

UNSTRESSED INITIAL SYLLABLE LOSS

The general process of deleting unstressed initial syllables in informal speech styles of Standard English (e.g., *because* → *'cause*; *around* → *'round*) is extended in vernacular varieties so that a wider range of word classes (e.g., verbs such as *'member* for *remember* or nouns such as *taters* for *potatoes*) and word-initial forms (e.g., *re-*, *po-*, *to-*, *sus-*, and so on) are affected by this rule.

INITIAL H RETENTION

The retention of *h* on the pronoun *it* [hIt] and the auxiliary *ain't* [hent] is still found in vernacular varieties retaining older English forms, such as Appalachia. This form is more prominent in stressed positions within a sentence. The pronunciation seems to be fading out among younger speakers.

NASALS

There are a number of processes that affect nasal sounds; there are also items that are influenced by the presence of nasals in the surrounding linguistic environment.

One widespread process in vernacular varieties is the so-called "g-dropping," in which the back nasal [ŋ], represented as *ng* in spelling is pronounced as [n]. This process takes place when the *ng* occurs in an un-stressed syllable, as in *swimmin'* for *swimming* or *buyin'* for *buying*.

Another general characteristic affecting nasals is the generalization of the form of the indefinite article *a* so that it occurs before words beginning with either a vowel or consonants (e.g., *a apple*, *a pear*).

A less widespread phenomenon affecting nasals is the use of a nasalized vowel (as in the production of the French nasalized vowel in words like *bon* [bõ]) when a nasal segment is in word-final position, particularly when the item is in a relatively unstressed position within the sentence. Thus *man*, *bum*, or *ring* may be pronounced as *ma'* [mæ̃], *bu'* [bʌ̃], or *ri'* [rĩ], respectively, with the vowel carrying a nasal quality. Most frequently, this process affects the segment *n*, although all final nasal segments may be affected to some extent. This process is typical of Vernacular Black English.

There are other nasal processes (e.g., the neutralization of the contrast between [I] and [ɛ] before nasals as in *pen* and *pin*), but these tend to be much more regionally than socially sensitive.

OTHER CONSONANTS

There are a number of other consonantal patterns that affect limited sets of items or single words. For example, the retention of the older form *aks* for *ask* is observed in several vernacular varieties, including Vernacular Black English. The form *chimley* or *chimbley* for *chimney* is also found in a number of southern-based vernaculars. The use of *k* in initial (*s*)*tr* clusters as in *skreet* for *street* or *skring* for *string* is found in Vernacular Black English, particularly rural southern varieties. Such items are quite socially obtrusive, but occur with such limited sets of words that they are best considered on an item-by-item basis.

VOWELS

There are many vowel patterns that differentiate the dialects of English, but the majority of these are more regionally than socially significant. The back vowel [ɔ] of *bought* or *coffee* and front vowel [æ] in *cat* and *ran* are particularly sensitive to regional variation, as are vowels before *r* (e.g., compare pronunciations of *merry, marry, Mary, Murray*) and *l* (compare *wheel, will, well, whale*). Although it is not possible here to indicate all the nuances of phonetic differences reflected in the vowels, several major patterns may be identified with respect to the dialects of English.

VOWEL SHIFTS

There are several shifts in the phonetic value of vowels that are currently taking place in American English. The important aspect of these shifts is the fact that vowels are not shifting their phonetic value in isolation, but as rotating subsystems of vowels in terms of a "push-pull" effect. One major rotation is the Northern Cities Vowel Shift. In this rotation, the phonetic values of two series of vowels are affected; the low long vowels are moving forward and upward and the short vowels are moving downward and backward. For example, the phonetic value of a vowel like the open *o* of *coffee* is moving downward and forward toward the /a/ of *father*. The low vowel in a word like *pop* or *lock*, in turn, moves towards the [æ] of *bat*, which, in turn, moves upward toward the vowel [ɛ] of bet. At the same time, another rotation moves the short vowel [I] of *bit* toward the [ɛ] of *bet*. The [ɛ], in turn, moves backward toward the mid vowel of *but* [ʌ], which is then pushed back (short vowels and long vowels tend to rotate as different subsystems within the overall vowel system). Diagrammatically, the shift may be represented as follows. The conventional vowel chart of English is set up schematically to represent relative tongue height and frontness in the vocal tract. For convenience only, key words in terms of an idealized Standard American English phonemes are given. The arrows point to the direction of the phonetic rotations taking place in the shift.

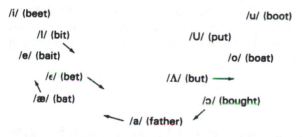

Vowel Rotation in Northern Cities Vowel Shift (from Labov "The Three Dialects of English" forthcoming, p. 25)

Regionally, the pattern of vowel rotation represented in the diagram starts in western New England, and goes eastward into the northern tier of Pennsylvania, northern Ohio, Indiana, Illinois, Michigan, Wisconsin, and is more concentrated in the larger metropolitan areas. More advanced stages of this change can be found in younger speakers in the largest metropolitan areas in this northern region, such as Buffalo, Albany, Cleveland, Detroit, and Chicago. Minority groups in these metropolitan areas tend not to participate in this phonetic shift.

The Southern Vowel Shift is quite different in its phonetic rotation of vowels. In this rotation pattern, the short front vowels (the vowels of words like *bed* and *bid*) are moving upward and taking on the gliding character of long vowels (a vowel like the long *e* of bait actually consists of a vowel nucleus [e] and an upward glide into [I]). Meanwhile, the long front vowels (the vowels of *beet* and *late*) are moving backward and the back vowels (the vowels of *boot* and *boat*) are moving forward. This phonetic rotation may be described in the following chart.

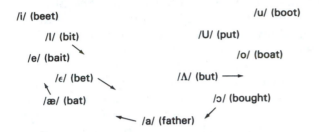

/i/ (beet)   /u/ (boot)

   /I/ (bit)   /U/ (put)

  /e/ (bait)   /o/ (boat)

   /ɛ/ (bet)   /ʌ/ (but) ——→

  /æ/ (bat)   /ɔ/ (bought)

    ←— /a/ (father)

Vowel Rotation in Northern Cities Vowel Shift (from Labov, "The Three Dialects of English" forthcoming, p. 35)

LOW BACK VOWEL MERGER

One of the major regional variations in vowels is the merger of low back vowels *a* and "open *o*." This merger means that words like *cot* and *caught*, or *hawk* and *hock*, are pronounced the same. This regional merger radiates from two centers, one in eastern New England, centered around Boston, and one centered around Pittsburgh in the Ohio Valley. Its western extension covers a large portion of the traditional West, excluding major metropolitan areas such as Los Angeles and San Francisco.

æ RAISING

The vowel of words such as *back* or *bag* may be heightened from its typical phonetic position so that it is produced closer to the [ɛ] of *beg* or *bet*. The feature is found in a number of northern areas and is often a part of the Northern Cities Vowel Shift.

aw CENTERING

The vowel nucleus of words like *out* and *bout*, which is often [a] or [æ] (e.g., [aUt] or [æUt] *out*) may be produced with a central vowel closer to the schwa [ə], as in [əUt]. This feature is often associated with the Tidewater region in the East, but is also found in some far northern regional dialects as well.

VOWEL UNGLIDING

The vowel glides, as in *ay* [aI] (e.g., *side*, *time*) and *oy* [oI] (e.g., *boy*, *toy*), may be unglided in items such as [tam] for *time* and [bɔ] for *boy*. Absence of the glide is more frequent when the following segment is voiced (e.g., *side, time*) than when it is *voiceless* (e.g., *sight, rice*). This variable is characteristic of practically all southern-based vernaculars, and is not particularly socially significant in the South.

FINAL UNSTRESSED OW

In word-final position, Standard English *ow*, as in *hollow* or *yellow*, may become an *r*, giving *holler* or *yeller*, respectively. This "intrusive *r*" also occurs when suffixes are attached, as in *fellers* for *fellows* or *narrers* for *narrows*. This production is characteristic of highland varieties such as those found in Appalachia or the Ozarks, although it is found to some extent in other rural varieties as well.

FINAL UNSTRESSED A[ə] RAISING

Final unstressed *a* (phonetically a schwa [ə]), as in *soda* or *extra*, may be raised to a high front vowel [i], giving productions such as *sody* (phonetically [sodi]) and *extry* [ɛkstri]). Again, this is a production found in highland rural vernaculars of the South.

IRE/OUR COLLAPSE

The sequence *ire*, which is usually produced as a two-syllable sequence in Standard English, including a diphthong [aI] (e.g., [taIɚ] *tire*; [faIɚ] *fire* can be collapsed into a one-syllable sequence, without the glide, as in *fa'r* [far] and *ta'r* [tar]. This process also affects those sequences formed by the addition of an *-er* suffix, such as *buyer* [bar] and *retired* [ritard]. A similar process affects *-our/ower* sequences which phonetically consist of a two-syllable sequence involving the [aU] diphthong and *r*, as in *flower* [flaUɚ] or *hour* [aUɚ], which are reduced to a single syllable, as in *fla'r* [flar] or *ha'r* [ar].

GRAMMATICAL STRUCTURES

The Verb Phrase

Many of the socially significant grammatical structures involve aspects of the verb phrase. Some of this variation follows the principles of readjustment discussed in Chapter 2, but there are also items unique to vernacular varieties because of their historical contact situations.

IRREGULAR VERBS

There are five categories of irregular verb patterns that differentiate the usage of these forms. For the most part, the shifts in subclasses of irregular forms have resulted from the process of analogy, including both regularization and minority pattern shifts. These differences are as follows:

1. past as participle form
   I *had went* down there.
   He may *have took* the wagon.
2. participle as past form
   He *seen* something out there.
   She *done* her homework.
3. bare root as past form
   She *come* to my house yesterday.
   She *give* him a nice present last year.
4. regularization
   Everybody *knowed* he was late.
   They *throwed* out the old food.
5. different irregular form
   I *hearn* something shut the church house door.
   She just *retch* up on the fireplace.

Various vernaculars of English participate in these patterns in slightly different ways, with the majority of vernaculars in the North and South having categories 1, 2, and 3. Southern-based rural vernaculars are more likely to have category 5. Varieties subject to the influence of second-language learning strategies (e.g., Vietnamese English) often reveal a higher incidence of regularization (category 4).

VERB SUBCLASS SHIFTS

There are a number of different types of verb patterns that include analogical shifts among subclasses of verbs. These patterns include the following:

1. shifts in the transitive status of verbs (i.e., whether or not the verb is required to take an object)
   If we *beat*, we will be champs.
   She *learned the students* how to do math.
2. verbs derived from other parts of speech (e.g., verbs derived from nouns)
   Our dog *treed a coon.*
   We doctored the sickness ourselves.
3. the formation of verb complement structures (i.e., the structures of items that occur with the verb)
   The kitchen *needs remodeled.*
   The students *started to messing* around.
   I'll *have* him *to do* it.
   The dog *wanted out.*

1. verb plus verb particle formations
   He *happened in* on the party.
   The coach *blessed out* his players.
5. shifts in the semantic reference (broadened or narrowed semantic domain) of the verb form
   He *carried* her to the movies.
   My kids *took* the chicken pox when they were young.
   I was *fixin'* to go there.
   I been *aimin'* to go there.

For the most part, the shifts in verb subclasses and the semantic reference of various verbs have to be dealt with on an item-by-item basis. All vernaculars and many regional varieties participate in these patterns to some extent.

COMPLETIVE DONE

The form *done* may function to mark a completed action or event in a way somewhat different from simple past, as in a sentence such as *There was one in there that done rotted away* or *I done forgot what you wanted.* In this use, the emphasis is on the completive aspect. It may also add intensification to the activity, as in *I done told you not to mess around.* This form is typically found in southern white and black vernaculars.

HABITUAL BE

The form *be* in sentences such as *Sometimes my ears be itching* or *She usually be home in the evening* may signify an event or activity distributed intermittently over time or space. The predominant construction for habitual *be* involves a form of *be* + verb -*ing*, as in *My ears be itching.* This unique aspectual meaning of *be* is typically associated with Vernacular Black English, although isolated and restricted constructions of this type have been found in some rural white varieties.

REMOTE TIME BEEN

The form *been* can also serve to mark a special aspectual function, indicating that the event or activity took place in the "distant past." In structures such as *I been had it there for about three years* or *I been known her*, the reference is to the event taking place, literally or figuratively, in a distant time frame. This use, which is associated with Vernacular Black English, is dying out in some varieties of the vernacular, but still prominent in those varieties more closely aligned with its creole predecessor, where the form was used much more extensively.

AUXILIARY COME

The use of the form *come* as an auxiliary in sentences such as *She come acting like she was real mad* or *He come telling me I didn't know what I was talking about* conveys a special sense of speaker indignation. It is a "camouflaged" form, in the sense that it appears to be much like a comparable Standard English construction (e.g., *She came running home*), but does not function in the same way as its standard counterpart. It is found in Vernacular Black English.

A-PREFIXING

An *a-* prefix may occur on Verb + *-ing* forms functioning as progressives (e.g., *He was a-comin' home*) or adverbial complements to the verb, as in *He kept a-wantin' to go out, She makes money a-sewin'* or *He starts a-laughin at you.* This form cannot occur on *-ing* forms that function as nouns or adjectives (i.e., sentences such as **He likes a-sailin'* or **The movie was a-charmin'* do *not* occur). The *a-* is also restricted phonologically, in that it occurs only on forms beginning with a consonant (i.e., sentences such as *He was a-drinkin'* but *not *He was a-eatin'*) and forms where the first syllable of the form is relatively stressed (e.g., sentences such as *She was a-following the trail* but *not* sentences such as **She was a-discoverin' the cave*). This structure may be used to indicate intensity by some speakers, but does not appear to have any unique aspectual marking analogous to habitual *be* or completive *done*. It is quite characteristic of Vernacular Appalachian English, but found in other rural varieties as well.

DOUBLE MODALS

Double modals involve constructions of two modal forms such as *might could, useta could, might should, might oughta,* and so forth. Sentences as *I might could go there* or *You might oughta take it* are typically southern vernacular structures; only modal clustering with *useta*, as in *He useta couldn't do it* or *He didn't useta go there* is found in northern varieties.

SPECIAL MODALS

The forms *liketa* and *(su)poseta* may be used as a special verb modifier to mark special speaker perceptions relating to significant events that were on the verge of happening. *Liketa* is "counterfactual," in that it is used to indicate that an event about to take place actually did not happen, as in the sentence *She liketa scared me to death* or *I liketa froze it was so cold in there*. It usually carries with it an exaggerated connotation. *Supposeta*, in sentences such as *You (su)poseta went there*, is used in a sense parallel to the Standard English construction *supposed to have*.

ABSENCE OF BE FORMS

Where contracted forms of *is* or *are* may occur in Standard English, these same forms may be deleted in some vernacular varieties. Thus, we get structures such as *You ugly* or *She taking the dog out* corresponding to the Standard English structures *You're ugly* and *She's taking the dog out*, respectively. It is important to note that this absence only takes place on "contractable" forms (e.g., it does not affect forms such are in *That's where they are* since this form cannot be contracted to *That's where they're*); furthermore, it does not typically apply to forms of *am* (e.g., sentences such as *I ugly* do not often occur). The deletion of *are* is typical of both white southern and black English vernaculars. A more general version, including *am* absence, is sometimes found in varieties developed in the process of learning English as a second language (e.g., Vietnamese English).

SUBJECT-VERB AGREEMENT

There are a number of different subject-verb agreement patterns that enter into the social differentiation of dialects. These include the following:

1. agreement with the existential *there*
   There was five people there.
   There's two women in the lobby.
2. agreement patterns with the general present and past tense forms of *be*
   The cars was out on the street.
   Most of the kids is younger up there.
3. agreement with the form *don't*
   She don't like the cat in the house.
   It don't seem like a holiday.
4. agreement with *have*
   My nerves has been on edge.
   My children hasn't been there much.
5. agreement with special kinds of plural subjects
   Some people likes to talk a lot.
   Me and my brother gets in a fight.
6. agreement with regular third person singular
   The dog stay outside in the afternoon.
   He usually like the evening news.

Different vernacular varieties participate in these patterns in varying ways. Virtually all vernacular varieties participate to some extent in the patterns of categories 1, 2, and 3 (in fact, standard varieties are moving towards the pattern found in 1), but in different degrees. The patterns illustrated in categories 4 and 5 are the most characteristic of highland southern and rural varieties in the South, and those found in category 6 are most typical of Vernacular Black English.

PAST TENSE ABSENCE

Much of the past tense absence in regular verb forms such as *Yesterday he mess up* or *She like the book that she got for a present* can be accounted for by phonological processes discussed earlier (e.g., consonant cluster reduction). However, there are instances in which past tense is unmarked as a function of a grammatical difference. This is particularly true of varieties influenced by other languages in their recent past. Thus, structures such as *He bring the food yesterday* or *He play a new song last night* may be the result of a grammatical process rather than a phonological one. Grammatically-based tense unmarking tends to be more frequent on regular verb forms than irregular forms, so that a structure such as *Yesterday he play a new song* is more likely than *Yesterday he is in a new store*, although both may occur. In some cases, both phonological and grammatical processes operate in a convergent way.

Tense unmarking has been found to be prominent in varieties such as Vietnamese English and American Indian English. In the latter case, unmarking is favored in habitual contexts (e.g., *In those days, we play a different kind of game*) as opposed to simple past time (e.g., *Yesterday, we play at a friend's house*).

HISTORICAL PRESENT

In the dramatic recounting of past time events, present tense verb forms may be used, as in *I go down there and this guy comes up to me. . . . In some cases an -s* suffix may be added to non-third person forms, particularly with first person forms of the verb *say* (e.g., *so I says to him . . .*). This structure is more prominent in white vernaculars than in Vernacular Black English.

ADVERBS

There are several different patterns that distinguish adverb usage among vernacular varieties. These involve differences in the placement of adverbs within the sentence, differences in the formation of adverbs, and differences in the use or meaning of particular adverbial forms.

ADVERB PLACEMENT

There are several differences in terms of the position of the adverb within the sentence, including the placement of certain time adverbs within the verb phrase, as in *We were all the time talking* or *We watched all the time "Little House on the Prairie."* These cases do not hold great social significance, and are not particularly socially stigmatized. More obtrusive is the change in order with various forms of *ever*, as in *everwhat*, *everwho*, or *everwhich* (e.g., *Everwho wanted to go could go*). These retentions of older English forms are generally found only in vernaculars retaining relic forms of English, but even in these contexts they are currently dying out.

COMPARATIVES AND SUPERLATIVES

Most vernacular varieties of English participate in adaptations of irregular comparative and superlative forms. One extension is the regularization of irregular forms, resulting in *badder* or *mostest*. Another extension involves the use of *-er* and *-est* on polysyllabic (two or more syllable) words where the standard variety uses *more* and *most* (e.g., *beautifulest*, *awfulest*). In some instances, the extension may result in double marking as in *most awfulest* or *more nicer*. Such natural regularization and generalization processes cut across the different kinds of vernacular varieties of English.

-ly ABSENCE

In present-day American English, some adverbs formed at an earlier period through the addition of the *-ly* suffix are losing the *-ly* (e.g., in Informal Standard English, most speakers say *He answered wrong* instead of *He answered wrongly*). The items affected by this absence can be extended to various degrees in different vernacular dialects, ranging from a relatively unobtrusive item such as *awful* in *She enjoyed life awful well* to a quite obtrusive form such as *original* in *I come from Virginia original*. Northern vernaculars tend to be less expansive in their extension of the items affected by this *-ly* absence than their southern counterparts, particularly the southern highland varieties.

INTENSIFYING ADVERBS

There is a set of adverbs found in southern-based vernaculars that can intensify particular attributes or activities. *Right* (which is currently limited to location or time in Standard English as in *He is right around the corner*) intensifies the degree of an attribute (e.g., *She is right nice*) whereas *plumb* intensifies the attribute in totality (e.g., *The students fell plumb asleep*). Other adverbial intensifiers found in these varieties include items such as *big old*, *little old*, *right smart*, and *right much*, among others.

A special function of the adverb *steady* has been described for Vernacular Black English, in which its use in a construction such as *They be steady messing with you* refers to an intense, continuous activity.

OTHER ADVERBIAL FORMS

There are a number of other cases in which the adverbial forms of vernacular varieties differ from their standard counterparts. Some of these involve word class changes, as in the use of *but* as an adverb meaning "only" as in *He ain't but thirteen years old* or the item *all* in *the corn got all*. In many midland dialects of American English, *anymore* may be used in positive constructions with a meaning of "nowadays," as in *She watches a lot of videos anymore*.

There are also a number of differences in the kinds of lexical items in included in the adverbial word class, such as *yonder* (e.g., *It's up yonder*) or *yet* (e.g., *I yet eat a lot of honey*). Another difference comes from the phonological fusion of items, such as *t'all* from *at all* (e.g., *It's not coming up t'all*) or *pert' near* (e.g., *She's pert' near seventy*), or *druther* (e.g., *Druther than lose the farm, he fought*). Again, such differences must be considered on an item-by-item basis.

Negation

The two major differences in negation involve the formation of the so-called double negatives, which involve the marking of a negative element at more than one point in the sentence, and the use of the lexical item *ain't*. Other forms, resulting directly from the acquisition of English as a second language (e.g., *He no like the man*) are found in the interlanguage of some developing varieties, but do not seem to be perpetuated as a continuing part of the English-based variety apart from this transitional process. (An exception may be the negative tag *no* as found in some Hispanic English varieties as in *He's going to the store, no?*).

MULTIPLE NEGATION

There are four different patterns of negative marking found in the vernacular varieties of English:

1. marking of the negative in the verb phrase and the indefinite(s) following the verb

The man *wasn't* saying *nothing.*
He *didn't* say *nothing* about *no* people bothering him or *nothing* like that.
2. negative marking of an indefinite before the verb phrase and within the verb phrase
Nobody didn't like the mess.
Nothing can't stop him from failing the course.
3. inversion of the negative element from the verb phrase and the preverbal indefinite
Didn't nobody like the mess.
Can't nothing stop him from failing the course.
4. multiple negative marking across different clauses
There *wasn't* much that I *couldn't* do (meaning "There wasn't much I could do")
I *wasn't* sure that *nothing* wasn't going to come up (meaning "I wasn't sure that anything was going to come up")

Virtually all vernacular varieties of English participate in the multiple negation of category 1 in the preceding inventory; restricted northern and most southern vernaculars participate in category 2, most southern vernaculars participate in category 3 and restricted southern and black English varieties participate in category 4.

THE AUXILIARY AIN'T

The item *ain't* may be used as a correspondence for various forms of Standard English auxiliaries, including the following:

1. forms of *be* + *not*
She *ain't* here now.
I *ain't* gonna do it.
2. forms of *have* + *not*
I *ain't* seen her in a long time.
She *ain't* gone to the movies in a long time.
3. *do* + *not*
He *ain't* tell him he was sorry.
I *ain't* go to school yesterday.

The first two types are found in most vernacular varieties, but the third type, as the correspondence of standard *didn't*, has only been found in Vernacular Black English varieties.

Nominals

Constructions involving nouns and pronouns are often affected by socially significant dialect variation. The major types of differences involve the attachment of various suffixes and the various case markings of forms.

PLURALS

There are several different ways in which plurals may be differentiated from the patterns found in standard varieties of English. These include the following:

1. general absence of plural suffix
    Lots of boy__ go to the school.
    All the girl__ liked the movie.
2. absence of plural suffix with restricted subclasses of nouns
    The station is four mile__ down the road.
    They hauled in a lotta bushel__ of corn.
3. regularization of various irregular plural noun forms.
    They saw the *deers* running across the field.
    The *firemans* liked the convention.

    Category 1 is found only among varieties where another language was spoken in the recent past and, to a limited degree, in Vernacular Black English. In category 2, plural suffix absence is limited to nouns of weights (e.g., *four pound, three ton*) and measures (e.g., *two foot, many mile, lotta acre*), including some temporal nouns (e.g., *two year, five month*); this pattern is found in many southern-based vernaculars. Category 3 includes regularization of plurals that are not marked overtly in Standard English (e.g., *deers, sheeps*), forms marked with irregular suffixes in the standard (e.g., *oxes*), and forms marked by nonsuffix plurals (e.g., *firearms, snowmans*). In the last case, plurals may be marked with both plural forms, as in *mens* or *childrens*. Some kinds of plurals in category 3 are quite widespread among the vernacular varieties of English (e.g., regularizing the nonmarked plurals such as *deers*), whereas others (e.g., the double marking in *mens*) are more limited.

POSSESSIVES

There are several patterns involving the possessive nouns and pronouns, including the following:

1. the absence of the possessive suffix
    The *man hat* is on the chair.
    John coat is here.
2. regularization of the possessive pronoun *mines*, on the basis of analogy with *yours, his, hers*, and so on
    Mines is here.
    It's *mines*.
3. the use of the special possessive form *his'n* or *your'n*. (This form can only be found in "absolute" sentence position, as in *It is his'n*; it is *not* found in structures such as **It is his'n book.*)

Is it *your'n?*
I think it's *his'n.*

The first two types of possessives are typical of Vernacular Black English, and the third type is found in Vernacular Appalachian English and other older, rural varieties, although it is now restricted to older speakers.

PRONOUNS

Pronoun differences typically originate in changes to the case forms or regularization by analogy. The categories of differences include the following:

1. regularization of reflexive forms by analogy with other possessive pronouns
   He hit *hisself* on the head.
   They shaved *theirselves* with the new razor.
2. extension of object forms to coordinate subjects
   Me and him will do it.
   John and them will be home soon.
3. adoption of a second person plural form to "fill out" the number-person paradigm
   a. *Y'all* won the game.
       I'm going to leave *y'all* now.
   b. *Youse* won the game.
       I'm going to leave *youse* now.
   c. *You'uns* won the game.
       I'm going to leave *you'uns* now.
4. extension of object forms to demonstratives
   Them books are on the shelf.
   She didn't like *them* there boys.
5. a special "personal dative" use of the object pronoun form.
   I got *me* a new car.
   We had *us* a little old dog.

The first four types of pronominal differences are well represented in most vernacular dialects of English, with the particular kind of second person plural pronoun sensitive to the regional locale. Example 3a is, of course, the southern form and 3b the northern form, with some specific regions (e.g., western Pennsylvania) using 3c. The so-called "personal dative" illustrated in example 5 is a southern feature, but it is not particularly stigmatized in that context.

Other pronoun forms, such as the use of an object form with a simple subject (e.g., *Her in the house*) and the use of subject or object forms in possessive structures (e.g., *It is she book*; *It is he book*) are quite rare in most current vernaculars, except for those still closely related to a prior creole state.

RELATIVE PRONOUNS

Differences affecting relative pronouns include the extension of relative pronoun forms and the generalized absence of relative pronouns under certain conditions. Form differences may range from the socially insignificant use of *that* for human subjects (e.g., *The man that I was telling you about is here*) to the quite stigmatized use of *what*, as in *The man what I was telling you about is here*. One form which is becoming more common, and spreading into informal varieties of Standard English, is the conjunctive use of *which*, as in the sentence *He gave me this cigar, which he knows I don't smoke cigars*.

In Standard English relative pronouns may be deleted if they are the object in the relative clause, so that *That's the dog that I bought* could alternately be rendered as *That's the dog I bought*. In most cases where it is the subject, however, the relative pronoun must be retained, as in *That's the dog that bit me*. A number of southern-based varieties, in varying degrees, may delete the relative pronoun whether object or subject, so that these varieties use *That's the dog bit me* or *The man come in here is my father*.

EXISTENTIAL IT/THEY

The Standard English form *there*, in sentences such as *There are four people in school* or *There's a picture on TV* functions as an existential rather than a locational adverb. In these cases, vernacular varieties may use *it* (*It's a picture on TV*) or *they* (*They's a picture on TV*) as the corresponding existential form. *They* and *there* seems to be found only in southern-based vernaculars; *it* is more general, and appears to be spreading.

OTHER GRAMMATICAL STRUCTURES

There are a number of structures that might have been considered here, but we have not treated them in detail. In some cases, empirical sociolinguistic investigation indicates that the presumed vernacular forms are more common in informal standard varieties than thought originally, so they are not discussed in detail here. For example, pronominal apposition, as in *My mother, she made my breakfast*, is such a case, as it is found in the spoken language of practically all social groups of American English speakers. Furthermore, it is not particularly obtrusive in spoken language. It has also been found that indirect questions such as *He asked could he go to the movies* (as compared with *He asked if he could go to the movies*) are becoming a part of informal spoken English standard varieties, and are not socially stigmatized. Other differences, such as those affecting prepositions, have to be treated item by item, and really qualify as lexical rather than grammatical differences. Thus, forms such as *of the evening* (in the evening), *upside the head* (on the side of the head), *leave out of there* (leave there), *the matter of him* (the matter with him), and so forth have to be treated individually. In most cases, their social significance is also secondary to their regional variation, so that we have not treated them in detail in this account. Traditional linguistic atlas surveys and the *Dictionary of American Regional English* give much more adequate detail about these forms than could be given in this overview.

GLOSSARY

absolute position   The position at the end of a clause or sentence (e.g., *his* is in absolute position in *The Book is his*, but *not* in *His book is here*).

accent   1. A popular label for dialect, with particular reference to pronunciation. 2. Speech influenced by another language (e.g., "She speaks with a French accent"). 3. See *stress*.

accommodation model   A model accounting for style variation in speech on the basis of a person's social psychological adjustment to the addressee; adjustment toward the addressee is *convergence*, adjustment away from addressee is *divergence*.

acronym   A word formed by combining the initial sounds or letters of words (e.g., *NATO*, *UN*).

address form   The title or label used in speaking to or referring to a person by title (e.g., *Mr.*, *Mrs/Miss/Ms.*, *Dr.*, *Professor*).

addressee   A person to whom speech is directed.

affix   A morpheme that attaches to the base word in some way, modifies the meaning of the word (in *retells*, *re-* and *-s* are affixes).

age grading   The language characterizing a particular age group (e.g., teen-ager slang).

agreement   A co-occurring relationship between grammatical forms, such as that between the subject and verb form (e.g., third person singular subject with the morpheme *-s* in *She likes dialectology*).

alveolar   A sound produced at the protruding small ridge just in back of the upper teeth.

analogy   The application of a pattern to forms not previously included in the set (e.g., the past tense of *bring/brang/brung* on the basis of *sing/sang/sung*).

Anglicist hypothesis   The contention that Vernacular Black English is derived historically from dialects found in the British Isles.

applied dialectology   The application of knowledge from the study of dialects to practical social and educational concerns.

argot   A specialized vocabulary or jargon, typically used in a way to conceal the contents of conversation from outsiders; often used with reference to criminal activity.

audience design model   A model of speech style maintaining that people adjust their speech primarily based on the attributes of people in the audience of listeners.

auditor   A person in a speech situation who is recognized as a legitimate part of the conversational group but not directly addressed.

auxiliary   A form occurring with a main verb form, traditionally referred to as a "helping verb" (e.g., *has* in *has made*, *done* in *done tried*).

back formation   A word formation process in which an affixed form is used as the basis for creating a new pattern by analogy with a pattern of (de)affixation (e.g., *burgle* from *burglar*, *orientate* from *orientation*).

back vowel   A vowel produced with the tongue drawn toward the back of the mouth (e.g., the [u] of *Luke*, the [o] of *boat*).

backchanneling   The linguistic and extralinguistic strategies used by a conversational participant to indicate that the participant is following the conversation of the speaker (e.g., *uhmm, right*).

bare root   With reference to irregular verbs, the use of the present tense form as a past tense form as well (e.g., the past tense of *set* in *Yesterday Walt set the table*; in vernacular dialects, the past tense of *give* in *Yesterday they give me a present*).

bidialectalism   The position in teaching Standard English that maintains that the standard should coexist with a vernacular variety rather than replace it.

blending   The creation of new words by taking portions of different words (e.g., words such as *smog* (*smoke* + *fog*) or *twirl* (*twist* + *whirl*).

borrowing   A language item that is taken from another language (e.g., *arroyo* from Spanish).

bound morpheme   A morpheme that must be attached to another item; it cannot occur alone (e.g., the *-s* in *boys*). Compare *free morpheme*.

breathiness   The quality of speaking with an audible emission of air.

broad _a_   The vowel found in words such as *bat* and *back*.

broadening   See *semantic broadening*.

bundle of isoglosses   A set of isoglosses that cluster together in the way that differentiates dialect forms on a map.

camouflaged form   A form in a vernacular variety that looks like a standard counterpart while being used in a structurally different way (e.g., *come* in Vernacular Black English *They come here talking that nonsense*, which appears to be like the standard form *They come running* but means something different).

case   A form that indicates a syntactic function, in relation to the verb of a sentence. For example, *I* is the subject of the sentence in *I hate cheaters*; it is therefore a *subjective case* pronoun. *Me* is the object of the verb in *Dogs hate me*; it is therefore an *objective case* pronoun.

cell   1. In implicational analysis, an intersecting point at which a row and column meet. 2. In sampling, a category set apart by a distinctive set of social characteristics (e.g., middle-class white males).

chain shifting   The shifting of vowels in phonetic space in response to the change of phonetic position in adjacent vowels. See *push-pull, vowel rotation*.

change from above   The change of a language form which speakers are aware of on a conscious level.

change from below   Language changes that speakers are not aware of on a conscious level.

change from outside   Changes that take place due to borrowing from other language groups.

change from within   Changes that are initiated within the language itself, due to the pressures from the patterning of the system.

citation form   The way a word is produced when recited in isolation (e.g., the pronunciation of *photograph* as an isolated word versus its pronunciation in normal conversation).

clipping   The formation of new words through the removal of syllables (e.g., *dormitory* — *dorm*).

code switching   A shift between different language systems; with reference to dialects, it refers to the change between *overall* dialect systems, such as that between a standard and vernacular dialect.

colloquial   Forms associated with informal language usage; associated with "common" speech.

communication network   The pattern of social interaction that determines who people talk to.

complement   Words or clauses that complete a predication; structures co-occurring with particular verb forms (e.g., *painting* in *The house needed painting*, the clause *the house was dirty* in *I told him that the house was dirty*).

complementizer   A form introducing a complement clause; *that* in *I told him that dialects were fun*.

completion task   A format used to elicit an item in which the subject responds to an incomplete sentence by completing it (e.g., "The hard inside of a peach is called a ____"). Also known as *fill-in-the-blank*.

completive   A form signaling that an action has been completed at a previous time, with emphasis on the completion (e.g., completive *done* in *He done took out the garbage*; *You done messed up this time*).

compound   A word created by combining two or more words (e.g., *lighthouse* from *light + house*).

concord   See *agreement*.

consonant   A sound produced with obstruction in the vocal tract (e.g., [b] and [t] in *bat*).

consonant cluster   The sequencing of two or more consecutive consonants without an intervening vowel (e.g., [st] in *stop*, [ld] in *wild*).

consonant cluster reduction   The elimination of a consonant in a cluster (e.g., [st] in *mist* [mIst] becoming *mis'* [mIs]). Also called *consonant cluster simplification*.

constraint (on variability)   A linguistic or social factor that increases or decreases the likelihood that a given variant in a fluctuating set of items will occur.

content validity   With respect to testing, the extent to which a test measures the content area it claims to measure.

content word   A word having referential meaning, such as the noun *dog* or the adjective *blue*. Compare *function word*.

context-dependent text   Discourse that assumes knowledge of the context as a basis for understanding and interpreting.

context-independent text   Discourse that does *not* assume a particular or local context for its interpretation.

contraction   The shortening of words by omitting sounds, often resulting in the phonological merger of words (e.g., *is + not → isn't*, *She will → She'll*).

contrastive drill   A language learning drill in which two structures are placed side by side to focus on the contrast between forms (e.g., A sentence pair such as *The man nice* versus *The man's nice* focuses on the contrast between copula absence and presence).

contrastive linguistics   The study of different languages or dialects by comparing structures in each of the varieties to pinpoint places at which the varieties are similar and different.

convenience sample   The selection of subjects based simply on their availability at the time a study is conducted.

conversion   The creation of a new word by using it as a different part of speech (e.g., the verb *run* being used as a noun in *They scored a run*).

conversion task   A format for eliciting data in which a subject is asked to change one structure into another (e.g., "Change the sentence *John is ugly* into its negative form").

copula   The form used to link a subject with a predicate complement (in English, a form of *be*, as in *She is nice*, *Tanya is the boss*).

copula deletion   The absence of the copula, as in *You ugly* for *You're ugly*; the term usually is extended to auxiliary uses of *be* forms as well, as in *He writing a book* for *He's writing a book*.

covert prestige   Language forms or patterns that are positively valued in a local setting or by a special group despite the fact that these items are socially stigmatized in the society at large.

creole hypothesis   The contention that Vernacular Black English developed historically from an ancestral creole language.

creole language   A special contact language in which the primary vocabulary of one language is superposed upon a specially adapted, somewhat restricted grammatical structure; used as a native language by speakers. See *pidgin language*.

critical age hypothesis   The hypothesis that true language mastery can only occur during a given age period, namely, during the prepubescent period.

dative   The recipient of an action, indirect object (e.g., *Terry* in *Todd gave the ball to Terry*, *Howard* in *Walt made a glossary for Howard*). See *personal dative*.

decoding   The process of breaking down the written word letter by letter and relating it to the spoken language sound units.

decreolization   The process whereby an historical creole language loses the distinguishing features of its creole predecessor, usually through contact with a standard variety of the language.

density   The extent to which an individual in a social network has independent contact with other people in a network; if members are independently in contact with each other, the network has *high density*, if not, it has *low density*. See *social network*.

derivation   The creation of a new word through the addition of a derivational affix (e.g., *bewitch-ed*, *forest-ry*).

derivational morpheme   A prefix or suffix that changes the basic meaning and/or word class of an item (e.g., *-er* in *buyer* changes the form from a verb to a noun).

determiner   A grammatical category of items that combines with nouns; items such as articles *the*, *a*, demonstratives such as *this*, *that*, and so forth.

devoicing   The phonetic change of voiced sounds to their voiceless counterparts, as [d] — [t], [b] — [p], or [z] — [s].

dialect   A variety of the language associated with a particular social or regional group.

dialect code switching   See *code switching*.

dialect discrimination   In testing, items that systematically penalize speakers of non-Standard English varieties on the basis of a dialect difference (e.g., in language acquisition testing, the treatment of a dialect form as an unacquired Standard English form).

dialect reader   A reading text that attempts to represent the speech of a nonmainstream dialect community, including the incorporation of nonstandard dialect forms.

dialect rights   A position advocating that students should not be asked to give up their dialect, either by replacing it or by adding a standard variety.

dialectally diagnostic   A linguistic form that has the potential to differentiate social and regional groups from each other.

diphthong   A vowel that changes its quality within the same syllable (e.g., the [aI] of *bite* or the [oI] of *boy*); consists of a *nucleus* or core vowel and a *glide*.

direct transfer model   A model accounting for dialect influence in writing on the basis of direct carryover from spoken to written language.

directive   A speech act in which the speaker orders the listener to do something (e.g., *Take the garbage out*).

discrimination drill   A drill in which two forms or structures are given side by side and the listener is asked if they sound the "same" or "different" (e.g., *She run* versus *She runs*: "different").

divergence hypothesis   The contention that modern Vernacular Black English is becoming increasingly dissimilar from corresponding white vernacular varieties.

double negative   See *multiple negation*.

dropped r   See *r-lessness*.

eavesdropper   A person who is not known to be part of the audience during a person's speaking.

elicitation frame   The way in which a question is formed to lead a subject to produce a word or structural item (e.g., *What is the hard inside part of a peach called?*).

ellipsis   The omission of words or phrases in a syntactic construction (e.g., *If (it is) possible, I'd like to omit this sentence*).

environment   See *linguistic environment*.

eradicationism   The position on teaching Standard English that maintains that the standard dialect should be taught in place of a vernacular one, thus eradicating the vernacular variety.

error analysis   An analytical procedure which starts with the set of the actual errors produced by a speaker rather than forms predicted on the basis of a structural comparison of the varieties.

ethnography   The description of culture; with reference to language, the description of the cultural events and routines related to speaking.

existential   A form having no referential meaning but filling a grammatical function, such as the form *there* in *There are four students taking the course.* Also called *expletive.*

expletive   1. An interjection, often used with reference to profane words (e.g., *Damn!*). 2. See *existential.*

eye dialect   The use of spelling to suggest dialect differences; the spelling does not reflect an actual dialect difference (e.g., *wuz* for *was*).

fine stratification   See *gradient stratification.*

first-order constraint   The factor that has the greatest systematic effect on the variability of an item (e.g., the effect of a following consonant on word-final cluster reduction). The second most important factor is referred to as the *second-order constraint.*

flap   A sound made by rapidly tapping the articulator at the point of articulation, as in the usual American English pronunciation of *t* in *butter* [bʌDɚ].

floor   The recognized speaker in a conversational exchange (e.g., *holding the floor*).

focal area   A regional area at the center of dialect innovation and change; changes radiate from this area outward.

forced choice task   A format for obtaining information from subjects in which they *must* choose between items (e.g., "Choose which sentence sounds better, *She was a-discovering a cave* or *She was a-following the leader*").

formal Standard English   The variety of English prescribed as the standard by language authorities; found primarily in written language and the most formal spoken language (e.g., spoken language relying on a version written initially).

fossilized form   A form that occurs during the learning of a second language and persists while other forms continue their development toward the second-language norm.

free morpheme   A morpheme that can occur alone as a word (e.g., *boy* in *boys*). Compare *bound morpheme.*

fricative   A sound produced with a continuous flow of air through a narrow opening so that there is friction at the point of articulation.

front vowel   A vowel produced with the tongue moved toward the front of the mouth, as in the [i] of *beet* or the [æ] of *bat.*

function word   A word having little or no referential meaning, such as the articles *the/a* or the prepositions *to/at.* Compare *content word.*

g dropping   The production of *ng* in unstressed syllables as *n'* (e.g., *swimmin'* for *swimming*); in spelling, this is usually indicated by *n'*, but the actual phonetic shift involves the change from the nasal [ŋ] to [n].

genderlect   A variety of a language characterizing only women or men; in American English it is used primarily with reference to features that may set apart women's speech.

general social significance   The social evaluation of a form that holds regardless of the geographical area in which it is found.

generalization   The process in which a linguistic pattern or rule extends its application to additional linguistic contexts or items.

generic (pro)noun   A noun or pronoun form that does not differentiate the referent by sex (e.g., *they* in *They took the course*; *man* is used generically in *Man shall not live by bread alone*).

glide   A vowel quality that is peripheral to the core or nucleus of a vowel (e.g., [I] in *bite* [baIt]).

gradient stratification   The correlation of socially significant linguistic structures on a continuous scale rather than on the basis of discrete breaks between adjacent social groups. Also referred to as *fine stratification.*

grammar   The patterning of units into sentences.

grammatical   Sentences and forms that fall within the specified boundaries of a linguistic rule, linguistically "well formed." Compare *ungrammatical.*

group exclusive   A linguistic pattern or form *only* found among a particular group of speakers.

group preferential   Linguistic forms or patterns that are shared by different social groups, but the members of one group are more likely to use the form or pattern than those in another group.

group reference   The group that a person identifies with in terms of sociopsychological self-definition.

habitual   An activity that takes place at intermittent intervals over time (e.g., as signaled by the use of *be* in Vernacular Black English *When I come home, I usually be taking a nap*).

hedge   To lessen the force of an utterance through various language devices (e.g., the use of *Well* in *Well, I don't know what to do*).

high vowel   A vowel made with the tongue in high position in the mouth, as in the [i] of *beet* or the [u] of *boot*.

historical present   The use of a present tense form in the recounting of a past time event (e.g., *Yesterday, I go down there and this guy comes up to me . . .*); generally used for dramatic vividness.

homophones/homophonous words   Different words that are pronounced the same (e.g., *dear/deer*, in some southern dialects of English *pin/pen*).

horizontal shift   A shift of speech style that takes place without a primary effect on the social evaluation of speech (e.g., shifting from one regional standard to another regional standard variety of the same social class).

hypercorrection   The extension of a language form beyond its regular linguistic boundaries when a speaker feels a need to use more standard or "correct" forms. See *structural* and *statistical hypercorrection*.

hypocorrection   The process of overextending or misapplying the rules of a vernacular dialect by a standard dialect speaker attempting to produce the vernacular.

identification drill   A drill in which forms or sentences are placed side by side and the student asked to "identify" the dialect of each sentence (e.g., *She likes class*: "formal"; *She like class*; "informal").

implicational relation   A condition in which one dialect form implies the existence of another; for example, if a speaker has copula absence for *is* (e.g., *He ugly*), the copula absence for *are* (e.g., *You ugly*) will also occur.

indirect speech act   The use of one speech act to carry out another one (e.g., The use of a statement such as *The garbage is overflowing* to request a person to empty the garbage).

inflectional morpheme   In English, a suffix that augments a word without changing its basic lexical meaning or changing its word class (e.g., *-s* in *dogs*, *-er* in *bigger*.)

Informal Standard English   The spoken variety of English considered socially acceptable in mainstream contexts; typically characterized by the absence of socially stigmatized linguistic structures.

inherent variability   Variability between items within a single dialect system; speakers sometimes produce one variant and sometimes another (e.g., sometimes speakers say *drinking* and other times they say *drinkin'* in the same social context).

interdental   A sound produced by placing the tongue tip between the upper and lower teeth; sounds such as the [θ] of *think* and the [ð] of *the* are interdentals.

interdialectal shift   A shift between different dialect systems.

interlanguage   The intermediate language system that a language learner uses in the process of acquiring a second language.

interlocutor   A person who takes part in a conversation.

interruption   "Breaking into" a person's speech without a recognized turn by the speaker "holding the floor" at the time.

intervocalic   Occurring between vowels (e.g., *r* in *Mary*, *t* in *butter*).

intonation   The pitch contours that accompany phrases and sentences (e.g., question intonation of *Are you going?* versus the statement intonation of *You are going*).

intradialectal shift   A shift of styles *within* a single dialect system (e.g., a shift of registers, a shift in the frequency of a variant within the system based on the formality of the situation).

intransitive verb   A verb that does *not* take an object (e.g., *The students jogged*).

intrusive   Adding a sound to a word, such as the *t* of *acrosst* or the *r* of *warsh*.

inversion   A reversal of the "typical" order of items (e.g., *You are going/Are you going*, *Nobody can't do it/Can't nobody do it*).

irregular form   An item that does not conform with the predominant pattern (e.g., the *-en* plural of *oxen*; the vowel change used to mark the past tense of *come* as *came*). Compare *regular form*.

isogloss   A line on a map indicating a boundary between the use and nonuse of particular linguistic items.

jargon   A vocabulary set characteristic of a special-interest group (e.g., computer vocabulary, sports vocabulary).

judgment sample   A procedure of subject selection in which the types of subjects are first identified and then a quota of subjects is selected to fill each of the categories.

labial   Sounds produced with the primary involvement of the lips; [p] in *pit* is *bilabial* (involving both lips), [f] in *four* is *labiodental* (involving the lower lip and upper teeth).

lame, linguistic lame   A person whose speech does not match the speaker's social group or social affiliation, used mostly in reference to those in vernacular communities whose speech is more standard.

language acquisition   As used with reference to language learning, the unconscious learning of language rules which results in implicit knowledge of language.

language learning   As used with respect to second-language or dialect acquisition, the conscious learning of rules of language which results in more explicit knowledge of language.

language register   See *register*.

language sample   Language data collected on the basis of a conversational interview, as opposed to the direct elicitation of items.

language transfer   See *transfer*.

lax vowel   A sound produced with less muscular tension; the [I] of *bit* is a lax vowel compared with the [i] of *beet*, which is a tense vowel. See *short vowel*.

layering   A hierarchical arrangement of dialect features in which successive areas show differing levels of shared dialect forms. See *primary, secondary, tertiary dialect area*.

lexical hypercorrection   The use of markedly formal words in less formal settings, typically calling attention to the fact that the speaker is using a "bigger word" than called for by the occasion (e.g., the use of *pusillanimous* for *cowardly* in an informal setting).

lexicon   The vocabulary of a language, including words and morphemes.

linguistic constraint   A linguistic factor, such as a type of linguistic environment or structural composition, which systematically affects the variability of fluctuating forms. Also referred to as *independent linguistic constraint*.

linguistic environment   The linguistic items that surround an element, such as the sounds that occur next to a given sound.

linguistic insecurity   The manifestation of uncertainty about the standard use of forms; usually exhibited in linguistic hypercorrection.

linguistic marketplace   The socioeconomic activity of a person most directly related to linguistic variation. A *linguistic market index* is a scale which measures these characteristics.

linguistic rule   An explicit statement about the patterning of linguistic forms; a precise statement describing where a form may occur structurally.

linguistic variable   A varying linguistic structure (e.g., *-ing/in'*) which may correlate with social factors (e.g., region, status), or other linguistic factors (e.g., linguistic environment).

long vowel   A tense vowel, as in words such as *feet, bait, boot*, and *vote*. Compare *short vowel*.

Low Back Vowel Merger   The merger of the vowels of words like *cot* and *caught* so that these words are pronounced the same.

low vowel   A vowel produced with the tongue in a lowered position of the mouth; vowels such as the [a] of *father*, the [ɔ] of *caught*, or the [æ] of *bat*.

malapropism   The mistaken semantic identity of a word, typically involving words that sound similar (e.g., *amnesia* for *amnesty*).

marker   See *social marker*.

merger   The process in which a contrastive difference between sounds is nullified or lost (e.g., *caught* and *cot* in some English dialects). Also called *neutralization*.

metalinguistic task   A task that involves using technical ways of talking about language to get language data from a subject.

mid vowel   A vowel produced with the tongue in the middle range of tongue height, as in the [ɛ] of *bet*, the [ʌ] of *but*, or the [o] of *boat*.

minimal word pair   A word pair that is identical except for one sound; word pairs such as *bit* and *pit*, or *bit* and *bet* are minimal word pairs.

minority pattern analogy   Change of a form on the basis of an irregular pattern (e.g., *bring/brang* on the basis of *sing/sang* rather than the regular *-ed* past tense pattern).

miscue analysis   A procedure for analyzing reading ability based on examining the kinds of miscues readers make when reading aloud; such miscues provide insight into the nature of the processing taking place on several different levels of language organization (e.g., semantic comprehension, syntactic processing, and so on).

modal   A form in the verb phrase referring to mood or intention; words such as *can, may, will, shall, must*.

monitoring   The act of paying attention to how one is speaking during the production of speech.

monosyllabic   Consisting of one syllable (e.g., *go, but*).

morpheme   The smallest meaningful unit of language (e.g., in *dogs, dog* and *-s* are morphemes).

morphology   The study of morphemes, with particular reference to the way in which morphemes are combined in words.

morphosyntactic, morpho-syntactic   Reflecting a syntactic relationship through a particular morpheme (e.g., third person *-es/s* in *Tyler works hard* indicates a relationship between the subject and verb).

multiple negation   A negative proposition in which a negative element occurs at more than one point in the sentence (e.g., *They didn't do nothing about nobody*). Also called *double negative*.

multiplex network   The interaction of individuals in a social network in a number of spheres of activity (e.g., work, leisure, neighborhood). See *social network*. Compare *uniplex network*.

narrowing   See *semantic narrowing*.

nasal   A segment produced by allowing air to pass through the nasal cavity, as in the *m* of *mom* or the *n* of *no*.

naturalistic speech   Speech that represents how people talk under normal, ordinary circumstances.

naturalness   Linguistic processes and changes that follow natural principles of production or perception.

Network Standard   A variety of English relatively free of marked regional characteristics; the ideal norm aimed for by national network announcers.

neutralization   The loss of a contrast between sounds in a particular linguistic environment (e.g., *pin/pen* in southern dialects, *shore/sure* in some northern dialects). See *merger*.

nominal   Pertaining to nouns, pronouns, noun phrases, and so forth.

nonstandard   Forms that are socially stigmatized through association with socially disfavored groups.

nonstandard dialect   A socially disfavored dialect of the language (a synonym with *vernacular dialect* as used in this book).

Northern Cities Vowel Shift   The rotation of vowels in which the low vowels are moved forward and upward; found predominantly in northern metropolitan areas.

nucleus   1. The core or base of a vowel sound; in a word like *bike* [baIk], the [a] is considered the nucleus. 2. The peak or core of a syllable, usually a vowel-like sound.

objective case   A morpheme denoting that an item is the object of a verb (e.g., *me* in *Tanya likes me*). See *case*.

observer's paradox   The situation which takes place when an investigator observes speech being collected for analysis even though it is recognized that the best speech for analysis is that which occurs when people are not being observed.

offglide   The vowel portion that follows the nucleus or core of a vowel; in a word like *bike* [baIk], the [I] is the offglide.

onglide   A transitional vowel that precedes the vowel nucleus (e.g., a glide before the first vowel of *Tuesday* [tiuzde] in some dialects of English).

open o   The vowel [ɔ] in words such as *caught* or *song*, as produced in some dialects of English.

orthography   The alphabetic or spelling system of a language.

overhearer   A person who is considered part of a speech audience, but not a recognized participant in conversation.

overt prestige   Language forms or patterns that are positively valued on a wide-scale basis in the society.

participle   A word derived from a verb, having qualities of an adjective or noun as well as a verb (e.g., *charming* in *He was charming, taken* in *It was taken*).

perceptual dialectology   The study of how people classify different dialects; the subjective viewpoint of dialect speakers themselves.

personal dative   An emphatic relationship between the agent and same-referent recipient of an action, as in *I got me a little old dog*; typically found in southern dialects of American English.

phoneme   A basic unit of contrast in phonology, usually established on the basis of minimal word pairs (e.g., /p/ and /b/ are different phonemes on the basis of *pit* and *bit*).

phonemic brackets   The slashes / / surrounding sounds which are used to indicate that the symbols represent the phonemic status of sound units, as opposed to their phonetic or orthographic value.

phonetic brackets   The symbols [ ] which are used around sounds to indicate they are being presented in their phonetic form, particularly as opposed to their phonemic or their orthographic value.

phonetic space   The area in the mouth which serves as the basis for positioning the tongue in the production of vowels.

phonics   An approach to reading based on a letter-by-letter processing of written symbols; letters are "sounded out" and combined with each other to decipher words.

phonology   The study of speech sounds.

phonotactics, phonotactic   Patterns relating to the arrangement of sounds in a sequence.

phrase timing   The timing of syllables in which stressed syllables in phrases are held longer and unstressed ones shortened by comparison.

pidgin language   A language used primarily for contact situations, having no native speakers; the vocabulary is taken primarily from one of the contact languages and the grammar is drastically reduced.

possessive   An item indicating possession, such as the suffix *-s* in *John's hat* or the pronoun *his* in *his hat*.

postconsonantal   Occurring immediately after a consonant, as in the segment *r* of *brought*.

postvocalic r   The sound *r* when it follows a vowel (e.g., *r* in *poor*).

pragmatics   The way in which language is used to communicate meaning, taking into account speakers' and hearers' beliefs, attitudes, and intentions.

prefix   An affix attached to the beginning of a word base (e.g., *re-* in *retell*).

preposing   The shift of an item to the beginning of a sentence (e.g., *Yesterday* in *Yesterday Marge ran*, as opposed to *Marge ran yesterday*).

prescriptive Standard   The variety ordained as the standard in grammar books and by recognized language "authorities." See *Formal Standard English*.

prestigious   See *socially prestigious*.

primary dialect area   The region in a more general area exhibiting the greatest concentration of shared dialect features.

pronominal apposition   A construction in which both a noun and pronoun functioning the same way syntactically have the same referent (e.g., *mother* and *she* in *My mother, she came home early.*)

prosody, prosodic   The aspects of pitch, intensity, and timing that accompany the segments of spoken language.

push-pull   The term used to describe the movement of a vowel in response to a shift in the phonetic space of an adjacent one.

quota sample   A procedure for selecting subjects according to predetermined social categories (e.g., female, middle-class, white subjects).

raising   The production of a vowel in a heightened tongue position, as compared to a previous position of production or the position considered typical, as in the raised tongue position of the vowel [æ] in some northern metropolitan dialects.

random sample   A sampling procedure in which each person in the population has a statistically equal chance of being selected.

redundancy reduction   The loss of an item that is indicated at more than one point linguistically (e.g., in *five acres*, the number *five* and suffix *-s* both denote plurality, thus *-s* may be viewed as being redundant).

reduplication   The process in which a word or part of a word is repeated (e.g., *teensy weensy*, *boo boo*).

regional standard   A variety considered to be standard for a given regional area (e.g., the standard variety in Mid-South or in Philadelphia, Pennsylvania).

register   A specialized use of language for well-defined situations of occasions (e.g., the math register, child register used in speaking to babies).

regular form   An item conforming with the predominant pattern (*-s* plural of *cats*; *-ed* past tense of *missed*). Compare *irregular*.

regularization   The process in which irregular forms are changed to conform with the predominant or regular pattern (e.g., *oxen* → *oxes*).

relative clause   A clause that modifies a noun; in *The man who took the course was demented*, *who took the course* is a relative clause.

relative pronoun   A pronoun that introduces a relative clause, such as *who* in *The woman who liked the class was a linguist*.

relic area   An area where earlier forms of the language survive after they have disappeared from other varieties of the language.

response drill   A drill used in language teaching in which the response to the stimulus is a reply which matches the stimulus in a patterned way (e.g., third person singular forms in *Mary like homework*; *No she don't*).

retroflex   A sound produced with the tip of the tongue curled upward; the consonant sound *r* in *run* or the vowel sound *ir* in *bird*.

r-lessness   The absence or reduction of the *r* sound in words such as *car* or *beard*.

rule   See *linguistic rule*.

saturated   Typifying the vast majority of speakers within a given speech community. A less pervasive pattern is *unsaturated*.

scalability   The extent to which an ideal implicational array is matched by actual cases; derived by dividing the number of nondeviant cells by the total number of filled cells.

schwa   A mid central vowel symbolized as [ə]; the first vowel in *appear* [əpír]; generally occurs in unstressed syllables in English.

second-order constraint   See *first-order constraint*.

secondary-dialect area   The region in a more general dialect area showing the second highest concentration of shared dialect features.

semantic broadening   A word that expands its semantic reference (e.g., *holiday* from *holy days*).

semantic derogation   The change of word meaning in which a word refers to something less worthy; used in gender studies with reference to paired male and female words (e.g., the word *mistress* was once the female counterpart of *mister*, but now has negative meanings not matched by its male counterpart).

semantic narrowing   A word that reduces the scope of its semantic reference (e.g., the change of *hound* as a reference for all dogs to a specific type of dog).

semantic shift   The shift of word meaning to refer to a class of referents (e.g., *neat* used to refer to *nice*).

semantics   The study of word meaning.

sharp stratification   A clear-cut break between social classes in the distribution of socially significant language structures.

short vowel   A "lax" vowel in words such as *bit, bet,* and *put*.

sibilant   A sound produced with a groove in the middle of the tongue through which the air passes; sounds such as [s] of *see* and [z] of *zoo* are sibilants.

slang   Words with special connotations of informality and solidarity that replace "normal" words (e.g., *wus* for *coward*, *rad* for *nice*).

social dialectology   The study of language variation in relation to social status or social relationships.

social indicator   A pattern of linguistic variation correlating with social stratification without having an effect on listeners' judgment of speech.

social marker   A pattern of social stratification in language that is recognized on a conscious level but not typically commented about in American society (e.g., *æ* raising).

social network   A set of social relationships between people in a group; an index based on these relationships is a *social network score*.

social stereotype   A socially stigmatized (or, in some instances, socially prestigious) form that is popularly discussed in terms of its stigmatizing (or prestigious) function (e.g., the use of *ain't*).

social variable   A social attribute or characteristic such as status, ethnicity, gender, and so forth; in sociolinguistics a social attribute that may correlate with linguistic variation.

socially diagnostic   Correlating with different social groupings of speakers (as applied to language structures).

socially prestigious   A socially favored language form or pattern, an item associated with high-status groups.

socially stigmatized   Socially disfavored, as in a language form or pattern associated with low-status groups (e.g., *He didn't do nothing to nobody*).

sociogram   A sociometric chart showing the structure of interpersonal relations of some type.

sociolect   A dialect defined on the basis of a social grouping, such as a social class or ethnic group, as opposed to a dialect defined primarily on the basis of region.

sociolinguistics   The study of language in relation to society; the study of language in its social context.

Southern Vowel Shift   The rotation of vowels in which the front short vowels (e.g., *bit*, *bet*) are moved upward, the long front vowels (e.g., *beet, bait*) are moved backward, and the back vowels (e.g., *boot, boat*) are moved forward.

speech accommodation model   See *accommodation model.*

speech act   The social action or behavior accomplished through the use of language structures (e.g., *Take the garbage out!* is a directive speech act in which the speaker directs a hearer to do something).

speech community   A group of speakers united on the basis of their shared language characteristics; also usually sharing a set of social and regional attributes as well.

spelling pronunciation   The pronunciation of an item in a way that follows its spelling as opposed to its conventional spoken form (e.g., *often with* [t]).

Standard American English   A standard variety of English that is relatively unmarked with respect to regional characteristics of English; generally the variety targeted in teaching English as a second language.

standard dialect   The dialect associated with those socially favored in society; the dialect considered acceptable for mainstream, institutional purposes. See *Formal Standard English, Informal Standard English, Network Standard, Regional Standard.*

statistical hypercorrection   The quantitative overuse of a prestigious linguistic pattern; usually found among those groups attempting to emulate a higher social group (e.g., the overuse of postvocalic *r* in New York City by the lower middle class in more formal speech style).

stigmatized   See *socially stigmatized.*

stopping   The process in which fricatives become stop consonants, as *these* [điz] becoming *dese* [diz].

stress   A particular force or intensity placed on a syllable of a word; syllables spoken with such force are *stressed syllables,* those without such force are *unstressed syllables* (e.g., in *pity* [pí] is a stressed syllable, [ti] is unstressed).

structural hypercorrection   The extension of a linguistic boundary in the attempt to produce more standard or correct English (e.g., *Whom* in *Whom is it,* where the objective form is extended to a subject function).

style   The variation of speech based on a set of contextual factors such as audience, occasion, participants, and so forth. See *horizontal shift, vertical shift.*

stylistics   The study of language style, particularly focused on predetermined stylistic genres (e.g., written versus spoken language, literary styles).

subjective case   A morpheme denoting the subject of a sentence in relation to the verb (e.g., *I* in *I like students*). See *case.*

subordinate dialect shift   An irregular shift characterizing the production of forms when a speaker of a socially stigmatized dialect is asked direct questions about the structure of the vernacular dialect.

substitution drill   A contrastive drill in which one form or structure is systematically used in place of another (e.g., pronoun for noun in *Mary works hard: She works hard*).

substitution process   A correspondence between sounds in which one sound may be viewed as replacing another sound (e.g., in *was*[z]*n't* → *wad*[d]*n't* [z] → [d]), in *th*[đ]*ese* → *d*[d]*ese,* [đ] → [d]).

substratum language effect   The influence of a language on another language variety after it has ceased to be a source for immediate transfer (e.g., the holdover effect of Italian vowels on Italian English even though Italian is no longer actively used in the community).

suffix   A form attached to the end of a word base, as in the *-s* of *bats.*

superstandard   Applied to forms or styles of speech more standard than currently necessary (*It is I who shall write this*).

syllable timing   The production of utterances in which each syllable in a phrase has approximately equal duration.

syntax   The organization of words into sentences.

taboo word   A word having a social prohibition against its ordinary use, such as the "four letter" words of English (e.g., *shit*, *damn*).

tag question   A special type of question formed by items attached to, or "tagged" onto the end of the sentence (e.g., *right* in *You're coming to class, right?* or *aren't you* in *You're coming to class, aren't you?*).

tense   1. Produced with more muscular tension (e.g., the sound [i] in *beet* is a tense vowel whereas the [I] of *bit* is a lax vowel. See *long vowel*. 2. The time reference of an activity or event (e.g., past tense in *Marge missed the lecture*).

tertiary dialect area   The third-ranked, outer area in the layered, hierarchical concentration of shared dialect features.

transfer   The adoption of a form from another language, usually a form from a first language carried over into the second language in the process of acquiring the second language.

transitional zone   An intermediate area existing between two established dialect areas.

transitive verb   A verb that takes an object (e.g., *like* in *Students like movies*).

translation drill   A drill in which a structure in one variety is used as the stimulus for translating into another variety (e.g., *She run* to *She runs*).

turn taking   The shift from one speaker to another in a conversational exchange.

unflapping   The production of *t* in words like *butter* and *better* with a stop (e.g., [bʌtɚ], [bɛtɚ]) instead of the flap sound more commonly found in American English varieties. See *flapping*.

ungliding   The loss or reduction of the glide that accompanies the vowel [a] in words like *time* [taIm] and *glide* [glaId]; typically associated with southern speech (e.g., [tam] *time*, [glad] *glide*).

ungrammatical   1. Outside the parameters of a given linguistic rule, usually indicated by placing an asterisk in front of the form or sentence (e.g., **She is tall very*). 2. Socially unacceptable (e.g., *I seen it*); although this sense of ungrammatical is often used popularly, linguists do not generally use it in this way, restricting its use to the technical sense given in 1.

uniplex network   Interaction between individuals in a social network which is limited to particular spheres of activity. See *multiplex*, *social network*.

variant   A form of language in a set of alternating items (e.g., *-ing* and *-in'* are variants).

velar   Sounds produced by touching the back of the tongue against the soft palate or *velum* at the back of the mouth; the [k] of *cow*, the [g] of *go* and the [ŋ] of *sing* are velar sounds.

vertical shift   A stylistic shift that affects the social evaluation of speech (e.g., shifting from a vernacular to a more standard variety).

voiced sound   A sound produced by bringing the vocal bands close together while allowing air to pass through the vibrating bands, such as the [z] of *zoo* or the [v] of *vote*.

voiceless sound   A sound produced with the vocal bands open and not vibrating, such as the [s] of *suit* or the [f] of *fight*.

vowel breaking   The process in which a single, unglided vowel is divided or broken into a nucleus and a glide, as in some southern pronunciations of words like *bed* [bɛId] and *bid* [bIid].

vowel nucleus   The segment that serves as the core or primary basis of a vowel diphthong.

vowel reduction   The change or neutralization of a vowel to the quality of a schaw [ə]; usually takes place in unstressed syllables (e.g., the second *o* of *photograph* [fot əgræf]).

vowel rotation   The systematic shifting of the phonetic value of a set of vowels, as in the Northern Cities Vowel Shift or the Southern Vowel Shift.

wave model   A viewpoint on language change in which changes proceed in progressive stages in a way that is likened to the rippling effect of spreading waves of water.

word-medial   Occurring in the middle of a word, as in the sound *k* of *baker*.

BIBLIOGRAPHY

ALLEN, HAROLD B. AND MICHAEL D. LINN. 1986. eds., *Dialect and Language Variation*. New York, NY: Academic Press.

The Ann Arbor Decision: Memorandum, Opinion, and Order & The Educational Plan. 1979. Washington, DC: Center for Applied Linguistics.

Arco's Practice for the Armed Forces Tests. 1973. New York, NY: Arco.

ARIES, E. 1976. "Interaction Patterns and Themes of Male, Female, and Mixed Groups," *Small Group Behavior* 7:7–18.

ASH, SHARON AND JOHN MYHILL. 1986. "Linguistic Correlates of Inter-Ethnic Contact," in *Diversity and Diachrony*, ed. David Sankoff. Philadelphia, PA: John Benjamins, pp. 33–44.

ATWOOD, E. BAGBY. 1953. *A Survey of Verb Forms in the Eastern United States*. Ann Arbor, MI: University of Michigan Press.

BAILEY, GUY AND MARVIN BASSETT. 1986. "Invariant *be* in the Lower South," in *Language Variety in the South: Perspectives in Black and White*, eds. Michael Montgomery and Guy Bailey. University, AL: University of Alabama Press.

BAILEY, GUY AND NATALIE MAYNOR. 1987. "Decreolization?" *Language in Society* 16:449–474.

BAUER, LAURIE, JOHN M. DIENHART, HANS H. HARTVIGSON, AND LIEF KVISTGAARD JAKOBSEN. 1984. *American English Pronunciation*. Copenhagen: Gyldendal.

BAUGH, JOHN. 1983. *Black Street Speech: Its History, Structure, and Survival*. Austin, TX: University of Texas Press.

BAUGH, JOHN. 1957. A History of the English Language. New York, NY: Appleton-Century-Crofts.

BAUGH, JOHN. 1984. "Steady: Progressive Aspect in Black Vernacular English," *American Speech* 59:3–12.

BAUGH, JOHN. 1988. "Language and Race: Some Implications for Linguistic Science" in *Linguistics: The Cambridge Survey Vol. IV. Language: The Socio-Cultural Context*, ed. Frederick J. Newmeyer. New York: Cambridge University Press.

BAUGH, JOHN. forthcoming. "Hypocorrection: Beyond Vernacular African American English," *Language in Society*.

BEEBE, LESLIE AND HOWARD GILES. 1984. "Speech-Accommodation Theories: A Discussion in Terms of Second Language Acquisition," *International Journal of the Sociology of Language* 46:5–32.

BELL, ALLAN. 1984. "Language Style as Audience Design," *Language in Society* 13:145–204.

BERKO, JEAN. 1958. "The Child's Learning of English Morphology," *Word* 14:150–177.

BERNSTEIN, BASIL. 1981. "Codes, Modalities, and the Process of Cultural Reproduction: A Model," *Language in Society* 10:327–363.

BICKERTON, DEREK. 1971. "Inherent Variability and Variable Rules," *Foundations of Language* 7:457–492.

BLOOM, LOIS AND MARGARET LAHEY. 1978. *Language Development and Language Disorders.* New York, NY: John Wiley & Sons.

BODINE, ANN. 1975a. "Sex Differentiation in Language," in *Language and Sex: Difference and Dominance,* eds. Barrie Thorne and Nancy Henley. Rowley, MA: Newbury House.

BODINE, ANN. 1975b. "Androcentrism in Prescriptive Grammar: Singular 'they.' Sex-indefinite 'he,' and 'he' or 'she,' " *Language in Society* 4:129–146.

BOE, S. KATHRYN. 1987. "Language as an Expression of Caring in Women," *Anthropological Linguistics* 29:271–284.

BRASCH, ILA WALES AND WALTER MILTON BRASCH. 1974. *A Comprehensive Annotated Bibliography of American Black English.* Baton Rouge, LA: Louisiana State University Press.

BREND, RUTH M. 1975. "Male-Female Intonation Patterns in American English," in *Language and Sex: Differences and Dominance,* eds. Barrie Thorne and Nancy Henley. Rowley, MA: Newbury House.

BROWN, CLAUDE. 1965. *Manchild in the Promised Land.* New York, NY: New American Library.

BROWN, PENELOPE AND STEPHEN C. LEVINSON. 1987. *Politeness: Some Universals in Language Usage.* New York, NY: Cambridge University Press.

BUTTERS, RONALD K. 1989. *The Death of Black English: Divergence and Convergence in White and Black Vernaculars.* Frankfurt, Germany: Lang.

CALLARY, ROBERT E. 1975. "Phonological Change and the Development of an Urban Dialect in Illinois," *Language in Society* 4:155–169.

CARVER, CRAIG M. 1987. *American Regional Dialects: A Word Geography.* Ann Arbor, MI: University of Michigan Press.

CASSIDY, FREDERIC G., ed. 1985. *Dictionary of American Regional English, Vol. 1, A–C.* Cambridge, MA: Harvard University Press, Belknap.

CHAMBERS, J. K. AND PETER TRUDGILL. 1980. *Dialectology.* New York, NY: Cambridge University Press.

CHAPMAN, ROBERT L., ed. 1986. *New Dictionary of American Slang.* New York, NY: Harper & Row.

CHRISTIAN, DONNA, WALT WOLFRAM, AND NANJO DUBE. 1988. *Variation and Change in Geographically Isolated Speech Communities: Appalachian and Ozark English.* Publication of the American Dialect Society No. 74. University, AL: University of Alabama Press.

Committee on CCCC Language Statement. 1974. "Students' Rights to Their Own Language," College Composition and Communication 25 (special issue, separately paginated). Champaign-Urbana, IL: National Council of Teachers of English.

CROSBY, FAYE AND LINDA NYQUIST. 1977. "The Female Register: An Empirical Study of Lakoff's Hypothesis," *Language and Society* 6:313–322.

DANIELS, HARVEY. 1983. *Famous Last Words: The American Language Crisis Reconsidered.* Carbondale, IL: Southern Illinois University Press.

DAVIS, LAWRENCE M. 1983. *English Dialectology: An Introduction.* Tuscaloosa, AL: University of Alabama Press.

DILLARD, J. L. 1972. *Black English: Its History and Usage in the United States.* New York, NY: Random House.

DOWNES, WILLIAM. 1984. *Language and Society.* London: Fontana.

DUBOIS, BETTY LOU AND ISABEL CROUCH. 1975. "The Question of Tag Questions in Women's Speech: They don't really use more of them, do they?" *Language in Society* 4:289–294.

DUMAS, BETHANY K. AND JONATHAN LIGHTER. 1976. "Is Slang a Word for Linguists?" *American Speech* 51:5–17.

EAKINS, B. AND G. EAKINS. 1978. *Sex Differences in Human Communication.* Boston, MA: Houghton Mifflin.

EBLE, CONNIE C. 1983. "Greetings and Farewells in College Slang," in *The Ninth LACUS Forum 1982,* ed. John Morreal. Columbia, SC: Hornbeam Press, pp. 433–442.

EBLE, CONNIE C. 1984. "Slang: Deviation or Norm?" in *The Tenth LACUS Forum 1983,* eds. Alan Manning, Pierre Martin, and Kim McCalla. Columbia, SC: Hornbeam Press, pp. 409–416.

EBLE, CONNIE C. 1989. *College Slang 101.* Georgetown, CT: Spectacle Lane Press.

EBLE, CONNIE C. 1985. "Slang: Variations in Dictionary Labelling Practices," in *The Eleventh LACUS Forum 1984,* ed. Robert A. Hall, Jr. Columbia, SC: Hornbeam Press, pp. 294–302.

EDELSKY, CAROLE. 1976. "Subjective Reactions to Sex-Linked Language," *Journal of Social Psychology* 99:97–104.

EDWARDS, VIV. 1986. *Language in a Black Community.* San Diego, CA: College-Hill Press.

EDWARDS, WALTER F. 1986. "Vernacular Language Use and Social Networking in Eastside Detroit," in *Proceedings of Eastern States Conference on Linguistics,* pp. 117–128.

FARR-WHITEMAN, MARCIA. 1981. "Dialect Influence in Writing," in *Writing: The Nature, Development, and Teaching of Written Communication,* Vol. 1, ed. Marcia Farr-Whiteman. Hillsdale, NJ: Lawrence Earlbaum Associates, pp. 153–166.

FASOLD, RALPH W. 1968. "A Sociolinguistic Study of the Pronunciation of Three Vowels in Detroit Speech," unpublished manuscript.

FASOLD, RALPH W. 1969. "Tense and the Form be in Black English," *Language* 45:763–776.

FASOLD, RALPH W. 1976. "One Hundred Years from Syntax to Phonology," in *Diachronic Syntax,* eds. Sanford Seever, Carol Walker, and Salikoko Mufweme. Chicago, IL: Chicago Linguistic Society, pp. 79–87.

FASOLD, RALPH W. 1981. "The Relation Between Black and White Speech in the South," *American Speech* 56:163–189.

FASOLD, RALPH W. 1984. *The Sociolinguistics of Society.* Oxford, England: Basil Blackwell.

FASOLD, RALPH W. 1989. *The Sociolinguistics of Language.* Oxford, England: Basil Blackwell.

FEAGIN, CRAWFORD. 1987. "A Closer Look at the Southern Drawl: Variation Taken to the Extremes," in *Variation in Language: NWAV-XV at Stanford* (Proceedings of the Fifteenth Annual Conference on New Ways of Analyzing Variation), eds. Keith M. Denning, Sharon Inkelas, Faye C. McNair-Knox, and John R. Rickford. Stanford: Stanford University.

FERGUSON, CHARLES A. AND SHIRLEY BRICE HEATH, eds. 1981. *Language in the USA.* New York, NY: Cambridge University Press.

FINEGAN, EDWARD. 1980. *Attitudes Toward English Words: The History of a War of Words.* New York, NY: Teachers College Press.

FISHER, JOHN L. 1958. "Social Influences on the Choice of a Linguistic Variant," *Word* 14:47–56.

FRANCIS, NELSON W. 1983. *Dialectology: An Introduction.* New York, NY: Longmans.

FRANK, FRANCINE AND FRANK ANSHEN. 1983. *Language and the Sexes.* Albany, NY: State University of New York Press.

FRAZER, TIMOTHY C. 1983. "Sound Change and Social Structure in a Rural Community," *Language in Society* 12:313–328.

GILES, HOWARD, ed. 1984. *The Dynamics of Speech Accommodation* (special issue of the *International Journal of the Sociology of Language* 46).

GILES, HOWARD AND PETER F. POWESLAND. 1975. *Speech Style and Social Evaluation.* London: Academic Press.

GOLD, DAVID L. 1981. "The Speech and Writing of Jews," in *Language in the USA,* eds. Charles A. Ferguson and Shirley Brice Heath. New York, NY: Cambridge University Press.

GOODMAN, KENNETH. 1973. *Miscue Analysis: Application to Reading.* Champaign-Urbana, IL: National Council of Teachers of English.

GOODWIN, M. H. 1980. "Directive Response Sequences in Girls' and Boys' Task Activities," in *Women and Language in Literature and Society,* eds. Sally McConnell-Ginet, Ruth Borker, and Nelly Furman. New York, NY: Praeger.

GUMPERZ, JOHN J. 1982. *Discourse Strategies.* New York, NY: Cambridge University Press.

GUY, GREGORY R. 1988. "Language and Social Class," in *Linguistics: The Cambridge Survey Vol.*

IV Language: The Socio-Cultural Context, ed. Frederick J. Newmeyer. New York, NY: Cambridge University Press, pp. 37–63.

HARTMAN, JAMES W. 1985. "Guide to Pronunciation," in *Dictionary of American Regional English*, *Vol. 1, A–C*, ed. Frederic G. Cassidy. Cambridge, MA: Harvard University Press, Belknap.

HEATH, SHIRLEY BRICE. 1976. "A National Language Academy? Debate in the New Nation," *International Journal of the Sociology of Language* 11:8–43.

HEATH, SHIRLEY BRICE. 1983. *Ways with Words: Language, Life and Work in Communities and Classrooms*. New York, NY: Cambridge University Press.

HOLMES, JANET. 1989. "Sex Differences and Apologies: One Aspect of Communicative Competence," *Applied Linguistics* 10:194–213.

HORVATH, BARBARA M. 1985. *Variation in Australian English: The Sociolects of Sydney*. New York, NY: Cambridge University Press.

HUFFINES, MARION LOIS. 1984. "The English of the Pennsylvania Germans," *German Quarterly* 57:173–182.

HUFFINES, MARION LOIS. 1986. "Intonation in Language Contact: Pennsylvania German English," in *Studies on the Language and the Verbal Behavior of the Pennsylvania Germans*, ed. Werner Enninger. Wiesbaden: Franz Steiner Verlag.

HYMES, DELL. 1974. *Foundations in Sociolinguistics: An Ethnographic Approach*. Philadelphia, PA: University of Pennsylvania Press.

Illinois Test of Psycholinguistic Abilities. 1968. Champaign-Urbana, Il: University of Illinois.

IVES, SUMNER. 1971a. "A Theory of Literary Dialect," in *A Various Language: Perspectives on American Dialects*, eds. Juanita V. Williamson and Virginia M. Burke. New York, NY: Holt, Rinehart and Winston.

IVES, SUMNER. 1971b. "Dialect Differentiation in the Stories of Joel Chandler Harris," in *A Various Language: Perspectives on American Dialects*, eds. Juanita V. Williamson and Virginia M. Burke. New York, NY: Holt, Rinehart and Winston.

KING, PAMELA. 1972. *An Analysis of the Northwestern Syntax Screening Test for Lower Class Black Children in Prince George's County*, unpublished M.A. thesis, Howard University.

KRAMERAE, CHERIS AND PAMELA A. TREICHLER. 1985. *A Feminist Dictionary*. Boston, MA: Pandora Press.

KRASHEN, STEPHEN D. 1981. *Second Language Acquisition and Second Language Learning*. Oxford, England: Pergammon Press.

KRASHEN, STEPHEN D. 1982. *Principles and Practice in Second Language Acquisition*. Oxford, England: Pergammon Press.

KRASHEN, STEPHEN D., ROBIN SCARCELLA, AND MICHAEL LONG, eds. 1982. *Child-Adult Differences in Second Language Acquisition*. Rowley, MA: Newbury House.

KROCH, ANTHONY. 1978. "Towards a Theory of Social Dialect Variation," *Language in Society* 7:17–36.

KURATH, HANS. 1939. *Handbook of the Linguistic Geography of New England*. Providence, RI: Brown University.

KURATH, HANS. 1949. *Handbook of the Linguistic Geography of New England*. Ann Arbor, MI: University of Michigan Press.

KURATH, HANS. 1971. "The Origins of the Dialectal Differences in Spoken American English," in *A Various Language: Perspectives on American Dialects*, eds. Juanita V. Williamson and Virginia M. Burke. New York, NY: Holt, Rinehart and Winston.

KURATH, HANS AND RAVEN I. MCDAVID JR. 1961. *The Pronunciation of English in the Atlantic States*. Ann Arbor, MI: University of Michigan Press.

LABOV, WILLIAM. 1964. "Phonological Correlates of Social Stratification," in *The Ethnography of Communication, American Anthropologist* 66, No. 6, Part 2.

LABOV, WILLIAM. 1966. *The Social Stratification of English in New York City*. Washington, DC: Center for Applied Linguistics.

LABOV, WILLIAM. 1972a. *Language in the Inner City: Studies in the Black English Vernacular*. Philadelphia, PA: University of Pennsylvania Press.

LABOV, WILLIAM. 1972b. *Sociolinguistic Patterns*. Philadelphia, PA: University of Pennsylvania Press.

LABOV, WILLIAM. 1972c. "Some Principles of Linguistic Methodology," *Language in Society* 1:97–120.

LABOV, WILLIAM. 1976. "Systematically Misleading Data From Test Questions," *Urban Review* 9:146–169.

LABOV, WILLIAM. 1985. "The Increasing Divergence of Black and White Vernaculars: Introduction to the Research Reports," unpublished manuscript.

LABOV, WILLIAM. 1987. "Are Black and White Vernaculars Diverging? Papers from the NWAVE XIV Panel Discussion," *American Speech* 62:5–12.

LABOV, WILLIAM. forthcoming. "The Three Dialects of English," in *Quantitative Analysis of Sound Change in Progress*, ed. Penelope Eckert. New York, NY: Academic Press.

LABOV, WILLIAM, PAUL COHEN, CLARENCE ROBINS, AND JOHN LEWIS. 1968. *A Study of the Non-Standard English of Negro and Puerto Rican Speakers in New York City*. USOE Final Report, Research Project 3288.

LAFERRIERE, MARTHA. 1979. "Ethnicity in Phonological Variation and Change," *Language* 55:603–617.

LAKOFF, ROBIN. 1975. *Language and Women's Place*. New York, NY: Harper & Row.

LAKOFF, ROBIN. 1986. "You Say What You Are: Acceptability and Gender-Related Language," in *Dialect and Language Variation*, eds. Harold B. Allen and Michael D. Linn. Orlando, FL: Academic Press.

LEAVERTON, LLOYD. 1973. "Dialect Readers: Rationale, Use, and Value," in *Language Differences: Do They Interfere?* ed. James L. Laffey and Roger W. Shuy. Newark, DE: International Reading Association.

LEVINE, LEWIS AND HARRY J. CROCKETT. 1966. "Speech Variation in a Piedmont Community: Postvocalic r," in *Explorations in Sociolinguistics*, ed. Stanley Lieberson. The Hague: Mouton, pp. 76–98.

LOURIE, MARGARET A. AND NANCY FAIRES CONKLIN, eds. 1978. *A Pluralistic Nation: The Language Issue in the United States*. Rowley, MA: Newbury House.

MACKAY, DONALD G. AND DAVID C. FULKERSON. 1979. "On the Comprehension and Production of Pronouns," *Journal of Verbal Learning and Verbal Behavior* 18:661–673.

MARTYNA, WENDY. 1980. "The Psychology of the Generic Masculine," in *Women and Language in Literature and Society*, eds. Sally McConnell-Ginet, Ruth Borker, and Nelly Furman. New York, NY: Praeger, pp. 69–77.

McCONNELL-GINET, SALLY. 1988. "Language and Gender," in *Linguistics: The Cambridge Survey Vol. IV. Language: The Socio-Cultural Context*, ed. Frederick J. Newmeyer. New York: Cambridge University Press, pp. 75–99.

McDAVID, RAVEN I., JR. 1979. *Dialects in Culture: Essays in General Dialectology*, ed. William A. Kretzschmar. Tuscaloosa, AL: University of Alabama Press.

McMILLAN, JAMES B. 1978. "American Lexicology, 1942–1973," *American Speech* 53:141–163.

McMILLAN, JAMES B. AND MICHAEL MONTGOMERY. 1989. *Annotated Bibliography of Southern American English*. Tuscaloosa, AL: University of Alabama Press.

MEIER, DEBORAH. 1973. "Reading Failure and the Tests," An Occasional Paper of the Workshop for Open Education, New York, NY.

MENCKEN, H. L. 1962. *The American Language: An Inquiry into the Development of English in the United States, Supplement 1*. New York, NY: Alfred A. Knopf.

MILROY, JAMES AND LESLEY MILROY. 1985. *Authority in Language: Investigating Language Prescription and Standardisation*. London, England: Routledge & Kegan.

MILROY, LESLEY. 1980. *Language and Social Networks*. Baltimore, MD: University Park Press.

MILROY, LESLEY. 1987. *Observing & Analyzing Natural Language: A Critical Account of Sociolinguistic Method*. New York, NY: Basil Blackwell.

MIMS, HOWARD A. AND CARL T. CAMDEN. 1986. "Congruity and Predictability between Two Measures of Nonstandard Dialect Usage on Four Grammatical Forms," *Journal of Speech and Hearing Disorders* 51:42–52.

National Council on Social Studies, Task Force on Ethnic Studies. 1976. *Curriculum Guidelines for Multiethnic Education*. Arlington, VA: National Council on Social Studies.

NICHOLS, PATRICIA. 1983. "Linguistic Options and Choices for Black Women in the Rural South," in *Language, Gender, and Society*, eds. Barrie Thorne, Cheris Kramerae, and Nancy Henley. Rowley, MA: Newbury House.

NILSEN, ALLEEN PACE. 1977. "Sexism as Shown through the English Vocabulary," in *Sexism and Language*, eds. Alleen Pace Nilsen, Haig Bosmajiian, H. Lee Gershuny, and Julia P. Stanley. Urbana, IL: National Council of Teachers of English.

O'BARR, WILLIAM M. AND BOWMAN K. ATKINS. 1980. " 'Women's Language or 'Powerless Language,' " in *Women and Language in Literature and Society*, eds. Sally McConnell-Ginet, Ruth Borker, and Nelly Furman. New York, NY: Praeger, pp. 93–110.

PAYNE, ARVILLA C. 1980. "Factors Controlling the Acquisition of the Philadelphia Dialect by Out-of-State Children," in *Locating Language in Time and Space*, ed. William Labov. New York, NY: Academic Press.

PEDERSON, LEE A., SUSAN LEA MCDANIEL, GUY BAILEY, AND MARVIN BASSETT. 1986. *Linguistic Atlas of the Gulf States, Vol. 1. Handbook for the Linguistic Atlas of the Gulf States*. Athens, GA: University of Georgia Press.

PEÑALOSA, FERNANDO. 1980. *Chicano Sociolinguistics: A Brief Introduction* Rowley, MA: Newbury.

PHILIPS, SUSAN U., SUSAN STEELE, AND CHRISTINE TANZ, eds. 1987. *Language, Gender, and Sex in Comparative Perspective*. New York, NY: Cambridge University Press.

PICKERING, JOHN. 1816. *A Vocabulary, or Collection of Words and Phrases which have been supposed to be peculiar to the United States of America*. Also in *The Beginnings of American English: Essays and Comments*, ed. M. M. Mathews. Chicago, IL: University of Chicago Press, 1931.

PICKFORD, GLENNA RUTH. 1956. "American Linguistic Geography: A Sociological Appraisal," *Word* 12:211–233.

POPLACK, SHANA AND DAVID SANKOFF. 1981. "A Formal Grammar for Code-Switching," *Papers in Linguistics* 14:3–46.

PRESTON, DENNIS R. 1986a. "Five Visions of America," *Language in Society* 15:221–240.

PRESTON, DENNIS R. 1986b. "Fifty Some-Odd Categories of Languge Variation," *International Journal of the Sociology of Language* 57:9–48.

PYLES, THOMAS. 1971. *The Origins and Development of the English Language*. New York, NY: Harcourt.

RASPBERRY, WILLIAM. 1986. "Black Kids Need Standard English," *The Washington Post*, October 1, p. 23.

RICKFORD, JOHN R. ARNETHA BALL, RENEE BLAKE, RAINA JACKSON, AND NOMI MARTIN. 1988. "Rappin on the Copula Coffin: Theoretical and Methodological Issues in the Variable Analysis of Contracted and Deleted *BE* in BEV." Paper presented at NWAV XVII, Montreal, Canada.

ROMAINE, SUZANNE. 1982. *Socio-Historical Linguistics: Its Status and Methodology*. Cambridge, England: Cambridge University Press.

RULON, CURT. 1971. "Geographical Delimitation of the Dialect Areas in The Adventures of Huckleberry Finn," in *A Various Language: Perspectives on American Dialects*, eds. Juanita V. Williamson and Virginia M. Burke. New York, NY: Holt, Rinehart and Winston.

SANKOFF, DAVID. VARBRUL version 2, unpublished manuscript.

SANKOFF, DAVID AND SUZANNE LABERGE. 1978. "The Linguistic Market and the Statistical Explanation of Variability," in *Linguistic Variation: Models and Methods*, ed. David Sankoff. New York, NY: Academic Press.

SCHIEFFELIN, BAMBI B. AND ELINOR OCHS. 1986. "Language Socialization," *Annual Review of Anthropology* 15:163–191.

SCHNEIDER, EDGAR W. 1983. "The Origin of the Verbal -*s* in Black English," *American Speech* 58:99–113.

SCHNEIDER, EDGAR W. 1989. *American Earlier Black English: Morphological and Syntactic Variables*. Tuscaloosa, AL: University of Alabama Press.

SCHULZ, MURIAL R. 1975. "The Semantic Derogation of Women," in *Language and Sex: Difference and Dominance*, eds. Barrie Thorne and Nancy Henley. Rowley, MA: Newbury House.

SHUY, ROGER W. 1967. *Discovering Dialects*. Champaign, IL: National Council of Teachers of English.

SHUY, ROGER W. AND FREDERICK WILLIAMS. 1973. "Stereotyped Attitudes of Selected English Dialect Communities," in *Language Attitudes: Current Trends and Prospects*, eds. Roger W. Shuy and Ralph W. Fasold. Washington, DC: Georgetown University Press.

SHUY, ROGER W., WALT WOLFRAM, AND WILLIAM K. RILEY. 1967. *Linguistic Correlates of Social Stratification in Detroit Speech*. USOE Final Report No. 6–1347.

SHUY, ROGER W., WALT WOLFRAM, AND WILLIAM K. RILEY. 1968. *Field Techniques in an Urban Language Study*. Washington, DC: Center for Applied Linguistics.

SIMPKINS, GARY C., C. SIMPKINS, AND GRACE HOLT. 1977. *Bridge: A Cross-Cultural Reading Program*. Boston, MA: Houghton Mifflin.

SLEDD, JAMES. 1976. "Language Differences and Literary Values: Divagations from a Theme," *College English* 38:224–231.

SMITH, PHILIP M. 1985. *Language, The Sexes and Society*. New York, NY: Basil Blackwell.

SMITHERMAN, GENEVA. 1977. *Talkin' and Testifyin': The Language of Black America.* Boston, MA: Houghton Mifflin.

SPEARS, ARTHUR K. 1982. "The Black English Semi-Auxiliary come," *Language* 58:850–872.

SPENDER, D. 1980. *Man Made Language.* Boston, MA: Routledge and Kegan Paul.

STANLEY, JULIA P. 1978. "Paradigmatic Woman: The Prostitute," in *Papers in Language Variation*, eds. David L. Shores and Carole P. Hines. University, AL: University of Alabama Press.

STEINMETZ, SOL. 1981. "Jewish English in the United States," *American Speech* 56:3–16.

STOCKMAN, IDA J. 1986. "Language Acquisition in Culturally Diverse Populations: The Black Child as a Case Study," in *Nature of Communication Disorders in Culturally and Linguistically Diverse Populations*, ed. Orlando L. Taylor. San Diego, CA: College-Hill Press.

STREVENS, PETER. 1985. "Standards and the Standard Language," *English Today* 2(April):5–8.

TARONE, ELAINE E. 1973. "Aspects of Intonation in Black English," *American Speech* 48:29–36.

TAYLOR, ORLANDO L. 1985. "Standard English as a Second Dialect," *English Today* 2(April): 9–12.

TAYLOR, ORLANDO, ed. 1986. *Nature of Comunication Disorders in Culturally and Linguistically Diverse Populations.* San Diego, CA: College-Hill Press.

THORNE, BARRIE AND NANCY HENLEY, eds. 1975. *Language and Sex: Difference and Dominance.* Rowley, MA: Newbury House.

THORNE, BARRIE, CHERIS KRAMERAE, AND NANCY HENLEY, eds. 1983. *Language, Gender, and Society.* Rowley, MA: Newbury House.

TRUDGILL, PETER. 1974. *The Social Differentiation of English in Norwich.* Cambridge, London: University of Cambridge Press.

TRUDGILL, PETER. 1983. *On Dialect: Social and Geographical Perspectives.* New York, NY: New York University Press.

VAUGHN-COOKE, FAY. 1980. "Evaluating the Language of Black English Speakers: Implications of the Ann Arbor Decision," in *Reactions to Ann Arbor: Vernacular Black English and Education*, ed. Marcia Farr-Whiteman. Washington, DC: Center for Applied Linguistics.

VAUGHN-COOKE, FAY. 1983. "Improving Language Assessment in Minority Children," *Asha* 25(June):29–34.

WARD, MARTHA COONFIELD. 1971. *Them Children: A Study in Language Learning.* New York, NY: Holt, Rinehart and Winston.

WEAVER, CONSTANCE W. 1970. *Analyzing Literary Representations of Recent Northern Urban Negro Speech: A Technique, with Application to Three Books*, unpublished Ph.D. dissertation, Michigan State University.

WENTWORTH, HAROLD AND STUART BERG FLEXNER. 1975. *Dictionary of American Slang. Second Supplemented Edition.* New York, NY: Thomas Y. Crowell Co.

WEST, CANDACE AND DON H. ZIMMERMAN. 1983. "Small Insults: A Study of Interruptions in Cross-Sex Interruptions between Unacquainted Persons," in *Language, Gender, and Society*, eds. Barrie Thorne, Cheris Kramerae, and Nancy Henley. Rowley, MA: Newbury House.

WHITEMAN, MARCIA F. 1976. *Dialect Influence and the Writing of Black and White Working Class Americans.* Ph.D. dissertation, Georgetown University.

WIGGINS, M. EUGENE. forthcoming. *An Investigation of Predicted Dialectal Bias of Speech/Language Assessment Instruments*, unpublished Ph.D. dissertation. Union for Experimenting Colleges and Universities.

WIGGINTON, ELIOT. 1986. *Sometimes a Shining Moment: The Foxfire Experience.* Garden City, NY: Anchor/Doubleday.

WILLIAMS, FREDERICK. 1973. "Some Research Notes on Dialect Attitudes and Stereotypes," in *Language Attitudes: Current Trends and Prospects*, eds. Roger W. Shuy and Ralph W. Fasold. Washington, DC: Georgetown University Press.

WILLIAMS, JOSEPH M. 1975. *The Origins of the English Language: A Social and Linguistic History.* New York, NY: The Free Press.

WILLIAMS, RONALD AND WALT WOLFRAM. 1977. "A Linguistic Description of Social Dialects," in *Social Dialects: Differences versus Disorders.* Rockville, MD: American Speech-Language-Hearing Association.

WILSON ORR, ELEANOR. 1987. *Twice as Less: Black English and the Performance of Black Students in Mathematics and Science.* New York, NY: Norton.

WOLFRAM, WALT. 1969. *A Linguistic Description of Detroit Negro Speech.* Washington, DC: Center for Applied Linguistics.

WOLFRAM, WALT. 1974. "The Relationship of Southern White Speech to Vernacular Black English," *Language* 50:498–527.

WOLFRAM, WALT. 1980. "*A*- Prefixing in Appalachian English," in *Locating Language in Time and Space*, ed. William Labov. New York, NY: Academic Press.

WOLFRAM, WALT. 1981. "Varieties of American English," in *Language in the USA*, eds. Charles A. Ferguson and Shirley Brice Heath. New York, NY: Cambridge University Press.

WOLFRAM, WALT. 1982. "Language Knowledge and Other Dialects," *American Speech* 57:3–18.

WOLFRAM, WALT. 1984. "Unmarked Tense in American Indian English," *American Speech* 59:31–50.

WOLFRAM, WALT. 1985. "Variability in Tense Marking: A Case for the Obvious," *Language Learning* 35:229–253.

WOLFRAM, WALT. 1986. "Language Variation in the United States," in *Nature of Communication Disorders in Culturally and Linguistically Diverse Populations*, ed. Orlando L. Taylor. San Diego, CA: College-Hill Press.

WOLFRAM, WALT. 1988. "Reconsidering the Semantics of *A*- Prefixing," *American Speech* 63:247–253.

WOLFRAM, WALT AND DONNA CHRISTIAN. 1976. *Appalachian Speech*. Washington, DC: Center for Applied Linguistics.

WOLFRAM, WALT AND RALPH W. FASOLD. 1974. *The Study of Social Dialects in the United States.* Englewood Cliffs, NJ: Prentice Hall.

WOLFRAM, WALT AND DEBORAH HATFIELD. 1984. *Tense Marking in Second Language Learning: Patterns of Spoken and Written Language in a Vietnamese Community.* National Institute of Education Final Report No. BNS 8208916.

WOLFRAM, WALT AND MARCIA WHITEMAN. 1971. "The Role of Dialect Interference in Composition," *The Florida FL Reporter* 9:34–38.

WRIGHT, RICHARD. 1961. *Native Son.* New York, NY: The New American Library (originally published 1941).

ZIMMERMAN, DON H. AND CANDACE WEST. 1975. "Sex Roles, Interruptions, and Silences in Conversation," in *Language and Sex: Difference and Dominance*, eds. Barrie Thorne and Nancy Henley. Rowley, MA: Newbury House.

INDEX